SAINT PIUS X

RESTORER OF THE CHURCH

YVES CHIRON

Translated by Graham Harrison

ANGELUS PRESS
2915 FOREST AVENUE
KANSAS CITY, MISSOURI 64109

Translated exclusively for Angelus Press from the French original, *Saint Pie X: Réformateur de l'Église* (by Yves Chiron) by Mr. Graham Harrison.

Yves Chiron, born in 1960, is Professor of History and a member of the Society of the Ecclesiastical History of France. He has published numerous works on religious history, including *Padre Pio the Stigmatist* (1999, 2nd ed.), *Paul VI* (1993), *Inquiry on the Apparitions of the Virgin* (1995); *Pius IX: Modern Pope* (1995); and *Inquiry on Canonizations* (1998).

Library of Congress Cataloging-in-Publication Data

Chiron, Yves, 1960-

[Saint Pie X. English]

    Saint Pius X: Restorer of the Church / Yves Chiron.

      p. cm.

    Includes bibliographical references and index.

    ISBN 1-892331-10-1

    1. Pius X, Pope, 1835-1914. I. Title.

BX1375 .C4813 2001

282'.092--dc21

[B]   2001053295

Photographs from *Saint Pius X* by Leonard von Matt are reprinted with permission from Gemeinnutzigen Stiftung Leonard von Matt (the Leonard von Matt Foundation).

ANGELUS PRESS

2915 FOREST AVENUE

KANSAS CITY, MISSOURI 64109

PHONE (816) 753-3150

FAX (816) 753-3557

ORDER LINE 1-800-966-7337

ISBN 1-892331-10-1

FIRST PRINTING—March 2002

Printed in the United States of America

Contents

ABBREVIATIONS OF MOST FREQUENTLY CITED SOURCES

AMAE: Archives of the Ministry of Foreign Affairs (Paris).

Articoli: *Articoli per il processo vaticano apostolico sulle virtù del Servo di Dio papa Pio X* (Rome: Tipografia della Pontificia Università Gregoriana, 1943).

ASV: Archivio Segreto Vaticano (Vatican).

Documents pontificaux: *Documents pontificaux* (Versailles: Publications du Courrier de Rome, 1993), two volumes.

Lettere: *Lettere di S. Pio X,* 2nd edition (Padua: Gregoriana Editrice, 1958).

Marchesan: Angelo Marchesan, *Pio X nella sua vita, nella sua parola e nelle sue opere* (Rome: Desclée & C. Editori Pontifici, 1910) (1st edition 1904-1905, in twelve parts).

Romanato: Gianpaolo Romanato, *Pio X. La vita di papa Sarto* (Milan: Rusconi, 1992).

Scritti inediti: Scritti inediti de San Pio X (Padua: Edizioni Laurenziane, 1971, vol. 1; 1974, vol. 2).

Summarium: *Romana Beatificationis et Canonizationis Servi Dei Pii Papae X. Positio super virtutibus. Summarium* (Vatican City: Typis Polyglottis Vaticanis, 1949).

INTRODUCTION

Pius X (his name in the world was Giuseppe Melchior Sarto) was, at the time of writing, the first pope of the 20th century to have been canonized. No pope had been declared a saint since Pius V in the 16th century. This is no small matter. It means that the Church recognizes in Pius X a man who practised the Christian virtues to a high degree, is worthy to be given to the faithful as an example to be followed and venerated. He has become both a model and an efficacious intercessor. Moreover, this applies to all the different stages of his life: the child, the young cleric, the bishop, the pope. Should the historian, in his work, take account of this decision on the part of the Church? He would be obliged to take account of it willy-nilly, even if only as a historical fact.

To this day there have been two predominant ways of speaking of St. Pius X. On the one hand there are the hagiographical works which describe the life of Giuseppe Sarto entirely surrounded by the halo of sanctity, and which reproduce a wealth of edifying anecdotes and scenes. The works of Marchesan, Cigala, Bazin, Dal-Gal, Mitchell, among others, while not denuded of historical truth, illustrate this aspect of the personality of St. Pius X.[1]

On the other hand there are the more general works which portray Pius X and his pontificate in sombre colors. Here he appears as a reactionary, obscurantist pontiff, "a prisoner of his infallibility as much as of the Curia," as the agnostic historian Charles Guignebert wrote. This verdict has been taken up by one of the most eminent French historians of the Church.[2] The most recent historian of atheism still regards Pius X as "one of the most retrograde popes in modern times."[3]

---

[1] The definitive edition of Marchesan's work was published in 1910. It remains irreplaceable although it only deals with the years preceding the pontificate. Angelo Marchesan had been a pupil at the Treviso Seminary when Msgr. Sarto was spiritual director there. He would eventually become professor there. The biography he first published in 1904 had been re-read and corrected by Pius X.
Dal-Gal's biography was the "official" one, recognized as such by the Postulator of the Cause and distributed at the beatification of Pius X in 1951. It contains a wealth of extracts and depositions from the canonical processes. Its main purpose is to evoke the virtues of Pius X and deals very sketchily with the pontificate (hardly more than a 100 pages out of 509, in the French translation).

[2] Yves-Marie Hilaire, *Histoire de la papauté* (Paris: Tallandier, 1996), p.430.

[3] Georges Minois, *Histoire de l'athéisme* (Paris: Fayard, 1998), p.477.

The present new book on St. Pius X would wish to take its place, beyond these antagonistic and reductionist visions, within a more recent current of historiography which endeavors to take a fresh look at the person and actions of the first pope of the 20th century. This historiographical current, illustrated by many publications in Italian, is still largely unknown in France.[4] This new historiography certainly does not speak with one voice, and is still very critical with regard to certain aspects of the pontificate. Roger Aubert, for example, who recognizes that Pius X is "one of the greatest reforming popes in history"[5] and who, in a well-balanced judgment, sees him as "simultaneously a precursor and a traditionalist," nonetheless accuses him of "personally protecting a kind of ecclesiastical secret police" in the "repression of Modernism."[6] This point, it seems to us, can be contested. Thus the question of Modernism will be the topic of a long chapter which is intended to contribute to a re-evaluation of Pius X's role and responsibilities.

However, as Maurilio Guasco rightly observes, Pius X's battle against Modernism must not obscure the other aspects of his pontificate: Pius X was

> one of the most extraordinary reforming popes. After a few years of his pontificate, he proceeded to reform the Roman Curia and started work on the codification of canon law. He profoundly modified the programs of study and of clerical formation and established regional seminaries— which meant closing many small seminaries which were no longer able to give their students a formation worthy of the name. He devoted much energy to improving catechesis, liturgy and sacred music. He revitalized eucharistic devotion and reduced the age for first communion; most of all, he put the Eucharist at the centre of all Christian life.[7]

The motto which Pius X adopted at the beginning of his pontificate, *Omnia instaurare in Christo* ("to restore all things in Christ"), should apply to all the areas of the life of Christians: the religious life, but also political life, social and intellectual life. For Pius X, there was no civilization worthy

---

[4]   For general views of the pontificate one can mention the works of the Italian historians Domenico Agasso and Gianpaolo Romanato, of Canon Roger Aubert (in French and Italian) and, more recently, the study by Marcel Launay.

[5]   Roger Aubert, "Pio X, un papa riformatore e conservatore a un tempo," in *La Chiesa negli stati moderni e i movimenti sociali, 1878-1914,* under the direction of Hubert Jedin, vol.IX of *Storia della Chiesa* (Milan: Jaca Book), p.466.

[6]   Roger Aubert, "Pio X tra restaurazione e riforma," in *La Chiesa e la società industriale, 1878-1922,* under the direction of Elio Guerriero and Annibale Zambarbieri, vol.XXII/1 of *Storia della Chiesa* (Cinisello Balsamo: Edizioni Paoline, 1990), p.123.

[7]   Maurilio Guasco, *Modernismo, I fatti, le idee, i personaggi* (Cinisello Balsamo: Edizione San Paolo), p.194.

of the name except Christian civilization; there could be no separation between the spiritual and the temporal.

Where did Pius acquire this "integralist" conception of the life of the Church and of believers? Had he already applied this conception in his earlier charges? Such questions make it legitimate to study his life before studying his pontificate. Before becoming pope, Pius X had gone through all the echelons of the ecclesiastical hierarchy: curate in Tombolo, parish priest at Salzano, canon at Treviso and spiritual director of the seminary, Bishop of Mantua, Patriarch of Venice. No pope in modern times had such a varied pastoral experience.

Statements of witnesses of the life of Pius X made during the canonical beatification processes naturally have their place here. History does not contradict hagiography, it sheds light on it. And hagiography is a different way of writing history. These statements from the beatification processes will be complemented by other sources. In Italy many collections of documents have been published concerning different periods of Pius X's life: there are personal letters, acts of the episcopate in Mantua and the Venice Patriarchate and, of course, the different aspects of the pontificate.[8]

As yet, however, not all the relevant archives have been utilized. Their importance is different in France and in Italy: they merit a deeper exploration. There are the Archives of the Ministry of Foreign Affairs in Paris, which enable us to have a better idea of the relations between France and the Holy See, and of the process which led to the break in diplomatic relations and to the law separating Church and State. Different archives shed light on Modernism, Italian political life and the Italian social movement. Most important of all there are the Secret Vatican Archives regarding the pontificate of St. Pius X and the life of the Church in his time. They have only been open to researchers for a few years, and while it is not yet possible to consult all the dossiers assembled, many of them are accessible.

It is my hope that these diverse sources have enabled me to shed some new light on a pope who was very widely venerated in his lifetime, and who, subsequently, has too long been caricatured and disparaged.

---

[8] To mention only one area, which is very sensitive nowadays, there are the volumes published by the *Centro Studi per la storia del modernismo*, which is attached to the Institute of History at the University of Urbino. To date, 24 volumes of *Fonti e documenti* have appeared, with a wealth of unedited documents and diverse studies (sometimes very debatable).

CHAPTER 1

A BOY IN RIESE

The man who was to become Pius X was born in Riese in the heart of the Venetian plain, between the rivers Brenta and Piave. This is an agricultural plain, rich in wheat, maize and vines. In the 1920s René Bazin, member of the Académie Française, described it splendidly as follows:

> The country around Riese is quite flat, grassy and leafy. From a distance, from the elevation of Asolo, this plain seems to be endless. Looking north from Riese, however, it is not always possible to discern Asolo, nor the *Monte Grappa,* nor the chain of the Trentino Alps behind, their encircling peaks barring the horizon. The view is short-ranged practically everywhere. The roads are full of turns and twists, and they are often lined with pollarded plane-trees. The fields, with their harvests of wheat, maize, barley, oats, their beans, their grapes hanging low in clusters, are separated by ditches carrying the water from the Avenale and other streams or rivers connecting with the Brenta and the Piave. Along the ditches one sees the great water-loving trees, the alders and willows. Sometimes, but not too often, the eye delights to glimpse the long rectangle of a neighboring field.[1]

This is the countryside the young Giuseppe Sarto had before him during his childhood and adolescence. It has hardly changed even today, and even the village has experienced no major transformations. The name Riese comes from the Raetri, a tribe conquered by Drusus Nero, son-in-law of Augustus, in 15 B.C. Certain members of this conquered tribe established themselves in the Venetian plain. The *Castrum Retium* of this period became, with the passage of time, *Resium* or *Rexium* or again *Rexum,* and then the Latin name was italianized as *Resio* and finally *Riese.*[2] In the Middle Ages Riese had been subject to the Bishop of Treviso, and then in the 16th century it came under the authority of the Most Serene Republic of Venice.

---

[1] René Bazin, *Pie X* (Tours: Maison Mame, n.d.), pp.7-8. 1st ed. Flammarion, 1928.

[2] In 1951, the year of the beatification, by decree of the President of the Italian Republic, the locality was allowed to add the name of its most famous son to its existing name: henceforth it would be called Riese Pio X. The town coat of arms also incorporated the pontifical arms of St. Pius X. On the history and geography of the locality cf. Fr. Fernando da Riese Pio X, *La Terra di san Pio X* (Riese: Opera San Pio X), 1987.

Napoleon Bonaparte's first Italian campaign (1796-1797) played havoc with the region. French and Austrians fought over the Republic of Venice. In the end the Austrians kept it and, joining it to territories they already possessed further west, created a Kingdom of Lombardy and Venice with the Austrian Emperor as its sovereign.

The Kingdom of Lombardy and Venice was vast, extending from Milan to Venice. The Austrian Emperor was represented at Milan by a viceroy. Of course, the Kingdom's "patriots" insisted that Lombardy and Venice should be free, but they disagreed as to the regime which should be established once the Austrians had been ejected. Some people, partisans of a united Italy, wanted to see Lombardy and Venice integrated into a Kingdom of Italy governed by the House of Savoy. Others simply looked forward to a time when the Republic of Venice would regain its historic independence.

The Sarto Family

When the future pope was born there in 1835, Riese consisted of about 500 families. Most of them lived by farming and sent their cereal harvests or silk to Venice. The Sarto family (otherwise called *Sartore*, a variant which recurs for a long time) had originally come from Villa d'Este in the province of Padua. The surname indicates a modest origin, since *sarto* in Italian means a tailor, a dressmaker. It was Angelo Sarto, the great-grandfather of the future pope, who came to settle in Riese around the year 1760.

Twenty-five years later the village experienced great distress when it was attacked by the French. First it was occupied by the French, and then, for half a century, it was dominated by Austria. The Sarto family, however, like many other families of the region, did not regard entering the Austrian administration as an act of disloyalty to their own country. Giuseppe Angelo Sarto (1762-1841), the future pope's grandfather, was, until his death, *agente* (that is, secretary) of the village of Riese. He had eleven children, many of whom died young. One of his sons, Giovanni Battista[3] (1792-1852), the future pope's father, was also employed in the Austrian administration; he was the village *cursore*. There is no contemporary equivalent of this office; at the beginning of the 20th century one of the first books devoted to the pope described the work of the municipal *cursore* in these terms: he was

> charged with the task of communicating the mayor's orders to the inhabitants, making sure that they were carried out, and informing the municipal authorities of any infractions committed. This was a delicate

---

[3] He was more commonly called Giambattista or Giambatta.

office, at the same time akin to that of the police commissioner, the bailiff and the parish clerk.[4]

Giambattista Sarto was already performing this office when, on February 13, 1833, in Riese, he married Margherita Sanson. She came from Vedelago, a village near Riese, between Castelfranco and Treviso. She was an innkeeper's daughter. The marriage register calls her a *cucitrice* (dressmaker) and shows that she could not write, since she could not sign her name. There was a big age difference between husband and wife: Giambattista was 41 and Margherita was only 20.

Ten children were born of this union, but the family was not spared trials, for two of the children—the first and the last—died in infancy. The first child was born in 1834 and named Giuseppe, like generations of Sartos. He died of "spasm" seven days later. A second boy was born on June 2, 1835, the future St. Pius X. He was baptized the following day in the parish church. In the parish baptismal register one can read:

> Born the 2nd June 1835, baptized on the 3rd of the same month by me, Pellizzari, curate, *Sarto Giuseppe Melchiorre*, legitimate child of Sanson Margherita, dwelling at No. 30 with her husband Giambatta, village *cursore* and proprietor. Married in Riese on 13th February 1833, Catholics and proprietors. Godparents: Sarto Antonio, domiciled at San Vito, proprietor; Zorzan Francesca, midwife.

Giuseppe Melchiore (Joseph, the Christian name of his paternal grandfather and Melchior, the Christian name of his maternal grandfather) was the eldest of a large family. Angelo was born next, in 1837, then six girls: Teresa, in 1839; Rosa, in 1841; Antonia, in 1843; Maria, in 1846; Lucia, in 1848; Anna, in 1850. Finally, on 30 April 1852, another boy was born, Pietro Gaetano, but he died six months later.

Little is known about the father of the family. At the time of the beatification process of Pius X, his sisters briefly recalled their father: "he was so good," said Lucia Sarto; both Maria and Anna Sarto said that he was "a good Christian."[5] So we can say that Giambattista Sarto was in keeping with the village, which was itself profoundly Christian. Historians have established that Riese was one of the most uniformly Christian and practising of the Venice province. Even at the middle of the 19th century, those who did not go to Confession and Communion at Easter represented only 1% of the population.[6]

---

[4] Albin de Cigala, *Vie intime de S.S. le pape Pie X* (Paris: Lethielleux, 1926), pp.3-4. 1st ed. 1904. René Bazin gave a less flattering description of the job of *cursore*: "He kept the mayor's house in order, swept it and did the mayor's errands" (*Pie X*, p.9).

[5] Depositions of Maria, Anna and Lucia Sarto, *Summarium*, pp.187, 215 and 820.

[6] Angelo Gambasin, *Parocci e contadini nel Veneto all fine dell'800* (Rome: Edizioni de Storia e Letteratura, n.d.), p.269, quoted by Romanato, p.294.

It is not idle hagiography to say that the Sarto family was a united and profoundly Christian family, even if it is true, as we shall see, that certain disagreements arose when Giuseppe was to enter the seminary. When his mother died, the future pope wrote the most beautiful eulogy of her when he composed the inscription to be placed on her tombstone:

To Margherita Sarto, née Sanson,
an exemplary woman,
a virtuous wife,
a mother beyond compare.
She raised eight children
and died at the age of 81
on 2 February 1894.
May she rest in peace!

The family was not destitute, and only became poor after the father's death.[7] Giambattista Sarto's job as *cursore* gave him a modest salary,[8] to which were added the proceeds of an annual collection in the village, authorized by the authorities. The family could also count on the produce and revenue drawn from three fields (each of which was about 33 yards wide and 109 yards long) and a cow. Thus the Sartos largely shared the traditional mode of life of the majority of Italians at this period, a mode of life governed by the three C's: *Chiesa, casa e campo* (the Church, the home and the field).[9]

The Sartos lived in a house they had inherited. This house still exists and is open to visitors. It has hardly changed.[10] It is not a middle-class house, but neither is it a poor peasant house. Apart from a kitchen and a living-room on the ground floor, it has four upstairs bedrooms. At the back of the house there is a little yard and a walled garden.

Between church and school

Giuseppe, whom his mother generally called *Beppi* or *Beppino* in the Trevisan dialect, was a good and pious boy. All the biographers of saints say

---

[7] Hieronymo Dal-Gal, *Pius X* (Dublin, 1953), p.1, yields to literary stereotype and a vague hagiography when he says: "They had...a small cottage...to which was attached a tiny plot of not very fertile land....The mother and father worked hard from early morning till late at night...."

[8] His daily wage was a half-*zwanzig* (it would be doubled after the first war of independence in 1849).

[9] The kind of life which Giuseppe Sarto knew as a child is well documented by the catalogue of the travelling exhibition organized in 1985: *Sulle orme di Pio X. Giuseppe Sarto (1835-1914) dal microcosmo veneto all dimensione universale,* Amministrazione Comunale de Salzano, 1986; hereafter *Sulle orme di Pio X.*

this about their subjects, and the reader will be tempted to regard it as nothing more than a hagiographical formula. But in the case of St. Pius X all the testimonies—of his sisters and of his playmates who were still alive at the time of the beatification process—concur in saying that he was a child with a deep piety who never strayed from the practice of religion. He is also described as a lively, intelligent and willing boy. His father could entrust him with a letter for someone in the village; his mother could trust him to look after his brothers and younger sisters. All the same, a saint would not be a saint if he did not have to restrain certain instincts, passions and defects of character in order to grow in virtue. One childhood friend thought the future St. Pius X was "perhaps too severe and boorish."[11] We also know that he had to learn how to suppress anger. His first schoolmaster, Francesco Gecherle, sometimes had to administer the stick to teach him discipline. Beppi was no angel even if, from his childhood, it was possible to sense in him certain qualities and virtues which were not shared by all the boys of his age.

From the age of six, as we know, he was an altar-boy. He used to serve Mass for the parish priest or his curate. He certainly did this with joy, piety and zeal, for from the age of ten he was put in charge of the altar-boys who served at the parish church. He also showed himself hardworking at his catechism and liked to visit the church on his own. The parish church dedicated to St. Matthew is strikingly beautiful with its broad white façade along Classical lines (dating from the 18th century). It contrasts with the adjacent campanile of red brick. Inside the three lateral chapels are decorated with paintings which well express the great popular devotions of the Venetian region: on the right one is dedicated to the Annunciation and the other to St. Anthony of Padua; on the left another chapel contains two paintings, one representing St. Dominic (being given a rosary by the Blessed Virgin) and the other showing St. Catherine of Siena (being given a rosary by the Child Jesus). On the High Altar the imposing tabernacle is surrounded by marble statues of the two patron saints of the parish, St. Matthew and St. Sylvester.

---

[10] When Giuseppe Sarto became Bishop of Mantua he had the ground floor porch changed into a sitting-room for his elderly mother. After he became Cardinal and Patriarch of Venice, he had the kitchen's earthen floor tiled with blue tiles, and replaced the wooden staircase with stone steps leading to the upper floor. In 1935, the centenary year, a little museum was built at the bottom of the garden behind the house. A visit to the various locations made it possible to complete the very useful monograph of Quirino Bortolato, *La Casa natale di Pio X ed il museo di s.Pio X* (Riese Pio X: Fondazione Giuseppe Sarto, 1992). The Giuseppe Sarto Foundation was set up in Riese Pio X in 1985 by the town's local authorities and the provincial administration in Treviso; it is housed in the library of the little town.

[11] *Summarium*, p.845.

The young Beppi loved to pray alone in this church. His child's piety was not artificial or done simply out of obligations arising from serving at the altar or from catechism. This piety was authentic, nourished by personal practice. During the beatification process two of the future pope's sisters testified that young Giuseppe used to spend time before the Blessed Sacrament every week.[12]

Another sanctuary should be mentioned, *i.e.*, that of the *Madonna delle Cendrole*. Giuseppe Sarto had visited it from his earliest childhood and remained attached to it all his life.[13] Nowadays this Marian sanctuary, situated in the fields just outside the village, is a fine building of yellow and white. As in the entire Venice region, the tall campanile is separate from the church. It rings the quarter hours. The origin of this sanctuary is very ancient; at one time it was the village's only church.

Debate continues as to what the word *Cendrole* means. Some writers think that the name comes from a Roman military cemetery, in which case it means "cinders," recalling the Roman practice of cremation. Others consider that it refers to burnt trees resulting from a fire which had ravaged the place long ago. Religious tradition gives another origin for the name: one day the Virgin Mary appeared to a young shepherdess who was a deaf-mute, cured her and commanded her to ask the priest to build a chapel there. To indicate the spot the Virgin herself traced the outline of the building with cinders from a thicket that had been destroyed by fire.

The most ancient document referring to the *Cendrole* dates from 972 but does not mention this double miracle. On the other hand we know that the Virgin Mary was venerated here in the mystery of her Assumption (*Maria Assunta*). At this time Riese did not yet have a parish church. When a church was built in the village—in 1270, dedicated to St. Sylvester—the *Cendrole* sanctuary remained much frequented. The cult of the *Madonna delle Cendrole* has been observed uninterruptedly down to the present day. For a very long time now the traditional pilgrimage has been fixed on Easter Monday. Pilgrims come in considerable numbers from Riese and the surrounding villages.

The Sarto family never missed this pilgrimage. In addition, on the occasion of other festivals, Margherita Sarto would regularly come to this sanctuary with her children. The young Giuseppe was not slow, either, on other occasions, to bring his playmates to the sanctuary, which was nearly

---

[12] Deposition of Maria and Anna Sarto, *Summarium,* pp.27-28, 57.
[13] Cf. Msgr. Lino Zanini, *S. Pio X e il Suo Santuario della Madonna delle Cendrole* (n.p., 1961). After presenting a historical sketch of the sanctuary, this little book contains a complete reproduction of the study published by Pius X himself in 1910: *Il Santuario delle Cendrole nella parocchia di Riese* (Rome: Tipografia Poliglotta Vaticana).

two kilometers from his home. Once he had become Pope, Pius X heaped benefits and privileges on the sanctuary that was so dear to him. This was not only a gesture of generosity on the part of the Church's leader towards his native region, but also an acknowledgment of a spiritual debt. "It is the Madonna who called me to the altar," he said one day.[14] Nello Vian, in a beautiful album of photographs on the theme of Pius X and his surroundings, observes:

> The two paintings on either side of the altar were bound to hold the attention of the young Giuseppe Sarto. The first, by Luca Giordano, shows Noah having disembarked from the Ark, building an altar for the new sacrifice. The other, by Gregorio Lazzarini, recalls the sacrifice of Elijah, the burnt-offering accepted by God, devoured by fire from heaven. These are images of priesthood, and a child who had been taught sacred history could easily have grasped their symbolic significance.[15]

So young Sarto's vocation germinated in this sanctuary, at the foot of the altar where, surrounded by the two paintings we have described, there stands the beautiful gilded wooden statue of the Madonna of the *Cendrole*. The Virgin is shown sitting, her head slightly inclined, her hands crossed on her breast, her feet placed on an elegant block of dressed stone representing the sky.

At this time, First Holy Communion used to be made fairly late, at about eleven or twelve, and often the sacrament of Confirmation was given a year or two before. So it was for Giuseppe. The parish priest, Don Tito Fusarini, prepared him, together with other children, to receive the sacrament of Confirmation. The ceremony took place on September 1, 1845, in the cathedral of Asolo. Msgr. Sartori Canova, Bishop of Mindo *in partibus*, officiated. That same year a new curate came to the parish of Riese, Don Pietro Jacuzzi. He too, like Don Fusarini, would have a great influence on the young Sarto. Marchesan, who knew Don Jacuzzi well, wrote this about him:

> ...an upright priest, good, wise, learned, animated by a living faith, and full of a practical understanding of men and things that was not at all common....He was always prompt and generous in dealing compassionately with everyone. He spoke little, but what he said was always sound and sensible; he did not bore his listeners....[16]

It was Don Jacuzzi who prepared young Sarto for his First Holy Communion. The ceremony took place on April 6, 1847. Once he had become

---

[14] Quote by Zanini, *ibid.*, p.17.
[15] Nello Vian, *Pie X*, 150 photographs by Léonard von Matt (Bruges: Desclée De Brouwer, 1954), p.41.
[16] Marchesan, p.68.

Pope, Pius X worked with determination for early and frequent Holy Communion. In 1912, in addressing at length a group of French first communicants, Pius X was no doubt recalling his own First Holy Communion. Perhaps we can sense, in his words that day, his regret at not having been able to communicate so early and so frequently in his own childhood:

> ...you have received our Saviour for the first time; but that is not enough. Every day we ask God for the bread to sustain our body; so we also need the bread to sustain the life of our soul. Therefore I urge you to come to the table of the Eucharist frequently, if not every day, to unite yourselves to your Saviour.[17]

When Giuseppe received his First Holy Communion he had already been a pupil for nearly a year at the College at Castelfranco. First, as we have seen, he attended the two elementary classes in Master Gecherle's school; then he took lessons in grammar from Don Luigi Orazio, curate of the parish. Later the parish priest, Don Tito Fusarini, had given him classes in Latin to prepare him to enter the College (*ginnasio*) of Castelfranco. In August 1846 he had to pass an entrance examination at Treviso. His marks were excellent in all subjects: catechism, Christian morality, sacred history, Gospel commentary, reading, writing, mathematics, Latin.[18] Beppi started at the College of Castelfranco the following November. (Classes commenced on November 11, the Feast of St. Martin, and ended on August 24, St. Bartholomew.)

Castelfranco is seven kilometers from Riese. It is a pretty little town crowned with a fortress. It was the hometown of Giorgione and of other less illustrious artists. The College—which in former times had housed a convent of Servites—consisted of impressive buildings and a beautiful chapel. When Giuseppe Sarto was a pupil there, the College was directed by secular priests.

He was eleven on entering. He was to spend four years there. Together with other boys, the young Sarto used to walk every day from Riese to Castelfranco. He had to get up at 5am. Three witnesses in the beatification process reported that Beppi often walked barefoot to save the soles of his shoes. The story is well known. It does not mean that the Sarto family were so poor that they could not re-sole their children's shoes. It was something which young Sarto did voluntarily, in order not to aggravate the financial burden which his college studies implied. In the region of Venice, the Austrian authorities directed that children were obliged to attend school until

---

[17] Address of April 14, 1912, *Documents pontificaux,* vol.II, p.428.
[18] Fr. Fernando da Riese Pio X, *San Pio X, un figlio di Riese* (Parocchia di Riese Pio X, 1991), p.8.

the age of 12. Soon, therefore, Beppi would be of an age to start work. He was the eldest child. It seems that his father would have preferred him to start to earn his living. Only when Don Fusarini insisted did he consent to his son continuing his studies at the College.

This is why Beppi deliberately made these sacrifices, going on foot with his shoes around his neck, taking a very light midday meal in his bag (a piece of bread and a slice of *polenta*—a maize pancake—and something else depending on the day). On the way to school and on the way back the little group of Riese boys would stop half-way under the shade of an oak; at the foot of this tree there was a spring where water-cress grew. In 1849 Giambattista Sarto, who had to go to Castelfranco twice a week to bring the mail, bought a donkey and cart. So from then on, on Tuesdays and Fridays, he would bring Beppi and his brother, who by this time had also become a College boy, by cart.

There was a further moderation in the strict regime Beppi submitted to for the four years. At Castelfranco he got to know the Finazzi family. Giovanni Battista Finazzi was the district tax inspector and a friend of the Sarto family. Giuseppe would often visit the Finazzis, one of whose sons was also a pupil at the College. On occasion he spent the night with them, and sometimes—no doubt in winter—he used to sleep there every week-night, returning to Riese on Saturday evenings. In return he used to hear the Finazzi children recite their lessons and would help them to do their homework.

Giuseppe was a good pupil. Count Lauro Quirini, a fellow-schoolboy, gave the following testimony:

> I was a boarder at the College when Sarto was a day-boy. He was modestly dressed in woolen clothes and at times I saw him take from his bag nothing more than a piece of bread for his meal. How good he was! He was very good-natured with everyone, jovial, calm, very studious. At school he was at the top of his class. The marks were posted up every month, and at the end of the year we took the examinations at Treviso: he always came first.[19]

This report is confirmed by archive documents. The pupils of the College of Castelfranco, like the children of the colleges of the surrounding towns, had to take an examination at the seminary at Treviso every six months. This seminary was the only diocesan educational establishment recognized by the state and accredited to assess the studies taken at the College. Sarto always came first in each of the eight examinations he had to take during his four years at Castelfranco. At the final examination of

---

[19] Quoted by Marchesan, p.41.

the fourth year he was given first place out of 43 and judged "eminent" in all subjects (religion, Latin, Greek, history and geography, arithmetic).

Of his teachers at Castelfranco, young Sarto would have the happiest memories of his religion teacher, Don Gaetano Marcon. He was a reputed orator, much requested to preach in the whole of the north of Italy, even as far as Milan. He was first and foremost a good and hearty priest, who knew practically all the townspeople personally, and who knew how to listen to them, give comfort and help, and remind them of the eternal verities in all circumstances. Along with the priests of Riese, he was one of the priestly figures who had the most marked effect on the young Sarto, incarnating the model of the priest he aspired to become.

At the Padua seminary

In 1850 Giuseppe entered the Padua seminary. There was nothing un-expected about this. For a long time young Sarto had shown himself to be a pious boy, attracted by the Church. Every evening, in Riese, he went to the church to pray in front of the Blessed Sacrament. We have already spo-ken of his devotion, since childhood, to the *Madonna delle Cendrole*. At Castelfranco, when he was staying with the Finazzi family, he had impro-vised a little altar in a corner of his room and he played at celebrating Mass using items made for him by Signora Finazzi. He was full of admiration for the Riese priests, Don Fusarini and Don Jacuzzi.

Giuseppe was probably 14 when he told his parents and the parish priest of his desire to be a priest. While his mother received the news with joy, his father was not happy. One of Giuseppe's sisters gave her testimony about this at the beatification process.[20] She said that Giambattista Sarto had not wanted to allow Giuseppe to serve Mass in Riese, and he was un-happy with his son's desire to enter the seminary. Lucia Sarto did not give the cause of their father's opposition, nor did she elaborate on the discus-sions which followed between father and mother. Giambattista was a prac-tising Catholic, so his reaction was not due to hostility towards the Church. Perhaps he was hoping that his eldest son would contribute to the family income by swiftly moving to the world of work. There is, however, another explanation.

At the time when the young Sarto presented his aspirations to his fam-ily, Venice had just emerged from a long insurrection against Austria. A government had been formed under Daniele Manin, the inspirer of the national resistance. The Austrians had only succeeded in re-establishing order after more than a year of troubles and hostilities. However, the anti-Austrian feeling had remained very much alive in the country. Both Riese

---

[20] Deposition of Lucia Sarto, *Summarium*, p.820.

priests, like a large part of the clergy of the diocese and of Venice, had been won over to patriotic ideas. After the insurrection Fusarini, the parish priest, was under close surveillance by the Austrian police. As for Giambattista Sarto, who was an employee of the Austrian administration, he had not joined in the enthusiasm for the 1848-1849 insurrection; it is possible, therefore, that when his son told him of his wish to be a priest, he was reluctant to see him identify himself more closely with the Riese priests, who were politically suspect.[21]

Was the young Sarto in sympathy with the patriotic ideas largely shared in Riese? His father was not, nor was his brother Angelo, who entered the Austrian army of occupation and would stay in it for about ten years, having no hesitation to fight against Italian troops in the Second War of Independence. We know little of the political feelings of Giuseppe during these years. He was only 14 at the time of the first insurrection. Ultimately, however, he came to feel Austrian tutelage as a foreign occupation. In private conversations, after he had become Patriarch of Venice, he would gladly speak of the events of this time: "He did not disguise his dislike of foreign rule; his judgment about it was balanced, but severe."[22]

Finally, Giambattista gave way. "If God wants him, let him have him"[23]—and Giuseppe was able to enter the seminary. The parish of Riese was part of the diocese of Treviso, so the young Sarto had to enter the seminary of this town; however, it was in Padua that he finished his secondary studies and received the whole of his priestly formation. Once he had expressed his intention to become a priest, the question of financing his studies arose. The Sarto family could not pay to keep him at the seminary. Don Fusarini explained the difficulty to Canon Casagrande, prefect of studies at the Treviso seminary and Vicar Capitular. The latter mentioned the case of young Sarto to Cardinal Monico, Patriarch of Venice. In virtue of an ancient privilege the Patriarchs of Venice could enable a number of poor young men to enter the seminary of Padua free of charge. Now Cardinal Monico had been born in Riese, and what was more, one of young Sarto's uncles on his father's side, Angelo Sarto, was the Cardinal's privy chamberlain. It was quite natural, therefore, that the Cardinal took an interest in his young Riese countryman and, by a letter dated August 22, 1850, provided a "free place" for him in the seminary of Padua.[24]

---

[21] Romanato, pp.28-29.

[22] Agostino Vian, *San Pio X e Venezia* (Rome, 1958), p.7, quoted in Romanato, p.29.

[23] Deposition of Lucia Sarto at the ordinary process of Treviso, quoted by Dal-Gal, p.4.

[24] The letter is photographically reproduced in Marchesan, p.54.

Padua Seminary was one of the most renowned in Italy.[25] It had been founded in 1570 following the orders of the Council of Trent, which said that all bishops should found an "ecclesiastical college" in their diocese, which would be "a kind of perpetual nursery (*seminarium*) of ministers of God."[26] It was during the period of Cardinal Gregorio Barbarigo (1623-1697)[27] that the Padua Seminary acquired the organization and reputation it long possessed. In 1671 Barbarigo issued a detailed and methodical code for his seminary, inspired by the rules fixed a century earlier by the great reforming Bishop of Milan, St. Charles Borromeo; subsequently, in 1690, he gave it a rule of studies inspired by the Jesuit model. In Barbarigo's time the seminary's good name also came from the quality of its professors and the important material means which the establishment enjoyed: it had a very large library and a printing press capable of producing characters in Latin, Greek and oriental languages.

The seminary in Padua had undergone various vicissitudes in the 18th and 19th centuries, but it experienced a renewal during the episcopate of Bishop Modesto Farina, bishop from 1821 to 1856. He desired to "improve the clergy's scientific instruction"—the term *science* at that time meaning scholarship in the broader sense.[28] In 1837 he published a very lengthy "Declaration of the Rules" designed to govern the seminary in its two departments, namely, general studies and theology.[29] This long "Declaration," very well put together, began by defining the seminary's special vocation. Next it contained a disciplinary code and a program of studies. It re-affirmed the primary vocation of the seminary: it was to form future clergy "in piety, discipline and knowledge." This "discipline" was still in force when Giuseppe Sarto was a pupil there.

He was 15 on arriving at the seminary.[30] Before beginning clerical studies properly so called, he had to complete his general school education at the Collegio Tornacense Campion which was lodged in the seminary building. As required by the Council of Trent, the pupils of the ecclesiastical colleges, "so that they should be more easily formed in ecclesiastical discipline, shall immediately and henceforth wear the tonsure and the clerical habit."[31] So, on September 19, 1850, Giuseppe received the ecclesiastical habit in the church of Riese from the hands of Don Fusarini, the par-

---

[25] Paolo Giurati, "Giuseppe Sarto seminarista a Padova," in *Sulle orme di Pio X,* p.55.

[26] Session XXIII of the Council of Trent, canon XVIII (entirely devoted to seminaries), *Les Conciles œcuméniques* (Paris: Cerf, 1994), vol.II/2, p.1527.

[27] Beatified in 1761, canonized in 1960.

[28] Letter of June 2, 1821, quoted in Angelo Gambasin, *Un Vescovo tra illuminismo e liberalismo. Modesto Farina e il seminario di Padova (1821-1856)* (Padua: Istituto per la storia ecclesiastica padovano, 1987), p.96.

[29] *Dichiarazione delle regole ai chierici del seminario (1837),* published in full in an appendix to Gambasin's, *Un Vescovo tra illuminismo e liberalismo,* pp.220-256.

ish priest. From now on he was an *abatino,* a young abbé. His mother told Giuseppe's brother and sisters henceforth to speak to him with the formal form of address as a sign of respect for the priest he would one day become. On November 13, accompanied by his father, Giuseppe travelled to Padua.[32] He would stay there for eight years, only coming to Riese for the summer holidays.

Young Sarto's studies lasted for eight years: four years of studies at the ecclesiastical college and four years at the seminary proper. Monsignore Anton Maria Fabris was rector of the seminary from 1850 to 1856. He was a man of great education—a doctor of letters and doctor of philosophy—who advocated a return to the constitutions and rule defined by Bl. Gregorio Barbarigo. Recently his way of governing the seminary and the type of formation given has been described in these terms:

> Students and masters, living together, advanced together in piety and learning. Prayer and studies, in a pedagogy of the heart and the spirit, converged on the reading of Holy Scripture, the Fathers of the Church, in particular St. Thomas, whose *Summa* guided the study of dogmatic and moral theology. Those who underwent this school of Christian humanism and of theology were prepared to develop a doctrinal synthesis that was interiorized and personal, an essential requisite for those who were to be catechists, sacred orators, ministers of the word and sacraments.[33]

This goal was still far off, however, and young Sarto's initial preparation was through solid general studies, in which he showed himself an earnest and brilliant pupil. His first year (1850-1851) was the class of humanities. After one month, in a letter to Don Jacuzzi, young Sarto expressed how pleased he was: "...for the moment, heaven be thanked, I am getting on well with my companions and superiors, and especially with the professor, who is very kind."[34] Schoolwork was serious, with exams every semes-

---

30 Apart from the information given by Marchesan, pp.49-100, many documents relating to the life and studies of the young *abatino* Sarto at the episcopal college and the seminary, can be found reproduced in Ireneo Daniele, *San Pio X alunno del Seminario vescovile di Padova (November 13, 1850-August 14, 1858)* (Padua: Istituto per la storia ecclesiastica padovana, 1987), and in *Una memoria ritrovata. Pio X, il Seminario e la diocesi di Padova,* under the direction of Paolo Giurati and Gianpaolo Romanato (Padua: Centro Ricerche Socio-Religiose and Centro Studi Antoniani, 1988); hereafter *Una memoria ritrovata.* Much light has been shed on the intellectual climate and the religious spirit of the period in Padua by Angelo Gambasin, *Un Vescovo tra illuminismo e liberalismo.*

31 *Les Conciles œcuméniques,* vol.II/2. p.1527.

32 We know this date from a letter which Giuseppe Sarto wrote to his cousin of the same name, Don Giuseppe Sarto, who would be ordained priest less than a year later. It is dated November 25, 1850, *Lettere,* p.3. This is the first known letter of Giuseppe Sarto/Pius X—who maintained an abundant correspondence.

33 Gambasin, *Un Vescovo tra illuminismo e liberalismo,* p.77.

ter as at Castelfranco. In the first examinations Sarto came first out of 55 pupils who registered. At the end of the year he received nothing but great praise: "Discipline irreproachable. Superior intelligence. Excellent memory. Very promising indeed." (*Disciplina nemini secundus; ingenii maximi; memoriae summae; spei maximae*). He was given first place and assessed as "eminent" in all departments (conduct, attention, application, religious instruction, Latin, Greek, Italian, history and geography, mathematics, natural science).

The second year (1851-1852) was the class of rhetoric. It began on September 20 with the ceremony of tonsure, which signifies a preliminary consecration to God. The ceremony took place in the Cathedral of Asolo, and was presided over by Monsignore Giannantonio Farina, Bishop of Treviso. A shadow was cast over this second year of studies by the death of Giambattista Sarto. Some writers have said that the young seminarian, moved by a supernatural presentiment of his father's grave state of health, obtained his superiors' permission to go to Riese to be with his father in his last hours. In fact it was a letter from Don Fusarini, dated May 2, which notified the rector of the seminary of Giambattista Sarto's grave state of health. His son just had time to get to Riese before his father died.

Giambattista Sarto died on May 4. The situation was all the more dramatic since the family had just been augmented by a ninth child, Pietro Gaetano, born only four days earlier.[35] The deceased had left no fortune, and his widow could not even benefit from a retirement pension granted by the Austrian administration. Some relations had hoped that Giuseppe would leave the seminary and return to Riese to help look after his family. One of his uncles suggested that he would succeed his father as municipal *cursore*. With infallible determination, young Sarto replied, "No, I shall be a priest."[36] This must not be seen as an egoistic stubbornness or a sign of a lack of concern for his family's fate, but rather as the desire to be faithful to a sure vocation and as a total confidence in Providence. As Pope, Giuseppe Sarto would always manifest an unshakable determination once he had taken a decision in conscience.

We can also suppose that Giuseppe knew that his mother supported him in his determination. In order to provide for the needs of her family she would instruct young girls of the village in cooking; later, she would open a little dressmaker's shop. As for Giuseppe, although he was still kept at the seminary free of charge, he wanted to spare his mother the other costs of his studies (books, various pieces of equipment, *etc.*). Before going

---

[34] Letter to Don Pietro Jacuzzi, December 21, 1850, *Lettere*, p.4.
[35] He died the following October.
[36] "*No, vado prete!*" deposition of Maria and Anna Sarto at the beatification process. *Summarium*, pp.190 and 217.

back to the seminary, in all humility and with the encouragement of the parish priest, he would go from door to door around the village asking for assistance. The Sarto family, from now on, would experience great poverty. At Padua, Giuseppe's soutane had become an object of curiosity: his comrades amused themselves counting the number of patches it exhibited.

Giuseppe continued to show himself a brilliant student. At the beginning of the school year 1852-1853, the first year of philosophy, his superiors appointed him "room prefect" *(prefetto di camera)*. He had to keep discipline and a good atmosphere in the common dormitory. He exercised this office for three of his four years of theology. This school year was also marked by the departure of the two Riese priests: in April 1853 Don Fusarini had to leave the pastoral ministry for health reasons and retire to Venice; and in the autumn Don Jacuzzi was appointed to another parish. The young Sarto had seen in them model priests: pious, modest, of conduct beyond reproach, inspired by a deep priestly ideal. He remained in regular correspondence with Don Jacuzzi, and when Don Fusarini died in 1877, Don Sarto was charged with preaching his funeral eulogy. After listing all the qualities of the former parish priest of Riese he made the following admission: "After God and my parents, it is to him alone that I owe everything."[37]

In Riese the young Sarto's relationship with the new parish priest, Don Pietro Pamio, was less close. Don Pamio, Sarto later observed, was "ill-tempered."[38] What was more, he did not get on with the new curate, Don Vattai. Soon the village was split into two factions, the supporters of Vattai and those of Pamio.[39] Whenever he came back to Riese the young seminarian tried not to take sides between the two priests and continued to offer his services to the parish.

At the end of the second year of philosophy (1853-1854) Giuseppe Sarto, as usual, was given first place and received very flattering comments:

> *Religion*: he has eminently distinguished himself and has taken great interest in all areas of the subject; *Philosophy*: he has distinguished himself by being a good thinker and has a great facility for setting forth the knowledge he has acquired in breadth and depth; *Italian*: he has distinguished himself by his great ability to commentate on the Classics, by his vast literary knowledge and by the very great correctness of his style; *Latin*: he has distinguished himself by his great ability to commentate correctly and

---

[37] Funeral eulogy of Tito Fusarini, *Scritti inediti,* vol.II, p.231. Romanato, p.27.

[38] Sarto wrote to Don Jacuzzi on September 9, 1854: "...and then the presbytery is a place of solitude, and the man who lives there, instead of devoting some hours to friendship, prefers to go for a walk every day. So he lives in his house practically all the time, separated from everyone," *Lettere,* p.15.

[39] Marchesan, p.85.

to translate, and by the great limpidity of his style; *Greek*: he has distinguished himself by his great ability to commentate and by his great skill in translating; *Geography and history*: he has distinguished himself by the extent and depth of the knowledge acquired, which is always clear, well-ordered and accurate; *Mathematics*: he has distinguished himself by his great ability, the clarity and precision of his calculations and proofs in all areas of this science; *Natural science, physics*: he has distinguished himself by the clarity, order and abundance of his knowledge, even in the mathematical parts....

At the end of his studies at the Collegio Tornacense Campion, Giuseppe Sarto was placed first in all subjects except philosophy, where he was only sixth. From his letters to Don Jacuzzi we also know that he had a great interest in music. In Riese, Don Jacuzzi had taught him the rudiments. Now Giuseppe knew how to read a score fluently and how to transcribe it.[40]

During the summer of 1854 Giuseppe frequented the circle which met in the villa of the Contessa Marina Loredan Gradenigo. When she was very young, this aged contessa had been a lady-in-waiting at the court of Napoleon I. She lived in a large, Palladian-style house near Riese and held her salon there. The leading citizens would meet there to discuss, listen to music or play cards. The priests of Riese regularly attended this salon and so, as a result of a rise in the social scale that was entirely natural, the son of the *cursore,* now a young cleric, was admitted also.

In the autumn, before returning to the seminary, *abate* Sarto preached for the first time, on All Souls' Day, in the parish church. We know little of this first sermon except what one of the villagers wrote to the former curate, Jacuzzi: "*Labatte* (the *abate,* the abbé) Sarto preached a good sermon on the Holy Souls; you would think he had already done a lot of preaching...."[41] The young cleric was 19, and in a few days he was about to begin theological studies leading to the priesthood. He would have preferred to attend classes at the university faculty of theology rather than those in the seminary, in order simultaneously to follow a course in oriental languages (in Padua four oriental languages were taught at this time: Arabic, Aramaic, Chaldean and Syriac). To do this he would have to live elsewhere. The Bishop of Treviso would not allow this, since young Sarto's "free place" was in the seminary, and not elsewhere.

What had attracted young Sarto to oriental languages? No doubt it was the seminary library, which had many works in Hebrew, Syriac and Chaldean. Cardinal Gregorio Barbarigo, long ago, had wanted the semi-

---

[40] Cf. Letter to Don Pietro Jacuzzi, January 29, 1853, *Lettere,* pp.7-8.
[41] Marchesan, p.89.

narians to study these languages "the better to interpret the Holy Scriptures." Giuseppe Sarto was not able to have his wish but, as Ireneo Daniele remarks,

> it is splendid to think that he who, 55 years later, was to found the Biblical Institute (where the study of the oriental languages would form the basis of the training of future professors of Holy Scripture), had already—at the age of just 19—sensed the importance of reading the sacred texts in the language in which God had inspired them.[42]

Student of theology

The study of theology at the seminary lasted for four years.[43] As in the last two years he spent at the Collegio Tornacense Campion, Sarto was "room prefect" (except for the third year). The seminarians were divided, by age and not by class, into small dormitories of ten to fifteen persons. Each of these "rooms"—there were eight of them—was dedicated to a saint and placed under the responsibility of a prefect appointed by the seminary superiors. As we have seen, the room prefect had to keep watch over the discipline and good atmosphere of the group of seminarians in his charge. Most of all, he had the delicate task, every semester, of writing a brief report on his fellow-seminarians with regard to "piety," "discipline" and "studies." The fact that he was entrusted with this task for three years in succession shows that the young Sarto enjoyed his superiors' full confidence. At the same time it seems that this responsibility of his, which could have been a formidable one, did not upset his fellow-seminarians. His written judgments were sometimes severe, but always very balanced.[44]

In the first year of theology, the young cleric Sarto studied church history, canon law, moral theology, patristics and Holy Scripture. His professor of Holy Scripture, Don Giuseppe De Rossi, director of studies and canon of the cathedral, had been nominated Bishop of Concordia. Out of modesty—he felt unequal to this task—he had refused. Another of his professors in this first year was Don Vincenzo Agostini, professor of moral theology and canon law. He had published a manual of casuistry in three volumes.

This year was interrupted, in April 1855, by an epidemic of cholera which ravaged Padua and all the region. The seminarians were sent home

---

[42] Daniele, *San Pio X alunno del Seminario,* p.29.

[43] Following Cigala, p.14, many writers have these theological studies begin in October 1855 instead of November 1854, at the Treviso Seminary, and not in Padua. Cigala is also responsible for errors concerning the dates of ordinations found in the different authors.

[44] A complete reproduction of these reports (in Latin) is given in Daniele, *San Pio X alunno del Seminario*, pp.55-64.

until mid-June. In Riese some tens of people fell victim to the epidemic. The second year of theology (1855-1856) was again dedicated to the study of canon law, moral theology and church history, but above all of dogmatic theology.

If we were to accept the reminiscences of some of Sarto's fellow-seminarians of the time, seminary life was suffering from a certain relaxation and the seminary was more like a boarding-house than an ecclesiastical establishment for the formation of clerics. In fact, this view of things is warped and a caricature. It can be explained by the circumstance that certain lay students were lodged in the seminary, while certain seminarians, for reasons of health or on some other pretext, lived in the town with some relation or family member, only coming to the seminary for classes. At the same time, however, there was a core of seminarians who were serious, studious and respected the rules. Young Sarto was one of these. In 1855, at the request of the Bishop of Treviso, the rector of the seminary compiled a report on the two seminarians from his diocese, Bortignon and Sarto. There is unreserved praise for the latter: "Sarto is a real angel and without dispute the first in his class. His haircut is exemplary, he gives no sign of discontent, he willingly lives under the discipline of the Institute (the seminary)."[45]

During the four years he spent at the seminary proper, apart from the summer vacations, he went home only twice, under exceptional circumstances. First on account of the cholera epidemic, as we have already said, and then, on another occasion, to preach on the Sacred Heart, as we shall see. At the seminary, anyone who wanted to could lead a life of study and piety and take part in the religious exercises provided. Every Sunday the seminary's spiritual director used to give a sermon on Christian doctrine. Every fortnight the seminarians were obliged to go to Confession and Holy Communion. Twice a year the Spiritual Exercises were conducted, lasting for a week.

It should be added that, ever since 1671, there had existed at the seminary a confraternity promoting a certain rivalry in discipline and piety: this was the "Congregation of clerics" (also called the Congregation of the Immaculate and of St. Philip, because the election to different duties in the Congregation took place every semester, on the feasts of the Immaculate Conception and of St. Philip Neri). Giuseppe Sarto had been a member of this confraternity ever since his first year at the Collegio Tornacense Campion. He was elected its chancellor in December 1851 and—uniquely in the entire annals of the Congregation—he was elected prefect three times.

---

[45] Report of Msgr. Fabris to Msgr. G. A. Farina, July 28, 1855, quoted in Daniele, *San Pio X alunno del Seminario*, p.40.

For the true student, according to the tradition inherited from Bl. Gregorio Barbarigo—and from St. Charles Borromeo—"masters are to be preferred to books, the works of great authors are to be preferred to manuals, and the thorough investigation of doctrine is to be preferred to the apprenticeship of memory which encourages repetition and erudition."[46] We know which were the great authors presiding over the theological formation of the young cleric Sarto. In dogmatic and moral theology the classic reference remained St. Thomas Aquinas. The work of St. Alphonsus Liguori was the standard text for the study of practical moral cases. St. Basil, St. John Chrysostom, St. Augustine and St. Gregory the Great were the masters of sacred eloquence. In addition to these authors we know that the young Sarto regularly borrowed from the seminary library the works of Aurelio Mutti (who had been Patriarch of Venice) on sacred eloquence and those of Augustin Calmet on the study of Holy Scripture.[47]

1856-1857 was the penultimate year at the seminary. In November 1856, in the chapel of the seminary of Treviso (his home diocese), Giuseppe Sarto received the two first minor orders (porter, lector) from the hands of Bishop Farina. At the same time several favors were granted the young cleric Sarto in virtue of his merit as a zealous and pious seminarian. He was relieved of his post as room prefect (different from his function as prefect of the Congregation); he was allotted a little room to himself, and from now on he did not have to take part in the gloomy communal walks, but, with permission, could walk around the town with one of his fellow-seminarians. He wrote to Don Jacuzzi to express his happiness:

> I'll not be going for walks any more in that long line which looks so dreary to people who see it, and is even more dreary for those who have to take part in it; instead I shall walk with a good school companion, my friend. I could not have wished for anything better. I do my different tasks in complete peace....The superiors call me "the jolly fellow" (*il giubilato*) and they are right....[48]

---

[46] Gambasin, *Un Vescovo tra illuminismo e liberalismo,* p.198.

[47] *Ibid.,* p.198. Dom Augustin Calmet (1672-1757), from Lorraine, of the Congregation of St. Vanne, was among others the author of a *Commentaire littéral sur tous les livres de l'Ancien et du Nouveau Testament* (in 23 vols.) and of a *Dictionnaire historique, critique, chronologique, géographique et littéral de la Bible* (4 vols.). He is judged very severely nowadays: "Dom Calmet's influence as an exegete was considerable. He is the representative figure of Catholic scholarship in the 18th century. But at that time biblical criticism had not recovered from the blows it had received from Bossuet. A partisan of the literal sense, Calmet did no more than make conscientious compilations denuded of all critical spirit." P. Auvray, "Calmet (dom Augustin)," *Catholicisme,* vol.II, col.392-393.

[48] Letter to Don Pietro Jacuzzi, November 25, 1856, *Lettere,* p.20.

The friend he mentions in this letter is Pietro Zamburlini, three years older, who had been his fellow-pupil ever since he arrived in Padua. The two clerics would remain close friends all their lives. Zamburlini was to become Bishop of Concordia and then Archbishop of Udine.

This third year of theology was devoted to moral theology, more canon law and dogmatic theology, as well as classes in sacred eloquence. On June 6, 1857, Giuseppe Sarto received the two remaining minor orders (exorcist and acolyte). Twelve days later he had to deliver the traditional panegyric in praise of Bl. Gregorio Barbarigo in the seminary church. This address was not in the nature of a scholastic test, but it was a solemn event since it was delivered in the presence of all the professors and students of the seminary. We can be sure that young Sarto had drawn the material for his panegyric from various authors. Far more important than its originality, which is completely relative, this address reveals the view of the priesthood this young man had—who was himself to be ordained priest one year later.[49] In the portrait of Bl. Gregorio Barbarigo drawn by the young Sarto, do we not see much of himself, or, at least, of the priestly ideal in which he wished to immerse himself? In Bl. Gregorio Barbarigo, Sarto extols the "gravity" and "mildness" which are not opposites, his "simplicity of habits" and his generosity towards the poor, his apostolic fervor and the concern to give his diocese a seminary eminent in both virtue and culture.

His priestly ordination was coming nearer. The young Sarto had been happy at the seminary even if, occasionally, he had been homesick for Riese and his family. Later he wrote that the eight years he spent at Padua were "the happiest years of my life."[50] At that time the Padua seminary was one of the best administered in Italy, and one of the few which effectively followed a "rule of studies." Gianpaolo Romanato rightly observes: "We would not be far wrong in thinking that, with regard to the reform of seminaries he would undertake as Pope (in 1907), he had the model of Padua before him."[51]

The fourth and last year of theology (1857-1858) was preceded, on September 19, 1857, by ordination to the subdiaconate. He was ordained deacon on February 27, 1858. This final year was dedicated once more to dogmatic theology and classes of sacred eloquence, but there was a new subject: pastoral theology, catechetics and methodology. Sarto the *abatino* was very enthusiastic about this course which was given by Dom Domenico Zarpellon, who was also the professor of eloquence. In all the pastoral positions he subsequently held (curate, parish priest, bishop and pope),

---

[49] Panegyric published in Daniele, *San Pio X alunno del seminario*, pp.69-74.
[50] Letter to Msgr. Dal Santo, rector of the Padua Seminary, December 31, 1894, photographically reproduced in *Una memoria ritrovata*, p.137.
[51] *Una memoria ritrovata*, p.11.

Giuseppe Sarto would give a central place to catechism and the teaching of Christian doctrine.

Without doubt he was also greatly influenced by what he read. We know from the *Regole* outlined by Bishop Farina what spiritual works were meant to guide the seminarians in their daily meditations. It is probable that the young Sarto read at least the majority of works recommended in the rules during his four years of theology. Apart from the *Imitation of Christ* we find some of the following authors recommended: St. Alphonsus Liguori, St. Leonard of Port-Maurice (whose *Via del Paradisio* had been reprinted on the seminary press), the Capuchin Gaetano Maria de Bergamo (1672-1753), an anti-Jansenist, the French Jesuits Crasset and Croiset. These last two wrote on subjects dear to the future priest right up to the time of his pontificate. Jean Crasset (1618-1692), known for his spiritual writings *Méthode d'oraison* and *Le chrétien en solitude,* was also an apostle of the popular catechism.[52] Every week, at the Hôtel-Dieu in Paris, he used to give small courses of religious instruction to the poor who were there. The other Jesuit, Fr. Croiset (1656-1738), was the mentor of Margaret-Mary Alacoque during the last two years of her life.[53] Subsequently he published *Abrégé de la vie de la Sœur Marguerite-Marie Alacoque* and *La dévotion au Sacré Cœur de N.S.J.-C.* We can imagine that the reading of one or other of these books, in Italian translation, nourished the young Sarto's devotion to the Sacred Heart, which we have already noted.

From the letters the young cleric wrote to Don Jacuzzi we also learn that he assembled a little library during his last year at the seminary. He had been able to buy the works of St. Cyprian and those of St. John Chrysostom (in 24 volumes). We can discern in this a new side of his taste for study, a taste which would never leave him and which has been so ignored by those who, during the period of Modernism and subsequently, would try to brand him as a pope with no great culture and little open to the things of the spirit.

In this last year at the seminary, young Sarto was once again appointed as room prefect. He was also given charge of the seminary choir. Here we see evidence of his taste for music. Classes in Gregorian chant were obligatory and were given once a week by a canon of the cathedral. One of the better singers was appointed to give lessons and organize rehearsals. Young Sarto was chosen for this task in his last year, showing that he had given evidence of a certain aptitude for chant and sacred music.

---

[52] Henri Bremond, *Histoire littéraire du sentiment religieux* (Paris: Bloud et Gay, 1920), vol.V, pp.311-339, and vol.VIII, 1928, pp.289-309, and "Jean Crasset," *Catholicisme,* vol.III, col.274-275.

[53] P. Mech, "Croiset (Jean)," *Catholicisme,* vol.III, col.320-321, and Ivan Gobry, *Sainte Marguerite Marie, la Messagère du Sacré-Cœur* (Paris: Téqui, 1989), pp.247-249.

In the archives of the seminary of Venice there is a little book of 24 pages containing pieces of music associated with the liturgy of Holy Week. It was long believed that this music had been copied out by our young cleric.[54] In fact they are pieces he himself composed while at the seminary.[55] Later, when he was Bishop of Mantua, he used two of them as chants for Holy Week. Once he had become Pope, the first of his great reforms was the restoration of sacred music.

In June 1858, a few weeks before leaving the seminary, Sarto the deacon went to Riese for the Feast of the Sacred Heart to give a sermon, which made a considerable impression. It made an impression because the preacher was a local boy, particularly worthy, and was not yet a priest. With modesty and realism, however, the young deacon announced his sermon as a "little discourse."[56] The art of public speaking which, later, he was to show as a curate and then as parish priest, was not something innate. He had to work at it and practice it. On the other hand, even if it is still somewhat awkward, the young cleric's sermon reveals one of the characteristics of his spirituality: devotion to the Sacred Heart of Jesus. In the following decades he would follow with great attention the various initiatives aiming to propagate the cult of the Sacred Heart and to establish a Feast of Christ the King. Once he had become Pope, the only decoration he allowed in his room was a "memento of Paray-le-Monial."

We can discern, in the adolescent and the young man who had spent eight years in the seminary at Padua, several traits of character, preoccupations and spiritual aspirations which are evident in the bishop and the Pope. The germ of the saint, Pius X, was largely already present in the young cleric of Padua. He left the seminary with the regard and admiration of his superiors; as the rector of the Padua Seminary wrote to the rector of Treviso, "Sarto left nothing to be desired. On the contrary, he gave a continual example of gravity and excellence in piety and conduct. In a word: may God grant us more young men of this calibre!"[57]

Marchesan, p.395; N. Vian, in a note to the letter of January 21, 1853, *Lettere*, p.8.
Guglielmo Zaggia, "Quadernetto autografo di musiche sacre di Giuseppe Sarto, chierico nel Seminario di Padova," in *Fonti e ricerche di storia ecclesiastica padovana* (Padua: Istituto per la storia ecclesiastica padovana, 1969), vol.II, pp.341-345.
"Discorsetto" is what he wrote to his cousin Don Giuseppe Sarto (June 11, 1858, *Lettere*, p.24); to Don Jacuzzi he referred to it as a *"piccolo discorso"* (June 22, 1858, quoted by Marchesan, p.96). There is no evidence, however, for preaching activity mentioned by Lucia Sarto: she said that her brother, still a seminarian, gave Lenten sermons in Pieve di Castelfranco (*Summarium*, p.820). Perhaps she confused this with some later preaching on his part.
Letter of Don D. Slaviero to Don F. Saccol, August 24, 1858, photographically reproduced in *Una memoria ritrovata*, p.86.

Giuseppe Sarto was ordained priest at Castelfranco in the church of St. Mary and St. Liberale. The canonical age for priestly ordination was 25, and the deacon Sarto was only 24 and three months. So he had to ask a dispensation from Rome, which was given. Before ordination he made a 10 day retreat. Then the ceremony took place on September 18, 1858. That day 22 seminarians of the diocese of Treviso were ordained priest by Bishop Farina.[58] Fifteen years later, in a letter to a newly-consecrated priest, Don Sarto would give his spiritual vision of the priesthood:

> ...you are about to set out along the path of Calvary, which is the only way to reach Mount Thabor, and so you will understand that the life of the priest is a life of sacrifice.—Unfortunately we live at a time when all the priest can expect is scorn, hatred and persecution. What comforts us, however, is that from this very circumstance springs a power which makes those who do not know its secret turn pale; you yourself will be filled with amazement when you put forth this power.[59]

Don Sarto celebrated his first Mass in Riese, on September 19, the Feast of the *Vergine Addolorata*. He celebrated the Mass for the intention of his deceased father and not for himself, as is usual for newly-consecrated priests. After the celebration, following the tradition, the faithful came to kiss the hands of the new priest. Many of the village inhabitants had been present at the ceremony, a sign of the esteem in which everyone already held Don Sarto. The same day, in the centre of the village, a little oratory was inaugurated containing a statue of the Madonna.

Don Sarto spent two months with his family before going to the first parish to which his bishop appointed him.

[58] The bishop who ordained Giuseppe Sarto, Msgr. Giovanni Antonio Farina, Bishop of Treviso, should not be confused with Msgr. Modesto Farina, Bishop of Padua.
[59] Letter to Don Pio Antonelli, September 18, 1873, *Lettere*, p.54.

CHAPTER 2

FROM TOMBOLO
TO TREVISO

After ordination, Don Sarto stayed in Riese, waiting to receive his first assignment. He was appointed *cappellano* (chaplain, curate) in Tombolo. This village was in the province of Padua, but belonged to the diocese of Treviso. It had about 1380 inhabitants, mostly dependent on farming. They grew cereals, bred silk worms and reared a few cattle, and there was a long tradition of some of the peasants being horse-dealers. The latter had given the whole village a bad reputation. The *Tombolani* were well known in all the markets of the Venice region, and even as far as Lombardy. At the end of the century, Marchesan could still describe them as follows: "They can be recognized from among a hundred different provincial types, so characteristic are they. Characteristic in the way they walk, speak, dress and work. These folk are very sturdy, indifferent to rain, snow, wind or sun."[1] They were also called rough, grasping and great drinkers. Of course this reputation was unjust, apart from certain individuals. Yet, when Don Sarto learned of his appointment, he seemed to share the common view, according to the testimony of his sister Maria. He told his mother the news in these terms: "Mamma, I have been appointed curate in Tombolo. I don't care for the place; they're said to be a rather bad lot (*cattivotto*)." Nonetheless he added immediately, "but I must obey and shall go."[2]

On November 13 Don Sarto left Riese, taking a bed (given him by his uncle Angelo), some clothing and books on a cart. At Tombolo the presbytery was not large. Also, the custom was for curates to look after themselves in their own lodging. Don Sarto found a room to rent in the house of Francesco Beghetto, a stonemason. He installed his few things and remained there for four years. After that he found a little house he could rent. Three of his sisters, first Rose, then Maria and Lucia, came to live with him and do the housework.[3]

The curate did not have a fixed income. His only resources were the wheat and maize he was entitled to ask for throughout the area once the

---

[1] Marchesan, p.105.
[2] Deposition of Maria Sarto, *Summarium*, p.31.
[3] Many statements regarding his mode of existence in Tombolo were taken during the beatification processes. They are collected and set in order in the *Articoli*, pp.10ff.

harvest had been gathered in. Furthermore, for the seven years he spent at
Tombolo, he very frequently had to trust in divine Providence. What is
more, we know that his father had left behind him considerable debts. It
was only after several years that Don Sarto, curate in Tombolo, was able to
pay them back.

The faithful regularly supplied him with various provisions: eggs,
wine, fruit and vegetables. When he preached outside the parish—and
that became increasingly frequent—he received some remuneration. At
Tombolo Don Sarto was always poor, which did not prevent him, as we
shall see, from giving away the little he had in the form of charity. His
ordinary dress was very simple and his shoes were shod with wooden soles,
which were less expensive and more sturdy than leather soles, but noisier
and less comfortable! The only objects of value the young curate had were
his priestly vestments. It seems that Cardinal Monico, who had died seven
years earlier, had left him, through his uncle Angelo, some albs, stoles and
chasubles.

The young priest's début

Don Sarto arrived in Tombolo on Saturday evening, and the next day
he celebrated his first Mass and gave his first sermon there.[4] Before beginning the Gospel of the day, he addressed his parishioners and asked them
to be "indulgent" and "patient" with him; at the same time he expressed
his determination to "take care" of their souls and to teach them the way
which leads to Paradise.

On November 29 Don Sarto began his priestly ministry. The parish
priest, Don Antonio Costantini, had been appointed to Tombolo the year
before. He was only 14 years older than his curate, but his health would be
soon in rapid decline. He was a good theologian, an expert in casuistics,
and he was also very well versed in Gregorian chant. Under his direction
Don Sarto continued his priestly formation; he was given advice about
how to preach: in the morning, when the church was empty, the parish
priest got his curate to go up into the pulpit and listened to him preach,
and then gave his comments on his preaching, showing him how to be
simple and clear, and encouraging him to overcome his fear of speaking in
public.[5]

More and more frequently, as Don Costantini's health declined—he
had contracted consumption—the young curate had to look after the entire pastoral work. From January 1, 1859 (the date of the first Baptism he
administered), until June 1867, when he left Tombolo, Don Sarto per-

[4]   The full text of this first sermon is printed in *Scritti*, vol.I, pp.15-20.
[5]   *Articoli*, p.11.

formed practically all the parish baptisms. We also know that he used to celebrate Mass every morning at 5am. Several witnesses at the beatification process reported the vivid and extraordinary impression made by the young curate celebrating Mass or venerating the Blessed Sacrament exposed: "At such moments," one witness recalled, "his face bore an almost superhuman expression. With his hands joined, his eyes fixed on the Blessed Sacrament, he seemed to radiate a great faith. There was something extraordinary about him."[6]

On holy days Don Sarto used to preach at the 9am high Mass and he used to give a doctrine class to adults (in dialogue form, as recommended by Don Costantini). He also took an interest in teaching the liturgical chant to children and young people—we have already noted his enthusiasm for this. He also gave special classes for a number of young men preparing to enter the seminary at Treviso, where Pietro Jacuzzi had become rector: he gave classes in Latin and Italian, but also in religion, Greek, algebra and history![7] Throughout his entire time in Tombolo he continued to study and to read (the Church Fathers, studies in Holy Scripture and treatises of moral theology). In 1860, in order the better to combat modern errors in his preaching and in the confessional, he asked his bishop for permission to read certain works that had been placed on the *Index librorum prohibitorum* (Index of prohibited books).[8]

One of the features of his apostolate had a definite effect on people's minds. In Tombolo, as in many villages and towns of Italy at this time, a certain sector of the population was strongly addicted to swearing. Don Sarto fought against this habit by giving admonitions, and even, when the opportunity presented itself, by giving a slap to recurrent offenders.[9]

As the years went by, Don Sarto's talent as a preacher became established. He was summoned to preach or to give the Lenten sermons in several parishes near Tombolo: at St. Martino di Lupari, Cittadella, Castelfranco, Godego, Fontaniva, Camposampiero, Galliera. Soon his reputation as a sacred orator grew, and he was called to preach even in the diocese of Vicenza, a neighboring diocese to Treviso. In 1866 his parish priest, Don Costantini, extolled his curate's talents to a fellow priest: "Don Beppi was greatly praised (*laudabiliter*) for his Lenten sermons at Godego. *Fama volat* (his fame is spreading). Yesterday he received a letter inviting him to deliver the panegyric of St. Anthony at Montebelluna, and he had

---

[6] Deposition of V. Pivato, quoted in Dal-Gal, *Pius X*, p.19.
[7] Letter of Don Sarto to Don Pietro Jacuzzi, October 22, 1860, *Lettere*, pp.27-29. One of these young men, Pio Antonelli, when a seminarian, would again be helped, this time financially, by Don Sarto.
[8] Letter to Msgr. Farina, September 13, 1860, *Scritti inediti*, vol.I, pp.20-21.
[9] Several testimonies are cited in *Articoli*, p.12.

to refuse because he had already been retained by the cathedral of Treviso."[10] Indeed, on June 13 this year Don Sarto gave the panegyric of St. Anthony in the cathedral of Treviso. It was a milestone of his talent as an orator. An educated local man wrote in his diary the impression made by this young preacher, hitherto unknown in Treviso: "At the cathedral for the solemnity in honor of St. Anthony of Padua. At 10:30 there was a sung Mass, with organ accompaniment, celebrated by Msgr. G. Martignago. After the Mass the panegyric of the wonder-working saint was given by Don Giuseppe Sarto, curate of Tombolo, 31 years of age. Humility was exalted; the fine work of a young talent. It lasted an hour and a quarter....A very full congregation, and most of them were deeply affected. All the canons were present, the 36 clerics of the seminary and numerous priests."[11]

This panegyric evidently appealed to the bishop and the faithful, for, next year, Don Sarto was summoned to the same place on June 10, to deliver the panegyric of Blessed Enrico of Bolzano. This panegyric was as important as that of St. Anthony, if not more so, since the body of Blessed Enrico (1250-1315), a lay saint, is interred in Treviso cathedral, where a phial of his incorrupt blood is also preserved.

Don Sarto, a devoted curate, an eloquent preacher, also showed himself to be a priest of an immense charity. There are innumerable incidents, reported in abundance in the process for his beatification. Anyone who came to knock on his door could count on being helped, rarely with money—for the curate had little of it—but most often with some gift in kind. The curate would give anything he had: linen, a measure of cereals or a piece of meat (even if it was already cooking in the pot!). And when he really had nothing, he would put his few precious objects in the pawnshop in Castelfranco or Cittadella. So it was that a silver table-setting, given to him by parents whose children he had taught, was sent to the pawnshop and recovered several times, together with a little silver clock he had been given by someone else.

To everyone, the curate of Tombolo was not "Don Sarto" but, more affectionately, "*Don Beppi.*" The young priest was too well aware of the social necessities to think that individual charity was sufficient. When he became Bishop of Mantua and then Patriarch of Venice, and subsequently Pope, he was very active in encouraging and organizing various social projects for the protection and improvement of the most needy. As curate of Tombolo he started a modest work, but one of great usefulness: with the

---

[10] Letter of Don Costantini to Don Tositti, April 20, 1866, cited in Marchesan, pp.11-12.

[11] Diary of Alessio Pozan, Wednesday, June 13, 1866, cited by Marchesan, p.131.

help of the village schoolmaster, he began an evening course for the illiterate, both children and adults.[12]

Don Sarto's activity in Tombolo was also a priestly work of making peace and concord. In 1859, when Napoleon III and Victor-Emmanuel II, the King of Piedmont-Sardinia, declared war on Austria in order to regain Lombardy, Venice was not affected by the hostilities. The battlefields were far from Tombolo, on the banks of the Ticino—at Montebello, Palestro, Magenta, Solferino. But in Tombolo, as throughout the region, they had to receive those wounded in the campaign. Don Sarto devoted himself to them.

After that, Victor-Emmanuel II, having annexed Lombardy and proclaimed himself King of Italy, wanted to liberate Venice also. Thanks to the military action of Prussia and the diplomatic support of France, Austria surrendered Venice (Treaty of the Peace of Vienna, October 3, 1866). A referendum was organized in the following weeks to seal Venice's definitive union with Italy. Don Sarto was not inactive in this historic moment. Unlike the parish priest, Don Costantini, Sarto had never been suspected of patriotic agitation by the Austrians. All the same, like most of the Venetian clergy, he favored the departure of the Austrians. His bishop, Msgr. Zinelli, after having met Victor-Emmanuel II, wrote to the Patriarch of Venice: "There will be no cessation of hatred towards us on the part of the sectaries who want to destroy religion; still, it is a comfort to know that the King's soul is religious."[13]

We can imagine that Don Sarto did all he could, in the face of the departure of the Austrian troops and administration, to prevent anarchy taking over and to preserve peace in society. It is said that the curate of Tombolo had the tricolour hoisted on the bell-tower of his church.[14] In any case, it is certain that he joined in organizing the referendum which took place in front of the village church. One of the Pope's first biographers adds: "In the town one is still shown the first electoral list, prepared by Don Giuseppe Sarto and copied out entirely by his hand. And when,

---

[12] It is worth noting, in a different field, Don Sarto's interest in making sun-dials. He had learned how to do this at the Padua Seminary where, as we have seen, he took courses in physics and astronomy. He made one for the front of the Tombolo presbytery and others for two neighboring parishes (Onara and Fontaniva). When he was elected Pope, the Fontaniva authorities affixed a plaque beneath the sun-dial he had erected in 1866.

[13] Letter of Msgr. Zinelli to Cardinal Agostini, November 6, 1866, quoted by Silvio Tramontin, "La diocesi nel passaggio dal dominio austriaco al Regno d'Italia," in *La Chiesa veneziana dal 1849 alle soglie del novecento,* under the direction of Gabriele Ingegneri (Venice: Edizioni Studium Cattolico Veneziano, 1987), p.45.

[14] Tramontin, "La diocesi nel passaggio," p.45, note 57.

soon afterwards, the National Guard was re-established, it even used to drill in the presbytery yard."[15]

Don Sarto's peacemaking efforts also explain his intervention on behalf of his brother Angelo. Angelo had joined the Austrian police and had served at Gorizia and Mantua. Not only was he now unemployed, he could also have been uneasy about the new authorities. Don Sarto very skilfully put together a letter on his behalf.

This priest, active, pious, charitable, was called to higher tasks. Many people had the feeling that this would happen, beginning with Don Costantini, who often praised his curate. In Italy in the second half of the 19th century all curates looked with envy towards the post of parish priest (*parocco*). Quite apart from assuring a regular income, it involved the effective and total government of a parish. Don Sarto, if we believe several witnesses, never aspired to this position. Similarly, when his bishop several times suggested that he become professor at the Treviso seminary, he refused. Don Sarto sought neither honors nor responsibilities.

In February 1866—and we do not know whether he did this on his own initiative or if he was invited—he presented himself as a candidate in a competition organized to provide a pastor for vacant parishes. Five parishes were to be provided, including the parish of Riese, and there were seven candidates. The examination took place on March 21, 1866. Don Sarto had to prepare a homily on the theme of the Good Shepherd and give written answer to three questions (one on the temporal power of the popes, one on the liceity of a renewal of baptism, and the third on the impediments of marriage).[16] Don Sarto was accepted as a candidate, but his results did not permit him to be appointed to one of the parishes. Next year the episcopal curia of Treviso conducted a new competition for appointment to five further vacant parishes. Perhaps cooled somewhat by his lack of success the previous year, the curate of Tombolo had not intended to present himself as a candidate. He only did so at the invitation of his bishop. Msgr. Zinelli told him, "If you do not enter the competition, I shall enter you myself."[17] The competition took place on May 21. Don Sarto went to Treviso accompanied by one of his friends, Don Carlo Mercante, curate at St. Martino di Lupari. Five candidates presented themselves for the competition, which took place in the presence of the bishop and four canons, prosynodal examiners. Don Sarto had to prepare a homily on one of Christ's sayings and give written answer to questions of moral

---

[15] Cigala, *Vie intime de S.S. le pape Pie X,* p.23.

[16] Don Sarto's replies are published in *Scritti inediti,* vol.I, pp.34-40.

[17] Report quoted by S. Pilotto, *Summarium,* p.581.

and doctrinal theology (the Church's doctrine on indulgences, the definition of scandal in moral matters, and the duties of the confessor).[18]

The five candidates were admitted. This time Don Sarto was given
first place. He was appointed parish priest of the most important parish of
the five: Salzano.

Parish priest of Salzano

Salzano is a little town about a dozen kilometers from Venice, but it is
still part of the ecclesiastical jurisdiction of Treviso. The locality, which
included Salzano and the hamlet of Robegano, had nearly 3,000 inhabitants. Don Sarto would have responsibility for about 2,200 souls, since
Robegano had its own parish.

Having been invested canonically on May 21, 1867, Don Sarto arrived in Salzano on July 13. He was to remain there until 1875.[19] The new
parish priest was young—he was just 32—and his reputation as a preacher,
if it had reached Treviso, had not got as far as Salzano, on the edge of the
diocese. The little town was accustomed to having priests of note, more
titled, older, who had already had charge of a parish or been seminary professors. Don Sarto, to the inhabitants of Salzano, was nothing but an unknown young priest. Initially, therefore, he was received coolly. Even Don
Costantini regarded the promotion of his former curate as too much, too
soon.[20] Don Sarto would have to convince his new parishioners that he
was not unworthy of the charge entrusted to him by his bishop.

On July 14 he celebrated his first Mass in the parish church and gave
an hour-long sermon. Then, on the following days, he went from house to
house: "I have devoted the first week to visiting all my parishioners...," he
wrote to his cousin.[21] In writing "all my parishioners" he does not mean
just the faithful who come to church, but all the families of Salzano, even
those of notorious unbelievers and Jewish families. Among the latter there
was one family with which Don Sarto had a close relationship: that of

---

[18] Replies published in *Scritti inediti,* vol.I, pp.44-51.

[19] The work of Eugenio Bacchion, *Pio X Giuseppe Sarto arciprete de Salzano (1867-1875)*
(Padua: Tipografia del seminario, 1925), contains many documents and testimonies
relating to this period, but they are primarily concerned with his public activity and
less with his pastoral action. In 1996 it was reprinted by the Salzano *Amministrazione
Comunale* and complemented by a volume of *Note integrative e indici* compiled by
Quirino Bortolato.

[20] "Why give a parish like that to Sarto when there are so many deserving parish priests,
so many zealous pastors of souls? Where is the bishop's wisdom, justice and equity? I
admit that he (Sarto) is a young man with qualities of distinction, that he is among the
first and that he must be promoted, *etc., etc.* But to Salzano!": letter of Don Costantini
to Don Marcello Tositti, May 31, 1867, published in Marchesan, p.144.

[21] Letter to Don Giuseppe Sarto, August 5, 1867, *Lettere,* p.39.

Moses Jacur, the principal landowner of Salzano. Gianpaolo Romanato thinks that Don Sarto "was not uninvolved in the decision of the Jacur family to create a silk factory in Salzano, near their villa; this factory was inaugurated in September 1872 and soon began to produce about a third of the raw silk of the province of Venice. The factory employed 200 work-ers and constituted a precious shot in the arm for the country."[22] Don Sar-to was frequently invited to dine with the family and he closely followed the education of the industrialist's nephews. One of them, Leone Roma-nin Jacur, a future senator and minister, came several times to visit the former parish priest after he had become pope.

People appreciated Don Sarto for his simplicity. A story will illustrate this quality—a quality which the future pope never abandoned. A priest passing through Salzano one evening, came to make himself known to Don Sarto. He found him in the presbytery kitchen, playing the game of "goose" [a board game] with some of the youngsters.[23] He always gave great attention to his parishioners. Witness to this are the death registers, where the name of the deceased is always followed by a few lines of person-al remarks penned by Don Sarto.[24]

He quickly won the regard of all, since, a few months after he arrived, the municipal authorities appointed him president of the local charitable organization. He was very active, and his first act was to open a subscrip-tion to buy 300 bushels of maize so that, once winter had come "it could be sold to the needy at a low price."[25] On May 4, 1869, Don Sarto was also appointed *Direttore Scolastico Comunale* by the town authorities.[26] This post meant that he had to ensure the good operation of the town's four schoolrooms: two at Salzano (one for boys and one for girls) and two at Robegano, the hamlet belonging to Salzano (one for boys and one for girls): the total number of schoolchildren was 320. Don Sarto, helped by a female inspector, took his responsibility to heart. As well as responding to needs as they arose, every year he would give a very detailed and concrete report to the municipal authorities. He was particularly vigilant lest there be any neglect of the teaching of the catechism.[27]

The Salzano presbytery had just been rebuilt, to the right of the parish church. It was a long, two-story house which no longer exists. It was large

---

[22] Romanato, p.85.

[23] Marchesan, p.154.

[24] The annotations of the years 1869 and 1870 are reproduced in *Scritti inediti*, vol.I, pp.93-100.

[25] The letter of nomination as president of the *Congregazione di Carità*, dated December 13, 1867, is published in Bacchion, *Pio X G. Sarto arciprete di Salzano*, pp.127-129. The first circular, dated December 23, is given on pp.132-133.

[26] Cf. Letter to Timoteo Scabello, *sindaco* of Salzano, May 11, 1869, *Lettere*, pp.43-44.

[27] Deposition of Msgr. E. Bacchion, *Summarium*, p.592.

and impressive. Several Sarto sisters came, by turns, to live with their brother and look after the household; two of them found husbands during their stay.

The work done in the parish was important. There had been nothing wrong with Don Sarto's predecessor, Don Antonio Bosa, but he had died at his post at an advanced age, having directed the parish for more than 20 years. Don Sarto had not come to turn Salzano upside down, but he amplified, corrected, ameliorated things, and made innovations. After a few months of work in his parish, he received his bishop's visitation. Msgr. Zinelli carried out a pastoral visitation, examining everything, questioning the faithful, the parish priest and his curates. At the end of his visitation he published a report in which he said how pleased he was "with the very good religious spirit in the parish," the increased number of the faithful who communicated, the good religious instruction of children and the excellent state of the church and of everything concerned with divine worship. The bishop also gave his "full approbation to the Very Reverend Archpriest Don Giuseppe Sarto, and to his zeal, to which, in large measure, we must attribute such an encouraging situation...."[28]

A zealous, untiring parish priest, Don Sarto also showed himself to be an innovator. Later on we shall refer to several of his initiatives, but for the moment let us mention just one: for the sake of his parishioners Don Sarto brought forward the time of the morning Mass to 4:30, so that those who worked in the fields could attend Mass before leaving for work.[29]

Although he was now parish priest and hence provided with a regular income and assisted by two curates, Don Sarto continued to lead a simple life. As at Tombolo, his charitable gifts were innumerable and supplemented the town's charitable works where they were deficient. Almost 200 families were entered in the *Congregazione di Carità* over which he presided—which meant 1,000 persons (one third of the inhabitants of the locality!). The municipal subsidies and private gifts were often not enough. At the approach of the winter of 1873, discouraged by the many difficulties he had encountered, Don Sarto resigned his post of president of the charitable works of the locality. However, yielding to the urgings of his friend Moses Jacur, a member of the local council, he withdrew his resignation.[30] Don Sarto held this responsibility until he left Salzano, but very often he himself had to supply the innumerable needs. There are many stories about the way in which he plundered his own reserves of firewood, wheat

[28] Decree dated December 20, 1867, published in Bacchion, *Pio X G. Sarto arciprete de Salzano,* pp.34-35.

[29] Deposition of Maria Sarto, *Summarium,* p.34.

[30] Letter of resignation, November 2, 1873; letter of retraction, November 29, 1873; documents published in Bacchion, *Pio X G. Sarto arciprete di Salzano,* pp.142-143.

or beans in order to help the unfortunate. "One day," one of his sisters recounted, "I had prepared for dinner a splendid soup with meat and vegetables. While I was out, someone came asking my brother for some help for a poor woman in labor: he had no more money. Saying not a word, he went to the kitchen, lifted the meat for our dinner from the pot and told the visitor to give it to the sick woman. When I came to serve the meal, however much I turned the ladle, I only brought up carrots. I ran to my brother to ask him if he hadn't seen the dogs of the hunters, who had arrived that morning, go into the kitchen. He started laughing...."[31] In such circumstances his favorite maxim was, "Don't get upset! Providence will always supply what is needed."

At the beginning of his ministry at Salzano he had been given a ring by the parish (a contemporary photograph shows it to have been large and very richly ornamented): on one occasion he deposited it at a Venice pawnshop. On another occasion he sold the horse which used to pull his little cart. The money he thus obtained was used to pay for the board of a poor seminarian or to help other young laymen to pursue their studies.

In 1873 a cholera epidemic spread throughout the Venice region and began to affect the surrounding provinces. Don Sarto did not want his young curates to be exposed to the disease. He, however, did not hesitate to accompany the doctor to the sick, acting as nurse, administering the sacraments and bringing the dead to the cemetery, which many people were slow to do for fear of catching the disease. "Once," reported a witness at the beatification process, "dressed in surplice and stole, he did not hesitate to help to transport a coffin—with some difficulty—across a canal." To his sisters, who were anxious about the danger of catching the disease, he replied with an unshakable faith in Providence: "Have no fear: the Lord is with us";[32] and he was to be seen wherever the epidemic struck. However, once the scourge had been stemmed, Don Sarto was considerably weakened, physically and emotionally—he was subject to bouts of weeping. He had to slow down his activities for a while.

This generosity and charity towards his neighbor extended to more lasting works too. He took to heart his position as president of the town's municipal hospital, which fell to him in July 1867, and in it he showed "an uncommon precision in administrative matters. The archives of Salzano contain many statements of account in his own handwriting, revealing his scrupulous management of public assets."[33] As in Tombolo, beginning in his second year in his new parish, he gave evening classes for illiterate chil-

[31] Story reported by Cigala, p.26.
[32] Depositions of Anna and Lucia Sarto, *Summarium,* pp.59 and 608.
[33] Romanato, p.104.

dren and adults. (From the marriage registers of this period we know that only one-sixth of the faithful could sign their names.)

Nor was his charity with regard to the faith any less. It was his duty as a priest to instruct both small and great in religion. In the area of religious instruction he showed personal initiative. One day, for instance, during the month of May (traditionally dedicated to the Blessed Virgin) he read to his parishioners, from the pulpit, extracts from a book on the due veneration of the Mother of God.[34] Another initiative of his was the editing of a catechism.

In 1872 the Bishop of Treviso, Msgr. Zinelli, had published an official catechism entitled *Dottrina Cristiana breve, ad uso della città e diocesi di Treviso* ("A short Christian Doctrine, for the use of the town and diocese of Treviso"). This was a work designed for priests, enabling them to teach the truths of the faith. It was inspired by a catechism which had circulated widely in Italy since the 17th century: the *Christian Doctrine* of St. Robert Bellarmine. Don Sarto, in turn, was inspired by the catechism published by his bishop to compile his own. The manuscript has been preserved, and it has recently been reproduced in book form.[35] The text, written in two ruled notebooks, consists of 577 questions (not numbered) and answers. It does not have parts or chapters, but gradually unfolds the faith, from the existence of God to the life of grace by prayer and the sacraments. Here we quote some of the first questions and answers:

Q. Who is God?

A. The Creator, Lord of heaven and earth *(padrone del cielo e della terra)*.

Q. Why do you say Creator of heaven and earth?

A. Because it is God who made heaven and earth of nothing.

Q. What does "create" mean?

A. To make from nothing.

The questions are always short and simple, but they do not avoid theological terms. There are questions on the meaning of the words "God's unity," "Trinity," "Incarnation," *etc.* The manuscript has 252 emendations: words added or replaced by others, and marginal notes. Here is an example of the latter, in connection with the three resurrection miracles worked by Jesus and recorded in the Gospels: "Tell children the story of these three miracles with plenty of detail." Or, on the question of the *"vi-*

---

[34] Marchesan, pp.163-164.
[35] The original manuscript has been fully reproduced under the title *Catechismo di don Giuseppe Sarto Arciprete di Salzano* (Cancellaria dell Curia Vescovile di Treviso, 1985).

aticum," we read Don Sarto's marginal note: "Give a good explanation of the word."

Thus we see the parish priest of Salzano constantly improving his catechism, finding more appropriate or more accessible terms, out of a concern to give clearer explanations. He wanted to enter into a living dialogue with his children to help them to grasp the mysteries of faith at a deep level.[36] It has been noted, furthermore, that this Salzano catechism is "biblical": "More than a third of the questions and answers are related to a semi-continuous reading of the Holy Scriptures, particularly the Gospel...Sarto—who never departs substantially from the structure which was traditional at the time—introduces the Bible in a more spontaneous, lively and immediate way. What we have is almost a generative relationship between the "word of God" and catechesis."[37]

Don Sarto was also concerned to teach the faith to adults, to refresh their religious knowledge, to open their souls and spirits more and more to the truths of the faith. Twice he organized a mission in his parish. Again we refer to the talks on doctrine (called "catechism") which were given to the faithful on Sunday afternoons and on feast-days. Don Sarto urged his parishioners not to miss this catechism, even if they had to miss Vespers. This adult religious instruction, in dialogue form, was given either by him or by a priest from a neighboring village, Don Giuseppe Menegazzi, who would eventually succeed him as parish priest of Salzano. They were a great success. The faithful came from surrounding parishes to attend the talks. Their parish priests took umbrage at this and complained to the bishop. Bishop Zinelli told them that they should follow Don Sarto's example![38]

The liturgy, according to the parish priest of Salzano, also had a part to play in the formation of souls. The beauty of the ceremonies elevates the soul, and the devotional practices lead them to an ever greater grasp of the different facets of the divine mystery. At Salzano, says one of his biographers, summing up a score of witness depositions, Don Sarto "also desired to enhance the splendor of the liturgical ceremonies. He demanded the greatest possible cleanliness in everything concerning the altar and the vestments. He introduced children and adults to the beauty of the chant, restored the Company of the Blessed Sacrament, instituted the Confraternity of the Sacred Heart, the adoration of the Forty Hours and the devotions of the month of Mary; he urged frequent Communion and imparted special solemnity to the First Communion of the children, who were ad-

---

[36] Francesco Tonolo, "Come da parocco Pio X insegno il catechismo. Il Catechismo manoscritto di don Giuseppe Sarto," *Catechesi*, 1954, pp.367-376.

[37] Giuseppe Badini, "I 'Quaderni di un parocco (il catechismo di Salzano)," *Annuario del Parocco*, XXI, 1975, pp.118-119.

[38] Depositions of Alessandro Bagaglio and A. Bottero, *Summarium*, pp.601 and 629.

mitted to the holy table at a much more tender age than was then custom-ary."[39] Also, in 1868, he began a *schola cantorum* to teach the sacred chant to men and youngsters.

All these external activities and pastoral initiatives should not obscure the spiritual life which animated them. Two events of 1870 allow us to make a concrete assessment of the profound spiritual life of the parish priest of Salzano. Firstly, as an extension of his longstanding devotion to the Sacred Heart, Don Sarto commissioned a Venetian artist to paint a picture which he installed in the parish church, and he erected a Confra-ternity of the Sacred Heart.[40] Secondly, that same year, he was received into the Franciscan Third Order by Don Onorato Bindoni, professor at the Treviso seminary. The Franciscan poverty and simplicity fitted in well with his priestly ideal.

A letter he wrote at this time to Pio Antonelli, recently ordained, gives us a better understanding of the supernatural vision of priesthood which Don Sarto had after 15 years as a priest, 15 years of experience in which there had been an alternation of trials and joys. Priesthood, wrote Don Sarto in this letter from which we have already quoted, is a "way of the Cross" (*via del Calvario*), "the only way to reach Mount Thabor." "...The life of the priest is a life of sacrifice," he went on. "Unfortunately we live at a time when all the priest can expect is scorn, hatred and persecution. What comforts us, however, is that from this very circumstance springs a power which makes those who do not know its secret turn pale; you your-self will be filled with amazement when you put forth this power."[41]

At Treviso

In April 1875 Don Sarto was summoned by the Bishop of Treviso. Msgr. Zinelli told him that he was appointing him canon of the cathedral, spiritual director of the seminary and chancellor of the episcopal curia. Henceforth he would be entitled to be called "Monsignore." The parish priest of Salzano took no pleasure in this appointment. To one of his former fellow-seminarians, writing to congratulate him on his appoint-ment, he spoke of it as "a new cross placed on my shoulders, to which obedience bids me submit."[42]

---

[39] Cf. Dal-Gal, *Pius X*, pp.33-34.

[40] Letter to the Episcopal Curia of Treviso, March 8, 1870, *Scritti inediti,* vol.I, p.102. In this letter Don Sarto sought authorization to affiliate the Confraternity he had just founded to the Arch-Confraternity in Rome. The following year he asked the Treviso Episcopal Chancellor for the same permission for the Confraternity erected, at his suggestion, in Cappelletta di Noale, a neighboring parish (*Scritti inediti,* vol.I, p.118).

[41] Letter to Don Pio Antonelli, September 18, 1873, *Lettere,* p.54.

[42] Letter to Don Angelo Gazzetta, May 14, 1875, *Lettere,* p.56.

Back in Salzano, Don Sarto seemed preoccupied. But when his sisters began to express their dislike of the impending change of situation, Don Sarto humbly replied, "I have become a priest and I must obey, and you too must do God's will."

While the Sarto sisters were upset to have to leave the house and a way of life they had got used to—for they had to return to Riese, since in future their brother would be living at the Treviso seminary—the parish priest of Salzano was affected by deeper concerns. From being a parish priest, directly responsible for the cure of souls, he was going to be an important man in the diocese, entrusted with different official functions. With regret, he was aware that when he left parish life he would have less contact with the faithful of diverse kinds and conditions. On the other hand it must be said, looking back, that the 17 years since his priestly ordination, spent first at Tombolo and then at Salzano, had been full of experience, which had enabled him to take the exact measure of the priesthood, its obligations, its joys and its sorrows. It was therefore a fully mature, 40 year-old priest who was to be faced with various important responsibilities in the diocese.

Msgr. Zinelli had wanted the man who was now to be called Monsignore Sarto (although, until he became Bishop of Mantua, he continued to sign himself "Don Sarto") to take up his new functions as soon as possible, but the parish priest of Salzano "did everything he could," in his own words, to stay at his post until the end of September.[43] Msgr. Sarto was invested as a residentiary canon on July 21, 1875, but he did not move to Treviso until the following November. This delay can be explained by practical concerns. The open-handedness of the parish priest of Salzano—of which we have already given several examples—was too extensive, and his list of debts had become longer and longer. He did not want to leave his parish without paying back the greater part of them. In a few months, his canon's prebends, which were more substantial than the income of a parish priest, enabled him to reimburse his creditors.

Regretfully, Msgr. Sarto left his parish on September 16. "This morning," he wrote to his cousin, "I finally left Salzano...I will not describe to you the dejection I felt at the moment of bitter separation, after having spent eight years with the people. I left this morning, two hours before dawn, without speaking to anyone, and now I feel terribly overwhelmed....Write me a line, for I need some word of comfort..."[44]

On November 28, 1875, the first Sunday of Advent, Canon Sarto took his place in his stall in the cathedral of Treviso for the first time, join-

---

[43] *Ibid.*, p.56.
[44] Letter to Don Giuseppe Sarto, September 16, 1875, *Lettere*, p.58.

ing his voice to those of the other canons. At 40 he was the youngest of the canons, and his beautiful voice added something special to the venerable choir.[45]

In this canonical responsibility, which was both honorific and symbolic, Canon Sarto impressed his colleagues by his piety and simplicity. A single significant detail will illustrate this: by a privilege granted by the Republic of Venice, the members of the Treviso chapter had long ago obtained the right to wear violet soutanes. With the passage of time, the soutane had come to be made of silk and ornamented with cord and ribbons, and the violet had given place to purple. In the Church, however, this color is reserved for cardinals. Msgr. Sarto refused to accept this inappropriate custom and kept his black soutane, ornamented simply with a violet collar to show his canon's rank and reflect the ancient privilege. This return to simplicity was soon followed by all the other colleagues of the chapter.[46]

Canon Sarto divided his time between the episcopal headquarters (where he had his chancellor's office) and the seminary (where he occupied two small rooms). Circumstances made the responsibility of the episcopal chancellor a very onerous one. In fact, the fragile health of the bishop—he had been the victim of a cerebral attack some time previously and was partially an invalid—and the advanced age of his vicar general, Msgr. Antonio De Paoli, meant that most of the administrative work which they should have carried out now devolved on Chancellor Sarto. He also had to perform other tasks normally carried out by the bishop or his vicar general, such as receiving parish priests of the diocese who had come to talk about their problems, mediating in conflicts between persons, and maintaining relations with the civil authorities.[47]

This was a heavy burden, for the diocese included some 350,000 inhabitants, 210 parishes and about 500 priests. A journalist who frequently saw him at this period—and who subsequently became a Salesian religious—recalls in his memoirs how Sarto, the episcopal chancellor, knew how to make himself all things to all men:

---

[45] From 1880, however, he obtained from the Pope a dispensation from choir office whenever his duties as chancellor and spiritual director of the seminary were too onerous (*Scritti inediti*, vol.I, pp.247-248).

[46] Deposition of Msgr. Zanotto, *Summarium*, p.78.

[47] Of his spiritual interventions we mention the following: he wrote a letter to the town's parish priests and curates inviting them to bring their parishioners to a triduum of prayers organized in the cathedral to implore an end to the drought which was causing devastation to the region. The letter is dated August 15, 1876; ten days later another letter from Msgr. Sarto invited the parish priests and curates to join in the thanksgiving ceremony to take place in the cathedral "to give thanks to the Lord...for granting the rain so urgently implored" (*Scritti inediti*, pp.170-171 and 173-174).

It was a pleasure to see him on the ground floor of the episcopal palace on days and at times when there were many people there, especially on Tuesdays, when parish priests and curates of the diocese took the occasion of the market to come to the town. His head slightly inclined, and with an inimitable gentleness, he used to receive the visitors, always kind and master of himself. He used to reply in a few clear, precise, quick words, illuminated by a broad smile which sprang from his heart....And, having seen him, everyone went home happy.[48]

Having spent the morning in the chancellery, Msgr. Sarto used to spend the rest of the day at the seminary. In his first years there he had the joy of the company of his old teacher from Riese, Don Jacuzzi, who had become rector. Apart from the seminarians, the establishment accepted lay pupils. In total there were more than 200 young men of different ages and levels. The spiritual director's task was very time-consuming. Msgr. Sarto gave himself to it with all his heart and in a spirit of faith. He knew that the candidates for the priesthood whose spiritual formation had been entrusted to him represented the future of the diocese. Every morning he directed the seminarians' meditation in the chapel; every week he gave them a spiritual conference; every month he preached a retreat to them. In addition, every Sunday, he gave a sermon on the Gospel. As well as that, every Wednesday and Saturday he heard the confessions of the seminarians and the pupils of the episcopal college attached to the seminary. One of the seminarians who had him as a spiritual director gave the following testimony:

> In the meditations, Msgr. Sarto succeeded without effort, without ostentation, and in a calm voice, as if entirely naturally, to lead the young men's spirits into the very depths of the Christian verities....In instruction he showed himself eminently practical, never getting lost in vain speculation.[49]

He would insist on the qualities necessary in the priest: "the priest must be holy, but humility is the basis of all the virtues"; "the priest must be like the Virgin Mary since, every day, the immaculate Lamb is born from his hands"; he must "know the infinite distance which exists between himself and God," but "he must be close to God"; and he must also be "kindly towards men," a "teacher of humility" (as St. Gregory expressed it); and he must give example.[50]

In this apostolate of spiritual direction Msgr. Sarto was not aloof from the more material anxieties of his charges. On occasion, he looked after

---

[48] Luigi Ferrari, quoted by Dal-Gal, *Pius X*, p.47.
[49] Deposition of Don Santinon, *Summarium*, p.610.
[50] All these recommendations feature in a "Note for conferences to be given to seminarians," in eight points (*Scritti inediti*, vol.II, pp.212-213).

and supported financially those who were poorest (and their families). In addition, for one year, he took upon himself the responsibility for lessons in religion for the college students attached to the seminary. He used no book, but, after each lesson, he used to distribute to his pupils a polycopied summary.

Canon, chancellor and spiritual director, Msgr. Sarto regularly preached in various Treviso churches. He gave a notable sermon, in the church of St. Mary Major, on the occasion of the 25th anniversary of the proclamation of the dogma of the Immaculate Conception. He was also invited to preach in Venice, Vicenza, Rovigo, Monselice, Mirano, Castelfranco and Padua. Finally, he was asked to preach the spiritual exercises to the clergy in several of the surrounding dioceses.

Msgr. Sarto's collaboration in the Catholic newspaper *L'Eco del Sile* should also be mentioned. The paper was edited by Luigi Ferrari, who became a friend of the Canon's. In this paper, under the pseudonym "Francesco Pan Molle," Don Sarto wrote homely, humorous dialogues in order to get across a number of wholesome ideas.

In June 1877 the episcopal jubilee of Pius IX was celebrated in Rome. Pilgrims swarmed to Rome from the whole world; they included Pedro II, the Emperor of Brazil, and the Bishop of Philadelphia at the head of a delegation of American faithful. Canon Sarto and Msgr. Saccol, rector of the seminary and a canon, were commissioned to represent the chapter of Treviso and Msgr. Zinelli, who was sick.

It is normal, of course, for two of the most important people of the diocese to represent their bishop in Rome. However, it emerges from many depositions and from Msgr. Sarto's correspondence that the bond between Msgr. Zinelli and Msgr. Sarto was closer than everyday administrative relationships would require. Msgr. Sarto saw in his bishop far more than a superior to whom he should give every assistance. Msgr. Zinelli, who was an *"intransigent"* (in the sense in which this word was employed in Italy in the last decades of the 19th century, meaning "intransigent with regard to the rights of the Church, including her temporal power"), had been at the First Vatican Council in 1870 as one of the members of the commission charged with preparing the dogmatic definition of papal infallibility. He had been one of the "reporters" for the project of this definition. At the very core of this commission, he had associated himself with Msgr. Pie, the Ultramontane Bishop of Poitiers. In all probability it was through Msgr. Zinelli that Msgr. Sarto got to know the works of Msgr. Pie (created cardinal by Leo XIII). Later Pius X expressed his doctrinal debt to Cardinal Pie: "I have all the Cardinal's works here," he told a priest of the diocese of Poitiers, "and for many years now hardly a day goes by but I read a few pages of him."[51]

The 1877 Jubilee took place in a climate of great hostility on the part of the anti-clericals and the government. Ever since 1870 the remainder of the pontifical estates and the city of Rome had been occupied, and annexed to the Kingdom of Italy. Pius IX had not accepted this despoliation and regarded himself as a "prisoner of the Vatican." What is more, the health of the 85 year-old pope was fragile, and this was the last of the great demonstrations of Catholic unanimity which punctuated his pontificate. He died some months later.

This time spent in Rome—the first time in his life—made a deep impression on Canon Sarto. Two letters show his admiration, and the piety which Christendom's capital and its leader inspired in him. "The only anxiety I have," he wrote on June 1, "is of not being able to see the Holy Father, since the reception on the 4th has been cancelled and I am greatly afraid that on Sunday there will be so many people that it will be difficult to see him."[52] In the end Don Sarto was able to see Pius IX, and, on another occasion, he was able to present him with the *album* (written expression of homage) and the diocesan *obole* (medal). He also visited the great places of Christendom: the major basilicas, the catacombs, and the *Scala santa*. During his stay he made the acquaintance of Msgr. Parocchi. At that time Msgr. Parocchi was Archbishop of Bologna and he was directing the "Italian Pilgrimage" which had come to render homage to Pius IX. Soon Msgr. Parocchi would be made cardinal and, in 1884, under the pontificate of Leo XIII, he would be appointed Vicar of Rome.

On June 12, 1879, as a reward for his "merits of piety and learning," Msgr. Zinelli appointed Msgr. Sarto "canon primate," *i.e.*, first in honor among the canons, not least because of the prebends attached to this office. He was also given two further responsibilities: he was made "prosynodal examiner" (which conferred authority to nominate and transfer parish priests) and "counsellor" at the eccesiastical tribunal. His cousin in Venice wrote to congratulate him and Msgr. Sarto wrote in reply: "A bit of smoke, Dear Cousin; you know how insignificant it is to me."[53] At this time there was also a rumor that he was going to be appointed auxiliary bishop of the diocese. To the same correspondent Msgr. Sarto humbly wrote:

> I am too well acquainted with my littleness to aspire to this position....The experience I have had for five years in the diocesan curia have

---

51   Carlo Snider, *I tempi di Pio X*, vol.II of *L'Episcopato del cardinale Andrea C. Ferrari* (Vicenza: Neri Pozza Editore, 1982), p.143, who cites another testimony to the same effect.

52   Letter to Msgr. Giovanni Battista Mander, secretary to Msgr. Zinelli, June 1, 1877, *Lettere*, p.65.

53   Letter to Don Giuseppe Sarto, August 3, 1879, *Lettere*, p.77.

shown me the thorns, the dangers and the responsibilities inherent in this post, which are not compensated for by the poor glory of a pectoral cross. After all, this glory soon fades when one remembers the words of St. Philip Neri: And then? And then? And then there is death!

This rumor kept recurring, and it was particularly current when Msgr. Zinelli died, on November 24. Msgr. Sarto, who was his bishop's spiritual director, had also become his nurse in recent times. He was given the task of delivering the funeral eulogy. On November 27, waiting for a new bishop to be appointed, the chapter elected as vicar-capitular Msgr. De Paoli, who was already vicar-general. The latter refused, however, and Msgr. Sarto was nominated. He was to govern the diocese for seven months until the arrival of a new bishop in June 1880.[54] At this date Msgr. Giuseppe Callegari, hitherto professor at the Venice Seminary, took possession of the See of Treviso.[55] He was six years younger than Msgr. Sarto, and the latter's experience seemed to promise him a certain stability. He confirmed Msgr. Sarto in all his titles and offices: canon-primate, episcopal chancellor and spiritual director of the diocesan seminary. In addition he appointed him pro-vicar-general.

In 1881 Chancellor Sarto made another pilgrimage to Rome. This time it was a pilgrimage of reparation and protest after the serious incidents which had marred the transfer of the remains of Pius IX, who had died three years earlier. In July 1881 the remains of Pius IX had been transferred from his provisional tomb in St. Peter's Basilica to the Basilica of St. Laurence-outside-the-walls, where a tomb had been prepared. While the remains were being transferred, the cortege was violently attacked by anti-clericals. In order to protest against this insult to the dead pope, and as a sign of reparation, pilgrimages from all Italy took place in the following months. The Treviso pilgrimage came to Rome in October. After visiting the Shrine of Our Lady of Loretto, and Assisi, Msgr. Sarto joined Msgr. Callegari in Rome. The Treviso pilgrims set a crown of flowers on the dead

---

[54] Acting in this capacity, Msgr. Sarto had occasion to manifest a rigorous impartiality. One of his cousins, Don Giacomo Sarto, priest of the diocese of Treviso, had become the pastor of a little parish without having passed an examination. He was not satisfying his parishioners, and his limited intellectual endowment did not fit him for such a position, however modest. Vicar-Capitular Sarto removed him from the position of pastor, and reduced him to the rank of vicar. (Cf. the letter of Msgr. Sarto to one of his cousins, Dom Giuseppe Sarto, February 24, 1883 in *Lettere*, pp.97-98.)

[55] Msgr. Callegari took possession of his episcopal see on June 26, 1880. A week beforehand, Msgr. Sarto felt it his duty to warn him of the bad reputation of a priest whom the new bishop intended to bring with him as secretary (letter to Msgr. Callegari, June 18, 1880, *Lettere*, pp.85-87). Msgr. Callegari decided to do without the services of this priest.

pope's new tomb. For the first time Canon Sarto was received at an audience by the new pope, Leo XIII.

In September 1882 Msgr. Callegari was nominated Bishop of Padua. Msgr. Sarto remained in touch with him by letter. They had become friends. Msgr. Callegari thought so highly of his former chancellor that he proposed to make him vicar-general of his new diocese, but Msgr. Sarto refused, knowing well that he would be regarded as an intruder by the clergy of a diocese which was not his native one.[56]

Msgr. Sarto remained at Treviso, and when a new bishop, Msgr. Apollonio, was appointed, Msgr. Sarto was confirmed in all his offices. Since he had been so long in his post, he had become indispensable to the good running of the diocese. In addition to the administrative and canonical duties which were proper to a diocesan chancellor, Msgr. Sarto had undertaken initiatives of his own. In 1883, for example, an earthquake had devastated the island of Ischia in the Bay of Naples, causing the deaths of about 5,000 people and a considerable amount of destruction; Msgr. Sarto took the initiative and opened a subscription, initially from among the clergy, for the victims. Ultimately he succeeded in involving more than 300 clergy and prominent people of Treviso in action on behalf of the victims, and three times he sent them significant financial help.[57]

These years which preceded his appointment to Mantua saw him involved in even more work outside Treviso. In 1884 he preached the Lenten sermons at Castelfranco, gave the panegyric of Blessed Beatrice at Este and, at Padua, gave the sermons called the *tredicina* in honor of St. Anthony. On this last occasion he was the guest of Msgr. Callegari at the episcopal palace. When people congratulated him on his sermons, he quipped: *"Roba copiara!"* ("It's only a copy!").[58]

This was no false modesty. In a letter written when he was about to enter his 50th year, we see a little of what constituted the habitual background of his thought: "What a meagre consolation! To have reached the half-century and, so close to the *redde rationem* (the "giving of one's account"), to be so far away from that state of mind and soul which will attract a favorable verdict from Him who judges justly. Do not be surprised at this; I have been thinking about this all day...."[59]

One day in September 1884 Msgr. Sarto was at his desk when he was summoned by Msgr. Apollonio. The latter bade him accompany him to his chapel, where he said, "Dear Monsignore, let us kneel down before the Blessed Sacrament, for we need to pray for a matter which concerns us

---

[56] Letter to Msgr. Callegari, May 19, 1883, *Lettere,* pp.99-100.
[57] Note dated October 5, 1883, *Scritti inediti,* vol.II, p.140.
[58] Depositions of Msgr. G. Peschini and Don G. Bianchi, *Summarium,* pp.711 and 792.
[59] Letter to Don Carlo Agnoletti, February 6, 1884, *Lettere,* p.109.

both."[60] After they had prayed together for a while, Msgr. Apollonio handed Msgr. Sarto the letter appointing him Bishop of Mantua.

Msgr. Sarto, according to many witnesses, was surprised at this appointment. He was even disconcerted, thinking himself incapable of filling such a weighty post. He wrote to Rome to try to avoid accepting it, but the Vatican authorities were not prepared to reconsider. Confirmation of his appointment arrived in Treviso on September 12. The following day Don Sarto, in a letter to Msgr. Callegari, opened his heart:

> Yesterday I received absolute confirmation that the Holy Father wishes me to be Bishop of Mantua. I have prayed, I have earnestly besought the Holy Father to leave me here, wretched as I am, in my poverty, but my prayers have not been heard....Ah! Pray to the Good Lord for me, that He may send some soothing ointment for this wound and give me the strength to bear the cross.[61]

---

[60] Depositions of A. Romanello, F. Zanotto, G. Beccegato and G. Bressan, *Summarium*, pp.29, 79, 783 and 832. Also Marchesan, pp.227-228.

[61] Letter to Msgr. Giuseppe Callegari, September 13, 1884, *Lettere*, p.113.

CHAPTER 3

BISHOP OF MANTUA

Msgr. Sarto's nomination as head of the diocese of Mantua was not the result of an administrative process. It was not some kind of automatic consequence whereby a good parish priest who had become a respected vicar-general would inevitably become a bishop one day. Msgr. Sarto was chosen for his own qualities and because it was thought that these qualities corresponded to the particular needs of the diocese. In fact, from two points of view, the Diocese of Mantua was in crisis. There was an old crisis, with many contributory causes, making it a diocese adrift, a diocese in decay. Furthermore, there was a more recent crisis which had made it necessary to appoint the current bishop to another see.

At the beginning of 1884 Msgr. Berengo, Bishop of Mantua, had been nominated Archbishop of Udine. Was this promotion a quiet way of getting rid of someone, as one of Pius X's first biographers had suggested? He wrote that Msgr. Berengo "had been at first an enthusiastic supporter of Austria; subsequently he was in constant battle with the authorities and alienated himself by his rash actions, not only from the faithful but also from a large portion of the clergy."[1] Certain of the Mantua clergy communicated their grievances to Cardinal Parocchi, Vicar of Rome. While the Cardinal Vicar, as such, has no role to play in episcopal appointments, Cardinal Parocchi was originally from Mantua and had been vicar-general of the diocese before being raised to the episcopate. So he continued to take a close interest in his original diocese.

Even if historians have by now established that Msgr. Berengo had not acted in any blameworthy manner, it does seem that he was not in a position to surmount the grave crisis through which his diocese was passing. Cardinal Parocchi admitted that a new bishop would have to be appointed. The bishops of the neighboring dioceses were consulted, and the name of Giuseppe Sarto was put forward. The report on Sarto which was drawn up in these circumstances—an unpublished report kept in the secret Vatican archives—after detailing his ecclesiastical career, speaks of his qualities: Msgr. Sarto "enjoys the best reputation" and is esteemed "by all those who have had to do with him."[2] He is exemplary "in faith, morals and

---

[1] Cigala, *Vie intime de S.S. le pape Pie X*, pp.36-37.
[2] "Testes pro persona," dated September 30, 1884, ASV, Processus consistoriale 275, no.30.

doctrine" and, so the researchers observe, even if the future bishop does not have a license in canon law or theology, he has sufficient knowledge of souls and of doctrine to be able to govern a diocese.

Officially appointed Bishop of Mantua in September 1884, Msgr. Sarto left for Rome on November 5, after a celebration given in his honor at the seminary. On route he wished to make a stop in Padua to greet his former bishop, Msgr. Callegari, and make a pilgrimage to the tomb of St. Anthony. He arrived in Rome on November 8 and was received at a first audience with Leo XIII, whom he presented with three works published by professors of the Treviso seminary. On November 10, the Consistory took place during which he was officially instituted as Bishop of Mantua. Then Msgr. Sarto prepared himself for the ceremony of episcopal consecration by making a retreat for some days with the Vincentian Fathers. There he followed the Spiritual Exercises and spent a long time studying the Pontifical. He also read Giussano's life of St. Charles Borromeo.[3] Cardinal Charles Borromeo, Archbishop of Milan 1564-1584, was a prime example of a bishop engaged in promoting restoration and reform, faithful to the prescriptions of the Council of Trent. During Msgr. Sarto's episcopate at Mantua, Giussano's work would be a much-consulted book of reference.

Two days before this episcopal consecration Msgr. Sarto wrote a long letter to Msgr. Bonomelli, Bishop of Cremona, one of the dioceses bordering on that of Mantua. Msgr. Bonomelli, who governed the diocese of Cremona from 1871 to 1914, was one of the most prominent bishops of Italy. He was regarded as a "conciliationist."[4] At this time Msgr. Sarto saw him simply as an older brother in the episcopate (Msgr. Bonomelli had been a bishop for eleven years). He sought his support, asking him to be "generous in protection, in counsel, and in help," adding with characteristic humility, "for I consider my virtue unequal to my weakness. Without your help I would be downhearted, since alone I cannot achieve even a tiny part of that good which the diocese of Mantua has the right to expect from its bishop."[5] Later, however, there would be disagreements between the Bishop of Mantua and the Bishop of Cremona.[6]

---

[3] Following Cigala, p.41, writers speak of a life of St. Charles Borromeo written by "Giussani." The work is in fact by Giovanni Pietro Giussano, *Vita di S. Carlo Borromeo* (Rome: Stampa della Camera apostolica, 1610). This is a classic work which went through many editions.

[4] In Italy, the "conciliatorists" were those who desired a reconciliation between the Italian State and the Church, even if it meant that the Church would have to renounce all territorial possessions.

[5] Letter of November 14, 1884, *Lettere*, p.116. This latter phrase would recur in the letter which Msgr. Sarto wrote some months later to the mayor of Mantua prior to taking possession of his see (letter of March 5, 1885, *Lettere*, p.123).

Msgr. Sarto had wanted to be consecrated bishop in Mantua, among his future faithful. But Cardinal Parocchi, as Cardinal Vicar, could not perform ordinations and consecrations outside the diocese of Rome. So Msgr. Sarto received episcopal consecration in the Eternal City on Sunday, November 16. The ceremony took place in the church of St. Apollinarius. The new bishops of Guastalla and Marsi were consecrated at the same time as the Bishop of Mantua. The consecration was conferred by Cardinal Parocchi, assisted by the two former bishops of Mantua, Msgr. Rota and Msgr. Berengo.

After his first meeting with Msgr. Sarto, Msgr. Rota wrote to one of his friends: "I have just seen the new Bishop of Mantua, Msgr. Giuseppe Sarto, and I thought he was a very apt choice for his gentleness, friendliness, modesty and humility."[7]

On the evening of the ceremony the new Bishop of Mantua was once more received at an audience by Leo XIII. This was not an audience of pure form, for it lasted more than an hour and much of it was devoted to the question of the diocese of Mantua and in particular to the situation of the seminary. No doubt the Pope referred to the different problems which had arisen in the diocese. At all events, in the letter in which Msgr. Sarto speaks of this audience, he tells his correspondent: "The thought of this diocese terrifies me...and causes me many a deep sigh."[8] As we shall see, the situation of Mantua, both material and spiritual, was highly disturbing.

During this second audience Leo XIII gave the new bishop a pectoral cross which had been worn by two of Msgr. Sarto's predecessors in the See of Mantua, a ring (bearing his effigy), a Pontifical and an altar missal. Having left Rome, Msgr. Sarto went as a pilgrim to two shrines close to his heart: Assisi and Loretto. He was not able to go to Mantua immediately because he had to obtain the *regio exequatur*, the government's authorization. He did not receive this until three months later. In the meantime he continued to reside at the Treviso seminary. He worked a lot, received many visits, learned all he could about the situation of the diocese he was to govern and, freed from all his former obligations, was able to visit his family and his former parishioners. He visited Riese and Treviso. He presided at ceremonies and preached. His former Salzano parishioners made a

---

6 "The Bishop of Cremona tells everyone that his greatest enemies are the Bishops of Pavia and Mantua," letter of Msgr. Sarto to Msgr. Callegari, August 4, 1887, photographically reproduced in *Una memoria ritrovata*, pp.131-134.
7 Letter cited by Marchesan, p.233.
8 Letter to Msgr. Giuseppe Callegari, November 20, 1884, *Lettere*, pp.119-120.

collection to present him with a pastoral ring; the Romanin-Jacur family, although they were Jewish, as we have seen, gave the amethyst which adorned the ring. Visiting Riese, Msgr. Sarto showed his mother his bishop's ring. Mamma Sarto showed her good sense in her reply, reported by all the authors: "Your ring is beautiful, Giuseppe; but—pointing to her wedding ring—you wouldn't have it if I hadn't got this one."

While he was waiting for the *exequatur*, Msgr. Sarto accepted many invitations to preach. On January 29, 1885, in the church of the Salesians in Venice (where his cousin was a curate) he delivered the panegyric of St. Francis de Sales. The following February 8, he went to visit his former parishioners in Salzano, celebrating the morning Mass and then, in the afternoon, giving a spiritual conference on the Sacred Heart of Jesus, at which he was surprised to see Msgr. Callegari present. That day his former parishioners presented him with a very beautiful episcopal crozier.

On February 26 the *exequatur* arrived. He could therefore officially inform the Mantua civil authorities of his appointment as bishop. The letter he sent on this occasion to the Mayor *(sindaco)* of Mantua gives a good idea of the state of mind in which he approached the political authorities of the time: respect for the legitimate authorities (even if their political convictions were contrary to the Church's doctrine), concern for the common good and insistence on the free exercise of his spiritual power. He assured the Mayor of Mantua: "If I know the charge entrusted to me by the Lord, I am also acquainted with the duty I have to be most loyal to the constituted authorities, and, as a minister of Religion, my banner is that of peace and my law is the law of charity." He also assured the political authorities that his first concern would be to "maintain harmony" and that he was ready to make "every honest sacrifice in order to avoid the least discord, which would be fatal not only to the prosperity of the region but also to the precious unity of hearts." He said that he wanted only to fulfil "the office of a father and friend" and that he had "no other aim than to promote the salvation of souls and to create of them one single family of friends and brothers."[9] We shall see that this irenic will, sincere yet flexible, would not stop Msgr. Sarto showing himself firm when the Church's laws and rights were challenged.[10]

On March 18, the Feast of St. Anselm, patron of the diocese of Mantua, Msgr. Sarto addressed his first pastoral letter to his clergy and the faithful of the diocese. It took the form of a commitment:

> For the good of souls I will spare neither toil, watchings nor fatigue, and nothing will be closer to my heart than your salvation. Some, perhaps, will wonder what is my basis for making such promises. It is *hope*, the

---

[9]   Letter to the *sindaco* of Mantua, March 5, 1885, *Lettere,* p.123.

emblem of which, the *anchor*, I have had displayed on my episcopal coat of arms; as Scripture says (Heb. 6:19), hope is the soul's sure and firm anchor; hope is the sole companion of my life, the greatest support in uncertainty, the strongest power in situations of weakness. Hope, yes; but not human hope, which is imagined to be the source of the greatest happiness even in the midst of the greatest misfortune; but the *hope of Christ*, which culminates in the heavenly promises and can strengthen the feeblest man with the greatness of soul and the help of God...I know that, for the salvation of my sheep, I shall have to fight battles, face dangers, accept insults, suffer storms, struggle against the plague which is attacking morality; but my flock...my flock will always find me gentle, kind and full of charity.[11]

After visiting his aged mother in Riese once more, Msgr. Sarto left his native Venice region for Lombardy, less smiling and more severe. He arrived in Mantua on April 18 and the next day officially took possession of his diocese. His first sermon in the town's cathedral was on the theme of the bishop's mission and the respective duties of pastor and faithful.

The cathedral (*Duomo*), a fine classical building, is situated at the end of the city square. The façade, of Carrara marble, dates from the 18th century and bears aloft statues of the great saints who have shone their light on Mantua. The interior, constructed in the 16th century according to the plans of Giulio Romano, consists of five naves separated by Corinthian columns, and at its transept there is a splendid octagonal cupola. The *Duomo* is flanked by two magnificent edifices. On the right there is the red brick palace of the Dukes of Gonzaga, who reigned over the city and its surrounding region for centuries. On the left there is the episcopal palace, a beautiful two-story building. Msgr. Sarto moved into this palace which, no doubt, he found far too big (soon, as we shall see, he rented out a part of it). His sisters Maria and Anna came to look after him, sometimes helped by two of his nieces. Msgr. Sarto also looked for a *maestro di camera* to act as both major-domo and private secretary. For some time a young priest from Treviso, Giuseppe Santinon, fulfilled this role and then, from

---

[10] Thus, from 1888, the tenth anniversary of the accession of the King of Italy, Humbert I, his *genetliaco* (birthday, which fell on March 14) was celebrated in all the country by civil and religious ceremonies. In Mantua the civil and military authorities attended a *Te Deum* in the cathedral, and then went to the Synagogue for a ceremony. This practice profoundly shook Msgr. Sarto. Formally, it contravened the first article of the Italian constitution at that time (the *Statuto*). On the religious level it amounted to putting the Catholic religion on the same level as the Jewish religion. The following year, as March 14th approached, Msgr. Sarto informed the town authorities that if they envisaged the same ceremonies, he would have to refuse them entry to his cathedral. After taking instructions from Rome, the mayor of Mantua decided not to have any religious ceremony.

[11] Pastoral letter of March 18, 1885, quoted by Marchesan, pp.238-239.

September 1885, another young priest, Giovanni Bressan, entered his service. He was 24 and stayed on as private secretary, active and influential, in Venice and subsequently in Rome.

The state of the diocese

The city of Mantua had enjoyed a prestigious past, illuminated particularly by the Gonzagas, one of Europe's richest ducal families. Arising from its location—it is built on a rocky spur on an island in the River Mincio—it had long been a strategic place of prime importance. In the 18th century and the first half of the 19th the Austrians had made it the keystone of the defensive system of their Lombardy possessions. First the Josephinist politics and then the war brought by Napoleon Bonaparte in 1796 had encouraged Mantua's decline. The French occupation had overturned the city's structures and led not only to a political revolution but also, for the first time, to a total laicization of social life and to the separation of Church and state. Once the French had gone, Austria (in 1815) recovered its authority over Mantua and placed it at the head of one of the nine provinces of its Lombardo-Venetian kingdom. The struggle between the Kingdom of Piedmont-Sardinia (the future Kingdom of Italy) and the Austrian Empire proceeded by stages. In 1859 part of the province of Mantua was attached to Italy, but not Mantua itself, which remained Austrian until 1866. When Msgr. Sarto arrived, nearly 20 years later, the signs of decadence were many and worrying.

The end of Austrian occupation and Mantua's incorporation into Italy had resulted in the city becoming isolated. Agriculture, dominated by large landholdings (*latifundia*), yielded little, due to the lack of land suitable for cultivation. In addition the countryside had been stirred up, since 1884, by a deep-seated agrarian revolt, with its war-cry of *"la boje!"* A few days after the new bishop arrived, some 160 peasants and their ringleaders were arrested. The social and economic situation seemed all the more dire since the city did not as yet have any important industries. The state of public sanitation was utterly deplorable. There were recurrent plagues of tuberculosis, malaria and pellagra due to the proximity of swamps, the place's particular climate and the people's defective diet. The mortality figures were 50% higher than the national average, and in some years the number of deaths exceeded the number of births. If the population of Mantua did not drop in the 19th century, it was because the exodus from the land came to swell the depleted ranks of the citizenry.[12]

The spiritual state of the diocese was also deplorable. Ever since the beginning of the century there had been no lack of disruption. From 1797 to 1803 the seminary was closed as a result of the French occupation of the city. Then for 16 years, from 1807 to 1823, the diocese had been without a bishop! This exceptional interregnum, added to other causes, plunged the clergy into a crisis which only came to an end when Msgr. Sarto arrived. In 1864, for example, five priests renounced the priesthood and ten in 1870. Msgr. Sarto's two predecessors knew much disappointment. Msgr. Rota, bishop from 1871 to 1879, without the government's *exequatur,* had been persistently attacked by the anti-clerical left and by Freemasonry, both of which were very active in Mantua. He was brought before a court and imprisoned. What is more, in 1871 the Congregation of the Council, which was responsible for seminaries, closed the Mantua seminary because of its doctrinal deviations. Not until the following year could it open its doors again. After that it was closed again on two other occasions, this time on the orders of the government. It did not function normally again until three years after Msgr. Berengo took over as head of the diocese. We have already referred to the grave difficulties the latter had to contend with. In five years as bishop he could ordain only six priests....When Msgr. Sarto took possession of his diocese, 16 parishes were without a parish priest and six had no priest at all.

The episcopal disappointments, added to the way in which people's thoughts were moving, had created a city and a diocese that was spiritually adrift. In the whole of Italy, and even further afield in the case of informed observers, the diocese of Mantua had become *"mala fama famosa"*—notorious. Msgr. Sarto knew what was waiting for him. In 1876 Pius IX had asked Msgr. Zinelli to present a report on the diocese of Mantua. No doubt Msgr. Sarto, Msgr. Zinelli's closest collaborator, was acquainted (at the very least) with the contents of this hard-hitting report.

When, less than ten years later, Msgr. Sarto arrived in Mantua, he set about a work of restoration with single-minded determination. As his episcopal coat of arms he had chosen an anchor within a sea illumined by a star. The anchor was a symbol of hope, according to the words of St. Paul quoted by Msgr. Sarto in his first pastoral letter.[13]

Once installed in the episcopal palace, and as the months went by, with meetings and audiences, he acquired a clearer vision of the problems that were to be solved and the reforms that needed to be made. For example, the reports sent to him prior to his first pastoral visitation show that in

---

[12] On Mantua and the Sarto episcopate: Roberto Brunelli, *Diocesi di Mantova* (Brescia: Editrice La Scuola, 1986), collection *Storia religiosa della Lombardia*; Stefano Siliberti, "Vescovo a Mantova (1884-1893)" and Rinaldo Salvadori, "Mantova" in *Pio X,* under the direction of G. Romanato (Milan: Edizione Paoline, 1987); Andrea Cappelletti, *Giuseppe Sarto, vescovo a Mantova* (Mantua: Arel-Padania, 1992); *Giuseppe Sarto. Un vescovo e la Società mantovana all fine dell'Ottocento* (various) (Mantua: Istituto Mantovano di storia contemporanea/Comune di Mantova/Diocese di Mantova-Archivio storico diocesano, 1995).

[13] Hope is "like an anchor of the soul, sure and steadfast" (Heb. 6:19).

three of the city parishes even the Paschal precept was little observed: at St. Maria della Carità and St. Apollonia only about a third of the parishioners made their confession and went to Communion; at St. Apollonia it was 800 faithful out of 1800 inhabitants of the parish.[14]

In December 1885, eight months after arriving, Msgr. Sarto sent to Rome a first report on the state of his diocese. This long unpublished document—17 large manuscript pages in Latin—gives a picture of the diocese as well as of the first reforms that had been begun.[15] Msgr. Sarto wrote that the diocese had 270,000 inhabitants and 153 parishes (of which 10 were in Mantua itself). These parishes, to which had to be added 214 public chapels, were served by 308 priests, which was few enough. The bishop deplores the fact that some of them "are so sluggish that they are oblivious or ignorant of the office and dignity of the priesthood, or get involved in secular affairs or, which is most regrettable, are distracted by worldly futilities or abandon themselves to drink."

Msgr. Sarto set himself to reform the clergy, beginning with an overhaul of the diocesan seminary.

"*Ego dilexi vos*"—restoration of the seminary

Msgr. Sarto's first concern in Mantua was for the seminary.[16] Only a street separated the seminary from the episcopal palace. He visited it in the very first days after he arrived. In the report we have already cited he wrote: "The seminary is the apple of my eye and I regard it as my natural dwelling-place. I am accustomed to go there almost every day, to keep an eye on everything."

He used a different mode of speech when, in a pastoral letter, some months after his arrival in Mantua, he told his diocesan faithful of his great interest in the seminary:

> I devote much thought to the serious matter of the seminary. It is the object of my desires and the focus of my affections; it either calms or arouses my anxieties, because the education of clerics is the basis of a diocese's discipline and government: it depends solely on them whether we are to have good priests. This is the most beautiful work that can emerge from a bishop's hands....
>
> How I would wish to dedicate myself entirely to guarding those who are the Church's precious hope, talking with them, being present at their exercises to discern their spirit, their inclinations, their habits; cultivating

---

[14] Figures cited in Cappelletti, *G. Sarto, vescovo a Mantova,* p.85.

[15] *Relatio,* dated December 1885, ASV, S. Congr. Concilii, Relationes, 485B.

[16] In addition to the sources already cited on the Sarto episcopate in Mantua, cf. Stefano Siliberti, "Mons. Giuseppe Sarto e il Seminario," in *Seminario vescovile di Mantova. Una storia da riscorire* (Mantua: 1995), pp.51-94.

in them the germs of the virtues; giving prompt remedies when disorder rears its head; discussing with the masters what are the best means of education; demonstrating, finally, that the clerics are the apple of my eye, and that the seminary, as a holy bishop once said, is "the heart of my heart."[17]

When he arrived the diocese had only 60 seminarians. Several professors had left the seminary in the preceding years. Discouraged, they had obtained some other ministry or even, in the case of some, given up the priesthood. The most famous instance is that of Roberto Ardigo (1828-1920).[18] Professor at the Mantua Seminary, he had been suspended *a divinis* after the publication of a study dedicated to Pietro Pomponazzi. He left the clerical state in 1871 and had become professor of the history of philosophy at the University of Padua and the leader of Italian positivism. Msgr. Sarto took an interest in what had happened to this former priest of the diocese, now living in the city of his friend Msgr. Callegari. After a journey to Rome, he wrote to the latter: "Cardinal Parocchi asked me to beg Your Eminence and Professor Alessi to think what might be the best way of converting Professor Ardigo. The Cardinal thinks that he will not be so stubborn as to refuse to listen to a word of grace. As God wills!"[19] The editors of Roberto Ardigo's correspondence have not published the letters Msgr. Sarto wrote to him and the replies he gave, but we know that Ardigo's response was a courteous but firm refusal to go back on his decision.[20]

Msgr. Sarto was fervently determined to restore his seminary. He met the seminarians and their professors, acquainted himself with the program of studies and with the seminary's material needs. Its material position was catastrophic: the lack of pupils meant a lack of resources. The intellectual level of their formation and the spiritual atmosphere left a lot to be desired.

One week after the aforementioned pastoral letter it was the end of the academic year at the seminary. Just as he had said he wanted to, Msgr. Sarto endeavoured to find out for himself the intellectual level and the religious tone of his seminarians. He was present at all their end-of-year examinations and desired to close the academic year with a solemn event at the episcopal palace. During this ceremony, which took place on July 14,

[17] Pastoral letter of July 7, 1885, cited by Pierre Fernessole, *Pie X. Essai historique* (Paris: Lethielleux, 1952), vol.I, p.78.

[18] Paolo Bonatelli, "Ardigo, Roberto," *Enciclopedia cattolica,* vol.I, col.1849-1850.

[19] Letter to Msgr. Callegari, December 22, 1891, photographically reproduced in *Una memoria ritrovata,* p.122.

[20] The edited correspondence of Roberto Ardigo *Carteggio 1868-1916* (Florence: La Nuova Italia Editrice, 1973), and *Lettere edite ed inedite* (Frankfurt/Main: Peter Lang, 1990), contain no letter from Msgr. Sarto and no mention of his name.

1885, Msgr. Sarto gave an address on the importance of studies for the clergy, particularly in modern times, and gave a brief summary of the teaching of St. Thomas Aquinas.[21] In doing this, the new bishop was in perfect harmony with the directives of Leo XIII who, in the Encyclical *Aeterni Patris* a few years earlier, had recalled "the origin and character and the excellence of the scholastic doctrine" and had urged that the "admirable doctrine of St. Thomas Aquinas—the Angelic Doctor—should be taken up with fresh vigor." Msgr. Sarto's address to his seminarians completely echoed the exhortation of Leo XIII, who had written:

> Nothing is dearer to Our heart, nor do We have any greater wish, than to see provided copiously to young students the pure waters of wisdom such as the Angelic Doctor pours forth so inexhaustibly.
>
> We have several reasons for this ardent desire of Ours: in the first place, since in our time the Christian faith is daily being attacked by the maneuvers and wiles of a certain false wisdom, it is necessary for all young people, especially those whose education is the Church's hope, to be nourished by a doctrine that is solid and strong, so that, full of energy and clad with a complete suit of armor, they will early acquire the habit of defending religion with valor and wisdom....[22]

From the earliest days, furthermore, Msgr. Sarto did not hesitate to appeal to the generosity of everyone, urging them to respond to the many material needs of the establishment.[23] However, considerable work had yet to be done to obtain a plentiful supply of well-trained clergy. At the end of this academic year 1884-1885 Msgr. Sarto could only ordain one priest and one deacon. It made him sad: "These are the only fruits my seminary has given me this year," he wrote to Don Bressan, adding, "how wretched it is, and how it pains me, when I would need at least 40...."[24] The situation was such that Msgr. Sarto could not find, among the Mantua clergy, a priest suitable to direct the seminary according to his views. He had to leave the existing rector in office, even though he regarded him as inade-

---

[21] Articoli, p.35.

[22] *Aeterni Patris*, August 4, 1879, *Actes de Léon XIII* (Paris: Maison de la Bonne Presse, 1925) vol.I, p.71. It is only right to point out that the Thomist Encyclical of Leo XIII was the culmination of a cultural and intellectual movement which had been prompted under the preceding pontificate; cf. Antonio Piolanti, *Pio X e la rinascita del tomismo,* (Vatican City: Libreria Editrice Vaticana, 1974).

[23] In the following years Msgr. Sarto established the principle that no seminarian could be admitted to the seminary free of charge, so that the sacrifices undertaken by his family should make him appreciate the value of what he was receiving. At the same time he paid a large part of the fees of the poorest students out of his own pocket (Marchesan, p.254, and the deposition of Don Pedrini, *Summarium,* p.532).

[24] Letter of July 24, 1885, quoted in *Articoli,* p.35.

quate for the task. Gradually, however, he was able to introduce the necessary improvements.

In December 1885, in his first report to Rome on the state of his diocese, he indicated that the seminary had 123 students, that is, more than double the number he had found on his arrival eight months earlier. Evidently Msgr. Sarto knew how to make the seminary attractive again by restoring discipline, studies and the spiritual life. In his report he states that the minor orders are conferred only after three-day spiritual exercises, and that the major orders are conferred only after ten-day spiritual exercises. "Besides, no one is admitted without a qualifying examination, nor without having provided proof, as required by the rules, of legitimate birth, dignity of temperament, progress in studies, good morals and a clerical spirit."[25] He is also known to have established a "disciplinary rule" which, once its effectiveness became evident, was adopted by other bishops for their seminaries. As regards the teaching, Msgr. Sarto adopted the methods he had seen practised in the Treviso seminary. He recruited professors of quality. Only in the following years did he find a man suitable to direct the seminary: a young priest, Giovanni Battista Rosa. Fr. Rosa was sent to Rome to pursue his studies at the Lombard Seminary, and was ordained priest in 1892. He was appointed vice-rector of the Mantua Seminary the following year. Since he was so young, Msgr. Sarto himself assumed the title of Rector.[26]

He was no less concerned about the seminary's financial position. To find the necessary resources for the establishment to function, Msgr. Sarto rented out part of the episcopal palace, put up for sale two fields he still possessed in Riese, and sold the amethyst from his pastoral ring.[27]

Msgr. Sarto was always watchful concerning the formation of his seminarians. He himself taught moral theology for one year and Gregorian chant for a while (this was the first time this subject had been introduced at the seminary). Gradually he replaced the professors who where missing in one or other discipline: dogmatic theology, Greek, mathematics, philos-

---

[25] *Relatio* of December 1885, ASV, S.Congr.Concilii, *Relationes*, 485B.

[26] Msgr. Sarto had attentively followed the young cleric's studies in Rome. G. B. Rosa had been at the Lombard Seminary for a few days, when he received this advice from his bishop: "I do not urge you to be devout, because I am sure that you have treasured your bishop's last recommendations. Always distrust yourself, love the virtue of humility and you will always enjoy heaven's blessings," letter of October 26, 1886, in *Lettere*, p.152. Rosa had a fine career under the pontificate of Pius X: in 1911 he was appointed *sostituto* at the Consistorial Congregation.

[27] He had the precious stone replaced by an imitation. One day, laughing, he showed it to Signora Romanin Jacur when she was visiting him in his episcopal palace in Mantua: "*el xe el fondo d'un goto*" (Bacchion, *Pio X, Giuseppe Sarto, arciprete di Salzano, 1867-1875* ([1996], p.65).

ophy, music. In 1891, after six years as bishop, in the third report he sent
to Rome on the state of his diocese, he laid stress on the curriculum of
studies in his seminary: Italian, Latin, Greek, philosophy "according to the
scholastic method," "without forgetting mathematics and physics." For
the four years of theology the subjects were: dogma, moral theology, biblical studies with particular attention to "a good interpretation of the
books of Holy Scripture" and to an exposition of "its authority and inspiration, following the rules of hermeneutics and sacred exegesis."[28] We also
know that he always entrusted the teaching of dogmatics and moral theology to Jesuit professors, whom he regarded as less subject to doctrinal de-
viation.

For spiritual formation he turned to a spiritual director who did not
belong to the diocesan clergy, and to two Jesuit confessors. Convinced,
through his own experience, of the importance of preaching in the priest's
apostolate, he desired that, during the month of May, the seminarians in
theology—*i.e.,* those who were close to ordination—should have to
preach at solemn Masses. He himself came to hear the sermons, and we
can be sure that he made the necessary remarks and suggestions.[29] In spite
of the great needs of his diocese, Msgr. Sarto always showed himself strict
with regard to admission to the priesthood: he refused to ordain young
men to the priesthood unless he was sure that they were worthy. In the case
of each one, he conducted an enquiry into their moral and spiritual qualities.[30] Finally, he wished that, for the first four years after ordination, all
priests should come before a commission presided over by him, to be examined on subjects both sacred and profane. According to Msgr. Sarto, a
good priest, apart from other qualities, must remain a man of study.

As Andrea Cappelletti has observed, "Msgr. Sarto established a relationship with his seminarians which was both paternal and magisterial."[31]
Seminary discipline was as dear to his heart as good teaching. He watched
over it closely and did not hesitate to intervene personally in grave cases, as
we learn from this article, published by a former seminarian on the day
after Giuseppe Sarto was elected to the pontificate:

> He loved us dearly, but with a great *intransigence*. Often, when we
> were least expecting it, he would appear and fix us with his probing gaze

---

[28] *Relatio,* November 24, 1891 (22 manuscript pages), ASV, S. Congr. Concilii,
Relationes, 485B.

[29] Depositions of Anna Sarto and Msgr. Sartori, *Summarium,* pp.64 and 537.

[30] Depositions of Msgr. Sartori and Don Martini, *Summarium,* pp.535 and 538. It
should also be noted that, out of concern for the dignity of his priests, Msgr. Sarto
prohibited all his priests from riding on bicycles.

[31] Cappelletti, *G. Sarto, vescovo a Mantova,* p.122.

as if demanding our attention—which was already stretched to the limit as soon as he opened his mouth. Anyone who had transgressed immediately began to tremble, because of the bishop's love for us, which so desired our good. Wasn't he right? He was implacable towards those who thought they were above others because they knew a bit more.

One day a storm erupted. Light-hearted as we were, like all young men, we had committed a serious act of insubordination. The following day the bishop arrived, his eyes flashing. We thought there would be an angry scene—a fist banging the table, a crushing word. We were afraid, wondering how it would all end. And suddenly we saw two big tears rolling down his face.

We never forgot those tears; they were the sign of the huge affection he had for us. No father could have loved us more.

The last time he came to see us, he said: "Perhaps we won't see each other again; but you must pray for me, because I have loved you."[32]

Reform of the clergy

Those who were to become priests were Msgr. Sarto's first concern since they represented the future of the diocese and of the Church. But he was also determined to reform the existing clergy. It was necessary to fight against the abuses and deviations which were to be found here and there, to revitalize a secular clergy which had been shaken by the many crises of recent decades, and to refashion the unity of a divided clergy. (In the preceding years three priests had allowed themselves to be elected parish priest by their parishioners, in rebellion against the bishop.)

So Msgr. Sarto worked on different fronts at the same time. To prevent ecclesiastical posts being the result of intrigue and favoritism, he reestablished competitions to supply them. To give an example of assiduous attention to priestly obligations, he did not spare his own person. Even today one is still shown the confessional in the cathedral of Mantua where he loved to go to hear his people's confessions. One day, to teach a lesson to a parish priest who rarely showed himself in the confessional, Msgr. Sarto turned up without warning and installed himself in the confession-box. The lesson had the desired effect. Such stories could be multiplied. From the first report he sent to Rome we know that Msgr. Sarto had introduced frequent spiritual conferences for the Mantua clergy: "Eight times a year there are exercises of this kind in the city, in the episcopal palace, attended by parish priests and confessors resident here."[33] We also know that the bishop did not hesitate to use his authority when exhortation and persuasion proved insufficient. Thus one day, for example, after having frequent-

---

[32] Article published in *Il Cittadino di Mantova,* August 8, 1903. Reproduced in Dal-Gal, *Pie X* (Paris: Éditions Saint-Paul, 1953), p.84.

[33] *Relatio* of December 1885, ASV, S. Congr. Concilii, *Relationes*, 485B.

ly reminded his priests of the necessity of attending these short retreats on a regular basis, he summoned to his palace two priests who had ignored his advice. He himself brought them to a convent to follow the spiritual exercises there....[34]

These edifying characteristics show the high and demanding ideal of the priest which inspired Msgr. Sarto. In a letter to his clergy—one of the last of his Mantua episcopate—he thus described the attitude the priest should have:

> The priest should regulate his actions, his bearing, his habits in harmony with the sublimity of his vocation, so that he will never lower himself to any unedifying act. The priest who, at the altar, leaves behind—in a certain way—his earthly condition and takes on a divine form, is still the same when he comes down from the holy mountain and leaves the temple of God. Wherever he is, wherever he goes, he never stops being a priest. His priestly dignity goes with him everywhere, and this is why he should maintain a certain gravity of bearing.
>
> The priest must be holy and serious; he must inspire respect; he must edify all those he meets by his words, his demeanor, his way of doing things. External dignity radiates a kind of eloquence which is better able to conquer souls than the most persuasive talk. The priest who never forgets the dignity of his state naturally inspires confidence in people; on the contrary, if he forgets it, if he does not show more gravity in his bearing than certain people of the world, he will incur the scorn even of those who may perhaps applaud his easy-going attitude; such people will start by despising him, and end by despising the sacred ministry and religion itself. When gravity is lacking in superiors, the inferiors will lack respect and veneration.[35]

Of course the bishop had a duty to give example to his priests. And at Mantua Msgr. Sarto never lost the gravity and the priestly awareness which he urged on his clergy. Zealous and indefatigable pastor that he was—frequently he slept for only four hours, as his secretary has attested—he had a high notion of his work. "To work is a pleasure," he wrote to a relative at this time, "and the soul is a fire which is fed solely by work."[36] A man of prayer and charity, the new bishop quickly acquired the reputation throughout the diocese of being a genuine man of God. One night, according to his secretary's testimony, he was summoned to the bedside of a teacher from the city's school, hitherto an unbeliever, who was not willing

---

[34] This severity went hand-in-hand with a great charity towards his priests. There exists a manuscript letter—and no doubt there are others—which was polycopied and sent to all the priests of the diocese: in it, Msgr. Sarto asked for financial aid for an elderly, sick priest who had neither ministry nor revenue (letter of September 28, 1887, *Lettere*, pp.158-159).

[35] Letter to the clergy of August 25, 1894, cf. Dal-Gal, *Pius X*, p.72.

[36] Letter of November 15, 1886, cited in Marchesan, p.284.

to receive any other priest but the new bishop. Msgr. Sarto came and stayed by his side for more than an hour and succeeded in convincing him to receive the Last Sacraments.[37]

Right from the start of his episcopate Msgr. Sarto insisted that his priests teach children the catechism in a progressive but complete manner. He also required them to give a conference on Christian doctrine to all the faithful on Sundays and holy days of obligation; this was to last an hour and a half, and should explain the origin and, most importantly, the meaning of the solemnity being celebrated that day. Msgr. Sarto could have insisted that his parish priests use the dialogue method he had used in Salzano, but did not do this. To give a stimulus to his clergy's zeal, he published a circular in which he offered a prize to the one who suggested the best method of teaching.[38]

One day he found out that a Mantua priest, the parish priest of Stradella, was not giving the required instruction. He went to the church unannounced and had the bells rung to call the faithful; then he himself began to teach Christian doctrine in connection with the feast of the day. The parish priest, who had also run to the church on hearing the bells, was astonished to find his bishop in his pulpit.[39]

There was a great deal to do. On August 18, 1885, he announced the beginning of the pastoral visitation of the diocese. According to the prescriptions of the Council of Trent he would visit in turn each of the parishes of his diocese. He would examine their material state and maintenance, and that of the objects employed in divine worship; he would also dispense the sacraments (in particular, Confirmation), preach to the faithful, question them, and question the parish priests and curates, giving reprimands and advice where necessary. Depending on the number of parishes to be visited, the bishop's visitation would take place more or less frequently. It was rare for a bishop to be able to visit all his parishes every year. It even happened that negligent bishops never visited their parishes, or at least not systematically.

At Mantua, as later in Venice, Msgr. Sarto always respected to the letter the prescriptions of the Council of Trent. In the letter announcing his first pastoral visitation, he defines it as "one of the bishop's first duties, one of his sweetest consolations." He also issued recommendations so that no additional expense should be incurred by the parish priests because of his visitation; as for the faithful, instead of lining the streets to receive him in a carnival atmosphere, he wished them to assemble at the church, ready to

---

[37] Testimony of Msgr. Bressan, reported by Cigala, p.48, and deposition of Msgr. G. B. Parolin, *Summarium,* p.141.

[38] Deposition of Msgr. G. B. Rosa, *Summarium,* p.215.

[39] Deposition of Msgr. Rizzi, *Summarium,* pp.674 and 675.

follow the Mass and come to Communion. The first pastoral visitation began in 1885 and was concluded in 1888; the second was begun in 1889 and was interrupted by his nomination to Venice. The purpose of pastoral visitations, according to the Council of Trent, is threefold: to defend or propagate sound doctrine against errors or deviations; to keep the clergy and the faithful in the path of good conduct, or bring them back to it; and to promote or re-awaken religion and concord in souls.

The different testimonies regarding Msgr. Sarto's pastoral visitations show us a bishop attentive to the spiritual and temporal needs of parish priests and their faithful. At least a week before his arrival, each parish had to present a report on its material and religious situation. During his visitations the Bishop of Mantua was eager to administer the sacraments himself (as well as the Eucharist, he heard confessions and gave Confirmation) and to preach at every Mass. He also took delight in explaining Christian doctrine to children and adults. He carefully examined the parish records and the church itself, nor did he omit to meet the parish priest in private, to listen to him and ask him questions, doing the same with the curates and any of the faithful who wished to meet him. The material and spiritual state of the parishes was very diverse. Sometimes they were very defective. The most spectacular case was that of a parish which had not seen its parish priest and curate for several months!

The parishes of the diocese of Mantua were often quite inferior to those Msgr. Sarto had known in the province of Venice. At his first pastoral visitation, in Canneto sull'Oglio, he observed this bitterly in a letter to Msgr. Callegari:

> It is very different from even the worst parishes of the dioceses of Treviso and Padua!...Here we are *in partibus infidelium.* Just imagine: here, in a parish of 3,000 souls, at the bishop's Mass, there were only 40 women, of whom eight received Communion; and at the lesson of Christian doctrine there were 100 children and about the same number of spectators. And the man who presides over the cure of souls even tried to tell me that the region was not as bad as I had perhaps imagined.[40]

Visiting all the parishes of the diocese took almost three years. There were many parishes—153—and the bishop had continually to interrupt his tour to return to his cathedral on Sundays, or else he had to give one or more days over to important affairs or special ceremonies (thus, for instance, he wanted to be present in his seminary on November 15, 1885, for the beginning of term and the arrival of those who would be future clerics).

---

[40] Letter to Msgr. Giuseppe Callegari, October 30, 1886, quoted in Siliberti, "Mons. Giuseppe Sarto e il Seminario," p.65.

This first pastoral visitation called for comprehensive solutions and new orientations. This was the subject of a diocesan synod. It was announced on February 16, 1887, in a pastoral letter. The bishop wrote that the aim of the synod would be to "draw up, after mature and deliberate reflection, a résumé of the diocesan statutes and establish suitable rules to meet new situations, new evils and new challenges—rules which earlier synods could not have imagined." It has been observed that this pastoral letter is also "a veritable declaration of holy war against errors of a nascent modernism,"[41] even if the word *Modernism* was not yet used. In fact, Msgr. Sarto was here opposing those who, "setting themselves up as masters, assert that the Church must always adapt herself to the demands of the times, and that it has become impossible to keep the primitive integrity of her laws." The Bishop of Mantua denounced "this modern Christianity which has forgotten the ancient folly of the Cross [and where] the dogmas of faith must be adapted to the requirements of the new philosophy...."[42] Here we see that the anti-Modernist battle waged by Pius X arises from a very ancient concern for the faith.

Announced in February 1887, the synod took place in September 1888, after the pastoral visitation had concluded. This long delay between its announcement and its opening facilitated much important preparatory work. There had been no diocesan synod for more than two centuries. Each vicar forane was invited to present written proposals and suggestions to the bishop. After that there were preparatory meetings in which the participants were the canons of the cathedral, the Mantua parish priests and the vicars forane.

In a letter to his former teacher, Msgr. Jacuzzi, Msgr. Sarto complained of the difficulties he encountered in assembling such a gathering of clergy: "I have worked alone for almost a year; I have used the greatest tact possible; I have not heeded any sacrifice, even from my own purse, to get the representatives of the clergy together from time to time...."[43] Finally 200 priests participated in the synod which took place on September 10, 11, and 12. The diocesan legislation was set forth, and new norms were promulgated for the clergy and for the faithful. The areas covered by these regulations were very diverse: for example, the discipline of marriage; the teaching of Christian doctrine; the Easter Communion; Communion of the sick and of children; the schedule of Masses; processions; the practice of indulgences; holy images; oratories; churches; the ecclesiastical tribunal; funerals; cemeteries; sacred music; relationships with Protestants and non-

---

[41] Pierluigi Occelli, quoted in Domenico Agasso, *L'Ultimo papa santo Pio X* (Cinisello Balsamo: Edizioni Paoline, 1985), p.48.

[42] Pastoral letter of February 16, 1887, quoted in Agasso, p.48.

[43] Letter to Msgr. Pietro Jacuzzi, September 28, 1888, *Lettere*, p.170.

Christians (Mantua had a strong Jewish community). The decisions of the synod were also published and sent to all the priests of the diocese.[44] Here, for instance, is the synod's injunction on the teaching of doctrine:

> A school of Christian doctrine shall be instituted in all the parishes. On Sundays and on holy days of obligation, catechism will be given in all churches. The parish priest will explain the Christian doctrine, and immediately afterwards, from the pulpit, he will give catechism to the people. During Lent and Advent there must be a special daily instruction for children to prepare them for confession and Communion. Parish priests must remember that parents, guardians and employers who habitually prevent their children or those who depend on them from attending instruction in Christian doctrine, cannot be absolved.[45]

On May 25, 1889, Msgr. Sarto began his second pastoral visitation of his diocese. Once again he insisted on the necessity of a good knowledge of Christian doctrine on the part of all the faithful. In the letter announcing the new pastoral visitation he reminded them:

> What will console me most will be progress in the teaching of Christian doctrine. This was my message to you when I had hardly set foot in the diocese; it is what I urged in all the parishes during my first pastoral visitation, and it will also be the first of my concerns—and I shall insist on it—in my second visitation.

In the parishes, he was often seen giving a detailed explanation of some point of Christian doctrine to all the faithful, assembled in the church, or else he would attend the lesson of doctrine given by the parish priest.

Vigilant that the teaching of the faith should be full and solid, Msgr. Sarto took a close interest in the first National Catechetical Congress which was held in Piacenza on September 24, 25, and 26, 1889. The Bishop of Mantua could not attend in person since he had reserved all his available time for the second pastoral visitation, which had begun some months earlier. But he took part by means of an address which was read to the assembly. The Congress, presided over by Msgr. Scalabrini, Bishop of Piacenza, examined different questions. Msgr. Sarto's contribution was on the subject of the "unitary catechism," *i.e.*, a catechism that could be imposed on all countries and would be obligatory for the whole Church. Msgr. Sarto explained why the existing catechisms were insufficient:

---

[44] Constitutiones Mantuanae ab Illmo et Revmo DD. Josepho Sarto S. E. Episcopo promulgatae in synodo diocesano dictus X. XI. XII mensis septembris anni MDCCCLXXXVIII habita. (Mantua: Typis Apollonio, 1888).

[45] Cf. Dal-Gal, *Pius X*, p.68.

As for the numerous catechisms which have been published, particularly in recent years, many are unsatisfactory not only in their form, but also in their dogmatic correctness; what is needed is to adopt one single text for the teaching of Christian doctrine.[46]

Here the Bishop of Mantua was voicing a wish that had been already expressed 20 years earlier, at the First Vatican Council. He did not want the Congress to discuss this matter all over again, but to formulate a wish that would be addressed to the Holy See. Msgr. Sarto who, as we have seen, had already compiled a catechism when he was in Salzano, had a clear idea of what a universal catechism could be: "In the same way that the Holy See has established a prayerbook for the Universal Church, it is very desirable that a people's catechism should be made, historical, dogmatic and moral, compiled in the manner of short questions and very short answers, which could be taught in all the schools of Christian doctrine and translated into all languages. This would form a basis for the more advanced instruction which parish priests and catechists would give, depending on the age, intelligence and conditions of their listeners."

The entire Congress assented to Msgr. Sarto's suggestion. Two years later, during their annual conference, the bishops of Lombardy again took up the idea advanced by Msgr. Sarto. Elected secretary of the episcopal conference, he was authorized to present this request to Leo XIII. He did this in a letter, which found hardly any echo in Rome.[47] At this date, no one suspected that the very author of this suggestion would become pope and would himself bring the project to its completion.

The social question

In Mantua, even more than in Treviso and Salzano, the "social question" was a dramatic one: a considerable part of the population was in poverty, illiteracy was widespread, unemployment was accentuated by the particular crisis which had affected the city and its region over several decades. The agrarian revolt (*la boje*) and the socialist solutions (the confiscation of large properties, the creation of co-operatives, *etc.*) had seemed to many people to be the best way of dealing with a desperate situation. One year after Msgr. Sarto arrived in Mantua, the election results showed that the socialist ideas were shared by a large segment of public opinion; in May 1886 the candidates of the left had achieved 64% of the vote.

Msgr. Sarto, of course, had a totally different response to the "social question." As he did in Venice and during his pontificate, he gave a *religious* response to the *social* question because, in his integralist view of the

---

[46] Acts and documents of the first Catechetical Congress, Dal-Gal, *Pius X,* p.71.
[47] Letter to Leo XIII of October 16, 1891, *Lettere,* pp.180-181.

faith, no area of life could be excluded from religion, and the Church and her teaching must illuminate every domain. *Omnia instaurare in Christo,* to restore all things in Christ—this was the watchword of his pontificate. In Mantua, in a pastoral letter in which he set forth the social question at length, he says very clearly: "I shall not, of course, be proposing new things to you; I would only urge my flock not to be taken in by the utopias of certain people who, not always in good faith, are trying to stir them up." "Only the Gospel," he asserted, "can lead subjects to observe the laws, the powerful to defend the weak, and all men to conquer the virtues (or at least respect them); only the Gospel can restore to society that feature of the early Church: *'the multitude of believers were of one heart and one soul.'*"[48]

Yet the Bishop of Mantua did not call on his faithful simply to take refuge in prayer and the assiduous practice of religion. Throughout his episcopate he encouraged associations of the faithful and social organizations: he wanted Catholics to be good Catholics in social life too, so that their example and their action would attract those who were alienated from the Church and seduced by socialism and other "utopias."

Msgr. Sarto was particularly interested in the "Congress Works" (*Opera di Congressi*). This organization, founded in 1875 by two Venetians, Vito D'Ondes Reggio and Giuseppe Sacchetti, was the expression of a Catholicism that was social, "intransigent," anti-conciliationist and anti-liberal. It created—or linked within a federation—charitable work, youth movements, as well as credit unions, mutual societies, peasants' leagues, and newspapers. Bishops and laypeople worked side by side: the *Opera di Congressi* was a federative umbrella for a multitude of diocesan and parish committees. Under the pontificate of Pius X it represented, until its demise, the most numerous and most active wing of the Italian *movimento cattolico.*[49]

In Mantua, in 1886, the year when the Left won the elections, Msgr. Sarto promoted the creation of "youth sections" attached to the *Opera di Congressi.* This same year the Bishop of Mantua was made an honorary member of the *Società operaia Cattolica* (Society of Catholic Workers) in Treviso. In 1888, among the decisions taken by the synod we have already mentioned, there was the approval to create emergency funds for agricultural workers, and similar ones for artisans and other workers. They would

---

[48] Pastoral letter of January 28, 1894, quoted in Cappelletti, *G. Sarto, vescovo a Mantova,* pp.170-171.

[49] Very full information on the founders and principle inspirers of the *Opera dei Congressi,* in all the regions of Italy, can be found in the *Dizionario storico del movimento catolico in Italia, 1860-1980* (Turin: Marietti, 1981-1984), six volumes.

be in competition with similar societies, of Socialist or laicist origin, which had already existed for several years.

This interest in the social question is a constant in his episcopate, and would be a constant in his pontificate also. This is well illustrated by the relations he had and consistently maintained, to the end of his life, with the great Catholic economist Giuseppe Toniolo (1845-1918).[50] Toniolo was professor of political economy at the University of Modena and subsequently at that of Pisa (where he was the teacher of Werner Sombart). The author of many works on capitalism and social policy and of a *Trattato di economia sociale,* his great idea was that of "economic ethics": the economy, including its applications, implies a moral conception. And this moral conception must have practical consequences.

Toniolo got to know Msgr. Sarto during his time as Bishop of Mantua. In Padua on December 29, 1889, Giuseppe Toniolo, the Count Medolago-Albani, of Bergamo, and about twenty laymen founded the *Unione cattolica per gli studi sociali* (Catholic Association for Social Studies); Msgr. Sarto was invited to this meeting. He had been asked if he would preside at the founding meeting, but he refused, saying that [it would be inappropriate for him to do so, because] Padua was an eminent university city. Msgr. Callegari presided at the meeting, and Msgr. Sarto was one of the invited guests.

We should also mention the part he played at the 8th Assembly of the Catholic *Opera di Congressi* which was held in October 1890 at Lodi. At its third general session, Msgr. Sarto urged unity between the different tendencies. But he also gave a definition of Catholic social action which always guided his work in this area, and which, once he had become pope, would lead him to take grave decisions. At Lodi, on the one hand, he defined the social action of Catholics, in its multiplicity of works, as an action that should always be carried out under the Church's strict control:

> One must know how to make the sacrifice of one's own self-love and one's opinions. Make this your guiding maxim: *In necessariis unitas, in omnibus caritas,* but remembering that the third phrase, *in dubiis libertas,* cannot apply to our program of practical work, because doubt is eliminated by the oracle of the Church, which always indicates the path to be followed.[51]

---

[50] Cf. Serafino Majerotto, "Toniolo, Giuseppe," *Enciclopedia cattolica,* vol.XII, col.305-308, and *Giuseppe Toniolo tra economia e società,* under the direction of Paolo Pecorari (Udine: Del Bianco Editore, 1990).

[51] Address of Msgr. Sarto at the 8th Italian Catholic Congress, quoted in Dal-Gal, *Pie X,* p.148. *In necessariis unitas, in omnibus caritas, in dubiis libertas:* unity in things necessary, charity in all things, liberty in secondary matters.

This principle, the subordination of laypeople to the Church's hierarchy, went along with another fundamental principle which, according to Msgr. Sarto, defined the very spirit of lay action: Catholic action, the works of charity and social work, in the most varied areas, must always be first and foremost "an apostolate"; in order to carry this out, the Catholic engaged in this work must not be simply active, enterprising and generous: he must also sanctify himself and others through his action and his example:

> Catholics have to exercise an apostolate governed by a rule fixed by Jesus Christ when he said: *Pro eis ego sanctifico meipsum, ut sint et ipsi sanctificati in veritate.* Evil exists, but, before doing battle with it in others, we must fight against it inside ourselves and show ourselves to be exemplary in everything.

Among the social phenomena which Msgr. Sarto closely observed, there was the factor of emigration, which was undergoing a great expansion at this time. Between 1881 and 1885, every year about 154,000 Italians left their county to settle in the industrialized countries of Europe or in the "new world" (United States, Canada, *etc.*). The annual figure reached 221,000 in the following years and about 310,000 in the last years of the century.[52] In the province of Mantua alone, between 1885 and the end of the century, 34,174 people left to settle abroad.[53] One August day in 1887, while he was carrying out a pastoral visitation in the little town of Castelforte, Msgr. Sarto learned that 305 inhabitants of the town were to leave for America in the next few days. The news deeply impressed and saddened him. To the faithful assembled in the church, including many of these future emigrants, he opened his heart:

> It is impossible to think of this without one's soul overflowing with pain, affection and compassion! My sons, we urge you always to keep your faith...to practise your religion and to seek out, even when you are *lontani* ["far away"], the succor of religion, which alone can console you and help you to bear life's miseries. Before you leave, I ask you to go to your parish priest; as well as advice and some keepsake, he will give you a copy of the diocesan catechism or some book of devotion....[54]

When he returned to Mantua, he immediately wrote his clergy a letter on this subject. He urged his priests to warn their faithful who were tempted to emigrate of the dangers lying in wait for them: the dubious characters who would abuse the emigrants' situation for their own evil ends, and

---

[52] Figures quoted by Agasso, *L'Ultimo papa santo,* p.52.
[53] Figures quoted by L. Cavazzoli, "Le campagne mantovane da '*la boje!*' a fine secolo" in *G. Sarto, un vescovo e la società mantovana,* p.169.
[54] Allocution quoted by Marchesan, p.278, and recalled by Don Sartori and Don Martini, *Summarium,* pp.540 and 549-550.

the scarcity of priests who could help them in their countries of destination.[55]

In a general way, Msgr. Sarto watched over the common good and social peace. Accordingly he paid great attention to the Catholic press. As he had no Catholic newspaper in Mantua, he recommended his collaborators to inform the region's Catholic newspapers—the Milan *Osservatore catolico*,[56] Venice's *la Difesa* and the *Verona fedele*—about the major work and events of the diocese. In 1892, when a small Catholic newspaper was started in Treviso, the *Vita del Popolo*, Msgr. Sarto wrote to congratulate its director and assured him that he would work to extend its circulation, recommending it on his visits throughout the diocese.

While as a bishop he was loyal to the government, Msgr. Sarto was no less attentive to defending the Church's rights, the natural law and Catholic doctrine when they were endangered by political decisions. Thus he opposed a twofold attempt of the Italian government to change the law to give pre-eminence to civil marriage over religious marriage, and to authorize divorce. Msgr. Sarto summoned the members of his diocesan committee to the palace and, after addressing them on the sanctity of Christian marriage and the evil effects, for the Church and for society, which the two new laws would have, the Bishop of Mantua invited them to protest against them.

Solemn ceremonies

In Mantua, as later in Venice, Msgr. Sarto took delight in honoring the saints of the city and diocese. It was an opportunity to renew the links the faithful of the diocese (and the inhabitants in general) had with their roots and their religious past. But also, like all the bishops of his time, Msgr. Sarto loved the great religious ceremonies when, from the whole diocese and beyond, a throng of faithful and clergy came together to celebrate the memory of a saint, to gather at a shrine or to solemnize a particular event. As well as being a collective expression of the faith, this was an opportunity for mutual support at a time when the social and political environment was frequently hostile or indifferent to religion.

---

[55] Cf. *L'Église et les migrations. Un précurseur G. B. Scalabrini,* under the direction of Antonio Perotti (Paris: CIEMI/L'Harmattan, 1997).

[56] This did not prevent him from occasionally cooling the ardor of certain people, *e.g.*, in the case of the *Osservatore catholico,* one of the most aggressive of the "intransigent" Italian newspapers, directed by a priest, Don Davide Albertario. On August 4, 1887, Msgr. Sarto asked Msgr. Callegari to write to Don Albertario to "show him how, in certain matters, he must be more moderate." Photographical reproduction of this letter in *Una memoria ritrovata,* pp.131-134.

The first of these great ceremonies expressing a single heart and mind took place in March 1886, which was the eighth centenary of the death of St. Anselm, the patron saint of the diocese. St. Anselm (1036-1086), a nephew of Pope Alexander II, had been Bishop of Lucca. The author of many works of spirituality and commentaries on Holy Scripture, an apostolic legate in Lombardy, he was reputed for his austerity and charity, and for his reforming activity along the lines of Gregory VII (*i.e.,* the reform of morals and the restoration of ecclesiastical discipline).[57] His zeal in the application of the Gregorian reform meant that he came into conflict with the Lucca civil authorities; he had to accept exile in Mantua, where he spent many years and finally died. He was canonized one year after his death.

Msgr. Sarto's predecessor, Msgr. Berengo, had announced his intention of celebrating the eighth centenary of the death of St. Anselm. It was his successor, Msgr. Sarto, who carried this project through. A commission was nominated to prepare the ceremonies, which were to take place from March 16 to 18, 1886, and to collect the offerings. Msgr. Sarto wanted these celebrations, splendid as they were—nothing is too beautiful to celebrate a saint—to maintain their religious character. In the weeks preceding the ceremonies, therefore, the faithful were prepared spiritually by talks on St. Anselm given in Mantua by Don Alessandra Puricelli, a priest of Ferrara. The celebrations made a big impression, underlined by the presence of the Bishop of Brescia, the Archbishop of Udine and Cardinal Agostini, Patriarch of Venice. The centenary celebrations also saw the foundation of the *Association of St. Anselm*, consisting of priests who devoted themselves to helping their brother-priests by preaching, spiritual exercises and missions.

Even more striking were the celebrations in honor of St. Aloysius Gonzaga (1568-1591), which Msgr. Sarto wanted to celebrate in a big way on the third centenary of his death. Once again the Bishop of Mantua, in his own words, desired to grasp "all opportunities to recall the great periods of our religious history, in order to revive the faith and cause the spiritual life to grow in souls."[58] The goal of these celebrations was most definitely religious. In honoring St. Aloysius Gonzaga, the diocese of Mantua would be honoring a young prince who, in the 16th century, had consecrated himself to the Virgin Mary at the age of nine, and who had renounced all honors and temporal power—he was the eldest—in order to put himself at the service of God. He entered the Jesuit order and was an

---

[57] M. Mähler, "Anselm de Lucques (saint)," *Dictionnaire de Spiritualité* (1937), vol.I, col.698-699.

[58] Letter to the clergy and faithful, May 10, 1889, quoted in Dal-Gal, *Pie X*, p.128.

exemplary religious, dying at the age of 23, eight months after having given devoted service during an epidemic of plague which was ravaging Rome. Canonized in 1726, he would be proclaimed "patron of youth" by Pius XI.

Even if, in Msgr. Sarto's time, this particular patronage had not been officially declared, St. Aloysius Gonzaga had long been regarded as patron of youth. The Bishop of Mantua wanted to present him as a model to the faithful, and more particularly to the young people, of his diocese.

In November 1888 Msgr. Sarto was in Castiglione delle Stiviere, where St. Aloysius (Luigi) Gonzaga was born, to discuss with the little town's clergy the most appropriate ways of commemorating the 300th anniversary of the saint's death. Then, the following year, the Bishop of Mantua wrote to all the bishops of Italy asking them to authorize a collection in their dioceses to help defray the cost of the coming celebrations and restore the parish church and other places where St. Aloysius Gonzaga had lived. So it was that, prior to the festivities, work could be put in hand to restore the sanctuary of Castiglione. However, Msgr. Sarto wanted the preparation for these celebrations to be an opportunity for spiritual renewal as well. On September 3, 1889, two years before the tercentenary celebrations, he published a pastoral letter in which he urged the faithful to make a pilgrimage to the sanctuary of Castiglione. He himself gave example by going to the sanctuary on September 12, with all his clergy. He went again three times in 1891 (on April 26, May 3 and 21), each time giving an address to the crowds of pilgrims who had come from Bergamo and its region. At the beginning of this year, Msgr. Sarto published a new pastoral letter exhorting young people to follow the example of St. Aloysius Gonzaga:

> Yes, you must be strong to triumph over the self and its passions, to remain faithful to virtue and truth, to conquer the demon of evil and deceit. You will need strength and courage to keep the faith when so many others are losing it, to remain attached to the Church when so many others are abandoning her, to keep the grace which so many others have banished from their souls. May God guard you from the apostasy which would cause you to secretly renounce your faith. Be strong, despising the foolish notions of a public opinion which claims to dominate the world; do not waver in the face of that degraded ghost of human respect which tries to shackle the holiest convictions.
>
> Do not take fright, imagining that you will be asked to make impossible sacrifices. All that is necessary is that your faith shall be docile, your virtue lovable, and that the discipline of your life may have some flexibility. Be kind to one another; let the best prove their pre-eminent virtue by their compassion for their brothers; let the weakest admire in others a perfection that can be the inheritance of all, and which they are making efforts to attain.[59]

In June 1891, over three days, the celebrations took place, culminating on June 21, the feast-day of St. Aloysius Gonzaga. Eight bishops from
Lombardy and Emilia took part. In connection with this event the clergy
of Mantua wanted to honor their bishop. On June 16, six Mantua parish
priests and their dean had sent Leo XIII a letter asking the Pope to grant
Msgr. Sarto "the honorific title of Assistant at the Pontifical Throne."[60] "In
the pages of the history of the Church in Mantua his name is already written in letters of gold (for these celebrations) and for other signal deeds."
Leo XIII was glad to grant their request and took care to hasten his reply so
that the honorific title should arrive in Mantua before Sunday, June 27,
the octave of St. Aloysius Gonzaga.

These celebrations had made a great stir and were widely welcomed
among the population because St. Aloysius was a native of the region.[61]
Local patriotism meant that many people wanted also to honor other
members of the Gonzaga family. Msgr. Sarto agreed to promote the cause
of Francesco Gonzaga (1546-1620), a Franciscan, who had been Bishop of
Mantua.[62] The decree introducing his cause had already been given in
1627, but the beatification process had hardly advanced at all. Msgr. Sarto
re-launched it, but without coming to a new decision. On the other hand,
despite the ill-feeling it produced among the population, Msgr. Sarto put
a stop to the inappropriate cult of three nieces of St. Aloysius Gonzaga:
Cinzia, Olimpia and Gridonia.[63]

In 1892 there was also the Feast of Blessed Battista Spagnoli (1447-
1516). This Carmelite religious, who was born and died in Mantua, had
always been the object of a popular cult. But it was not until the Congregation of Rites gave a decree dated December 17, 1885, that the cult was
confirmed as legitimate and canonically authorized.[64] Perhaps in order to
avoid interfering with the ceremonies in honor of St. Anselm and St. Aloysius Gonzaga, which had been long in preparation, it was only on March
20, 1892 (the anniversary day of his death), that the cult of Blessed Spagnoli was solemnly inaugurated in the cathedral of Mantua. Msgr. Sarto
presided at the ceremony and delivered the panegyric of blessed Battista.

---

[59] Pastoral letter of January 25, 1891, quoted in Dal-Gal, *Pie X*, p.131.

[60] Letter of June 16, 1891, in a dossier containing the other documentation relative to
this title, ASV, Sec. Brev. 5908, f.511-516.

[61] On August 9, 1891, during a diocesan pilgrimage to Castiglione, many faithful came
from other dioceses, notably 1,500 who came from Parma in seven special trains (letter
of Msgr. Sarto to a parish priest in Sermide, July 30, 1891, quoted in Silibert, "Vescovo
a Mantova," p.124).

[62] *Index ac Status causarum* (Vatican City, 1988), p.101.

[63] Depositions of Don Pedrini and Msgr. Parolin, *Summarium,* pp.532 and 726.

[64] *Index ac Status causarum*, p.310.

In these three cases, St. Anselm, St. Aloysius Gonzaga, and Blessed Battista Spagnoli, Msgr. Sarto was concerned to help people in his diocese rediscover their Christian roots, to evoke once again the great days and the great religious figures of the past in order to revitalize the present.

In February 1893, in Rome, there took place the jubilee celebrations of Leo XIII,[65] with which Msgr. Sarto had urged his flock to associate themselves. With Cardinal Parocchi and the Bishop of Perugia, Msgr. Sarto was among those called upon to preach. His sermon, in the basilica of St. Laurence in Panisperna, was much applauded.

Msgr. Sarto, a connoisseur of great religious ceremonies which solemnly manifested the Church's unity of heart, was very attentive to the quality of the singing and the music which was sung. We have seen that, right from his time in the Padua Seminary, the young Sarto had shown a great interest in music and sacred chant. Both in Tombolo and in Salzano he had started a choir and had shown himself very attached to the beauty of the liturgy. During his episcopate at Mantua, various meetings and events enabled him to expand his knowledge in this area and gave him a better grasp of what would be involved in a restoration of sacred music and chant.

One of his first measures arising out of a concern for the dignity of liturgical services was a ruling of the diocesan synod which forbade bands to play in the churches. This practice was widespread in Italy at that time. One day, having found out that a parish priest was intending to take no notice of this ruling on the parish's patronal feast, the bishop turned up at the church unexpectedly, ascended the pulpit and delivered an emphatic address to convince the faithful of the incongruity of profane music in a holy place.[66] Another initiative of his was the creation of a *schola cantorum* at the seminary to teach the young clerics correctly to sing and appreciate sacred music.

His Mantua episcopate saw the development of the National Congresses of Sacred Music. The first was held in 1891 in Milan. While he could not participate in it since he was too preoccupied by diocesan affairs, Msgr. Sarto took an interest in it. Then, in October 1892, together with many bishops from Venetia and Lombardy, he took part in ceremonies at Pavia celebrating both the third centenary of Blessed Alessandro Sauli[67] (a Barnabite religious of the 16th century, who had been bishop of the city) and the fourth centenary of Christopher Columbus's discovery of Ameri-

---

[65] He had already gone to Rome to take part in the priestly jubilee of Leo XIII in January 1888. Some months earlier, in a pastoral letter, he had called on his faithful to associate themselves with this celebration since "the Church's whole strength resides in the Pope, and our faith's whole solidity is founded on the Successor of St. Peter."

[66] Deposition of Msgr. Rizzi, *Summarium,* p.950.

ca; for this occasion Msgr. Sarto composed a Latin poem of five lines which deserves to be brought forth from a century of oblivion:[68]

B.ALEXANDRO SAULI
TRECENTESIMO VERTENTE ANNO
A FELICI EXITU VITAE EIUS
Sint alii, dilecte, tuas qui laudibus ornent
Immensas animi dotes, praeclaraque facta
Cantent. Non ea vis, nec tanta potentia nobis.
Nos tacitos coluisse tuae tot nomina laudis
Praesidiumque tuum semper petiisse iuvabit.[69]

Part of the religious festivities marking these days was a concert of sacred music. Those in charge of this concert were Canon Tebaldini, professor at the Venice *schola cantorum,* and Professor Terrabugio. Msgr. Sarto kept in touch with them because he had taken a great interest in their work. On his return to Mantua he wrote to congratulate each of them. In the regional episcopal conference he also acted as contact with the *Società regionale lombarda di S. Gregorio* (Lombardy Region Society of St. Gregory) which they had just founded to promote the study and performance of sacred music and Gregorian chant.

Did Don Tebaldini tell Msgr. Sarto, at the Pavia ceremonies, about his recent stay in Solesmes?[70] At any rate, the years 1892-1894 were very important from this point of view: they saw the genesis of the crucial *motu proprio* on sacred music that Pius X would produce soon after his election,

---

[67] Alessandro Sauli (1534-1592), a Barnabite religious, was "the apostle of the young" of Pavia. At the age of 32 he was appointed General of his order. In 1570 he was appointed Bishop of Aleria in Corsica. One year before his death his was appointed Bishop of Pavia. "An angel in human flesh," according to Pope Gregory XIV, Alessandro Sauli was beatified in 1741. Once he had become pope, Pius X canonized him, on December 11, 1904, at the same time as Gerard Majella. These were the first two canonizations (of only four) of the pontificate.

[68] It was published, together with texts written by other bishops, in a booklet brought out for the occasion: *Il Beato Alessandro Sauli. Strenna-Ricordo del terzo centenario della sua morte 1592-1892* (Pavia: Tipografia del Privato Istituto Artigianelli, 1892), p.22.

[69] "It is for others, greatly beloved, to heap praise upon the immense merits of your soul and to sing of your famed deeds. We have not this skill and power. But we rejoice to have honored, in silence, your many titles and to have always implored your protection." Philippe de Gavriloff, who translated this poem [into French] assesses it thus: "A graceful little poem in dactylic hexameters (an elevated style recalling Virgilian epic), with well-placed caesuras and sound rhythm, written by an elegant and literate person used to constructing Latin verse. The words are all appropriately placed. The whole is harmonious, expressing a humble and sincere regard."

[70] Dom Pierre Combe refers to this visit in his *Histoire de la restauration du chant grégorien d'après des documents inédits* (Abbey of Solesmes, 1969), p.177.

and in which he would define Gregorian chant as "the chant proper to the Roman Church, the only chant which she has inherited from the ancient fathers and which she has jealously guarded for centuries in her liturgical regulations."

During his episcopate at Mantua, Gregorian chant experienced a renaissance—though not without difficulties—after several centuries of decadence.

"Decadence," a Gregorian specialist has written,

> began with the rhythm, and before it appears in history, its first symptoms are found in the manuscripts. First of all there is the progressive abandoning of the rhythmical signs by the copyists; this is followed by their total omission when line-notation is adopted, which is concerned only with the intervals. Finally, in the 13th century, there is the purely arbitrary duration allotted to the different forms of notes by proportional notation. When the neglect of rhythm passes from the notation into the execution of the chant, we can say that Gregorian chant has been lost. Its melodies were nothing more than a body without a soul, and in due course they were bound to succumb also, which is what happened. Having become incomprehensible and disfigured by being misrepresented in large notes, and executed heavily and clumsily, the long and graceful melismas seemed to have no beauty; they seemed unbearable, and amputation and contraction seemed to be the only remedy. This was mutilation of the melodies by decree.[71]

The restoration of Gregorian chant in its authentic form originated in France between 1856 and 1860. Its leading light was Dom Guéranger, who restored the Abbey of St. Peter in Solesmes. He laid down the principles, consisting "essentially, for the singing of the chant, in a return to free speech-rhythm; for the restoration of the melodies it was necessary to go back to the manuscripts."[72] Those who implemented this restoration were Dom Jausions, Dom Pothier and, subsequently, Dom Mocquereau. A lengthy process was begun: researching the manuscripts (from the whole of Europe), transcribing them into pure neums and restoring the melodies. As the years went by, the Solesmes printing press produced different books of Gregorian chant in traditional notation and, in particular, a treatise on the Gregorian melodies (1880) which had great influence also in Germany and Italy. Yet the advocates of the deformed transcription of Gregorian chant (and hence of its incorrect manner of performance) could boast of official support. In 1883, against all expectation, Leo XIII, in his decree *Romanorum Pontificium sollicitudo*, had retained the privileges of

---

[71] Dom Maur Sablayrolles, "Le chant grégorien," in *Liturgia,* under the direction of René Aigrain (Paris: Bloud et Gay, 1931), pp.445-446.

[72] Dom Combe, *Histoire de la restauration du chant grégorien*, p.109. Cf. also Dom Cuthbert Johnson, *Dom Guéranger et le renouveau liturgique* (Paris: Téqui, 1988).

the so-called "Ratisbon" [Regensburg] edition, a symbol of the decadent form of Gregorian chant.

It was a real battle, intellectual and musical, with partisans of Solesmes on one side and "Ratisbon men" on the other (led by the editor Pustet). Msgr. Sarto took the side of Solesmes. As well as Don Tebaldini, another Italian, Fr. De Santi, a Jesuit, helped to keep Msgr. Sarto informed about the restoration work of the Solesmes enterprise. Fr. Angelo De Santi, former professor of music at the seminary of Zara, and then director of the Padua *Scola puerorum,* had been appointed to the editorial board of the great Roman Jesuit review, *Civiltà Cattolica.* Converted to the cause of the restoration of authentic Gregorian chant, he supported it in his articles and through his contacts with the Curia, and by having the Gregorian melodies performed in the Pope's presence.

The work of Solesmes became more and more well-known. In 1891 Leo XIII ordered the Congregation of Rites to draw up new regulations for sacred music. The Church's most famous musicians and the presidents of the episcopal conferences of Italy were consulted. Then a commission was charged with the task of studying the replies received and preparing a *schema.* In July 1893, when he was no longer Bishop of Mantua—he had just been created Cardinal and appointed Patriarch of Venice—Msgr. Sarto, in turn, was consulted.

It was known in Rome that he was interested in sacred music, and his experienced opinion was valued. Aware of the current disputes, he called on the expertise of Fr. De Santi. The latter, together with his friends in Solesmes, prepared the long response—the *votum*—which Cardinal Sarto delivered to the Congregation of Rites. This *votum* consisted of a memorandum on sacred music and the desirable reforms, and draft regulations.[73] The new draft regulations elaborated in 1893 reappeared, in large measure, in the *Instruction* which would accompany the 1903 *motu proprio* on sacred music.

Some time after this *votum* had been sent off to the Congregation of Rites, the third National Congress of Sacred Music was held at the episcopal college of Thiene. It took place from October 10 to 13, on the initiative of Msgr. Callegari. Cardinal Sarto could not attend but, in a letter to Msgr. Callegari, president of the Congress, he urged the cause of authentic Gregorian music:

> We must promote Gregorian chant and ways of making it popular. Oh, if only I could get all the faithful to sing the *Kyrie,* the *Gloria,* the *Credo,* the *Sanctus,* the *Agnus Dei* in the same way that they sing the Lita-

---

[73] "Origine et présentation du *votum*" in Dom Combe, *Histoire de la restauration du chant grégorien,* pp.182-183.

nies and the *Tantum ergo*. To me, this would be the most beautiful victory for sacred music, because it is by really taking part in the liturgy that the faithful will maintain their devotion. Sometimes I just imagine a thousand voices singing the *Missa de Angelis* or the psalms in a country church; this thought utterly delights me. I prefer the *Tantum ergo*, the *Te Deum* and the Litanies chanted by the people to all the polyphonic music.[74]

An important meeting should be mentioned here, since it would have consequences in the future. On May 22, 1894, in Mantua, Cardinal Sarto met Lorenzo Perosi, at that time a seminarian in Imola. Fr. De Santi may have suggested the young musician's name to the Cardinal. He was not yet a priest, yet his reputation was already considerable, and Cardinal Sarto proposed, that very day, that he should become choirmaster at St. Mark's Basilica in Venice.

The following July Don Lorenzo Perosi went to Solesmes to make direct contact with the restorers of Gregorian chant and to complete his musical formation. In particular he got to know Dom Mocquereau. From Mantua, Cardinal Sarto wrote to Don Perosi of how he was looking forward to a restoration of the Gregorian chant: "The mere mention, in your letter, of the Vespers you heard chanted by these venerable monks has increased in me the desire to hear the Lord praised in the same way here in Italy. This work will take a long time, but I hope I shall not die before having tasted its fruit."[75]

At this very moment a new decree on sacred music had been promulgated. Cardinal Sarto's *votum* on the necessary Gregorian reform had not been followed. The Ratisbon edition had been confirmed in its "official" character, but at the same time bishops had been granted liberty to use other editions (including, of course, that of Solesmes).

In Venice, and even more when he had become Pope, Cardinal Sarto would be able to work for a complete restoration of the sacred chant.

---

[74] Quoted in Dal-Gal, *Pius X*, p.115.
[75] Letter of July 11, 1894, *Lettere*, p.217.

CHAPTER 4

PATRIARCH OF VENICE

Ever since 1451 the Bishops of Venice have borne the title "Patriarch." Traditionally a cardinal's dignity goes with the patriarchal see. The see is one of the most prestigious in Italy, even if the diocese is not one of the most populous of the country. When Cardinal Agostini, Patriarch of Venice, died on December 31, 1891, the rumor began to spread that Msgr. Sarto would succeed him.[1] In fact Msgr. Apollonio, Bishop of Treviso, was first approached with regard to the see of Venice. He refused this prestigious promotion on the grounds of his poor health. Then Msgr. Sarto's name was put forward, but he asked his friend Msgr. Callegari to intervene on his behalf in Rome to prevent such an offer being made to him.[2] He even suggested that another bishop should be promoted to Venice: Msgr. Riboldi, Bishop of Parma. We also know that another bishop was approached: Msgr. Pellegrini, Bishop of Brescia; but he refused.

These rumors did not escape the political authorities, who did what they could to obtain information on the persons who had been approached. In a letter to the Minister of Justice and Religion, the Prefect of Mantua sent an interesting portrait of the man who was still the bishop of the city:

> He has been well received by the population and has applied himself to raise the moral condition of his clergy, which had slipped somewhat under his predecessor's rule....He enjoys general regard in virtue of his conduct in the civil and ecclesiastical realms. In all the acts of his episcopal ministry he has never given occasion for any complaint, and gives evidence, on diverse occasions, of much prudence and a conciliatory and respectful spirit *vis-à-vis* the authorities. He is also known and appreciated as a good administrator. Nonetheless he leaves a little to be desired with regard to the formalities, but this is due more to a lack of polish (*rozza educazione*) than to any rudeness. Among the Mantuan clergy it is gener-

---

[1] Msgr. Sarto, in a letter to a Venetian correspondent, March 19, 1892, dismisses the idea and says, "... however heavy this cross is (governing the Diocese of Mantua), I have no desire to abandon it," *Lettere,* p.185.

[2] Cf. letter to Msgr. Giuseppe Callegari, June 10, 1892, *Lettere,* p.187. Gianpaolo Romanato makes a blunder in giving the following commentary on the letter: "[Msgr.] Callegari was one of those who worked to have Sarto nominated to the Patriarchal See of Venice," *Una memoria ritrovata.* p.109.

ally said that the Monsignore does not hold his clergy in very high esteem, and so he is respected and feared rather than loved. Because of his intelligence and his doctrine he is held in high regard by the episcopate of the ecclesiastical province of Lombardy, and particularly so by the Vatican Curia.[3]

This portrait is all the more interesting in that it comes from an authority that is independent of, and at times hostile to, the Church. Whatever one may say about the relevance of some of these observations, what is clear is the good reputation Msgr. Sarto enjoyed among the local political authorities.

Back at the Vatican, there had been no lessening in the desire to name the Bishop of Mantua to the see of Venice. Finally, on May 8, 1893, Cardinal Rampolla, Secretary of State of Leo XIII, sent a telegram to Msgr. Sarto urging him to "bend to the wishes of the Holy Father, who desired to have him as Patriarch of Venice." Once again the man at the centre of these moves attempted to escape. "I wrote straight away and explained the reasons which should induce the Holy Father to dispense me (from such a responsibility), and now I am caught between fear and hope, but more depressed by fear than comforted by hope. May God's will be done."[4] He was told that a refusal would greatly displease Leo XIII. Msgr. Sarto therefore accepted the new responsibility entrusted to him.

Leo XIII's insistence that Msgr. Sarto should accept the Patriarchate of Venice shows the esteem in which he held him. All the same, relations between the Pope and the Bishop of Mantua had not been so many, or so close, as to explain Msgr. Sarto's promotion. We must see it rather as the result of his good management of the diocese of Mantua. He had known how to pull it out of a catastrophic situation. No doubt the reports he regularly sent in concerning the state of his diocese were not read by the Pope himself, but nonetheless they were noted. In particular they were noted by a man who had long been Msgr. Sarto's protector at the Vatican: Cardinal Parocchi. The latter was fond of saying of Msgr. Sarto: "He is the best bishop in Lombardy."[5]

---

[3] Letter dated August 13, 1892, quoted by Annibale Zambarbieri, "Il Patriarca Sarto," in *La Chiesa veneziana dal 1849 alle soglie del novecento,* pp.137-138. This joint work, which is the 8th volume of the collection "Contributi alla storia della chiesa veneziana," together with the 9th volume, *La Chiesa di Venezia nel primo novecento,* appeared under the direction of Silvio Tramontin (Venice: Edizioni Studium Cattolico Veneziano, 1995). It contains a wealth of archive documentation.

[4] Letter to Mgr Giussepe Callegari, May 9, 1893, *Lettere,* p.203.

[5] Testimony of Senator Crispolti, *Pio IX, Leone XIII, Pio X, Benedetto XV. Ricordi personali* (Milan-Rome, 1932), p.89. Quoted in Dal-Gal, *Pius X,* p.94.

At the beginning of June Msgr. Sarto travelled to Rome accompanied by his secretary, Don Bressan. As usual, he stayed in the Lombard Seminary. On June 7, he was received by Leo XIII, who confirmed his nomination as Patriarch of Venice. But the Pope also indicated that he hoped to create him cardinal in advance, so that this honor should not appear to come merely as a consequence of his nomination to the patriarchate, but should be seen to be the reward of his merit achieved as Bishop of Mantua.

On June 12, during a secret consistory, Leo XIII officially collated Msgr. Sarto cardinal. At the same time four other bishops were created cardinal: Graniello, Bishop of Cesarea del Ponto; Lecot, Archbishop of Bordeaux; Bourret, Bishop of Rodez; and Schlauch, Bishop of Grosswardein (Oradea). It was a little later that Cardinal Parocchi presented the Bishop of Mantua with the letter creating him Cardinal. Two days later, at a public consistory held in the throne-room, Leo XIII put the cardinal's biretta on his head. At the same hour, in honor of their cardinal, all the bells of the churches of Mantua started ringing.

On June 15, in the Sixtine Chapel, the newly promoted cardinals took the oath prescribed in the rite and received the cardinal's hat from the Pope's hands. Immediately afterwards a secret consistory was held, during which Leo XIII nominated Cardinal Sarto to the patriarchal See of Venice,[6] Cardinal Svampa to the archiepiscopal See of Bologna, and Cardinal Ferrari to the archiepiscopal See of Milan.

Cardinal Sarto did not hide the great emotion which gripped him in these solemn hours: "I will not say anything about the turmoil and anxieties of these last days. I will only tell you that, at the public consistory and even more at the secret consistory, I thought I would die. I held up as well as I could but, when it came to taking the oath, I could no longer either see or speak; I was ashamed of myself in front of the Pope and the cardinals, because I could not hold back my tears."[7]

The new cardinal's authentic spirit of poverty and humility is well shown by an anecdote: in order to gladden the faithful of the diocese of Mantua, whom he would be leaving, he wanted to celebrate among them the Feast of Sts. Peter and Paul, on June 29, clothed in his new cardinal's robes. However, he had no money, since he had given his last funds to the town hospital at Corpus Christi. So he suggested to his sister that she should take his bishop's vestments, which were violet, and have them dyed scarlet. No doubt the result would not have been a very happy one. Discreetly, his sister explained the situation to the ladies of the town who met

---

[6]   Canonically, the new cardinal was Cardinal-Priest of the Roman church of San Bernardo alle Termi.
[7]   Letter to Msgr. Giuseppe Callegari, June 17, 1893. Cf. Dal-Gal, *Pius X*, p.95.

every week to look after the clothes of the poor. They got together, bought sufficient red cloth and made the cardinal's garments for the appointed day.[8]

Though created cardinal, Patriarch Sarto could not enter his new diocese for more than a year because of a dispute in which the Church and the government were embroiled. When the province of Venetia had fallen under Austrian domination, the Emperor, according to the terms of the concordat which regulated the relationships between his country and the Holy See, had retained the right to nominate the Patriarch of Venice. When, subsequently, Venetia was attached to the Kingdom of Italy, the King and his government did not initially claim the exercise of this right. But on the death of Patriarch Agostini, the government once more claimed the right—unjustifiably, according to all legal opinion. Such were the difficulties in obtaining the *exequatur* (the authorization) that Cardinal Sarto even considered renouncing the See of Venice.[9]

While waiting for the crisis to work itself out, and continuing to govern the diocese of Mantua, he undertook a number of visits. In August 1893 he went to Pavia for the Feast of St. Augustine and in order to participate in the fifth regional assembly of the bishops of Lombardy. In September, in Verona, he met Cardinal Canossa and then, on the 16th, he took part in the celebrations at the famous mountain shrine of the *Madonna della Corona*. During the religious festivities at this shrine, he heard confessions for many long hours like a simple priest, and he also administered Confirmation. The following October he travelled to Borgo San Donnino for the feast of the local saint (St. Donatian, a martyr from the beginning of the 4th century, whose feast-day is on October 8). Then he went to Riese. It was the last time he was able to see his elderly (octogenarian) mother. In the village, the new Cardinal was fêted by the population and, on a suggestion of Don Bressan's, he showed himself to his mother in all his cardinal's attire: purple soutane and *cappa magna,* and his wide-brimmed cardinal's hat. *Mamma Sarto*, bed-ridden, was very moved and asked her son's blessing. She died four months later.

This was February 2, 1894. We have already quoted the epitaph, the mark of a great filial devotion, which the new Cardinal had put on his

[8]   In order to defray the other expenses of his cardinalate Msgr. Sarto had to borrow money from the Marquis Di Bagno, Senator of Mantua (deposition of Msgr. G. B. Parolin, *Summarium,* p.144).

[9]   Cardinal Dalla Costa, who knew of this document, recalls a letter written by Cardinal Sarto to the Archbishop of Florence in which he said that he was "entirely prepared to accept the most modest diocese in Italy if thereby all these difficulties at the Holy See could be avoided." (Cardinal Elia Dalla Costa, preface to the memoirs of Cardinal Merry del Val, *Pie X, Impressions et souvenirs* [CH-Saint-Maurice: Éditions de l'œuvre Saint-Augustin, 1951], p.12.)

mother's tomb. Two days after her death he wrote to his friend Msgr. Cal-legari: "I was prepared for the death of her who gave me life. But however resigned I was, the terrible news has torn me apart. I cannot think of my blessed mother—and I think of her all the time—without profound emo-tion. Thank you, Monsignore, for your affectionate condolences and above all for remembering her at the holy sacrifice of the Mass. The poor little woman! She worked so hard and suffered so much! She deserves to be in the thoughts of everyone who knows the meaning of the words 'work' and 'suffering.'"[10]

The months went by, the Cardinal waiting for an agreement with the Italian government. Finally, more than a year after his promotion to the See of Venice, he received the government's *exequatur*. There had been a change of government in 1893: Crispi had once more become President of the Council. Several groups were in favor of an agreement with the Church. Crispi was hoping to extend his political support by gaining Catholic votes, and so he showed himself to be conciliatory. In addition, Italy wanted to consolidate its presence in Eritrea and Ethiopia, and the Church's assistance could be valuable. The Holy See created an Apostolic Prefecture in the region, served entirely by Italian missionaries. In ex-change, the government finally gave the *exequatur* for Cardinal Sarto's ap-pointment to Venice.

This was on September 5, 1894. Three days later, on the Feast of the Nativity of the Blessed Virgin, Cardinal Sarto addressed his first pastoral letter to the clergy of Venice; the letter was also addressed to the clergy of Mantua as a kind of pastoral last testament. Since he had many weeks to prepare it, it was not an occasional writing but a long exhortation, as well as a warning against Catholic liberalism which seemed, to the Patriarch of Venice, to be spreading more and more at the heart of the Church.[11] In it, the new Patriarch of Venice called priests to be united in fidelity to the Holy See: "...the Bishop alone is the guardian and interpreter of the Sover-eign Pontiff's commands, and the priests must be intimately united to the Bishop...." This unity is more indispensable than ever, because, in our days, the Church "practically at every moment has to fight to defend her

---

[10] Letter of February 4, 1894, quoted in Dal-Gal, *Pie X*, p.153.

[11] This first pastoral letter, written in Latin, was immediately translated into Italian by a Mantua priest and published in booklet form. This translation, which was approved by Cardinal Sarto, is reproduced in the collection entitled: Giuseppe card. Sarto (S. Pio X), *Le Pastorali del periodo veneziano 1894-1898* (Riese Pio X: Quaderni della Fondazione Giuseppe Sarto, 1990), vol.I, pp.31-45; hereafter, *Le Pastorali*. In 1905, however, Marchesan (pp.322-329) quoted considerable extracts from this pastoral letter in an Italian version that is markedly different. This is the version which Dal-Gal and Fernessole quote. Here we are referring to the Italian text approved by Cardinal Sarto.

liberty, her dignity and her rights." The Church's enemies are "the baneful sects" and "rotten materialism," but they would not have so much success if "certain people, under cover of the glorious name of Catholic, did not come to their aid." These "liberal Catholics" (*cattolici-liberali*) "dream of a kind of peace, or rather, a conciliation between light and darkness": they stigmatize "all Catholics who think differently from them as 'the clerical party,'" and they say that "in all things that concern the State, the civil authority ought to have the pre-eminence over the authority of the Church" and "under the pretext of liberty they permit the licence of irreligion and insult." These liberal Catholics, wrote Cardinal Sarto again, "always preach charity and prudence, as if it were charitable to let the wolf devour the lamb, and as if it were a virtue to cultivate this prudence of the flesh, which God has condemned, as it is written: *I will destroy the wisdom of the wise, and the prudence of the prudent I will thwart* (1 Cor 1:19)." Liberal Catholics are "wolves in sheep's clothing; it is more important than anything else that their murky designs should be exposed to the light and denounced."

After these warnings, the Patriarch of Venice indicated the remedy: "But what doctrine should we defend and preach? That which comes from God and which is set forth by the Church's infallible magisterium." He urged the priests, "you must cultivate piety if you are to keep the integrity of doctrine," because the priest's preaching must be "confirmed by the authority and innocence of his life."

This first pastoral letter, a veritable anti-liberal manifesto in the tradition of 19th century anti-liberalism (from the Popes Gregory XVI and Pius IX to the great ecclesiastical and lay writers) was also an exhortation to the priest to be holy—a constant and characteristic concern of Msgr. Sarto.

He left Mantua on November 22. He spent a day in Treviso and visited the beloved seminary where he had been spiritual director. On November 24, having arrived by train, he made his entrance into Venice. The entire city, it seemed, was waiting for him. The crowd pressed forward to acclaim him all the way from the railway station to the episcopal palace. The municipal authorities, however, politically leftist and fairly anti-clerical, held themselves aloof from the welcome to the new Patriarch. A contemporary photograph shows him coming out of the church of the Discalced Carmelites, near the station: he is getting ready to step into a steam launch which will take him to St. Mark's Basilica. There is a great crowd of people, eager to see their Cardinal in his *cappa magna*. Preceded by a large cross, he is blessing those thronged around him.

His journey to the Basilica was accompanied by a swarm of gondolas, each one more ornate than the other, and *vaporini*. Each institution (the clergy, the municipal authorities, the magistrature, the military authorities) and each corporation had its own vessel. When the Patriarch arrived at the esplanade of St. Mark's, all the city's bells pealed forth: the three bells of the Campanile, the bell of the Palace of the Doges and those of the churches of the Lagoon.

The white patriarchal palace adjoins St. Mark's Basilica.[12] If Cardinal Sarto were to renounce all this marble and gold, he would be slighting the Venetian patrimony. He preferred to apply the evangelical precept: "use riches as if not using them." He reduced his private apartment to two rooms: one where he put a bed and the simplest suite of furniture, and the other which served as an office.[13] One of his first biographers also observes:

> Three of his sisters had come with him from Mantua to Venice. The family quarters were organized just like a convent under rule. The hours of work were fixed, as were the hours of prayer and recreation. The bishop's relations never entered the Patriarch's rooms. Not only did they never interfere in the affairs of the diocese, they were not even acquainted with them. Furthermore they were held in great esteem everywhere.[14]

It should also be said that the Mantua custom of the daily recitation of the Rosary with his sisters was maintained here in Venice.

On Sunday November 25, he celebrated his first pontifical Mass in St. Mark's; the simple eloquence of his sermon conquered the faithful.

> Parish priests, clergy, magistrates, nobles, the rich, sons of the people and the poor, you are my family, you are the object of my love, and I hope that you will love me in return. I want you to be able to say with utter sincerity: "Our Patriarch is a man of right intentions, who hates compromises, who holds aloft the unsullied standard of the Vicar of Christ, and who desires nothing else but to defend the truth and do good." If, some day, I were to set aside in any way this program I have solemnly announced to you, may God let me die...[15]

The Patriarch's motto could have been "defence of the truth and charity to all." The very first letter he wrote to his faithful, two days after the homily we have just cited, was to appeal for an act of charity. A serious earthquake had struck Calabria and Sicily on November 17, and then again on the 25th of the same month. On the 27th Cardinal Sarto wrote to his faithful and clergy, ordering that the next Sunday's collection would be for the faithful of the Calabrian and Sicilian dioceses; he asked for gifts to be sent to the Curia, the Chapter or the local Catholic newspaper, *La*

---

[12] To show his attachment to his new diocese, Cardinal Sarto added the Lion of St. Mark (symbol of the City of Venice) to his episcopal coat of arms.
[13] Deposition of Don F. Saccardo and Msgr. G. Peschini, *Summarium,* pp.434 and 710.
[14] Cigala, *Vie intime de S. S. le pape Pie X,* pp.59-60.
[15] Cf. Dal-Gal, *Pius X,* p.107.

Difesa.[16] It is worth noting that the first public figures received by the new Patriarch were the score or so of foreign consuls resident in Venice. On this occasion Cardinal Sarto raised the problem of Italian emigrants with those whom it concerned. As we have seen, the question was close to his heart. In this same period, on November 27, he visited Venice's civil hospital; on December 2 the city's prisons for men and for women and St. Anne's Hospital; on December 4, the Foundlings' Hostel; on 13th the military hospital and on 14th the night shelter. Wherever he went he learned of the difficulties of running these establishments, and everywhere he left some financial aid.

Encouragement of the clergy

At that time Venice had about 150,000 inhabitants. The diocese included 43 parishes (30 urban parishes and 13 outside), 10 monasteries or convents for men and 7 for women. Certainly, when Cardinal Sarto took over the direction of the diocese of Venice, it was not in the lamentable state Mantua had been in in 1885. However, signs of a growing religious crisis were visible: a clear diminution in the number of priests (from 418 in 1866 it had fallen to 290 in 1890); an increase in the numbers no longer practising; the growing influence of Socialist ideas and Freemasonry; and increasingly active preaching on the part of Protestants.[17] Furthermore, according to several witnesses at the beatification process, Cardinal Sarto observed that after a three-year interregnum in the patriarchal See a number of parish priests in the City of the Doges had been affected by a certain laxity: on Sundays they neglected to give a commentary on the Gospel of the day or dispensed themselves from giving Christian doctrine class; the Catholic apostolate was not encouraged and assisted as much as it should have been; there were other kinds of deficiency too.[18]

As at Mantua, Cardinal Sarto used various methods of improving the conduct and pastoral spirit of his clergy. The formation of future clerics was, of course, one of his continual preoccupations. He frequently went to the patriarchal Seminary to question the students and ascertain himself the level of their instruction and their spirit. For a certain period, at least, he went there every week.[19] He was scrupulous with regard to their admission to the various ecclesiastical orders, and refused or postponed the admission

---

[16] Letter to the clergy and faithful, dated November 27, 1894, *Le Pastorali,* vol.I, pp.48-49.
[17] Soon Cardinal Sarto established the Opera pia delle Signore visitatrici dell'Ospedale (Pious association of hospital visitors) to combat the Protestant influence at the heart of the Venice Hospital.
[18] *Summarium,* pp.145, 453, 466, 495.
[19] Depositions of Maria Sarto and Msgr. Jeremich, *Summarium,* pp.45 and 386.

of those who had shown themselves to be deficient in moral conduct or discipline or whose level of attainment was insufficient. To improve the discipline and functioning of the Seminary, he detached from it its dependent ecclesiastical college and drew up new regulations for the Seminary, in substance more in keeping with the norms of the Council of Trent. Taking up his predecessor's project, in 1902, he also created a faculty of canon law for the priests not only of the diocese but also of all the dioceses of the province of Venetia. He obtained permission from the Holy See to give university degrees but, elected pope the following year, did not have the time to give to the elaboration of this project. Since 1894 he had had the idea of a Catholic university open to clerics and laity.[20] This idea was taken up by others, but did not come to fruition until much later, in Milan, under the pontificate of Benedict XV.

Generally speaking, Cardinal Sarto regarded teaching as a royal road in the formation of secular priests. He liked to appoint his priests to teaching posts (in seminaries or Catholic schools) before entrusting other responsibilities to them.

Testimony to his concern to have good priests are the efforts made by the Venetian episcopal conference which took place on his initiative a few months after he arrived. This was in connection with the festivities in honor of the eighth centenary of the Basilica of St. Mark, to which we shall return. All the bishops of Venetia had come together around their Patriarch. Several sessions were devoted to examining and discussing different practical points regarding the life and conduct of priests, parish life and the apostolate of Catholics. At the end of the various sessions of the episcopal conference different resolutions were adopted over a wide range of topics: priests were obliged to preach on Sunday, they were forbidden to attend public theatrical performances, they were urged to promote the catechism; cremation was forbidden; support was urged for Catholic newspapers and associations; ecclesiastical censorship was insisted upon; parish records should be diligently kept. In the diocese of Venice these resolutions were followed up by a number of different initiatives.

Catechetical work

As in Mantua, the teaching of Christian doctrine was one of the principal pillars of the Patriarch of Venice's pastoral action. Only a few months after he arrived in the City of the Doges, he addressed a circular letter to the priests, insisting on the teaching of catechism to children and instruction in Christian doctrine for adults.[21] Citing the Council of Trent, the

---

[20] Letters to Msgr. Zamburlini, Archbishop of Udine, and Msgr. Callegari, Bishop of Padua, both dated December 20, 1894, Romanato, p.213.

Cardinal pointed out that parish priests had two obligations in the teaching of souls: on feast-days they should give the faithful a sermon "on divine matters" and they should instruct the *"pueros et rudiores"* (children and the ignorant) in the rudiments of the faith and the divine law. The Cardinal added that, very often, the faithful are also the *rudiores*.

> Furthermore it is necessary to overcome the grave misconception that the catechism is taught only to children; as if the Church, which has nourished us with her milk while we were children, would leave us without food now that we have become adults.

Henceforth this would be a recurring theme in his pastoral action. On November 21, 1895, in an open letter "to parents of the city of Venice" published in the newspaper *La Difesa,* the Cardinal recommended that "schools of religion" be established in the parishes of San Felice and San Cassiano.[22] The idea of these schools was to give courses of religious instruction to the adolescents who were no longer following the catechism. The very next day after the publication of the letter, another of the city's newspapers reported that a club was being started for workmen's children, without making any reference to religion: Cardinal Sarto immediately wrote an open letter to the director of *La Difesa,* warning parents against it and urging them to support the parish-based initiatives instead.[23]

One of the most important resources in catechetical work was the 1896 publication of a common catechism for all the dioceses of Venetia.[24] Its origin went back a long way.[25] As early as 1858 the episcopal conference of Venetia had decided to publish a catechism. But not until 1891 could Cardinal Agostini, then in charge of the See of Venice, submit the completed project to the Holy See. Cardinal Sarto, who published this text five years later, had not, therefore, taken a conspicuous part in compiling this catechism; but he put his personal imprint on the use he made of it. In publishing it, he introduced it in these terms: the aim was "to set forth, in simple words, adapted to the intelligence of simple people and especially of children, those truths which every Christian should know." Furthermore, since the Venetian dialect was still widely spoken,[26] the Patriarch recommended priests to question the children "often freely...and in differ-

---

[21] Circular letter of January 17, 1895, in *Le Pastorali*, vol.I, pp.51-55.

[22] *Le Pastorali*, vol.I, pp.85-86.

[23] Letter of November 11, 1895, *Le Pastorali*, vol.I, p.87.

[24] *Catechismo approvato nelle conferenze Episcopali della Regione Veneta* (Ed. Seminario de Padova, 1896).

[25] Bruno Bertoli, "La pastorale di fronte ai mutamenti culturali e politici della società veneziana," in *La Chiesa veneziana dal 1849 alle soglie del novecento*, pp.70-71.

[26] The Patriarch of Venice himself used it every day and, even as Pope, he frequently used dialect expressions in his private conversation.

ent ways," encouraging them to "reply in the dialect of the region, so that at an early age they will be attached to the spirit of the teaching rather than to the mechanical word." Ultimately it was a question of helping young minds to be familiar with the supernatural realities and the truths of the faith, so that they could assimilate them interiorly. Later, notably during the synod which we shall be describing, much attention would be given to the way in which the catechism was to be taught. It was not simply a case of addressing the memory and the intelligence, but the heart too. Those who teach catechism must know how to touch children's hearts and show how the truths of the faith they are teaching are bound up with sacred history or liturgy. Those who teach catechism must not be merely good teachers: they must also be collaborators with the Holy Spirit.

As a way of extending this catechism—and this time he did take a pre-eminent part in the compilation—Cardinal Sarto had two manuals published, designed to be used by families, namely, *Brevi cenni della storia della religione approvati per l'arcidiocesi di Venezia,* and *Brevi istruzioni sulle principali solennità della santa Chiesa approvate per l'arcidiocesi di Venezia.* The first volume consisted of a short history of the Old Testament, the New Testament and the great events of the Church's history (councils and heresies). The second volume contained spiritual teaching on the great liturgical feasts. These two manuals show Cardinal Sarto's concern that the truths of the faith be linked, in an integrated and vivid manner and in a supernatural spirit, to the Church's life, past and present. When he had become pope, he would inspire the publication of the *Roman Catechism*; the first two parts of this work would contain an "instruction on the feasts of the Church" and a "short history of religion"—with the same content and structure as the two Venetian manuals.

Pastoral letters

Cardinal Sarto had a privileged means of inspiring his diocese with that Christian ardor which was his: his pastoral letters addressed to clergy and faithful, and the circular letters to parish priests. In the ten years in which he was effectively present in the Patriarchate of Venice, Cardinal Sarto published scores of them, as well as his public letters published in the local Catholic newspaper.[27] The Catholic newspaper *La Difesa* received financial assistance from the Cardinal, who many times urged the faithful to support it and read it rather than the other local dailies (*La Gazzetta* and

---

[27] They have all been edited and annotated under the aegis of Antonio Niero: *Le Pastorali del period veneziano, 1894-1898* (Riese Pio X: Quaderni della Fondazione Giuseppe Sarto, 1990), no.2, and *Le Pastorali del periodo veneziano, 1899-1903* (Riese Pio X: Quaderni della Fondazione Giuseppe Sarto, 1991), no.3. Hereinafter cited as *Le Pastorali* with volume number: I for the years 1894-1898, II for the years 1899-1903.

L'Adriatico), which had a Masonic tendency: One of his first circular letters was on the subject of Sunday Mass and the instruction of adults in Christian doctrine. Developing a theme which was close to his heart, he wrote: "Can there be any other city like Venice for the number of Lenten sermons, octaves, novenas and panegyrics? But why, then, does all this bear so little fruit?" His verdict was that Christian instruction was too insubstantial here. "Give up that kind of eloquence," the Patriarch of Venice told his parish priests, "which belongs to the stage rather than the church, and which is more profane than sacred...and is bereft of any supernatural effectiveness. The faithful do not profit from it; it may fill the church, but it leaves their souls empty; it may draw their applause, but it will not make them weep, and they will leave the church in the same state in which they entered: *mirabantur,* as St. Augustine said, *sed non convertebantur* (they admired, but were not converted)."[28]

His pastoral letters for Lent were also used by the Patriarch to try to dissuade the faithful from profaning this liturgical season, notably by taking part in a carnival which, even at that time, lasted much longer than Shrove Tuesday, even if it had not reached the heights of current extravagances. Year after year Cardinal Sarto devoted his Lenten pastorals to temperance (1895),[29] abstinence, fasting and the practice of good works (1896), the sacred celebration of holy-days (1897), concord between Catholics and obedience to the Church's laws (1898), and other themes in succeeding years. His most famous Lenten pastoral, which was mocked by the anti-clericals, was the one published in 1901. It instituted a "league against blasphemy, obscenity and the profanation of holy-days."[30]

Pastoral visitation and diocesan synod

The pastoral visitation was also a classic and traditional means whereby Cardinal Sarto could make contact with the clergy, assess their needs and those of the faithful, and re-awaken the spiritual life of everyone. On May 21, 1895, a mere few weeks after the aforementioned resolutions of the Venetian episcopal conference, Cardinal Sarto announced the first visitation of his diocese.[31] In his announcement to the parish priests, the Pa-

---

[28] Circular to parish priests, January 17, 1895, in *Le Pastorali,* vol.I, pp.51-55.
[29] We cannot analyze them all, but this one, in the judgment of Romanato (p.207), is "one of the finest of the Venetian period." In it, Cardinal Sarto explains to everyone that temperance does not mean "abandoning the world," or even "treating one's body with austerity," but "mortifying the passions." Temperance, the Cardinal goes on, must also be spiritual: we must extinguish in ourselves "the spirit of impatience," we must "speak to others with gentleness, treat them with love, and do good, if the occasion presents itself, with a sincere and generous heart" (*Le Pastorali,* vol.I, pp.57-58).
[30] Pastoral letter of February 4, 1901, in *Le Pastorali,* vol.II, pp.72-81.
[31] Pastoral letter of May 21, 1895, in *Le Pastorali,* vol.I, pp.75-80.

triarch recommended that there should be a triduum of sermons prior to his visitation, so that the faithful could be prepared for their bishop's coming, and to demonstrate its spiritual importance. His fundamental aim, in this first pastoral visitation, was to re-awaken the spirit of faith and to correct abuses. "I come," he wrote, "to get to know your needs, to wipe away your tears, to calm your fears and, while looking after your spiritual good, to provide for your temporal necessities." It is necessary to re-awaken faith in the face of the new threats to it: "How necessary it is to stir up again the spirit of faith, at a time when there is a growth of that malignant fever which would discredit everything and deny every dogma of revealed religion! How necessary it is at this present time when people are trying to dismiss the mysteries of our faith, when people are claiming to explain them—while Christ has demanded the submission of the intellect—when they are casting doubt on the most established prophecies, when they are denying the most manifest miracles, when they are rejecting the sacraments, deriding pious practices, and discrediting the magisterium of the Church and her ministers!"

Cardinal Sarto, clearly, had in mind not only the rationalists outside the Church, but also those who, inside the Church, were beginning to dismiss her dogmas because of their own historical presuppositions and their erroneous philosophies. Even if the name *Modernism* does not appear in this pastoral letter, Cardinal Sarto had identified its initial symptoms, as he had in Mantua. It was during this period, moreover, that he began to take notice of the works of Alfred Loisy, "forcefully reproving the affirmations contrary to the faith" which they contained, as a witness in the beatification process tells us.[32]

Compared with his predecessors in Mantua and Venice, Cardinal Sarto spoke equally as bishop and father, equally with charity and faith. It was his hallmark. His care, which did not exclude severity, can be seen in another of his initiatives: on the last Thursday of each month he used to

---

[32] Deposition of Msgr. F. Petich, *Summarium*, p.530. We do not know which of Loisy's works Cardinal Sarto had read at this time. During the Cardinal's years in Venice, five works of the French exegete (and figurehead of Modernism) were published: *Études bibliques* (1901), *Les Mythes babyloniens et les premiers chapitres de la Genèse* (1901), *La Religion d'Israël* (1901), *Études Évangéliques* (1902). It was the latter, which became known as the first "little red book," which made Loisy's name known outside the circle of specialists in exegesis. It was in Venice itself that one of the first Italian anti-Modernist works appeared, with the aim of refuting this latter book of Loisy's, namely, Federico Brunetti, *La scienza umana e la coscienza messianica di N. Signore Gesù Cristo. A proposito di una publicazione recente* (1903). Here we add the testimony (probably unreliable) of the Italian Modernist Salvatore Minocchi: in 1911 he said that he had discussed Loisy's works with Cardinal Sarto long ago, and that the latter had shown himself well-disposed towards the French exegete (cf. Lorenzo Bedeschi, *Il modernismo italiano. Voci e volti* [Cinisello Balsamo: Edizioni San Paolo, 1995], p.116).

invite his priests to a period of recollection in the church of La Fava. He would give them spiritual talks on the priestly state and its duties. And of course he also preached by his own example. From among the many characteristics reported in the acts of the beatification process, we mention this: one year, at the Military Marine Hospital, the chaplain gave a series of sermons during the days before Easter, to prepare the sick for Confession and for Communion on the day of the Feast, as every Christian is obliged to. About 30 of the patients refused to confess and communicate. The Patriarch of Venice learned of this. Several days later he went to the hospital, celebrated Mass and gave a moving sermon on the necessity of Confession and the meaning of Communion. The 30 recalcitrant patients decided to make their Confession and received Communion from the hand of Cardinal Sarto.[33]

After the first pastoral visitation, as at Mantua, Cardinal Sarto decided to convoke a diocesan synod. The last one had been held in 1865 during the patriarchate of Cardinal Trevisanato, following an organic and very well-structured plan. When Cardinal Sarto announced the new synod, he saw it in express continuity with its predecessor, as bringing the latter up to date.[34] The Patriarch of Venice observed that there had been a deterioration in the situation since the last synod: attacks against the Church had got worse and society was becoming more and more dechristianized (*le nuove e perniciose massime disseminate fra il popolo*). But he also looked forward to making sure that doctrine and ecclesiastical discipline conformed to the teachings of Pius IX, the Vatican Council and Leo XIII.

In a pastoral letter of November 1, 1897, he asked his clergy to join him in the preparatory work. Preparatory meetings took place in each deanery. As a working basis they took the six-part constitutions of the previous synod. The reports drawn up at the conclusion of these meetings were examined during the presynodal assemblies: these consisted of the Patriarch, all the canons of the cathedral and the vicars forane, and took place in the patriarchal palace on April 29, and May 24, 1898. In addition, in order that this synod should be informed by a genuinely spiritual atmosphere that would contribute to its success, the Patriarch asked all the participating priests to follow spiritual exercises in the preceding weeks.

The synod was held from August 8 to 10 in St. Mark's Basilica. In his sermon at the solemn opening Mass, the Cardinal painted a clear picture

---

[33] Deposition of Dr. F. Saccardo, *Summarium*, p.435.

[34] In addition to the information contained in the two volumes to which we have already referred (*La Chiesa veneziana dal 1849 alla soglie del novecento*, and *La Chiesa di Venezia nel primo novecento*), cf. Mario Ronzini, "Il sinodo del card. G. Sarto e le associazioni laicali," *Quaderni della Fondazione Giuseppe Sarto*, year 1, no.1, January 1990, pp.47-92.

of the situation: "Good people are attacked and mocked in their most noble sentiments, and for the irreligious nothing is sacred any more apart from the sanctuary of conscience. Many are ashamed even to be called Catholic—a word which they cannot utter without blushing, while Christ's enemies keep waving their banners and, with the formidable weapons they have at their disposal, wreak destruction and ruin." He also identified the objectives the diocesan synod should pursue: "We must build a dyke against the torrent of evil which is spreading everywhere; we must find the antidote to the poison which is threatening the life of society; we must give this sick world the remedies which will cure it; we must save, by a single word, even the souls of those who hate that word and persecute it, because for them too Jesus Christ shed His precious blood."

The resolutions adopted by this synod were of very different kinds. In many areas they brought the resolutions of the 1865 synod up to date. For example, as a reaction against the laws of the government which had reduced the number of holy-days, there was an insistence on the obligation to respect the solemn religious feasts by going to Mass and by not sending children to school on those days. There were also decisions which reflected Cardinal Sarto's personal convictions. Examples of this were the drawing-up of rules for the teaching of catechism, or the creation of "ecclesiastical conferences" for young clerics, so that they could deepen their knowledge in all the religious subjects. The aim was to make the priests capable of "promoting the cause, the rights and the advantages of Christian knowledge in the face of the pretensions of modern laicist culture," in six areas: dogmatic theology; moral theology; biblical studies; ecclesiastical history; Christian archaeology; and social and political economics. It should also be mentioned that in each parish there was to be set up a confraternity of St. Lorenzo Giustiniani, to help the diocesan seminary by prayers and financial aid.

It was confirmed that all parish priests and curates were obliged to preach at the Sunday Mass and on holy-days of obligation (such preaching should not last longer than twenty minutes). To help the priests to prepare their homily, Cardinal Sarto had a book of commentaries published, explaining the readings in the lectionary. His admonitions were evidently effective, for, during the Apostolic Visitation of 1906, the Visitor noted that there was preaching on Sundays in all the parishes of Venice (whereas, when Cardinal Sarto arrived, there was never any preaching in a third of the city's churches).[35]

---

[35] Figures given by Bertoli, "Una diocesa all'ombra di Pio X," in *La Chiesa di Venezia nel primo novecento*, p.25.

Several of the synod's decrees concerned the life of priests. Notably there was a reminder of the obligation always to wear priestly dress, and that priests should make their confession at least every week. The final decree obliged all priests to follow the spiritual exercises regularly. Those who had not followed the spiritual exercises for three years were obliged to do so before November, or else be forbidden to celebrate Mass.

To Cardinal Sarto, the sanctification of the clergy was one of the most dependable instruments of the apostolate.

The *Opera dei Congressi*

It would be a mistake to think of Cardinal Sarto, at the end of the 19th century, as some kind of conservative ecclesiastical dignitary, concerned only with keeping his clergy on an orthodox doctrinal path and in a state of priestly rectitude. These concerns were uppermost to the Patriarch of Venice, but, to external observers, he appeared bolder and far more innovatory. Soon he would be described as one of Italy's great "social bishops."

His reputation as a charitable priest had accompanied him without interruption ever since Tombolo. In Venice, amid the gold and marble of the patriarchal palace, he always showed himself to be generous to the poor. The stories told by witnesses at the beatification process are well known: one day he gives his entire purse to a poor man; another time, having no money left to give, he gives a poor woman a rich ivory crucifix which had been presented to him.

When the situation was beyond his personal resources, he would appeal to the generosity of faithful and clergy. In 1896 he supported a *Pro Armenia* committee which had been created in Venice to come to the aid of Armenian Christians.[36] The following year, to give another example, he intervened to help a lace factory that was in difficulties. This factory, situated on the island of Burano, trained 400 apprentices. Once he had learned of the difficulties it was undergoing and of the deserving nature of the enterprise, Cardinal Sarto, in a circular letter dated March 24, 1897, addressed the bishops of the region, parish priests and rectors, urging them to purchase their lace requirements (for the making of liturgical vestments, *etc.*) from the Burano factory.[37] Several months later, in August, at Calle Redivivo, some workers who had gone to the assistance of the inhabitants of several houses that had caught fire were themselves buried under the debris. The day after the tragedy, Cardinal Sarto, by means of a circular

---

[36] Armenia, at that time in the Ottoman Empire, experienced terrible massacres of Christians in the years 1894-1896.
[37] Text of the circular in Marchesan, p.406.

letter to clergy and faithful, invited the members of his diocese to come to the aid of the victims' families.[38] He visited the wounded and, on September 3, he assisted at the funerals of the victims, which he desired to be celebrated in St. Mark's Basilica. Nor is it strange—after all, he was a Franciscan tertiary—that he encouraged the charitable work of St. Anthony's Bread in his diocese.

Individual acts of charity, however, are inadequate to resolve the great social problems which emerge in a diocese in economic and social turmoil, as was the Diocese of Venice at the end of the 19th century. Furthermore, Cardinal Sarto was not only a charitable prelate. He was a prelate troubled by social questions and eager to find collective, institutional and legislative solutions to them. At Mantua we have already seen him interested in the *Opera dei Congressi*. When he arrived in Venice, 26 of the 43 parishes had a committee of the *Opera*.[39] A testimony to Venetian dynamism was the fact that a city advocate, Giovanni Battista Paganuzzi, had been national president of the *Opera dei Congressi* since 1889.

Cardinal Sarto was an indefatigable promoter of the *Opera*. Three months after he arrived in the diocese, he wrote to the vice-president of the diocesan committee, Antonio De Angelo, a priest and professor, to encourage him to develop the parish committees and the different Catholic social works. He also encouraged the beginnings of the Women's Catholic Action in Venice.

On November 23, 1895, on the occasion of the 10th regional assembly of the *Opera dei Congressi,* Cardinal Sarto gave an important address. In it he saluted the "parish committees," the structures at the base of the *Opera,* as "the elite army of the Holy Father." At the same time he gave them their objectives: to help the laity grow in the faith and to perfect their Christian moral conduct by means of actions performed in submission to the Church's hierarchy and in a disinterested spirit of self-denial.[40]

It is worth noting that he was in favor, in 1895, of setting up a Catholic bank in Venice, the *Banca di San Marco*.[41] This bank, which was to have spectacular success, was the first anonymous limited company set up by Catholics. Cardinal Sarto bought the first of the 100 shares (at 1,000 lire each) which constituted the foundation's capital. Two years later he saluted the creation of the first Catholic assurance company, founded in Verona. He saw this as the realization of "a Christian social ideal responding per-

---

[38] Circular to the clergy and people, August 31, 1897, *Le Pastorali,* vol.I, pp.136-137.
[39] Tramontin, "La diocesi nel passaggio dal dominio austriaco al regno d'Italia," in *La Chiesa veneziana dal 1849 alle soglie del novecento,* p.39.
[40] Extracts cited by Marchesan, pp.417-418.
[41] As witness the lawyer Tagliapietra, one of the founders of the bank, *Summarium,* p.285.

fectly to the economic and moral needs of our time."[42] In 1900 Cardinal Sarto signed a life-assurance contract in favor of his brother and his sisters. In 1901, however—and this shows the quality of his vigilance—he got the Bishop of Verona, Msgr. Bacilieri, to dismiss two priest-members of the company from its administrative council. He wrote that he did not want "the Catholic world to be dragged in the mire."[43]

In August 1896, in Padua, the second Congress of the Catholic Union for Social Studies took place. We have already seen that this organization had been created seven years earlier by Professor Giuseppe Toniolo, in the presence of the then Bishop of Mantua. This time, eight bishops were present and several directors of the *Opera dei Congressi* took part. All the eminent representatives of the Italian Catholic Movement were present (Medolago, Paganuzzi, Alessi and others). Cardinal Sarto's address attracted considerable notice.[44] Faced with "ardent enemies" (unbelief and revolution) "...menacing and trying to destroy the social fabric," the Patriarch of Venice invited the participants to make Jesus Christ the foundation of their work: "the only peace treaty is the Gospel." He warned them against what is now called the "welfare state," the state which provides everything and shapes all socialization: "substituting public almsgiving for private almsgiving involves the complete destruction of Christianity and is a terrible attack on the principle of ownership. Christianity cannot exist without charity, and the difference between charity and justice is that justice may have recourse to laws and even to force, depending on the circumstances, whereas charity can only be imposed by the tribunal of God and of conscience." If public assistance and the redistribution of wealth are institutionalized, "poverty becomes a function, a way of life, a public trade...."

These are not the views of someone indifferent to social problems. This was clearly seen in 1901, when a dispute arose between manager and staff in the city's tobacco industry (which employed some 2,000 workers, male and female). The socialists organized a demonstration, called for a strike and campaigned for the tobacco workers to join a national union. Cardinal Sarto visited the plant, tried to calm people down and warned them against the evil results of a strike, offering to defend their rights and interests.[45] The strike was avoided.

These initiatives of Cardinal Sarto, and his eminently religious concept of the social question, were not unanimously shared, even at the heart

---

[42] Letter to the director of the *Società Cattolica d'Assicurazione,* March 4, 1897, *Lettere,* p.252.
[43] Letter of Cardinal Sarto to Msgr. Bacilieri, November 18, 1901, quoted in Romanato, p.211.
[44] Extracts in Marchesan, pp.421-422.
[45] Marchesan, p.404.

of the Catholic movement. It was at this time that a young priest, Romolo Murri, who would eventually emerge as the leader of the Christian Democrats, got into conflict with the Patriarch of Venice. Leo XIII's directives with regard to the ideas of the Christian Democrats, understood as "benevolent action on behalf of the people" and not as political action, had put the movement represented by Murri and his review, *La Cultura sociale,* in a difficult position. On August 16, 1902, Don Murri published a virulent attack on Paganuzzi, the president of the *Opera dei Congressi,* whom he considered too conservative. The following day, in an open letter published in *La Difesa,* Cardinal Sarto came to the defence of Count Paganuzzi and protested against "the disloyal campaign being made against the foremost of the illustrious and respected champions of Catholic works," denouncing "those who, under the pretext of suggesting necessary reforms, import discord into the *Opera dei Congressi.*"[46] Fr. Murri made a spirited reply. Later, as Pope, Cardinal Sarto would have to go to the length of excommunicating Murri.

Sacred music and liturgy

Cardinal Sarto used to smile and say, "I only wanted to be Patriarch of Venice for the sake of the lace." This quip clearly shows his long-evident taste for beautiful and solemn religious ceremonies. Not out of a love of pomp and vanity, but because the Patriarch of Venice was convinced that beautiful ceremonies, through their ornaments, their music and the quality of the chant, inspire people to devotion and help the soul to open itself to spiritual goods. On the occasion of major feasts, the Cardinal had the Persian tapestries and the liturgical vestments of lace brought out from the Basilica's treasury, where they had previously been kept untouched.

In matters liturgical one of his greatest concerns was the restoration of Gregorian chant in Venice. Young Don Perosi, whom (as we have seen) he had appointed as choirmaster, was the architect of this restoration. A few weeks before Cardinal Sarto's arrival in Venice, Perosi complained of the calamitous situation of music in St. Mark's Basilica: "I find everything here in disarray; there is practically no Gregorian chant...."[47] A month later he ordered 30 copies of the *Kyriale* from Solesmes so that the Gregorian chant could be sung during Cardinal Sarto's inaugural Mass.[48]

After this, all the great solemnities presented an opportunity to make the Venetians more familiar with the traditional plainchant. The celebra-

---

[46] Letter of August 17, 1902, *Le Pastorali,* vol.II, pp.288-289.
[47] Letter of Don Perosi to Dom Mocquereau, October 9, 1894, Archives of the Abbey of St. Pierre de Solesmes.
[48] Postcard from Don Perosi to Dom Mocquereau, no date (Nov. 1894), Archives of the Abbey of St. Pierre de Solesmes.

tions for the eighth centenary of the building of St. Mark's Basilica were particularly magnificent. The Basilica had been begun in 976 and finished in 1071, and was solemnly consecrated on October 8, 1094. Accordingly, the eighth centenary should have been celebrated in October 1894. At that date, however, Venice could not yet receive its new Patriarch, and Cardinal Sarto was waiting to take possession of his See. Once he was installed in Venice, however, he fixed the date of the ceremonies for the April 22, 23, 24 and 25, 1895 (April 25 being the Feast of St. Mark). All the bishops of the province of Venice took part. Cardinal Sarto took advantage of the occasion to organize a solemn assembly of the Venetian episcopal conference (we have already noted its very concrete resolutions). The celebrations were concluded by a solemn pontifical Mass and a panegyric pronounced by Cardinal Sarto on the subject of "St. Mark and Venice." The manuscript of this address has been preserved; it shows the many corrections the Cardinal made to it. The eighth centenary celebrations attracted a large crowd of people, and the Patriarch of Venice wished to address them "in a simple and familiar way" in order to put across his pastoral aim, that is, to bring Venice back to Christianity. Cardinal Sarto spoke of Venice's glorious hours and showed how the true greatness of a society is grounded in religion:

> If it is true that a nation's principal strength resides in its alliances, we can say "Blessed are the people who have God himself for their ally."...Venice was glorious because, above everything else, she brought her sons to St. Mark, teaching them that religion alone can open the triumphal path; that there can be no victory without the shield of faith and the Cross of Christ; that nothing lasting can be built without heaven's protection; and that there is no civilization and no greatness outside the Gospel of Jesus Christ.

In Venice's hey-day, the Patriarch went on, at the time of its victories against the Tartars, the Moslems, and when it dominated the Mediterranean and brought peace to it, the city magistrates

> not only called themselves Christians but showed it, not only at home and in their private chapels, but publicly, in all the circumstances in which they had to act...those who wielded power at that time were respected, venerated and feared....True liberty does not consist in absolute independence and anarchy: these are nothing but the most savage tyranny. For, as the wise dictum has it, where there is no master, all are masters, and a nation without a master is a nation of slaves.

"The decline of Venice came about," continued the Patriarch, when, "having arrived at the peak of her power, she began to forget the blessings she had received from heaven and ceased scrupulously to respect God's holy laws."

This address, which made a great impression, ended with invocations to St. Mark, asking him to protect and pray for Venice. The Cardinal concluded: "It is justice, faith and religion which constitute the greatness of nations. It is sin which makes peoples unhappy and scatters them."[49]

In the succeeding years, following his practice in Mantua, Cardinal Sarto would make a point of honoring the great figures of Venice's Christian past by means of splendid celebrations. In January 1897 there was the commemoration of St. Pietro Orseolo (Doge of Venice from 991 to 1009); in March 1900 there was the commemoration of the centenary of the election of Pius VII (the only Conclave in history to have taken place in Venice); in September 1900 there was the commemoration of St. Gerardo Sagredo (a native of Venice, and not Patriarch as certain authors say; he was Bishop of Csanád in Hungary in the 11th century).

For Cardinal Sarto the Christian past was not only an object of history. It should be a light for the present. Venice should re-establish connections with its Christian past and, if necessary, defend it against its despisers. One fact illustrates this conviction of his.

The very day Cardinal Sarto pronounced the panegyric of St. Mark, he signed a letter addressed to all the deans of the diocese, showing that he was not disposed to compromise where the respect due to religion was concerned. This year, 1895, for the first time, the City of Venice was organizing an international art exhibition (the "Biennale" which was to become famous as the years went by). The anti-clerical City fathers wanted to provide a foil to the religious festivities by means of this prestigious artistic display. The exhibition contained a scandalous painting by the contemporary artist Giacomo Grosso, entitled *Supremo Convegno*. It was a crude caricature of the Last Supper, which the Cardinal, in a private letter, termed "filth."[50] In a letter dated the Feast of St. Mark, the Patriarch of Venice forbade all his priests to attend this first Biennale.[51]

In the immediate wake of the celebrations in honor of St. Mark, Cardinal Sarto published a very important pastoral letter on sacred music.[52] Developing ideas which were dear to him, he established strict norms regarding sacred music and the ecclesiastical chant. His predecessor, Cardinal Agostini, having due respect for a ruling which issued from the Congregation of Rites (September 24, 1884), had created the Diocesan

---

[49] Panegyric of St. Mark, April 25, 1895, published under the title of *San Marco. Feste centenarie,* under the aegis of Quirino Bortolato and Giuseppe Carretta (Riese Pio X: Fondazione G. Sarto/Amministrazione Provinciale di Treviso, 1995).

[50] Letter to Federico Pellegrini, September 20, 1895, *Lettere,* p.239. The picture had just been awarded the *premio populare* ("people's prize").

[51] Letter to the deans of clergy, April 25, 1895, *Le Pastorali,* vol.I, pp.64-65.

[52] Pastoral letter on sacred music, May 1, 1895, *Le Pastorali,* vol.I, pp.66-74.

Commission of St. Cecilia to watch over sacred music and chant. The first circular letter published by the Commission forbade the playing of operatic music and dance-tunes in churches. Ten years later, Cardinal Sarto's pastoral letter would offer a more precise vision of what the chant and church music should be.

Music performed in church, wrote the Cardinal, should be subject to the liturgy and share its qualities. Sacred music and chant should exclude not only what is "light, vulgar, trivial and ridiculous," but also "all that is profane and theatrical, either in its composition or in its execution." The Cardinal affirmed that Gregorian chant, "by the *holiness* of its origin and its forms, is the only music which the Church acknowledges to be her very own"; since it is an art form that all recognize, it is "genuinely *universal*." Polyphony, culminating in the 16th century in the works of Palestrina, is "alone worthy of being placed alongside Gregorian chant" in churches, because it is inspired by the chant.

So the Cardinal ordered that, at least once a month, in all the churches, the *Kyrie, Gloria, Credo, Sanctus, Agnus Dei* should be sung in Gregorian chant, as well as the *Introit,* the gradual, the offertory, the communion chant and the office of vespers. He forbade the piano and bands in churches, and ordered that every parish should set up a school of Gregorian chant. He also created a Sacred Music Commission, with the task of promoting the study and performance of sacred music and chant, and of making sure that the prescribed norms were observed. The Commission consisted of five members, of whom Don Perosi was one.

In addition, Cardinal Sarto commanded that sacred chant should be taught in the Seminary. He entrusted this task to Don Perosi. In December 1898, Don Perosi, having performed an oratorio of his own composition in St. Peter's Basilica, was appointed choirmaster of the Sixtine Chapel. Msgr. Magri was chosen to succeed him at the patriarchal Seminary. During the beatification process, Mgr Magri testified that the teaching of sacred chant, and its execution in the parishes, was always close to Cardinal Sarto's heart, and that he took pains to be present at the Seminary examinations in sacred chant, giving encouragement or correction by his own example.[53]

The Patriarch of the Eucharist

It has often been said that, because of the great decisions he took in this area, Pius X was "the Pope of the Eucharist." If we look at the pastoral charges he issued before coming to Venice, it is normal to find there a great attachment to Eucharistic worship. This devotion was rooted in him since

---

[53] Deposition of Msgr. Magri, *Summarium,* pp.459-461.

childhood. Furthermore, as time went on his attachment to it increased, the more it was threatened and mocked by others. The response to those who attacked and denigrated religious faith and miracles, who wanted to distance man from God, was to bring the faithful Catholic closer to God through the exaltation of the Eucharist, the Sacrament in which the mystery is all the greater since it conjoins the most ordinary material reality (bread) with the most staggering supernatural reality (transubstantiation and the Real Presence).[54]

In Venice Cardinal Sarto organized perpetual adoration of the Blessed Sacrament as it was already being done in Rome and in many French dioceses. He also encouraged frequent communion and, as he had already done in Salzano and Mantua, he prompted children to communicate early (and not at the age of 12 or 14, as was then the custom). As Pope he would fix the age for First Communion at "seven years, more or even less." In Venice, in the statutes of the synod to which we have referred, he was less generous, but he established the conditions and provided arguments to which we shall return. At the synod he prescribed that "children of ten years, if they can distinguish the bread of the Eucharist from ordinary bread, if they have been well instructed in Christian doctrine, and if they are of good conduct, can laudably be admitted to the Eucharistic table before the tempter can soil their innocence."

In the early days of his patriarchate there was an incident in which the Eucharist had been profaned; he was deeply upset and he ordered ceremonies of reparation to be held. On the morning of April 2, 1895, in the church of Santa Maria in Nazareth, which was maintained by Discalced Carmelites, sacrilegious hands had forced open the door of the tabernacle, stolen the precious ciboria and thrown the hosts on the ground. As soon as he heard the news, Cardinal Sarto had a letter printed in the form of a poster calling on the clergy and faithful to make a work of spiritual reparation.[55] For three afternoons in succession, in the church where the sacrilege had been committed, an expiatory ceremony was organized; on the following Sunday, in all the churches of the city, an hour's Eucharistic adoration was kept.

Cardinal Sarto's veneration for the Eucharist was also shown on the occasion of the fifth National Eucharistic Congress. Since the first International Eucharistic Congress, which took place in Lille in 1886, many others had been held. Italy, which had not been associated with the first International Congresses, organized national ones. They took place successively

54 Zambarbieri, "Il Patriarca Sarto," in *La Chiesa veneziana dal 1849 alle soglie de novecento,* p.154.
55 Letter to the clergy and faithful, April 2, 1895, *Le Pastorali,* vol.I, pp.62-63.

in Naples, Turin, Milan and Orvieto. In September 1896, during the annual conference of the bishops of the Venetian province, the decision was taken to organize a National Eucharistic Congress in Venice. The decision was approved by the Holy See.

Cardinal Sarto announced the news in a letter dated November 1, 1896.[56] He gave the Congress a twofold aim: to re-awaken faith in the Eucharistic mystery and stimulate an increase in devotion and religious practice, but at the same time to make the Congress into a public affirmation of the social Kingdom of Christ. "Jesus is our King and our Father: we owe Him, so to speak, a vassal's homage and love....In the Eucharistic Congresses, Jesus shows himself in a light of splendor which compels even the wretched and ignorant to turn their gaze to Him, to contemplate His beauty, His greatness, His love, and to realize their duty to be Christian, not by halves, not in private, but wholly, in full submission of the intellect to revealed truth, in total obedience of the will to all His holy laws, and in the subjection of the passions to the rule of reason illuminated by faith."

This Eucharistic Congress was prepared over a long period of time. In addition to the two meetings with the Cardinal to draw up a detailed program and assess the material requirements, there was an intense spiritual preparation. Missions were preached in the five Venice churches. On August 8, 1897, an inaugural ceremony took place in St. Mark's Basilica. The opening address was given by Cardinal Svampa, Archbishop of Bologna, and then the Blessed Sacrament was exposed to the veneration of the faithful while the *schola cantorum*, under Perosi's direction, sang the *Pange lingua*, *Veni Creator* and *Tantum ergo*. The Congress properly speaking was held on August 9, 10 and 11, in the church of San Giovanni e San Paolo, the biggest in Venice. In his opening address, Cardinal Sarto reminded his audience of the aim of the Eucharistic Congresses: "to make an act of veneration to Jesus Christ, who is so often outraged; to obtain the grace that His mind may govern our intellects, His moral teaching our moral conduct, His truth our institutions, His justice our legislation, His worship our religion, His life our life."[57]

Addresses alternated with liturgical offices, while day and night, in the other city churches, the Blessed Sacrament was exposed. The talks dealt with the most diverse aspects of the Eucharist, of Eucharistic worship and its influence. Laymen were invited to give some of the addresses, notably Professor Toniolo, who spoke on "The Eucharist and the Future of Society."[58] It is interesting to note that two religious priests who, some years

---

[56] *Le Pastorali,* vol.I, pp.103-111.
[57] Address of August 9, 1897, cf. Dal-Gal, *Pius X,* pp.122-3.
[58] The Eucharistic Congress is portrayed in detail by Marchesan, pp.368-380.

later, were to be suspected of Modernism, took part in this Eucharistic Congress: Fr. Ghignoni spoke on "Heresies of our century against the Eucharist" and Fr. Semeria spoke on "The Eucharist and the Catholic movement."

Three cardinals (Svampa, Manara and Ferrari) in addition to 28 archbishops and bishops from all over Italy participated in this Congress. Its final act took place in St. Mark's Basilica: Cardinal Ferrari, Archbishop of Milan, celebrated a pontifical Mass. In the afternoon a solemn Eucharistic procession led the faithful from the Basilica to the Lagoon for the traditional Blessing of the Sea.

Another great manifestation of popular piety was the blessing of the Virgin of Monte Grappa, at a height of 1,779 meters. Ever since he had had a cardiac crisis, in January 1899—his first serious illness, from which he recovered in two weeks, to the amazement of all—Cardinal Sarto liked to go and rest in the neighborhood of Monte Grappa, not far from Riese. Towards the end of the summer, when the air became unbreathable and the sirocco and the mosquitoes used to invade the town, the Patriarch left for a week or two in Crespano, where some nuns lent him a remote little octagonal house in the midst of hills and fields. Sometimes he used to go to the little village of Possagno where his nephew Parolin had become parish priest. Monte Grappa was situated in the diocese of Padua. The bishop, Msgr. Callegari, had wanted to establish an oratory here, dedicated to the Blessed Virgin. However, when the day of its inauguration came, a sick Msgr. Callegari could not carry out the blessing so long awaited. He appealed to his friend and superior: Cardinal Sarto was glad to take his place.

On August 3, 1901, he ascended as far as Campo Santa Croce, a village at the foot of Monte Grappa, at an altitude of 1,000 meters. The Cardinal spent the night in a forest house and then, in the early hours, accompanied by a large crowd carrying torches and lanterns, he went to the top of the mountain. A photograph shows the Cardinal who was to become Pope exactly two years later: perched on a white mule, he wears a long black coat and a black hat, a white scarf is knotted about his neck and his face, sleek and round, gives an intimation of a great joy. The sun was coming over the horizon when the Patriarch of Venice reached the summit. Amid 10,000 pilgrims he celebrated Mass, distributed Communion to many faithful and blessed the large statue of the Virgin bearing the infant Jesus in her arms.

God in the city

We have already seen that when he arrived in Venice, the municipal authorities, who had connections with Freemasonry, had refused to join in the official and popular welcome given to the new Patriarch. This intolerant attitude was only a public manifestation of a sectarian war against the Church and her influence. The municipal authorities had taken certain measures which had scandalized Catholics, such as suppressing the teaching of catechism in publicly-administered schools, removing crucifixes from hospital rooms and refusing to erect the "votive bridges."[59] Some months later, in July 1895, the municipal elections were to take place. Catholics were divided on the attitude they should adopt.

Ever since the annexation of the Papal States and of Rome by the Kingdom of Italy, in 1870, Pius IX had given this political instruction to Catholics: *Non expedit.* "It is not appropriate" for Catholics to take part in national (legislative) elections and present candidates. To do otherwise would be to recognize, as a *fait accompli*, the "usurpation" practised by the King's regime. This instruction, therefore, was followed by the great majority of Catholics. On the other hand the Holy See did not forbid Catholics to take part in "administrative" elections (*i.e.,* municipal and provincial elections). However, there was a minority of Catholics who urged abstention, even at the local level. At the very moment of the 1895 elections an influential newspaper, the *Osservatore cattolico,* published in Milan by Don Albertario, was still supporting this view as being absolutely the only possible one. It recommended Catholics either to present separate lists, without looking for support from parties that were not openly Catholic, or to abstain.

Cardinal Sarto did not share this view. He believed that Catholics should take an active part in municipal elections. In Venice he showed a certain boldness in his approach to this issue. When he had been Bishop of Mantua he had categorically opposed the idea of Catholics voting for candidates who were Liberals. In a letter to the president of the *Opera dei Congressi* he wrote: "No Catholic should give his vote to Liberals, of whatever hue. I am an 'intransigent' to the very marrow of my bones, and am convinced that this is a duty in conscience."[60] Five years later, in Venice, he was more pragmatic and more flexible. He considered that, in the City of the Doges, in order to put an end to the reign of the "radical democrats," who were anti-clericals, Catholics should enter an electoral alliance with certain of the Liberals.[61] He therefore favored a political alliance between

---

[59] These "votive bridges" were temporary bridges traditionally put in place by the city authorities on the Giudecca Canal and the Grand Canal for the occasion of the Feasts of two sanctuaries (the Holy Redeemer, on the 3rd Sunday of July, and the Madonna della Salute, on November 21). These bridges made it easier for the faithful to visit these sanctuaries.

[60] "... *Intransigente fino al midollo...*," letter to Paganuzzi, March 1, 1890, quoted by Zambarbieri, "Il Patriarca Sarto," in *La Chiesa veneziana dal 1849 alle soglie del novecento,* p.136.

Catholics and the moderate Liberals; these Liberals, in political matters, were not the same as the liberals in religion whom Cardinal Sarto had often denounced. A common list of candidates was drawn up under the direction of a Catholic. This agreement was not initially accepted by all the Catholics. Some of them were afraid that a political pact with Liberals, even moderate Liberals, would end in compromises and concessions. The Patriarch of Venice succeeded in commending these electoral tactics to them; his watchword was "Work, pray, vote!" In order to do this he made sure that the common program that had been worked out contained guarantees that Catholics could live their faith in the city, and that were favorable to the restoration of a Christian city: the re-establishment of prayer and religious instruction in public schools; Sunday rest and respect for the holy days of obligation on the part of the town's employees; the participation of the municipal authorities in the votive feasts of the city and respect for the desires expressed in last wills and testaments.[62]

Committees were set up representing the various quarters of the city and meetings took place in the patriarchal palace, attended by the Cardinal, priests and political activists. All the Catholic associations were urged to participate in the electoral battle and the religious communities were asked to pray for the victory of Christian principles. The Catholic-Liberal list won the elections on July 18. The anti-clerical radicals were beaten. The Catholic-Liberal coalition was largely victorious with 60 elected members (24 outright Catholics, 6 Conservatives and 30 Liberals). On the evening of the elections, Catholic young people noisily showed their approval on St. Mark's Square, in front of the Patriarchate. Cardinal Sarto had two enormous candelabra placed on the balcony and stepped on to the balcony to bless the crowd. The victory of the Catholics allied to the moderate Liberals was largely a victory of Cardinal Sarto himself. Count Filippo Grimani was designated *sindaco* (mayor).

After the electoral victory, certain people reproached Cardinal Sarto for having allied himself with Liberals. Fr. Gaetano Zocchi, a Jesuit and director of *La Difesa,* who in fact had strong ties with the Patriarch of Venice, complained of the latter's decision in a letter to Cardinal Rampolla, Leo XIII's Secretary of State.[63] Cardinal Sarto explained his actions to the

---

[61] This disagreement with Don Davide Albertario did not prevent him supporting him when he was imprisoned by the authorities (from June 1898 to May 1899), and when he was gravely ill (letter of March 22, 1902, *Lettere,* pp.285-286).

[62] Depositions of Msgr. Jeremich, F. Pellegrini and A. De Blasi, *Summarium,* pp.389, 410 and 476-477.

[63] Bertoli, "La pastorale di fronte au mutamenti culturali e politici della società veneziana" and Zambarbieri, "Il Patriarca Sarto," in *La Chiesa veneziana dal 1849 alle soglie del novecento,* pp.78 and 159.

Pope when on a visit to Rome. Speaking of the moderate Liberals, he said: "These are men who publicly receive Communion at Easter, and not only at Easter; they attend Sunday Mass; they do not miss any of the city's votive feasts and, during the Corpus Christi procession, they do not hesitate to carry the canopy." As a result Leo XIII silenced the critics: he addressed a letter to the young Catholics of Venice, congratulating them on their electoral victory.[64]

History has vindicated Cardinal Sarto. The promises made by the moderate Liberals before the election were kept. The new municipal authorities implemented an extensive program of social—and sanitary—policy: institutional social aid; the fight against disease; urban hygiene (a network of sewers, *etc.*), and the building of community halls.[65] The political alliance permitted by Cardinal Sarto continued: Filippo Grimani (known to history as the *sindaco d'oro*) governed the city until December 1919, which is itself a sign that the majority found his policies satisfactory.

In addition to this political involvement of Cardinal Sarto, we must draw attention to the support he gave on many occasions to the anti-Masonic movement, which was more energetic in Venice because, for decades, Freemasonry had been very influential at the highest levels of the city. He wanted the diocese to be officially represented at the heart of the *Comitato antimassonico*, which had been set up to prepare for a great international anti-Masonic congress which took place in Trento in 1896. Cardinal Sarto regarded the anti-Masonic struggle as a work of prime importance. This is quite clear from the person he chose to direct the *Comitato antimassonico*: he appointed Don Antonio De Angelo who, as we have seen, was also vice-president of the diocesan committee of the *Opera dei Congressi*. In a public letter he wrote to him on August 29, 1896, he said: "Fighting Freemasonry is simultaneously a religious work and an eminently social work, because this sect is not only hostile to everything which pertains to our holy Religion, but it is intent on subverting the tranquillity of the social order."[66] The following month an anti-Masonic meeting took place in the patriarchal palace in the presence of the Cardinal. The meeting looked forward to the creation of an international anti-Masonic league, with the watchword: *"Pro fide et pro patria libertas! Fuori la massoneria!"* ("Liberty for faith and homeland! Away with Freemasonry!").

Nowadays some people may regard this hostility towards Freemasonry as a reactionary campaign, as evidence of a conspiratorial and obscurantist

---

[64] Dal-Gal, *Pius X*, p.120. Fr. Zocchi had to withdraw from his position as editor of the newspaper and was called to Rome, where he worked on *La Civiltà Cattolica*.

[65] Cf. Casimira Grandi, "Bonifica sociale e bonifica urbana nell'operato della giunta Grimani tra 1895 e 1914," in *La Chiesa di Venezia nel primo novecento*, pp.63-83.

[66] Letter quoted in Marchesan, pp.425-426.

mentality. This was not the case with Cardinal Sarto. Freemasonry was one of those powers which, openly or in a more shadowy way, was fighting against the Church. The Patriarch of Venice judged that no compromise was possible with the Church's enemies. However, fighting against error was not the same thing as fighting against persons. Giuseppe Sarto's motto in Venice, and later in the Vatican, was, "War against error, and charity towards those in error." This is attested by a fact reported by one of his first biographers and confirmed by history. In September 1900, the Patriarch of Venice did not hesitate to spend several days in the city's prison hearing the confessions of some 200 people detained there.[67]

Cardinal Sarto's last battle in Venice was against divorce. At the end of 1901 a draft law for the authorization of divorce was put before parliament. Cardinal Sarto opposed it with determination. In January 1902, on his initiative, all the bishops of Venetia signed an open letter to the Italian members of parliament, urging rejection of the draft law on divorce. Identical action was taken by the bishops of other regions.

Then the Patriarch of Venice dedicated his Lenten letter to the same subject.[68] In this long pastoral letter he recalled the greatness of marriage, "the sacrament which sanctifies man and woman in the very act which unites them, and which builds up, so to speak, a church in each particular family." Conversely, even in the context of the natural law, divorce is to be condemned; "in no case is it permissible to separate what God has joined."

Some time afterwards, in the patriarchal palace, he organized a conference against the draft law. It brought together the clergy, the lay Catholic movements, but also Mayor Grimani and several city councillors. At the end of the same year he returned to the argument in a letter to clergy and faithful.[69] He asked for public prayers in the churches and he called for a total mobilization against the "sacrilegious attack": "We must protest even in public and without fear, without human respect...in every way the laws permit."

A notable speech

There was one event which attracted attention to Cardinal Sarto from around the world and enhanced his reputation as someone who was *papabile*: this was the ceremony marking the start of reconstruction of the Ven-

---

[67] Marchesan, p.410 and Romanato, pp.217-218.
[68] Lenten pastoral *Il Matrimonio e il Divorzio,* dated January 30, 1902, *Le Pastorali,* vol.II, pp.91-110.
[69] Letter of December 9, 1902, *Le Pastorali,* vol.II, pp.125-127.

ice Campanile. On this occasion the Patriarch of Venice showed great skill, while not surrendering his principles in the least.

On July 14, 1902, the city's Campanile had collapsed. The following day, in a letter to the population, the Cardinal had ordered three days of prayers in thanksgiving to God that the catastrophe had not caused the death of anyone.[70] On July 23, 24 and 25, a triduum was celebrated in St. Mark's Basilica in front of the venerated painting of the Blessed Virgin, which was exposed on the altar. Cardinal Sarto was also the first to appeal to the public's generosity to hasten the rebuilding of the Campanile. His appeal was relayed by the municipal authorities and soon, in a few months, 5 million lire were collected. The Venetians, the province and the government made their contributions and there were also some important gifts from abroad. On April 25, 1903, the Feast of St. Mark, the first stone of the new Campanile was laid. This ceremony and the Patriarch's address attracted even more attention to him, both in Italy and abroad.

This was a grand ceremony, both civil and religious, since the municipal authorities had asked Cardinal Sarto to bless the foundation-stone. The Italian government was represented at the ceremony by a minister, Nunzio Nasi, and King Victor-Emmanuel III by his first cousin, the Count of Turin. Furthermore, the presence of the French minister for public education, M. Chaumié, symbolized the assistance of foreign donors.

A huge official stage had been erected between the Basilica and the Doges' Palace. The event was historic not only because of Venice's prestige but also because, for the first time since the annexation of the Papal States and Rome by the Kingdom of Italy, a prince of the Church and a representative of the King were officially participating in the same ceremony. Everyone was curious to hear what these two would say. Minister Nasi thought it necessary to insert a polemical note into his speech, recalling Venice's 17th century struggle against Pope Paul V. He repeated the apocryphal watchword attributed to a doge of that time: "Venetians first, Christians second!"

Cardinal Sarto could not leave such an inappropriate verbal attack without a reply. He showed great skill in dealing with it. After the rite of blessing the foundation stone, he gave an address in which, rather than replying directly to Minister Nasi, he said how good it was that the Venetians, and the municipal authorities, had wished to put the reconstruction of the Campanile under divine protection: "What an admirable sight it is to see people who, beginning some enterprise, ask God to bless it; for the genius of man is never so great as when it bows before the Eternal Flame

---

[70] *Le Pastorali,* vol.II, pp.111-112.

whence Light radiates forth, and man's works exhibit a more majestic and solemn character when he has recourse to that Supreme Power which consecrates them.

"I rejoice with you, noble representatives of Venice, *faithful spokesmen of the city's true citizens,* who have decided to inaugurate the reconstruction of the Campanile by a public act of religion—and that on the day dedicated to the evangelist St. Mark—so that Venice, which has flourished for so many centuries under such a Protector, should see a new era of prosperity opening up before her."[71] Far from opposing religion and patriotism, Church and State, he spoke of the "twofold love" which had united Venetians for so long: the love of religion, which had been "the source of their good fortune" and the love of their motherland, to which Venetians had always given "affection, respect and heroic sacrifice."

This language, in the mouth of Cardinal Sarto, attracted wide interest. The Italian press devoted several articles to this parallel praise of the love of the Church and the love of the motherland. It seemed like a first step towards a reconciliation between the Holy See and the Italian royalty, more than 30 years after the annexation of the Papal States and Rome.[72] This interpretation of Cardinal Sarto's speech was mistaken: when he became Pope, it became clear that he was not a *conciliationist.* In fact, this speech of April 25, 1903, was in complete continuity with the stance adopted by the Patriarchs of Venice since the former Republic became attached to the Kingdom of Italy: namely, radical condemnation of the ideology of the liberal state and the rejection of the anti-clerical and anti-Catholic politics of the government, and at the same time loyalty towards the authority of a state and regime that were acknowledged to be legitimate.[73]

Though misinterpreted by some, the speech of April 25 aroused great interest, even in diplomatic spheres. Cardinal Sarto's *papabile* reputation began to spread. This is attested by a report sent six days later by Nissard, the French ambassador to the Holy See, to his minister Delcassé. After writing, at length, on the ceremony and Cardinal Sarto's striking speech, Nisard observed: "This is the first time that a Cardinal has associated himself, in such an express manner, with a public event under the auspices of a Prince of the Royal House....This event throws an interesting light on the

---

[71] Dal-Gal, *Pie X*, pp.230-231.

[72] In other circumstances Cardinal Sarto had already publicly affirmed his loyalty to the Italian State: in 1897, after King Umberto I had escaped from an attempt on his life, the Patriarch of Venice had ordered the celebration of a *Te Deum* in thanksgiving. In July 1900, following the assassination of the King in Monza, Cardinal Sarto, in a letter to his clergy and faithful (July 31, 1900), had asked them to pray for the deceased sovereign, and on August 4 he had celebrated a funeral Mass in St. Mark's Basilica.

[73] Bertoli, "La pastorale di fronte ai mutamenti culturali e politici della società veneziana," in *La Chiesa veneziana dal 1849 alle soglie del novecento*, p.61.

situation of the Patriarch of Venice from the point of view of the future Conclave."[74]

The French ambassador added that Cardinal Sarto had "the reputation of being *papabile,* and that this was agreeable to the Italian government," and that by his attitude and his speech he had wanted "to attract the favorable attention of the Italian government." This first observation is interesting; the second is utterly without foundation, as we shall see. Cardinal Sarto never wanted to be Pope. He became Pope as a result of events which no one could have foreseen.

---

[74] Dispatch from Nisard to Delcassé, May 1, 1903, AMAE, Holy See, NS 3, f.52-53.

CHAPTER 5

POPE

On July 20, 1903, Leo XIII died. His death was not unexpected. Leo XIII had reigned for more than a quarter of a century. After having given serious cause for alarm in the preceding years, his health gravely deteriorated during the summer of 1903. For several months, diplomats stationed in Rome had been speculating on the chances of this or that cardinal becoming pope.[1]

At the beginning of July Cardinal Sarto, like many other Italian bishops, wrote to clergy and faithful ordering prayers for the Pope's recovery.[2] But on the 21st, "after a painful alternation between fear and hope," he published another letter announcing to clergy and people the death of Leo XIII which had taken place the day before, and asking them to pray that God would give the Church a new pope worthy of the task.[3]

On July 26 the Patriarch left Venice for Rome with his secretary, Bressan, and his valet, Abbiategrosso. On the very morning of his departure, in the church of Santa Maria della Salute, he had performed 27 priestly ordinations and administered Confirmation to several sick children. Before leaving the patriarchal palace he prayed in the chapel with his sisters.

Several authors think that Cardinal Sarto did not set out for the Conclave as someone already *papabile*—i.e., with a chance of becoming pope—let alone as a candidate for the pontificate. In their view, the Patriarch of Venice not only never wished to be pope, but did not even know that he was one of the *papabili* (although Leo XIII had asserted this,[4] as had certain cardinals, many diplomats and a section of the press). Cardinal Sarto was so sure that he would not be elected pope and that he would return to Venice that he is supposed to have told his secretary, "Get return tickets, it will be cheaper."

---

[1] The Archives of the Ministry of Foreign Affairs (AMAE) in Paris contain many dispatches on this subject by Nisard, French Ambassador to the Holy See, and by Barrère, French Ambassador in Rome (in particular there is a long, 20-page dispatch from Nisard of June 1903). We shall quote these along with other diplomatic sources.
[2] Letter of July 6, 1903, published in *Le Pastorali*, vol.II p.145.
[3] *Ibid.*, pp.146-148.
[4] Don Lorenzo Perosi stated on oath at the beatification process that, when he was received in 1898 by Leo XIII, the latter told him: "You will be able to render even greater service when the Patriarch of Venice becomes Pope." Other prophecies or expressions of certainty could be quoted.

In fact, this incident is apocryphal. On the contrary, two of his sisters asserted that he had not taken a return ticket.[5] Does this mean that Cardinal Sarto was sure that he would be elected pope? No. All the testimonies agree that he did not expect it at all. During the Conclave he had to be urged many times to accept the post. At the same time, however, he was not unaware that he was among the *papabili.* How could he have been ignorant of what the press, other cardinals, and many diplomats had been saying for years? He was far from being the only *papabile,* nor did he even have the greatest chance of being elected, yet he was one of those mentioned when people spoke of Leo XIII's successor.

So we can imagine that, on leaving Venice, Cardinal Sarto knew that he had a certain chance of being elected pope and that at the same time he dreaded that it might happen. To those who, after the death of Leo XIII, had mentioned to him the possibility of his election to the See of Peter, he invariably replied, with some severity: "Cannot you suggest some worse misfortune for me?"[6] He was in tears as he left Venice.[7]

Cardinal Sarto arrived in Rome by the night train on July 27. As at each of his previous stays in Rome since he had become Bishop of Mantua, he lodged at the Lombard Seminary, waiting for the opening of the Conclave, which was fixed for July 31, that is, the tenth day after the Pope's death. Rumors and speculations were rife in the city.

One of his first biographers cited two anecdotes which well show two of the Cardinal's virtues—his simplicity and humility—on the eve of the Conclave which would turn his life upside down. At the Lombard Seminary he was visited by two Venetian priests. He wanted to offer them some refreshment. "Only one glass could be found in the cell," Cigala recounts.

> The good Cardinal began to wash it himself.
> "Eminence! Eminence!" his visitors cried out.
> "Do you think St. Paul acted any differently when he arrived at the banks of the Tiber?" replied the Patriarch with his fatherly smile.

---

[5] Depositions of Maria Sarto and Anna Sarto, *Summarium,* pp.49 and 68.

[6] Testimony of Msgr. Bacchion, cf. Dal-Gal, *Pius X,* p.133.

[7] Reported by Marchesan, and all the authors dependent on him, is the well-known promise made by the Patriarch to the faithful who said farewell to him on his departure: "Living or dead, I shall return." After he was elected to the Sovereign Pontificate, this promise seemed illusory. In fact, however, it was a prophecy because, in April and May 1959, the mortal remains of St. Pius X came to Venice to be venerated by the faithful before returning to St. Peter's in Rome; cf. *San Pio X a Venezia. Celebrazioni e documenti,* special issue of the *Rivista diocesana del Patriarcato di Venezia,* June 1959, 207 pages.

He continued with his task, and the three friends drank water-and-tamarind from the same glass."[8]

On another occasion he was visited by the Contessa de Carpegna, who belonged to the best Venetian society. When she expressed her wish that he would become pope, he replied, in Venetian dialect: "I think it is quite enough that God should use intermediaries like me to make the Pope."[9]

However, the fact was that Cardinal Sarto was well up in the list of *papabili.*

The *papabili*

Nowadays we have at our disposal two sources which enable us to reconstruct the ambience of these pre-Conclave days: the accounts or personal diaries of certain ecclesiastics who participated in it, and the reports of diplomats.

At that time the Sacred College consisted of 64 cardinals. Two of them could not take part in the Conclave: Cardinal Pietro Celesia, Archbishop of Palermo, was too old to come to Rome; Cardinal Patrick Moran, Archbishop of Sydney, could not arrive in time for the opening of the Conclave. Of the 62 cardinals who proceeded to elect a successor to Leo XIII, 58 belonged to the "Great Powers" of the age: Italy, France, Spain, Austria-Hungary, Germany.[10] Each of these Great Powers, naturally, had its own recognized candidate or, at least, had made its preference known to the cardinal-electors.

France supported the candidature of Cardinal Rampolla. Leo XIII's former Secretary of State was regarded as a francophile, and, most importantly, as the French ambassador stressed with the Holy See: "It is under his ministry that the Holy See has formally adhered to the form of government which has ruled France for more than 30 years."[11] Delcassé, the Minister of Foreign Affairs, had told Cardinal Langénieux, Archbishop of Rheims, that the man who had been Leo XIII's Secretary of State was the favored candidate of his government: "Yesterday," he wrote to Barrère, "I had a conversation with Cardinal Langénieux which left me with a very

---

[8]   Cigala, *Vie intime de S.S. le pape Pie X*, p.27.
[9]   *Ibid.*, p.88.
[10] The Italian Cardinals were most numerous (38) in the Conclave. There were 7
      Frenchmen, 5 Spaniards, 5 cardinals of the Austro-Hungarian Empire and 3 Germans.
      There were also 1 Portuguese, 1 Belgian, 1 Irishman. Only one cardinal taking part in
      the Conclave was not from Europe: Cardinal James Gibbons, Archbishop of
      Baltimore. It was the first time the United States was represented at a Conclave.
[11] Dispatch from Nisard to Delcassé, April 19, 1903, AMAE, NS 3, f.42-45.

satisfactory impression. I did not mention any name, for which he thanked me, but he took the hint and understood me perfectly."[12]

At a meeting in Rome on July 29 the seven French cardinals decided to vote unanimously for Cardinal Rampolla at the first ballot.[13] This does not mean, however, that all the French cardinals wanted to see Rampolla elected. Some of them were not satisfied with his policies and hoped that another cardinal would be elected. For them, the first ballot was a matter of showing their homage to Leo XIII.[14]

Russia also supported Cardinal Rampolla because, during the pontificate of Leo XIII, he had shown himself very slavophile and had entered into conflict with Austria-Hungary, Russia's great enemy, on various questions.

Austria and Germany, on the other hand, had a long-standing aversion to Rampolla.[15] They signified their preference for Cardinals Gotti and Vannutelli.[16]

Cardinal Gotti was prefect of the Congregation of Propaganda (the Congregation in charge of missions). He was a virtuous man, not a politician like Rampolla, but it went against him that he was a religious—he was a Carmelite—and not a secular priest familiar with the world's affairs. Soon people were saying, "Gotti is well thought of here in Rome, but he is a sphinx: you never know what he is thinking or what he will do. Serafino Vannutelli would be better."[17]

Serafino Vannutelli was the Grand Penitentiary. Remarkably, one of his brothers, Vincenzo Vannutelli, was also a cardinal. It was said that the brothers Vannutelli were among those who conducted an active campaign. But the fact that they were brothers worked against them...In June, Ambassador Nisard gave his view that "Cardinal Serafino (Vannutelli) has maintained his position, but there is still resistance in the Curia to a family pontificate represented by two brothers."[18]

---

[12] Dispatch from Delcassé to Barrère, July 26, 1903, AMAE, NS 3, f.294. Nonetheless, the preference of the head of the government, Émile Combes, was for another candidate: Svampa, Archbishop of Bologna (Emmanuel Barbier, *Histoire du catholicisme libéral et du catholicisme social en France* [Cadoret, 1923], vol.IV, p.18).

[13] Testimony of Maurice Landrieux, "Le Conclave de 1903. Journal d'un conclaviste," *Études*, November 1958, p.169. Fr. Landrieux, vicar-general of Rheims, was *conclaviste* (assistant) to Cardinal Langénieux at the Conclave.

[14] "... I know that some will be disappointed if the manœuvre results in a candidate being elected," Fr. Landrieux observed on the eve of the first ballot, see article cited, p.172.

[15] Dispatch of Jules Cambon, French Ambassador in Madrid, to Delcassé, March 28, 1903, AMAE, NS 3, f.21-22.

[16] Dispatch of Reverseaux, French Ambassador in Vienna, to Delcassé, July 9, 1903, AMAE, NS 3, f.157.

[17] Landrieux, "Le Conclave de 1903," p.162.

[18] Dispatch of Nisard to Delcassé, June 8, 1903, AMAE, NS 3, f.66-75.

The Austrian authorities, however, did not order any explicit vote. At a meeting of the Austrian cardinals in Vienna, before their departure for Rome, Count Goluchowski, Minister of Foreign Affairs, invited them to "give their vote to the candidate who would seem to them to be the most moderate, someone foreign to political struggles, without naming any names."[19]

Spain initially had objections to Rampolla, but finally came round to his side, persuaded by the arguments of the French ambassador in Madrid, Cambon, and because it had been learned that the Spanish Cardinal Vivès y Tuto, a Capuchin, supported him.[20]

Nothing, however, was decided in advance. Cardinal Sarto's name continued to circulate. He was doubtless one of the most popular cardinals in Italy. On July 10 the French ambassador reported that, according to the Italian press, of those cardinals who did not belong to the Curia, "the chances of Patriarch Sarto are the most favorable."[21] Yet, three days before the Conclave, in the list of most likely *papabili* which Nisard sent to Delcassé, there were seven names, which did not include that of Cardinal Sarto....[22]

The Conclave

The electors entered into Conclave on Friday, July 31, at 5pm in the afternoon. The cardinals could be accompanied only by two persons, before whom they were to maintain the most absolute secrecy: a "conclavist" and a "noble guard." Cardinal Sarto chose his secretary Msgr. Bressan, as his conclavist and Count Stanislao Muccioli as his noble guard.

In charge of the Conclave was the Dean of the Sacred College and Camerlengo, Cardinal Oreglia di San Stefano, the only living cardinal created by Pius IX. Msgr. Merry del Val, president of the Academy of Noble Ecclesiastics, was secretary to the Conclave. Msgr. Cagiado De Azevedo and Prince Mario Chigi were respectively governor and marshal of the Conclave.

Sixty-two Cardinals assembled in the Sixtine Chapel to take the oath.[23] The Sixtine Chapel served both as a place of prayer and as a room for counting the ballot-papers. As 8pm approached, the ceremonial officers went through the corridors giving the traditional cry *extra omnes* ("ev-

---

[19] Dispatch of Reverseaux to Delcassé, July 9, 1903, AMAE, NS 3, f.157.
[20] Dispatch of Cambon to Delcassé, July 15, 1903, AMAE, NS 3, f.197-198.
[21] Dispatch of Nisard to Delcassé, July 10, 1903, AMAE, NS 3, f.163-164.
[22] Dispatch of Nisard to Delcassé, July 27, 1903, AMAE, NS 3, f.295.
[23] Of the 62 cardinals present at the Conclave, two (Herrero and Cretoni) were sick and had to stay in bed; they could not be present at the voting sessions in the Sixtine Chapel.

eryone out!") while Cardinal Oreglia and his assistants made sure that all the doors were closed and all openings were walled-up, so that there could be no communication between the cardinals and the outside world.

The following day Cardinal Sarto told his secretary that he had not been able to sleep. He had passed a great part of the night in prayer. On the morning of the first day, after the Mass called "of communion"—the cardinals did not say the Mass, but assisted at the Mass celebrated by the Cardinal Dean and received Communion from his hand—the first vote took place.

The election to the Sovereign Pontificate cannot be compared to the political elections which take place in democracies. While there can be meetings between cardinals before they enter into Conclave and during it, there is no "election campaign"—or at least there should not be. There are no candidates, promises, or pacts—or at least there should not be. Before each vote, the cardinals take an oath on the Gospel to vote according to their consciences: "I call Christ to witness, who will one day be my Judge, that I am voting for the one whom, before God, I believe to be most worthy to be elected." There is a further difference: the election does not proceed according to a simple majority of votes. To be elected, the future pope needs to have gained at least two-thirds of the votes. The new pope must not appear to have been elected by one camp in opposition to another: there should be the greatest possible consensus.

Historically, Conclaves have been longer or shorter. Three ballots were necessary to elect Leo XIII, and seven were required to elect him who would take the name of Pius X. The course of the Conclave which elected the latter is well known, from the accounts given by several of the participants, in writings published very soon after the Conclave or posthumously: the French Cardinals Mathieu and Perraud, the conclavist Maurice Landrieux, the Conclave secretary Merry del Val.[24] To these sources we can add the reconstruction made by the "authorized" biographer, Marchesan.

---

[24] A Witness (Cardinal Mathieu), "Les dernier jours de Léon XIII et le conclave de 1903," *Revue des Deux-Mondes,* March 15, 1904, pp.341-285 (article reprinted as a booklet); Cardinal Perraud, "Journal du Conclave de 1903," *Oratoriana,* no.12, May 1966, pp.57-68; Maurice Landrieux, "Le Conclave de 1903. Journal d'un conclaviste," *Études,* November 1958, pp.157-183; Cardinal Merry del Val, *Pie X. Impressions et souvenirs* (CH-Saint-Maurice: Éditions de l'Œuvre de St-Augustin, 1951; Italian edition 1949), pp.17-21. These first-hand accounts can be complemented by the report of Fr. Albin de Cigala, who was chaplain to the Marshal of the Conclave (Prince Chigi), *Vie intime de Sa Sainteté le pape Pie X,* pp.94-134, and the reports sent by Nisard, French Ambassador to the Holy See, to Minister Delcassé in August 1903, Archives of the Ministry of Foreign Affairs (Paris), Saint-Siège, NS 4.

The results obtained by the three principal "candidates" over seven ballots can be shown thus[25]:

	1 Aug		2 Aug		3 Aug		4 Aug
	a.m.	p.m.	a.m.	p.m.	a.m.	p.m.	a.m.
Rampolla	24	29	29	30	24	16	10
Gotti	17	16	9	3	6	7	2
Sarto	5	10	21	24	27	35	50

For the sake of completeness it should be noted that Cardinals Serafino Vannutelli, Oreglia di San Stefano, Capecelatro, Di Pietro, Agliardi, Ferrata, Cassetta, Portanova, Segna, Tripepi and Richelmy each received one or more votes in the first or succeeding ballots. But they never figured among the favourites and in the seventh and last ballot only Cardinals Sarto, Rampolla and Gotti entered the lists. Sarto had obtained 5 votes in the first ballot, then 10 in the second, which prompted him to say, in Latin, to his neighbor, Cardinal Lecot: *"Volunt jocare super nomen meum"* (they are having a joke at my expense).

The veto against Rampolla

Until the fifth ballot Rampolla had been the best placed "candidate," at least the one with the most votes. For many non-ecclesiastical observers, and for a certain number of cardinals, as we have said, he was the obvious candidate to succeed Leo XIII since people were sure that he would pursue the policies of the Pope whom he had served as Secretary of State. This explains the high number of votes cast in his favor in the first ballots. Relatively little attention, however, has been paid to the fact that the increase in his vote, from one ballot to another, was not impressive. From the second to the third ballot he stagnated at 29, a sign that his name was encountering strong opposition at the heart of the Sacred College and that he had perhaps reached his maximum possible. At this point, before the fourth ballot, there took place what has come to be known as Cardinal Puzyna's "veto."

---

[25] Marchesan and the other sources quoted agree on the number of votes cast, on each occasion, by the principal *papabile*. On the other hand there is disagreement or silence on the number of votes cast by the marginal candidates. We have given the numbers provided by the French Embassy at the Holy See, AMAE, NS 4, f.36-37.

Cardinal Puzyna, Prince Kozielsko, Bishop of Cracow (at that time within the Austrian Empire), rose to read a declaration in Latin.[26] He declared "...officially and in the name and by the authority of Franz-Josef, Emperor of Austria and King of Hungary, that His Majesty, in virtue of an ancient right and privilege, pronounces the *veto* of exclusion against my Most Eminent Lord, Cardinal Mariano Rampolla del Tindaro."[27]

Cardinal Puzyna had spoken very quickly, with much emotion. Many cardinals had not understood what his declaration meant, and some had not even heard it completely. An Italian cardinal therefore read the declaration again in a clear voice. Everyone grasped that a veto had been entered against Cardinal Rampolla.

None of the participants at the Conclave, in the written accounts we have cited, have given the reasons which caused Austria to utter this veto. Nor did the first biographers of Pius X risk speculating on the reason for this exclusion of the former Secretary of State to Leo XIII. Since that time, historians have advanced reasons of a political nature.[28] Austria was dissatisfied with the support given by the former Secretary of State to the aspirations of Slavs in the Balkans, and Cardinal Puzyna himself had accused Rampolla of having sacrificed the interest of Poles to his pro-Russian policies.

Some of his criticism is echoed in the reports of French diplomats at the time of the election. Just as the Conclave was about to begin, Bihourd, French ambassador to Berlin, wrote to his government: "What the Austro-Hungarian government is most afraid of is the possible success of Cardinal Rampolla. In Vienna it is feared that his election would only encourage the aspirations towards independence on the part of Catholic Slavs in Croatia, Carniola, Bohemia and other parts of the Monarchy."[29]...After the election, however, France's consul-general in Hungary would give a further reason: "It is not so much the hostility of the former Secretary of State *vis-à-vis* the Triple Alliance which brought about this direct intervention from Austria, as his obstinate thwarting, on several occasions, of the wishes of Hungary," and he gave as examples the difficulties encountered with re-

---

[26] He did this "at a sign from Cardinal Kopp," says Landrieux, informed by a cardinal ("Le Conclave de 1903," p.177). Cardinal Kopp was Bishop of Breslau [now Wroclaw, Poland].

[27] Cardinal Mathieu, "Les derniers jours de Léon XIII et le conclave de 1903," p.280, gives the full Latin text of the declaration; Marchesan, p.483, has reproduced this. The other sources give the substance of the text, with notable differences (Cardinal Perraud insisted on the "semi-official" nature of the veto).

[28] Cf. Aubert, "Pio X tra restaurazione e riforma," *Storia della Chiesa,* vol.XXII/1, *La Chiesa e la società industriale,* pp.108-109, which refers to the studies of F. Engel-Janosi and Z. Obertynski.

[29] Bihourd to Delcassé, August 1, 1903, AMAE, NS 4, f.2.

gard to episcopal appointments in Hungary and its rejection—opposed by the Holy See—of the Empire's desire to see the cardinalate given to Msgr. Samossa.[30]

Certain other writers have advanced another reason for the Austrian veto, a strictly religious reason: Cardinal Rampolla is supposed to have been a Freemason.[31] At the time there was never any mention of this, neither in diplomats' reports nor in the writings of the Conclave participants, nor even by the "integrists" of *La Sapinière*.[32] Only after the pontificate of Pius X did this rumor begin to spread.[33] We can imagine that if there had been the least suspicion on this subject in 1903, Cardinal Sarto, once he had become Pope, would have removed Cardinal Rampolla from every public function in the Church. Rampolla, however, while he lost the post of Secretary of State, kept most of his other offices under the pontificate of Pius X, and even acquired new ones. Furthermore we shall see that, if he only exercised a second-order role, it was because he volontarily went into semi-retirement.

At this moment, however, faced with the veto entered against him, Cardinal Rampolla rose and replied, calmly, in Latin: "In the name of the principles I protest against this attack on the liberty and dignity of the Sacred College. As far as my own person is concerned, I declare that nothing more agreeable and honorable (*nihil jucundius, nihil honorabilius*) could happen to me." Oreglia, the Cardinal Dean made a declaration protesting against this alien intervention and asserted that the Conclave would maintain its complete liberty. Later Cardinal Perraud, on behalf of the French Cardinals, made his protest too.[34]

---

[30] Report of the French Consul-General in Hungary to the Minister of Foreign Affairs, August 12, 1903, AMAE, NS 4, f.46-49.

[31] The Marquis de la Franquerie, in his booklet *Saint Pie X sauveur de l'Église et de la France* (Montsûrs: Éditions Résiac, 1976), p.3, writes: "We should bear in mind that Cardinal Rampolla was practically elected, but the Emperor of Austria—no doubt aware that Leo XIII's Secretary of State belonged to the Freemasons—raised his veto. This veto providentially prevented a tool of Lucifer ascending the pontifical Throne, and happily resulted in a Saint ascending it."

[32] In August 1913, in a list drawn up by Msgr. Benigni and some of his friends in anticipation of a future conclave, only one cardinal was suspected of being a Freemason: Agliardi Rampolla was judged very severely: "a superior type of man, his mind full of illusions, a dreamer, the Jules Verne of ecclesiastical politics, the Crispi of the papal government, a megalomaniac" (list published in Émile Poulat, *Intégrisme et catholicisme intégral* [Tournai-Paris: Casterman, 1969], pp.329-330).

[33] The rumor that he belonged to the Freemasons only began to spread in public after 1929, as a result of articles which appeared in counter-revolutionary publications: cf. the quotations found in Georges Virabeau, *Prélats et francs-maçons* (Paris: Publications HC, 1978), pp.26-31.

Initially this Austrian veto had no effect since, in the fourth ballot, Cardinal Rampolla continued to have the most votes, even if he had only gained one vote more than in the previous ballot and was far from obtaining the required two-thirds of all votes. In contrast Cardinal Sarto continued to advance smoothly. He received 24 votes in this fourth ballot and 27 in the next—the highest number of votes for any cardinal in this fifth ballot. It became more and more certain that he would be elected to the Sovereign Pontificate.

The reasons behind the election

The election of a cardinal to the Sovereign Pontificate is always the result of many considerations, political and spiritual. If Sarto was elected, it was because there was broad agreement on his name. Not that a great majority of cardinals shared the same view of him but, rather, there was an accumulation of the various reasons they individually had for wanting him Pope. Gianpaolo Romanato summarized these reasons thus:

> The Patriarch of Venice seemed to be the most satisfactory person. His biographical traits represented a kind of guarantee. He was a man of the people, very humble and not of the nobility; he had been born, not in the Papal States but in the Kingdom of Lombardy-Venice; he had never served as a pontifical diplomat; he was a discreetly cultured man, but not an intellectual; he had spent his entire career in the cure of souls; it was known that, if necessary, he knew how to command and make himself obeyed. Furthermore he was known for his deep piety; he was totally aloof from the Roman lobbies and devoid of personal interest. And, last but not least, he was exactly the right age (68) to give everyone the necessary guarantees of discernment and prudence.[35]

In short, in many ways he was the anti-Rampolla. Up until the veto, the Conclave had been largely a reflection of the struggles for influence between the great power-blocks. The Austrian veto had scandalized many cardinals and had made them see that the criteria for choosing a successor to St. Peter should be essentially religious ones. It is also possible that, even if the Conclave participants did not yet have sufficient information to assess all the results of Leo XIII's pontificate, they did have some of his weaknesses in mind. While the social encyclicals of Leo XIII, his prestige with certain governments and his encouragement of a Christian intellectual renewal (notably through a return to Thomist philosophy and the renewal

---

[34] Some months after his election, in the Apostolic Constitution *Commissum nobis* (January 20, 1904), Pius X formally condemned this practice of *veto* or *exclusive* and threatened with excommunication any cardinal who, in future, agreed to present such in a conclave (*Documents pontificaux,* vol.I, pp.85-87).

[35] Romanato, "Pio X: profilo storico," in *Sulle orme di Pio X*, p.13.

of biblical studies) were to his credit, the most attentive observers could not fail to see the problems that had remained unsolved: the inadequate formation of the Italian clergy and its laxity, the growing laicization of consciences and states, the first signs of Modernism, *etc.* By giving their votes increasingly to Cardinal Sarto, the cardinals of the 1903 Conclave, evidently, wanted to break with a certain kind of pontificate and a certain mode in which the Church presented herself to the world. Without crudely exaggerating the differences—for there was continuity too—we can say that the cardinals wanted to see a pre-eminently political pope succeeded by a religious pope who would bring the Church "back to the centre"— the centre being Christ—by uniting the Christian people on the basis of discipline and the defence of the faith.

Cardinal Sarto, however, did not aspire to the Sovereign Pontificate. There is a wealth of detailed evidence to the effect that he was not acting out of a feigned humility; nor is this picture the result of hagiographical rewriting after the event. As the votes rose for the Patriarch of Venice, so did his apprehension. After the fourth ballot he declared "that he was not made for the Papacy, and that people had been using his name without consulting him."[36] Several cardinals came to his cell to encourage him not to reject the pontifical office if it fell to him. Cardinal Satolli repeated to him Christ's words to St. Peter, walking on the water: *"Ego sum, nolite timere!"* and, smiling, told him: "God who helped you to steer St. Mark's gondola will help you to steer St. Peter's barque." After the fifth ballot it seemed that the movement in favor of the Patriarch of Venice could only go on from strength to strength. But, as the conclavist Landrieux reports, "after the ballot, Sarto got up and declared that he was unworthy of the choice which so many were making of him, and begged them to vote for others."[37]

Cardinal Sarto's scruples and refusals were so insistent that the Cardinal Dean, Oreglia di San Stefano, asked Msgr. Merry del Val to go and see him. Msgr. Merry del Val has given an account of this first meeting with the man whose principal collaborator he was to be:

> His Eminence (Cardinal Oreglia di San Stefano) felt bound in conscience to ensure that things should not drag on, and he sent me to Cardinal Sarto to ask whether he was insisting on his refusal and, if so, did he wish and authorize His Eminence the Cardinal Dean to make a public and definitive declaration of this fact to the Conclave during the afternoon session. In this case the Cardinal Dean would invite his colleagues to reflect and at least consider the possibility of applying their choice to another candidate.

---

[36] Landrieux, "Le Conclave de 1903, p.176.
[37] *Ibid.*, p.178.

I left immediately to look for Cardinal Sarto. I had been told that he was not in his room and that I would probably find him in the Paolina chapel.

It was close to midnight when I entered the silent, shadowy chapel...

I noticed a cardinal kneeling on the marble floor near the altar, lost in prayer, his head in his hands and his elbows resting on a little bench.

It was Cardinal Sarto.

I knelt beside him and, in a low voice, gave him the message with which I had been entrusted.

His Eminence, as soon as he had understood me, raised his eyes and slowly turned his head towards me, with tears pouring from his eyes....

"Yes, yes, Monsignore," he added gently, "ask the Cardinal Dean to do me this charity...."

The only words I had the strength to utter, which came to my lips spontaneously, were:

"Eminence, have courage, the Lord will help you!"[38]

When Pius X wrote, in the first lines of his first encyclical, "It is unnecessary to tell you with what tears and ardent prayers We tried to avert from Us the heavy responsibility of the Supreme Pontificate,"[39] it was no mere customary form of words.

Election and coronation

Meanwhile, Cardinal Sarto had recovered from his apprehensions. Other cardinals, notably Cardinals Ferrari and Satolli, came to make "a pressing appeal to his conscience, to persuade him to accept the sacrifice."[40] Cardinal Rampolla, despite the fact that his votes were crumbling, maintained his candidature. He did so, he said, "as a matter of principle" and was acting "on the formal advice of his confessor."[41] This attitude ultimately delayed the election of Cardinal Sarto. It even seemed, after various approaches reported by Cardinal Perraud, that Rampolla's obstinacy was a deliberate tactic of obstruction against Sarto.[42]

---

[38] Cardinal Merry del Val, *Pie X. Impressions et souvenirs,* p.51.
[39] *E Supremi Apostolatus,* October 4, 1903, *Documents pontificaux,* vol.I, p.33.
[40] Cardinal Mathieu, "Les derniers jours," p.283.
[41] Cardinal Perraud, "Journal du Conclave de 1903," pp.65-66.
[42] Cardinal Perraud reports two visits Cardinal Rampolla made to him on August 4: *Ibid.*, p.67. Fr. Landrieux, for his part, reports in his Diary the efforts made by the French cardinals to persuade Rampolla to retire "nobly." The latter's refusal astonished them. Landrieux observes, on the penultimate day of the Conclave, after the 6th ballot in which Rampolla received only 16 votes (only half as many as the day before): "Rampolla's behavior is incomprehensible. He has achieved nothing. In four ballots he has kept 30 votes in his favor, and for no purpose. He has been unable and unwilling to give any direction to those who have supported him. He refused to withdraw when he found himself compromised, and he let the psychological moment go by when he could have saved everything by a dignified and honorable retreat" ("Le Conclave de 1903," p.179).

Finally, in the ballot—the seventh—on the morning of August 4, Cardinal Sarto received 50 votes, against only 10 for Cardinal Rampolla and 2 for Cardinal Gotti. "Cardinal Sarto was crushed," Cardinal Mathieu records; "his eyes were full of tears, drops of sweat were like pearls on his cheeks, and he seemed close to fainting." According to the ritual, Cardinal Oreglia, Dean of the Sacred College, went up to him with two other cardinals, to ask the newly-elected:

> "Do you accept the election which canonically makes you Sovereign Pontiff?"
> Cardinal Sarto replied, humbly:
> "*Quoniam calix non potest transire, fiat voluntas Dei!* (Since I cannot be spared this chalice, may God's will be done)."
> This was not the canonically correct reply. Cardinal Oreglia asked again:
> "Do you accept or not?"
> Then Cardinal Sarto replied with the required formula:
> "*Accepto!*"
> And when he was asked what name he wished henceforth to bear, he declared:
> "*Pius Decimus* (Pius X)."

He then explained that he was choosing this name in memory of the "holy pontiffs who have borne this name, and of those who, in recent times, have been persecuted for the Church...."[43]

For a moment the new Pope had considered taking the name Benedict XV in memory of Blessed Benedict XI, a pope of the 14th century, who was also from the diocese of Treviso. But the series of popes named "Pius" commended itself to him by the great courage and determination shown by the more recent bearers of that name. Pius VI was hounded out of Rome by French troops, and died in exile in 1799; Pius VII, elected under difficult conditions in Venice in 1800, was also carried off by force into France; Pius IX, forced by revolutionaries to leave Rome in 1848 and then robbed of the Papal States in 1870, the pope who considered himself "the prisoner of the Vatican" until his death.[44]

---

[43] This reason for choosing the name is given in *Articoli,* p.75, according to a manuscript of Pius X himself, the "property of Msgr. Bressan." Fr. Landrieux, who, that same day, reported an explanation given by Cardinal Svampa (a neighbor of Cardinal Sarto at the Conclave), gives a more down-to-earth version: "... the holy pontiffs who bore the name Pius, particularly those who, in the last century, battled courageously against sects and ever-multiplying errors (*contra sectas et errores crassantes*)" ("Le Conclave de 1903," p.182).

[44] The new Pope may have forgotten, but eight years earlier an elderly nun prophesied that in the future he would bear the name of the Sovereign Pontiff. In June 1895, while he was visiting the convent of Franciscans of Gemona, a nun, struck by the physical resemblance between Pope Pius IX and the then Patriarch of Venice, exclaimed, "What a fine Pius X!" (Marchesan, p.134).

At the end of the morning session, having put on the white pontifical robes, the new Pope gave his first blessing to the faithful. He had two possibilities: he could follow the custom of his predecessor who, in protest at the despoliation of the Papal States by the Italian government, had refused to appear at the outside loggia of St. Peter's which opens on to the square and hence the city; or he could break with this custom and, as a sign of a conciliatory attitude towards the regime, appear on the balcony of the façade. Pius X wanted to have the advice of the College of Cardinals. They counselled prudence. So the blessing was given from an internal loggia opening on the interior of the Basilica. The new Pope was received by an enthusiastic and impatient crowd. Fr. Landrieux, who witnessed the scene, noted in his diary that evening:

> ...the Pope, escorted by the cardinals, went to the Loggia to bless the people who had flooded into the Basilica. It was a magnificent spectacle; a delirious crowd thronged with shouts and acclamations in the immense nave, without guards, without barriers, freely, under the impulse of a sudden common emotion which had no time to recollect, to reason, or to acquire poise.
>
> In the wink of an eye the Basilica was filled with an enthusiastic throng crying out in agitated expectation: *Evviva il Papa! Evviva il Papa!...*
>
> When Sarto appeared at the loggia, grave, moved, and as if crushed under the weight of the responsibility which he had three times attempted to shrug from his shoulders, the acclamations redoubled in intensity. Then, at a sign, the crowd grew calm and, in a religious silence, heads inclined and a strong voice resounded: *Benedicat vos...!* Pius X was blessing his people for the first time.[45]

After this first blessing, Pius X went to visit Cardinal Herrero, who was sick, and who had participated in the Conclave from his bed.

In the evening the new Pope returned to the room he had occupied during the Conclave and refused the apartments which had been prepared for him. He lived there for a further two months, until he finally agreed to move into a bigger apartment in the Vatican Palace. One of the first letters he wrote that evening was to take various measures concerning the diocese of Venice. In a letter to the vicar-general of the diocese, a letter which began with an act of humility—"though I am the most unworthy and unfit of all the cardinals, Divine Providence has wished to elevate me to the Apostolic See of the Roman Pontificate"—Pius X announced that for the present he intended to reserve to himself the administration of the Patriarchate of Venice, while granting the powers necessary for the good government of the diocese to the vicar-general and another canon, Msgr. Pantaleo.[46] This decision reveals two traits that were characteristic of the new

---

[45] Landrieux, "Le Conclave de 1903," p.181.

Pope's manner of governing: a practical sense which enabled him quickly to find a solution to problems, and, at the same time, a refusal to make hasty decisions and a readiness to reflect and consult before making a definitive choice.[47]

Exactly the same attitude can be seen when, that same evening, the new Pope chose Msgr. Merry del Val as his principal collaborator. Few people, no doubt, expected that Cardinal Rampolla would take up again the functions of Secretary of State which he had exercised under the preceding pontificate. There was too great a difference between the new Pope and the former Secretary of State. Furthermore, Cardinal Rampolla's attitude in these last days of the Conclave had shown a far too visible hostility. On the other hand, few thought that he would be so quickly replaced.[48] The evening of August 4, Pius X appointed Msgr. Merry del Val pro-Secretary of State for the time being, until he had made a definite decision.[49] His choice would be confirmed several months later, to the astonishment of many, both diplomats and members of the Curia.

The day after his accession, Pius X had generous alms distributed to the poor of Rome and of Venice. When a cardinal suggested that these sums were too high, the Pope replied: "Are you too, perhaps, mistrustful of Providence?"[50]

Those cardinals who knew the former Patriarch of Venice little, or not at all, gradually acquired a better estimate of his temperament and qualities as he began to take his first decisions and make his first reactions. Two days after the election, the French consul in Venice drew a moral portrait which is strikingly correct; it could profitably have been put before those in the Curia who would have to work under the orders of the new Pontiff: "The new Pope is a very simple man, of irreproachable conduct, of an aus-

[46] Letter to Msgr. Francesco Mion, August 4, 1903, *Lettere,* pp.307-308.
[47] His successor to the Patriarchate of Venice (Msgr. Aristide Cavallari) was not appointed until March 3, 1904. It is possible that, by not proceeding hastily to appoint his successor to Venice, Pius wanted to avoid getting into immediate conflict with the government in the matter of the *exequatur* and subjecting the patriarchal See to a long interregnum. Cf. Bruno Bertoli, "Una diocesa all'ombra di Pio X," in *La Chiesa di Venezia nel primo novecento,* under the direction of Silvio Tramontin (Edizioni Studium Cattolico Veneziano, 1995), p.11.
[48] On August 6, already two days after the Pope had asked Merry del Val, Ambassador Nisard believed himself justified in saying—according to a French cardinal—that Pius X "had asked Cardinal Rampolla to give him his co-operation for a time," telegram of August 6, 1903, to Delcassé, AMAE, NS 4, f.20.
[49] "I have taken no decision as yet. I do not know what I shall do. For the moment, I have no-one; stay with me as pro-Secretary of State... and then we shall see. Do me this service as a friend," Pius X declared on the evening of August 4. This is reported in Cardinal Merry del Val, *Pie X. Impressions et souvenirs,* p.26.
[50] Cigala, *Vie intime de S.S. le pape Pie X,* p.212.

tere manner of life, intransigent in the exercise of his functions, and who always acts with authority, and even severity. On the other hand he is said to be kind, affable and charitable."[51]

For a short while the plan was to postpone the Pope's coronation until December to allow a great number of the faithful to attend. But finally it was fixed for August 9. Leo XIII, fearing hostile demonstrations even in St. Peter's Basilica, had been crowned in the Sixtine Chapel. Pius X's coronation rite took place in the Basilica. The ceremony lasted for five hours. The French ambassador to the Holy See gave his impressions in a report to his minister: "An immense crowd, estimated at about 60,000, thronged in the vast Basilica. Placards said that all acclamations were forbidden; of course this prohibition was violated more than once, but does it not sum up, nevertheless, both the character of the man and his whole program?" He also gave a very lifelike description of the Pope: "Everyone could see that the Holy Father was subject to the deepest emotion; his extremely pale face, the sound of his voice when he gave the blessing, his eyes several times in tears—all this showed that the Head whom the cardinals have given to the Church is vividly aware of the heavy burden laid upon him."[52]

The Pope's day

Msgr. Bressan remained very close to Pius X. Officially his title was *primo cappellano segreto di numero* (private chaplain). In fact, he directed the private secretariat which, as Émile Poulat observed, "played a role that was so important (or so interfering, as those who were incommoded by it will say) during the whole pontificate: Pius X liked to use it to deal with questions he reserved to himself, or which he wanted to withdraw from the slow procedures of the Congregations."[53]

Apart from Bressan, four other priests made up this private secretariat: Giuseppe Pescini, Cardinal Sarto's other secretary in Venice; Francesco Gasoni, known to the Pope from his episcopate at Mantua; and Vincenzo Ugherini and Attilio Bianchi, who had worked under Leo XIII and were kept on in their posts.

Msgr. Bressan was also one of the Pope's confessors, a function he had already been exercising hitherto. This is a sign of the confidence which Pius X placed in his secretary. The other confessor was Msgr. Pifferi, a Vatican prelate. We also know that Fr. Cormier, the Master General of the

---

[51] Dispatch of the French Consul in Venice, addressed to Delcassé, August 6, 1903, AMAE, NS 4, f.22-25.

[52] Report of Nisard to Delcassé, August 11, 1903, AMAE, NS 4, f.40-41.

[53] Poulat, *Intégrisme et catholicisme intégral,* p.588.

Dominicans, while he was not, perhaps, the Pope's spiritual director, regularly had spiritual talks with him.[54]

According to the testimony of many witnesses at the beatification process, the Pope lived "like a monk," that is, in great simplicity. When he put on the pontifical habit for the first time, he was given a magnificent pectoral cross of gold, covered in diamonds. He wore it for a few days, thinking that it was the cross traditionally worn by all the popes. But when the jeweller who had made it sent in his bill, Pius X stopped using the cross and had it sent back, saying, "I have no intention of spending money on myself." After that he habitually used to wear the pectoral cross he had worn when Patriarch of Venice.[55]

Pius X desired the same simplicity for his household. He did not grant them any honor, title or function. His sisters Rosa, Maria and Anna, who had remained unmarried, and his niece, Ermenegilda Parolin, came to settle in Rome in a modest *palazzo* on the Piazza Rusticucci, near the Vatican. Pius X received them regularly twice a week, on Wednesday and Sunday mornings. But when a member of the Heraldic Commission came to discuss the title to be conferred on his sisters, he exclaimed in horror: *"Che titoli, che titoli! Si chiameranno Sorelle del Papa, e basta"* (What titles! What titles! They will be called the Pope's sisters, and that's enough).[56]

After several months the Pope agreed to occupy an apartment on the third floor of the Vatican Palace. He rose very early in the morning, after 4am. At six he celebrated his Mass, then assisted at that of his private chaplain and began to read his breviary. At seven, he took a collation and then went to his private library or, when the weather was good, he took a short walk in the Vatican gardens. Very soon he dispensed with the officers of the Noble Guards whose only function was to accompany him on his walks. At 8am, without fail, his daily work began. At 9am he received his Secretary of State; they used to say that it was "the diplomacy hour." At 10am his audiences began. First came the audiences of the *tabella* ("of the table," *i.e.,* those regularly fixed for the different heads of the Roman Congregations), and then the private audiences. At midday, after reciting the *Angelus*, the public audiences began. At 1pm the Pope took his meal in the company of Msgr. Bressan and one or other of his secretaries. The Pope dispensed with the services of the carver (a servant who carved the meat at meals), but kept paying his honorarium for life. After a siesta, the Pope went to his library at about 3pm, dealt with his correspondence (which was always very heavy) or read, making notes. From 5pm to 7:30 or 8pm

---

[54] Deposition of Cardinal Merry del Val, *Summarium,* p.187.
[55] Deposition of Cardinal Merry del Val and Msgr. Pescini, *Summarium,* p.187 and 711; also Cardinal Merry del Val, *Pie X. Impressions et souvenirs,* p.87.
[56] Deposition of Cardinal Merry del Val, *Summarium,* pp.750-751.

there were further audiences. At 8pm, after a visit to the Blessed Sacrament in his private chapel and the recitation of the Rosary with his household, the Pope retired to his apartment. While waiting for his meal, which was served punctually at 9pm, he read the newspapers or the press extracts prepared by the Secretary of State. After the meal, taken with Msgr. Bressan and one or other secretary, he conversed a little with them or they listened to music (a gramophone and a mechanical piano were installed in a drawing-room). At 10:30pm the Pope retired to his room.

Cardinal Merry del Val also gave this account of the temperament of Pius X:

> His favorite subjects seemed to be Sacred Scripture, theology and history. In spite of his everyday cares and his incessant work, to my own knowledge he managed to read many volumes and keep himself in touch with modern thought.
>
> I have often been surprised by his perfect understanding of nations and peoples, their traditions, their customs and their special character.
>
> This explains the ease with which he could appreciate the situation, the views and the sentiments of countries very different from his own and which he had never visited.[57]

This indubitable characteristic, which is confirmed by other testimonies with regard to these special areas of interest (Sacred Scripture, for example), contradicts the negative (and often scornful) judgment which some people—over-hastily—made of the new Pope. Many Modernists regarded Pius X as a Pope out of touch with the progress of religious studies, incapable of grasping the new questions; that, they said, explains his repeated condemnations of innovative writings and daring theses.

This pejorative judgment on Pius X has been repeated up to the present day by certain historians. However, Pius X was anything but an obtuse or chilly conservative. Right from the start he was eminently a Pope of reform.

---

[57] Cf. Dal-Gal, *Pius X*, pp.187-188.

CHAPTER 6

A POPE OF REFORM

The pontificate of Pius X lasted for eleven years. During this short pontificate he accomplished a considerable work. We shall examine this work in the following chapters, more thematically than chronologically, in order to bring out more clearly the central thrusts of his pontificate. Furthermore, Pius X's achievement requires this kind of presentation: this Pope was not a man of startling deeds, of spectacular or unexpected action. He preferred the long span of time, the deep transformation, perseverance in combat. In certain areas he inspired a work of reform, of restoration; in other areas (Modernism, or relations with the French government) his work was a work of defence.

In this chapter we shall examine his pontificate's principal reforms. These were, chronologically: the restoration of sacred music, apostolic visitations, the reform of seminaries, the codification of canon law, the reform of the Roman Curia. To these could be added his liturgical reforms, the catechism and the decrees on Communion (which seemed revolutionary to some); they will be examined in a later chapter.

"Instaurare omnia in Christo"

The first of his 17 encyclicals, *E Supremi Apostolatus,* appeared on October 4, 1903.[1] It contains the program for his pontificate, summed up in the motto: *Instaurare omnia in Christo* (to restore all things in Christ).[2] Two years later Pius X would recall that this was, indeed, his watchword: *"To restore all things in Christ* has always been the Church's watchword, and it is Ours most particularly, in the perilous times We are going through. To restore all things, not anyhow, but in Christ."[3]

In his first encyclical the Pope shows himself concerned about the world situation: "We feel a species of deep dread when we consider the disastrous condition of humanity at the present time. Is it possible to ignore the profound and grave disease which, now far more than in the past, afflicts human society, and which is getting worse from day to day, gnaw-

---

[1]   *Documents pontificaux*, vol.I, pp.33-41.

ing at the very marrow of its bones and dragging it to its ruin?" Pius X diagnoses this disease: "it is the abandoning of God, apostasy."

It is the ruin, not only of souls, but also of societies: "...in the majority of cases it is a total rejection of all respect for God. Hence those habits of life, both private and public, where no account is paid to His sovereignty." The disorders are so great and the "perversion of minds" is so strong, the Pope continues, that one might fear that "the beginning of those evils predicted for the end of time have arrived and made contact with the earth; and that, indeed, *the son of perdition* of whom the Apostle speaks has already come among us."

In this situation—and here this first encyclical sets out a kind of manifesto—the Pope invites everyone to respond "by persevering in prayer...by word and by works." It is pointless to look for peace "apart from God," for "to drive God out is to banish justice; and once justice has been eliminated, all hope of peace becomes an illusion." Nor is there anything to be gained by setting up a "party of *order*": "Alas, vain hopes, wasted efforts! There is only one party capable of re-establishing tranquillity in the midst of the turmoil of things, and that is the party of God."

What is needed is *"to restore all things in Christ,"* "to bring the human race back to the reign of Christ." Piux X points out three ways. First, "to form the clergy in holiness," to take special care of the seminaries so that "integrity of teaching shall be seen to flourish side by side with holiness of life." Next, to inspire once more in priests the "zeal for the divine honor" and to see that their first task is religious education ("the principal means of giving God back his reign over souls").[4] Thirdly, to make laypeople the

---

[2] Barbier, *Histoire du catholicisme libéral et du catholicisme social en France,* vol.IV, p.4, observed that the motto of the pontificate and a large part of the first encyclical were taken from the Pastoral Letter published by Msgr. Pie when he took possession of his See of Poitiers in 1849. There is nothing strange about this. We have seen that, since his time in Treviso, Msgr. Sarto was acquainted with the writings of this great French anti-Liberal bishop. If we compare the text of the Encyclical with that of the Pastoral Letter (*Œuvres de Msgr. l'éveque de Poitiers* [Paris-Poitiers: Oudin, 1883], vol.I, pp.96-119), there is a clear literary dependence in the first part of the Encyclical. On the other hand, the three-point program set forth by Pius X is his own. On two other occasions, at least, direct literary dependence can be seen between a writing of Msgr. Pie and a pontifical act of Pius X (cf. Grégoire Celier, *Essai bibliographique sur l'antilibéralisme catholique* [CH-Riddes: Procure du Séminaire Saint-Pie X, 1986], pp.127-129).

[3] Encyclical *Il Fermo Proposito,* June 11, 1905, *Documents pontificaux,* vol.I, p.298.

[4] Although the word is not used, we can see here a first warning against *Modernism*: "the members of the clergy must not let themselves be led astray by the insidious maneuvers of a certain new science which assumes the mask of truth and which does not breathe forth the fragrance of Jesus Christ. This is a mendacious science which, using fallacious and treacherous arguments, is trying to insinuate the errors of rationalism or semi-rationalism."

"auxiliaries" of the clergy: "It is not only the men clothed with the priest-hood who should devote themselves to the interests of God and of souls, but all the faithful without exception; not, of course, that everyone should follow his own wish and his own inclinations in this, but always as the bishops desire and direct."

With regard to this encyclical, Émile Poulat has rightly said: "One should note the date: October 7, the Feast of the Rosary, and read the 15 encyclicals of Leo XIII which were all given the date of this feast. There are analogous texts there, all marked by this threat of an apocalyptic future, a future which is in store for our Babel-like human race unless it turns from its ways and embraces the vision of Eden offered to it by the Church. From this point of view it would be a mistake to make too much of an opposi-tion between Leo XIII and Pius X, the political and liberal Pope, open to the modern world, and the religious Pope, outmoded and outclassed. In both cases, the same model of Catholicism was being transmitted and im-posed: a Catholicism which was "intransigent," as they say in Italy, that comes from the Counter-Reformation but was forged all through the last century in the wake of the trials of the [French] Revolution, of the other revolutions, confronted with modern times and the modern spirit."[5]

Merry del Val

Several days after the Encyclical appeared, Msgr. Merry del Val was officially appointed Secretary of State. He was to be one of the most active and influential collaborators of Pius X throughout the pontificate.

We have seen how Piux X named him pro-Secretary of State on the evening of the pontifical election. This was a provisional title, to be borne until the Pope would appoint a Secretary of State. Pius X did not decide the issue until two and a half months later. Many people felt that this was a long interval. Pius X did not want to hurry over such an important ap-pointment. As was his wont in a number of important decisions, he want-ed first of all to take advice: "He frequently questioned those cardinals who had most authority and experience in this matter and devoted constant meditation and continual prayer to it."[6] Some of the cardinals to whom the Pope had talked about the matter could have thought that he was thinking of them....Thus Cardinals Agliardi and Vincenzo Vannutelli let it be known that they had been "sounded out," and that Msgr. Merry del Val had little chance of being chosen because he was too young—he was 38.[7]

---

[5] Émile Poulat, *Modernistica* (Paris: Nouvelles Éditions Latines, 1982), p.230.
[6] Cardinal Merry del Val, *Pie X. Impressions et souvenirs*, p.38.
[7] Dispatch from Nisard to Delcassé, August 27, 1903, AMAE, NS 4, f.83-85.

At the beginning of October Pius X still had not made his choice. Then, on October 18, the Pope placed a letter into Msgr. Merry del Val's own hands announcing that he was appointing him Secretary of State, and that he was going to create him a cardinal. The chargé d'affaires of the French Embassy to the Holy See reported that this appointment was displeasing to a number of cardinals:

> The Holy Father's decision has provoked more discontent than surprise at the heart of the Sacred College...many princes of the Church feel hurt to see a prelate of 38 years ascend to the highest rank, without any transition....They are saying publicly that, by tradition, the Secretariat of State belonged to the "nationals"; and they recalled the fact that the father of the newly-appointed Secretary of State had distinguished himself, when he was representing Spain at the Holy See, by his hatred of Italy and his intransigence.[8]

In fact, Pius X had made his choice after mature reflection. He did not regard Merry del Val's youth as an obstacle. No doubt he appreciated his culture, his knowledge of several languages and his diplomatic experience. Born in London of an English mother and a Spanish father (of Irish origin), the son of an ambassador, Rafael Merry del Val had pursued his ecclesiastical studies in Rome. A former student of the Pontifical Academy of Noble Ecclesiastics (which served to train the Holy See's future diplomats), he had carried out several missions in foreign parts: in England (1887), Germany (1888), Austria (1889) and Canada (1897).[9] Then he had been summoned to direct the Academy of Noble Ecclesiastics, and in 1900 he was consecrated Archbishop. However brilliant this career was, it would not have been sufficient to impress Pius X. By appointing a Spaniard to the post of Secretary of State he expressed his desire to "internationalize the Curia," to use an expression much used in later pontificates, and to choose a man who was independent of the factions and coteries which are so influential at the heart of the Curia. Most of all, in the interval of more than two months between his election to the pontificate and the appointment of Merry del Val, he had got to know him and appreciate his style of work. In October 1903 a French diplomat well summed up the qualities which had so attracted Pius X: Merry del Val, he wrote, is "a highly cultivated ecclesiastic, of irreproachable conduct, of friendly and distinguished manners, diligent, prudent and devoted" and "ever since he took over from Rampolla he has wanted to acquire a deep understanding of the questions he is asked to deal with; he works conscientiously with the Sec-

---

[8]   Dispatch from Navenne to Delcassé, October 18, 1903, AMAE, NS 4, f.116-119.
[9]   Cf. Pio Cenci, *Il Cardinal Raffaele Merry del Val, Segretario di Stato di San Pio X Papa* (Rome-Turin: LICE-Roberto Berruti & Co., 1955), and Dal-Gal, *Le Cardinal Merry del Val* (Paris: Nouvelles Éditions Latines, 1955).

retary of State's *sostituto* and with the Secretary of the Congregation of Extraordinary Ecclesiastical Affairs."[10]

At Pius X's first consistory, on November 9, 1903, the Secretary of State and Msgr. Callegari, the new Pope's old friend, were created cardinals.

Merry del Val's double promotion aroused jealousies. Soon the Secretary of State was target of new criticisms from other quarters. The Modernists and those who were critical of the pontificate linked his name with those of two other cardinals—De Lai and Vivès y Tuto—and called them the Pope's "dark soul," *i.e.,* those who incited him to adopt an intransigent attitude and exercised a disproportionate influence over him. The rumor was so persistent that, towards the end of his pontificate, Pius X thought it necessary to contradict it in the severest terms: "words fail me to describe all those who keep saying that there are three cardinals who give the orders; there have always been such people in the Church; trying to avoid giving their due submission, they endeavor to persuade themselves that they are not obliged in conscience because it is not the Pope who is commanding."[11]

Certainly, the three cardinals indicated did play an important part in the Pope's entourage. Cardinal Merry del Val had a decisive role in the work of Pius X, and certain matters would have been treated differently if someone else had been Secretary of State. Gaetano De Lai, initially Secretary of the Congregation of the Council, was created cardinal in 1907 and then, the following year, he became Secretary of the powerful Consistorial Congregation (henceforth in charge of seminaries).[12] José Calasanz Vivès y Tuto, a Spanish Capuchin, a cardinal since 1899, had become Prefect of the Congregation of Religious. *"Vivès est tout"* (Vivès is everything) punned those who regarded him as one of the most influential advisors of Pius X.[13]

These three cardinals had an influence on Pius X, but—as we shall see—their influence was not all of one kind. They were very different by origin and training, and also by the kind of work they had already done. So the advice they gave Pius X and the service they rendered him was not all concentrated at the same time, nor necessarily in the same direction. Furthermore, they were not the only ones with influence. All popes have recourse to collaborators, whether occasionally or constantly, in the drawing

---

[10] Dispatch from Navenne to Delcassé, October 20, 1903, AMAE, NS 4, f.116-119.

[11] Letter *Je réponds de ma main*, October 20, 1912, *Documents pontificaux,* vol.II, p.480.

[12] "One of ours!"—this was the verdict of the leadership of *La Sapinière* with regard to a list drawn up in 1913 (document published by Poulat, *Intégrisme et catholicisme intégral*, pp.329-330).

[13] "Very good"—the verdict of the leadership of *La Sapinière*, cf. previous note.

up of the more important documents of their pontificate: thus, for example, Fr. Lemius was the principal compiler of the encyclical *Pascendi*; to say
nothing of the essential part which Msgr. Gasparri played in the elaboration of the Code of Canon Law—and Gasparri was doctrinally very far
removed from the three cardinals here mentioned.

Here again we must emphasize a feature of Pius X's character which is
rarely noticed: it was his custom to ask advice—and not only from those
close to him—before taking a decision. Cardinal Scapinelli di Leguigno,
for example, says that this was one of the Pope's maxims: "Whenever I
have to make a decision, I pray and I ask advice." Cardinal Merry del Val
explains: "In all his actions he was always inspired by supernatural
thoughts and showed that he was united to God. In the most important
matters he would look at the crucifix and draw inspiration from it. Where
there was doubt, he would postpone his decision and, gazing at the crucifix, would say, *He will decide*. Many bishops, priests and laity have told me
the same thing."[14]

Pius X was not an authoritarian pope, taking decisions high-handedly.
If he showed that he could act with authority on many occasions, he was
not led by any impulsiveness. Cardinal Merry del Val, who had an audience with him every day, sums up the Pope's character in two words:
"goodness and firmness."[15] More explicitly: "All those who, in one way or
another, had dealings with him speak of his amiable character and the innate goodness of his soul. People are unanimous in extolling his goodness....This goodness, this gentleness, were allied to an invincible strength
of character and a power of will to which those who lived with him can
bear witness; this strength was all the more striking to us who habitually
witnessed his constant gentleness." "He knew how to master the impulses
of his ardent temperament." For instance, goodness and firmness are the
two qualities which characterize his conduct in the battle against Modernism.[16]

---

[14] Cf. Dal-Gal, *Pius X*, pp.173 and 187.

[15] Cardinal Merry del Val, *Pie X. Impressions et souvenirs*, pp.44-45.

[16] Cardinal Mercier, Archbishop of Malines, uttered a similar verdict on the day after the
Pope died: "The captivating goodness of the Holy Father had nothing of the sickly
sweetness of the weak. Pius X was strong....If I am not mistaken, the characteristic of
the deceased Pope was a marvellous union of fatherly tenderness and a strength of
character which, because it was master of itself, communicated a poise to his soul and
spread over his countenance this mixture of gravity, serenity, condescension, almost
playfulness, to which the world was so strongly attracted....Pius X was a man of clear-
sightedness and decision," Pastoral letter of February 2, 1915, quoted in Cardinal
Merry del Val, *Pie X. Impressions et souvenirs*, pp.48-49.

Thus the great reforms introduced by Pius X, which all originate in the first year of his pontificate, were willed by him personally, even if he used advisors and executives as his collaborators.

The reform of sacred music

Ever since his Mantua episcopate, as we have seen, Msgr. Sarto had been concerned to restore dignity to church music and the chant. He had fought against the invasion of the churches by profane music, by rhythms, words and instruments threatening the simplicity of worship and causing it to lose its religious character. Sacred music must keep an eminently religious character; it must be at the service of the liturgy and encourage devotion. In Venice, his support for the Gregorian renewal and his acquaintance with Fr. De Santi and with Perosi had signalled a new stage of his struggle for the restoration of sacred music.

Once he had become Pope, it was natural that his first great reform was in this area. He was elected on August 4, and as early as August 27 he received Msgr. Carlo Respighi, who was in charge of *Rassegna Gregoriana* (Fr. De Santi collaborated very actively, but anonymously, in this review), and spoke of his desire for musical reform.[17] The following month he received Fr. De Santi. On October 14, the French musician Camille Bellaigue, a friend of Perosi's, came to ask him to reform church music and the chant as he had done in Venice. The Pope, already convinced of the necessity of this, replied, "Yes, it will be done, and soon. But do not say anything about it....No doubt *we shall have some battles* in this matter."[18]

In fact, four days later he requested Cardinal Respighi, Vicar of Rome, to draw up an instruction on the subject. The Cardinal referred it to his nephew, Msgr. Carlo Respighi, who invited his friend De Santi to collaborate with him. As we have seen, De Santi had worked very actively on the *votum* which Cardinal Sarto had sent to the Congregation of Rites in 1893, and on the pastoral letter published in Venice in 1895. It was these texts, partly re-worked and recast, which formed the substance of the motu proprio of November 22, applying to the entire Church.

This motu proprio on sacred music included very precise instructions.[19] It was designed to counteract "abuses in everything concerning chant and sacred music" and to "contribute to the holiness and dignity of the church where the faithful assemble." Pius X wanted the Instruction on

---

[17] The standard study remains that of Dom Pierre Combe, *Histoire de la restauration du chant grégorien d'après des documents inédits* (Abbey of Solesmes, 1969).

[18] Camille Bellaigue, *Pie X et Rome. Notes et souvenirs, 1903-1914* (Paris: Nouvelles Éditions Latines, 1916), p.12.

[19] *Tra le Sollecitudini,* November 22, 1903, *Documents pontificaux,* vol.I, pp.49-55.

Sacred Music promulgated this day to become "the legal code for sacred music."

In its first part it defined general principles:

> Sacred music must possess to the highest degree the qualities proper to the liturgy: *holiness,* and that excellence of form which gives birth spontaneously to its other character: *universality.*
>
> It must be *holy,* and so it must exclude all that would make it profane, not only in itself, but also in the way it is performed.
>
> It must be *true art*; otherwise it would not be able to have that felicitous influence on its hearers which the Church intends in admitting music into her liturgy.
>
> Yet it must also be *universal,* in the sense that, while every nation is permitted, in ecclesiastical compositions, to adopt those forms which are, in a certain way, particular to that nation, such forms must be subordinated to the general characteristics of sacred music, so that no one from another nation could be disconcerted by what he hears.

The motu proprio went on to specify which "kinds of sacred music" were to be promoted. In first place was Gregorian chant, defined as "the Roman Church's own chant": it should be "widely re-established in worship," and more particularly "among the people, so that the faithful, as in earlier times, can once more take a more active part in the celebration of the offices." Given its specific qualities, classical polyphony is worthy of being associated with the Gregorian chant. Finally, modern musical compositions can be "admitted" into the Church provided they "contain nothing profane, in no way recall the themes used in the theatre, and do not, even in their external forms, give the impression of being profane pieces."

Next, very detailed rules determined the use of the vernacular language in the liturgy, the role of singers in the liturgy, the use of musical instruments ("It is forbidden to use the piano in church, and also noisy or frivolous instruments such as the drum, bass drum, cymbals, handbells, *etc.*").

Finally all bishops were recommended to set up a Musical Commission in every diocese, a *schola cantorum* in every seminary and in the main churches, and to encourage the establishing of institutes of sacred music for the training of choirmasters, organists and singers.

Several days later, in the wake of this motu proprio, Pius X addressed a letter to Cardinal Respighi, Vicar of Rome, requiring him to implement these new rules without delay in the premier diocese of Christendom.[20]

In following years, in different circumstances, Pius X kept urging this restoration of Gregorian chant and sacred music. In 1904, on the 13th centenary of St. Gregory the Great (which was marked by the publication

---

[20] Letter *Il Desiderio,* December 8, 1903, *Documents pontificaux,* vol.I, pp.58-61.

of the encyclical *Iucunda Sane*, March 5), the Pope was able to admire the first-fruits of his first great reform. On April 11, in St. Peter's Basilica, a pontifical High Mass was celebrated: 1,200 seminarians and students of the Roman ecclesiastical colleges sang the *Missa de Angelis* in Gregorian chant.

A few days later a second motu proprio was published, prescribing a Vatican edition of the liturgical books.[21] This text contained a fine homage to the Benedictines of Solesmes, who for decades had been undertaking the vast labor of collating manuscripts and publishing critical editions. A pontifical Commission of Gregorian liturgical books was created to co-ordinate the prescribed edition. This commission included all those who had been working for years to restore Gregorian chant: Dom Pothier (Abbot of Saint-Wadrille, of the Solesmes Congregation), Dom Mocquereau (Prior of Solesmes), Fr. De Santi, Don Perosi, Msgr. Carlo Respighi, and others.

Once again Pius X had responded to a request on the part of the monks of the Solesmes Congregation and of Fr. De Santi. As we have seen, however, Pius X did not want to exclude from churches all music except the Gregorian. He permitted the use of polyphonic music. Cardinal Merry del Val explains: "He did not agree with the attitude of certain fanatics who wanted to exclude from our churches all music except Gregorian. This, he said, was an exaggeration."[22]

Here we shall not go into the work of the Commission, nor the arguments between Dom Pothier and the Abbey of Solesmes. Nor shall we speak of the expansion of Gregorian chant in the different countries. We simply observe that the desire to see an institute of sacred music established in Rome was fulfilled on January 1, 1911. Its direction was entrusted to Fr. De Santi. From the start it was open to students of all nationalities, and its aim was to train teachers of chant. In July 1914, it was erected into a faculty and authorized to give diplomas in four subjects: Gregorian chant, musical composition, choral conducting and organ.

Apostolic visitations

The apostolic visitations ordered by Pius X, beginning in 1904, seem to be far more austere than the renewal of sacred music promoted by the same Pope. Nonetheless there is a coherence between the two reforms. In his first motu proprio on sacred music, Pius X expressed his wish that "nothing should be done in church which troubles or even merely diminishes the piety and devotion of the faithful; there should be nothing which

[21] *Col Nostro Motu Proprio*, April 25, 1904, *Documents pontificaux*, vol.I, pp.169-171.
[22] Cardinal Merry del Val, *Pie X. Impressions et souvenirs*, p.82.

gives reasonable cause for abhorrence and scandal; and, most of all, there should be nothing which directly offends the honor and holiness of the sacred functions—which would therefore be unworthy of the house of prayer and of the majesty of God."

If we substitute, for the words "church" and "house of prayer," the words "diocese" and "seminary," we have practically the exact reason why Pius X, all through his pontificate, prescribed the apostolic visitations. In the Church, the apostolic visitation is a traditional means of resolving difficulties, putting an end to abuses, redressing injustices and keeping a watch on things. It is, as it were, the equivalent of the pastoral visitation which a bishop makes in his diocese, the only difference being that the apostolic visitation is ordered by the Pope and may be concerned with a single religious house, a seminary, or an entire diocese.

These apostolic visitations are one of the major facts of the pontificate, and their importance has long been misunderstood.[23] They began in 1904 with the diocese of Rome, and then were extended to the other dioceses of Italy and to all the seminaries of Italy from 1907; a new series of visitations was ordered in 1911. The apostolic visitations in Italy totalled almost 1,000. (Certain dioceses and seminaries underwent two visitations.)

At whatever time, and whatever its object (diocese or seminary), the principle of the apostolic visitation is the same: the apostolic visitor, appointed by the Pope, spends several weeks or months in the place he is visiting; he is empowered to interrogate whomsoever and see whatsoever he wishes, as he judges fit. Then he draws up a report (*relazione*). This manuscript report is reduced to a summary (*sunto*) and a limited number of copies is printed, which are then distributed to the members of the Congregation which is canonically in charge of the place visited. Dioceses were under the aegis of the Congregation of the Council and seminaries under that of the Congregation of Bishops and Regulars; then, after the

---

[23] They are the object of a recent doctoral thesis: Giovanni Vian, *La Riforma della Chiesa per la restaurazione cristiana della società. Le visite apostoliche delle diocesi e dei seminari d'Italia promosse durante il pontificate di Pio X, 1903-1914* (Rome: Herder Editrice e Libreria, 1998), 2 vols. Cf. also the long article by the same author: "Sviluppi ed esiti dell'antimodernismo durante il pontificato di Pio X attraverso le relazioni dell visite apostoliche," *Rivista di Stori e Letteratura religiose*, 32, 1996, pp.591-615. The *Fonti e Documenti* published by the *Centro Studi per la storia del modernismo* attached to the University of Urbino contain several studies on the subject by Lorenzo Bedeschi, followed by the publication of extracts from the reports drawn up by the Apostolic Visitors: "Antimodernismo piemontese—Relazioni dei Visitatori apostolici," vol.IX, pp.55-95; "Le analisi dei visitatori apostolici e l'antimodernismo in Toscana," vol.XI-XII, pp.7-78; "Radiografie nell relazioni dei visitatori apostolici," vol.XX-XXI, pp.343-386.

1908 reform of the Curia, dioceses and seminaries were both under the aegis of the Consistorial Congregation.

Here we shall not examine what these visits revealed (or confirmed) regarding Modernism's infiltration in the dioceses and seminaries. We shall turn to this in a later chapter. We shall simply indicate who the visitors were, what their mission was and in what way their reports succeeded in prompting reforms, in particular the reform of seminaries begun in 1907.

This long series of visitations which constituted the apostolic visitation began with all the churches, convents and monasteries of Rome. Pius X had been Pope for only six months—a sign that the visitation seemed to him both necessary and urgent. There had been no apostolic visitation of Rome since 1831. In the apostolic letter *Quum Arcano* the Pope linked this apostolic visit to the great task of his pontificate: "The restoration of all things in Christ, which We have set before us, must begin with the clergy and people of Rome, so that, by renewing their Christian spirit, all the ecclesiastics and laypeople of this City, even at this time which presents such difficulties to virtue, may walk with greater joy in the paths of holiness and justice."[24] Under the authority of Cardinal Respighi, Vicar of Rome, several bishops and religious were commanded to report to all the basilicas, churches, chapels, convents, monasteries, confraternities and ecclesiastical colleges of the city. Then, on March 3 the Pope issued a *brief* granting the broadest powers to Cardinal Respighi and the other visitors so that they could fulfil their mission.

A very detailed questionnaire was drawn up and sent in advance to all the relevant places to prepare for the visitation. For example, every parish priest of a church had to reply to 51 questions, themselves divided into several questions.[25] Sometimes what was required was very concrete information, for example question 27: "Has the church a bell-tower? Is it carefully locked? Who has the key? Does it need repairing? How many bells does it have?" The interrogations also concerned piety, for example question 39: "Have new devotions been introduced in recent times? Have new paintings been placed in the church? When? By whom? Why and on what authority have they been placed there? How have the new ceremonies required by these new devotions been provided for?" There were also questions concerning the clergy, for example question 41: "Who are the priests who officiate at the church? (Surnames and Christian names, family, nationality, age and domicile). Are they remunerated? How much does each

---

[24] *Quum Arcano,* February 11, 1904, *Documents pontificaux,* vol.I, pp.107-109.
[25] The complete text of the questionnaires, which differ according to the various places visited, is published in *Documents pontificaux,* vol.I, pp.793-822.

of them receive, at maximum? Who pays these remunerations? Who appoints these priests? Are they prompt and diligent in their duties?"

In addition, the visitors were helped in their task by a list of "special rules" to be observed: they were given a list of places to visit, objects to be examined, and regulations on whose observance they were to insist.

Shortly after the announcement of the apostolic visitation of Rome, that of all the dioceses of Italy was announced.[26] This visitation had been decided upon by Leo XIII but "its execution had been suspended by his death." As a result, "in order to come to the assistance of the bishops themselves and enable them to confirm their clergy and their faithful flock in their duty, or to deal more rapidly with matters on which they should consult the Apostolic See," Pius X put Leo XIII's project into action. This visitation would be succeeded, or rather redoubled, by an apostolic visitation of all the seminaries of Italy. This was decided in the spring of 1907.

Over a period of a few years, hundreds of apostolic visitors went all over Italy and finally produced, for the Pope and the Congregations, a kind of X-ray of the religious vitality of the country and the clergy. The primary aim of these visitations was not the repression of Modernism, as certain authors—who have never read a *relazione* or a *sunto*—have written, but the reform of the clergy, "considered as the basic nucleus of the project of the Christian restoration of society."[27]

Great care was taken in the choice of apostolic visitors. They had to be men of piety, integrity, quick to grasp situations and expose problems. Most often they were religious whom Pius X knew personally or who were known by people in whom the Pope had complete trust. Thus, for instance, in 1907 Abbot Beda Cardinale, Abbot of the Benedictine monastery of Praglia, in the diocese of Padua, was appointed apostolic visitor of the seminaries of Lombardy and the Abruzzi.

The four dioceses of southern Umbria were also entrusted to religious: Fr. Pontecorvi, of the Congregation of the Precious Blood, visited the diocese of Orvieto; Fr. Eugenio de Senigallia, a Capuchin, visited the dioceses of Norcia and Rieti; and Fr. Salvati, a Dominican, visited the diocese of Amelia.

Certain bishops were also sent as apostolic visitors; *e.g.,* Msgr. Pietro La Fontaine, Bishop of Cassano Jonio, was sent to the diocese of Massa Maritima. It would be a mistake, however, to think that only the most doctrinally "intransigent" religious or bishops were chosen. Thus Cardinal Maffi, Archbishop of Pisa, who opposed the Vatican and Pius X on the

---

[26] Decree *Constat apud Omnes,* March 7, 1904, *Décrets pontificaux,* vol.I, pp.667-668.
[27] Vian, "Sviluppi," p.600.

role of the Catholic press, was nonetheless sent as apostolic visitor to two dioceses: Livorno and San Miniato.

Fairly frequently, it is worth noting, if the visitors had given satisfaction, they were subsequently promoted. Thus Fr. Pontecorvi was appointed Archbishop of Urbino.

Of course, the results and consequences of the apostolic visitations were very diverse, as some examples will show. Strangely enough, while the visitors enjoyed full power to conduct their investigations, the Holy See did not always proceed to remove the persons concerned who had been shown to be less than worthy. Sometimes, too, the recommendations made at the conclusion of the visitation were sufficient.

In Venice, a diocese governed by Patriarch Cavallari (chosen by Pius X as his successor there), the Benedictine Abbot Mauro Serafini was appointed apostolic visitor. After the apostolic visitation, the Congregation of the Council reproached the Patriarch for having too centralized and too personal a mode of government. He was requested to see to it that the different diocesan commissions "worked actively," to choose advisors from them, and to get to know his priests better.[28]

In Livorno, a diocese governed by Msgr. Giani, two apostolic visitations were made. One was carried out by Fr. Pietro Paolo, a Passionist, in 1905, and the other by Cardinal Maffi in 1909. Both visitors were very severe, not only with regard to "the wretched moral and religious condition of the population, the insufficiency and apathy of the clergy," but also regarding the personal qualities of the clergy: "their imprudence in speaking...their over-hasty decisions and judgments...their vanity, their habit of breaking secrecy...."[29] While the first visitor suggested that the bishop of the diocese should be changed, the second hesitated and seemed to hope for some change of attitude. Pius X adopted the second course, no doubt after having made written observations to Msgr. Giani, who remained Bishop of Livorno until his death in 1921.

In Lucca, by contrast, the apostolic visitation seems to have resulted in the departure of the bishop, Msgr. Lorenzelli, the former apostolic nuncio in Paris. He was appointed Archbishop of Lucca in December 1905, and in 1906 his diocese underwent an apostolic visitation conducted by Fr. Germano di Stanislao, a Passionist. The report drawn up by the latter was very severe on the Archbishop: "...he is heartless....The clergy live under what one must call a reign of terror...." Initially this Archbishop, a man of sound doctrine and moral conduct, but who lacked the art of directing his

---

[28] Quoted by Bertoli, "Una diocesi all'ombra di Pio X," pp.16 and 47, note 39.
[29] Extracts from the *relazione* of Cardinal Maffi, published in *Fonti e Documenti,* vol.XI-XII, pp.26-28.

clergy and living in harmony with them, was left in place. He was created cardinal in 1907. Then, in 1909, he was invited to retire from his diocese.

Here is another case, in Florence, a diocese governed by Msgr. Mistrangelo. This visitation was also carried out by Fr. Germano. He was troubled by the high number of inhabitants who did not respect the Paschal precept: from 5% to 25% in the countryside, but about 40% in Florence and its surroundings.[30] The clergy were divided in their view of the bishop, and a section of the press scoffed at their sumptuous style of living. After the apostolic visitation, Msgr. Mistrangelo wrote a long letter (12 pages) rejecting its findings. He remained in place, but Pius X never made him a cardinal although the cardinalitial title is traditionally attached to the See of Florence.

The situation in the seminaries often attracted negative reports. The apostolic visitor to the diocese of Venice reported that the young clerics showed little enthusiasm for their studies. Having interrogated many of them, he found that, while "practically all felt inclined to parish life, several had shown a preference for the education of the young, but *not one* had shown any interest in sacred or profane studies."[31] This worried him. As for the apostolic visitors of the four dioceses of southern Umbria, they observed that in one out of every two cases the seminarians' studies were more than unsatisfactory: "At Rieti they only learned four subjects (Holy Scripture, Church history, sacred eloquence and Gregorian chant), and in Norcia even the professors' level of attainment was lamentable: the professor of philosophy restricted himself to translating a text, while the professor of dogmatic theology did not succeed in making himself understood."[32]

We can understand that facts such as these stimulated Pius X to develop the reform of the seminaries he had already begun.

The reform of the seminaries

Ever since his first encyclical, as we have seen, Pius X had been concerned about the seminaries. His experience in this area, in Treviso, Mantua and Venice, and the reforms he had carried out in the seminaries, had led him to write to the bishops of the entire Church: "How great should be your care to form your clergy in holiness! No work should take precedence over this. It follows that your best and principal zeal should concern your Seminaries, to give them such a regular structure and such a direction that

---

[30] Extracts from the *relazione* of Fr. Germano, *ibid.*, pp.62-68.
[31] *Relazione* quoted by Bertoli, "Una diocesi all'ombra di Pio X," pp.28-29.
[32] Bedeschi, "Radiografia," p.355.

you may see integrity of teaching flourish side by side with holiness of conduct. Make the seminary your heart's delight, and neglect nothing of what the Council of Trent prescribed, in its lofty wisdom, to guarantee the prosperity of this institution."[33]

As in the case of a number of Pius X's reforms, that of the seminaries and the formation of the clergy began by applying to Rome, since the centre of Christendom should serve as a model and an example to be imitated. Like all the reforms, the *raison d'être* of this one was "the restoration of all things in Christ." This expression is repeated in the letter the Pope addressed to Cardinal Respighi in May 1904 concerning the clergy's discipline.[34] Convinced that "in order that Jesus Christ shall reign in the world, nothing is as necessary as the holiness of the clergy, so that the clergy may be the guide of the faithful in example, word and knowledge," Pius X, practical as ever, drew up eight precise rules concerning the young clerics residing in Rome. Particularly in the 19th century, the Eternal City experienced a great influx, from Italy and abroad, of priests who had come to complete their training and of young religious or seminarians who were pursuing their studies. Not all of them lived in seminaries, convents or monasteries. A certain number of them prolonged their stay in Rome for no good reason, or seemed to be independent of all ecclesiastical authority. To put an end to these abuses, the document stipulated that if young clerics, Italians or foreigners, wished to come to Rome to study, they would need the permission of the bishop of their home diocese and would have to live in a seminary or ecclesiastical college. In July 1905, in a motu proprio, Pius X published seven detailed rules to be observed concerning the examinations to be taken by those receiving the different orders in Rome.[35] In December of the same year, a decree of the Congregation of the Council forbade bishops to accept into their seminaries any young cleric who had been dismissed from another seminary, and ordered them not to ordain more priests than were needed for their diocese.[36]

In March 1906 an apostolic letter fixed the rules for the teaching of Holy Scripture in all Catholic seminaries.[37] The same year the Congregation of Bishops and Regulars, which was in charge of seminaries, ordered the establishment of regional seminaries. Italy had a large number of dio-

---

[33] Encyclical *E Supremi Apostolatus,* October 4, 1903, *Documents pontificaux,* vol.I, p.37.
[34] Letter *La Ristorazione,* May 5, 1904, *Documents pontificaux,* vol.I, pp.178-180.
[35] Motu proprio *Sacrosancta Tridentina Synodus,* July 16, 1905, *Documents pontificaux,* vol.I, pp.313-314.
[36] Decree *Vetuit Sacra Tridentina,* December 22. 1905, *Documents pontificaux,* vol.I, pp.677.678.
[37] Apostolic Letter *Quoniam in Re Biblica,* March 24, 1906, *Documents pontificaux,* vol.I, pp.354-356. This document will be analyzed in the chapter on Modernism.

ceses, which were often quite small in compass; accordingly, the number of seminaries was very significant. A good number of them had few students and, as the apostolic visitations had begun to show, the quality of the teaching (and, indeed, of the professors) sometimes left a lot to be desired. It was therefore decided to regroup the seminarians of several dioceses in larger establishments; this would facilitate the recruitment of qualified professors and better equipment, *etc.* So, as the years went on, several big regional seminaries were created: at Bologna there was the *Flaminio Regional Seminary* for the seminarians of all the dioceses of the Romagna under the Archbishop of Bologna; at Chieti there was the *Appruntino Regional Seminary* for seminarians of the dioceses of the Abruzzi; at Anagni there was the *Regional Major Seminary of Latium inferior* for the dioceses to the south of Rome; and so on for all the regions of Italy.

This restructuring did not proceed without difficulties. Bishops who hitherto had been in charge of a diocesan seminary were reluctant to see it disappear and to entrust the education of their future priests to other authorities. This regrouping of the seminaries, which began in 1906, had not been totally completed at the death of Pius X. The last big seminaries established while he was alive were, in June 1913, the *Roman Major Seminary,* replacing all the seminaries then existing in Rome for Italian students (except the *Almo Collegio Capranica)* and, in March 1914, the *Major Seminary of Calabria,* established at Catanzaro.

The other important aspect of the restoration of seminaries was the reform of studies and the rule of discipline. These were announced in 1907 and 1908 respectively and applied to all the seminaries of Italy.[38]

Preparation for the reform of studies began in 1905. At the heart of the special Commission for his reorganization of seminaries, the Pope entrusted Fr. Genocchi, a reputed exegete (and who would be suspected of Modernism, as we shall see, but who was always protected by Pius X), with the task of preparing a program of studies for theology and Holy Scripture.[39]

The reform of studies published in 1907 represents a remarkable exposition, from a twofold point of view. Firstly, it stipulates that the boys in the ecclesiastical colleges (which we know as "minor seminaries") supplying the seminaries should follow the same curriculum as those in state colleges and schools. "Not that they are perfect," as the document comments,

---

[38] *Circular Letter to the Archbishops and Bishops of Italy on seminary studies,* dated May 10, 1907, and *Rules for the direction of education and discipline in the seminaries of Italy,* dated January 1, 1908, *Documents pontificaux,* vol.I, pp.709-710 and 711-731.

[39] Francesco Turvasi, *Giovanni Genocchi e la controversia modernista* (Rome: Edizioni di Storia e Letteratura, 1974); also by the same author, "Genocchi (Giovanni)," *Dictionnaire d'histoire et de géographie ecclésiastiques,* vol.XX, pp.488-493.

but they "mirror the level of cultural development which is demanded in today's society." In other words, future priests must not be put in a situation of inferiority *vis-à-vis* modern culture. The other innovative aspect of the reform of studies was to make obligatory, in clerical training, the teaching of certain subjects which were hitherto lacking in a number of seminaries: Hebrew, biblical Greek, exegesis. As we shall see in a later chapter, the curriculum would be modified in 1911, at the height of the Modernist crisis; but this would be a matter of greater definition, not an upheaval.

The *Rules for the direction of education and discipline* were even more precise: 169 articles concerning the internal organization of seminaries, their administration, and the rules they were to follow. They were complemented by 29 articles spelling out very specific "rules of hygiene" and a detailed example timetable.

This desire to establish precise norms binding on everyone is also found, of course, in the codification of canon law, another great reform of the pontificate.

The codification of Canon Law

Cardinal Merry del Val testified that only "two or three days" after he was elected Pope, Pius X declared his intention of codifying the laws of the Church.[40] For a long time, first as a priest, and then as a bishop, he had become aware of the inconvenience presented by the multiplicity of laws, decrees, special provisions, exemptions, and the fact that they were scattered throughout compendia of diverse origin and unequal authority. It had been a long-expressed wish in the Church to unify all these legislative provisions, to set them in order and adapt them to new conditions of life. In 1865, during a consultation which took place with a view to preparing for the Ecumenical Council which was to take place at the Vatican, many bishops had requested this codification of canon law.

Neither Pius IX, who was preoccupied by the grave *Roman question*, nor Leo XIII during his long pontificate, had felt able to carry this out, even if both of them undertook expositions of canonical themes in limited

---

[40] Cardinal Merry del Val, *Pie X. Impressions et souvenirs,* p.90. The historical sketch accompanying the draft motu proprio submitted to the cardinals (*"Codificazione del diritto canonico"*) affirms the same thing: "The Sovereign Pontiff gloriously reigning, before assuming the Tiara, was already convinced of this necessity," ASV, S.Congregazione degli Affari Ecclesiastici Straordinari, fondo "Codex Juri Canonici," scatola 1, busta I, pp.25-26. This very rich collection of archives composed of 97 *scatole,* will henceforth be referred to as ASV, AA.EE.SS., CIC. It has also been explored, from a perspective different from ours, by Giorgio Feliciani, "La codificazione del diritto canonico e la riforma della Curia romana," in *Storia della Chiesa,* vol.XXII/2, *La Chiesa e la società industriale 1878-1922* (Cinisello Balsamo: Edizioni Paoline, 1990), pp.293-315.

areas. Pius X, at the début of his pontificate, did not hesitate to grasp the nettle. Once again his boldness, or his strength of will, would see the realization of something which many had looked and hoped for, yet had not envisaged the means to bring it about. The matter was directed with determination and method, and resulted in the compilation of a Code of Canon Law which ruled the Church for 80 years until it was replaced, under the pontificate of John Paul II, by a new Code which, basing itself on part of Pius X's Code, adapted it to "the spirit of the Second Vatican Council."[41]

In February 1904 a draft motu proprio entitled *De Ecclesiae legibus in novum corpus redigendis* was submitted to the cardinals of the Congregation of Extraordinary Ecclesiastical Affairs. This motu proprio was preceded by a historical sketch of the evolution of canon law in the Church, and suggestions as to how it might be unified. The document distinguishes three types of ecclesiastical laws:

ius antiquum: laws existing prior to the Decree of Gratian (1139-1150), which collated all the ancient canons and set them in order;

ius novum: the laws adopted between the Decree of Gratian and the Council of Trent (1545);

ius novissimum: the laws adopted since the Council of Trent.

Three questions were submitted to the cardinals consulted. The first was, "Is it fitting to give canon law a new structure and a new form?" The replies were affirmative, even if they led to a large-scale modification of the draft motu proprio.

Even before this was published, the Pope, on March 2, sent a very detailed note to his secretary on the initial decisions and directions to be taken.[42] This note, "so characteristic in its style and precision," wrote Cardinal Merry del Val, shows the great interest which Pius X took in the project right to the end of his pontificate.

The date of the published motu proprio was March 19, 1904, and its title was *Arduum Sane Munus*.[43] Here the Pope expressed his desire to unify ecclesiastical laws under one Code in order "fully to remedy the current defective state of things": "Many laws have been enacted in the course of the centuries. They are contained in a great number of books. Several of them, which at an earlier time were appropriate to the needs of their age, have either been abrogated or fallen into desuetude. Several of them, furthermore, because of changed times and circumstances, have become hard

---

[41]   *Code de droit canonique* (Centurion/Cerf/Tardy, 1984), p.10.
[42]   Note fully reproduced in Cardinal Merry del Val, *Pie X. Impressions et souvenirs,* pp.92-93.
[43]   *Documents pontificaux,* vol.I, pp.152-154.

to carry out, or have become less serviceable, at the present time, for the good of souls."

To execute this work of unification, rationalization and necessary adaptation, Pius X announced the creation of a *Pontifical Commission for the codification of canon law.* Presided over by the Pope, it would consist of cardinals chosen by him and consultors, and it would collate the views of "the entire episcopate."

Four cardinals were chosen for this Commission: Ferrata, Gennari, Vivès y Tuto and Cavagnis. But the mainspring of the Commission was a prelate: Msgr. Pietro Gasparri, who was already secretary of the Congregation for Extraordinary Ecclesiastical Affairs and consultor of the Congregation of the Holy Inquisition. He was appointed secretary of the Commission and was its indefatigable leader. He was created cardinal in 1907 and, under the pontificate of Pius XI, he would be one of the Secretaries of State who made an impact on the Church. It is interesting to note that one of the members of the Commission was Eugenio Pacelli, the future Pius XII. Under Pius X he was entrusted with important missions: he was under-secretary of the Congregation of Extraordinary Ecclesiastical Affairs in 1911, then pro-secretary in 1912 and secretary in 1914; at the same time he was appointed a consultor of the Holy Office (1912) and of the Consistorial Congregation (1914).

As foreseen in the motu proprio, clerics who were specialists in canon law were appointed as consultors. They were chosen from among the canonists resident in Rome. In the first list drawn up, which consists of 17 names, three Frenchmen are found: Fr. Albert Pillet; Fr. Alphonse Eschbach, procurator general of the Holy Ghost Fathers and already consultor of four Congregations; and Fr. Pie de Langogne, a Capuchin, who was also already a member of four Congregations.

In a letter dated March 25 following, Cardinal Merry del Val wrote to all the bishops informing them of the motu proprio and inviting them to share their observations during these four months. They were also given the list of consultors and they could suggest other names.[44] Their replies are of unequal interest.[45] As far as the French bishops were concerned, a great number did not take the trouble to reply. Others (such as the Bishops of Sées, Carthage and Troyes) only sent an acknowledgment. On the other

---

[44] Letter of Cardinal Merry del Val to all the archbishops and bishops, March 25, 1904, ASV, AA.EE.SS., CIC, scatola 1, busta IV. The following April 6, by a letter from Msgr. Gasparri, the Catholic universities were also consulted.

[45] These replies were summarized, in a synthesis containing almost 300 pages, by Fr. Bernardino Klumper, consultor: *Codex Iuris Canonici. Postulata Episcoporum in ordinem digesta,* ASV, AA.EE.SS., CIC, scatola 4. We refer to the original text of certain replies that are contained in the preceding *scatole.*

hand Msgr. Turinaz, Bishop of Nancy, showed himself very supercilious about the choice of consultors.[46] He rejected the three Frenchmen already appointed: Eschbach, he complained, had been "the protector of all the errors which the Pope had condemned for a certain number of years" (he cited Americanism and Christian Democracy); Pillet "is more inclined to the left than the right," whereas Fr. Pie de Langogne "has a good heart, is very intelligent, very correct and very learned, but he has been out of France for a very long time." Instead Msgr. Turinaz suggested that Canon Deshayes, superior of the seminary at Le Mans, author of a work on canon law, should be appointed consultor.

In the Rome of Pius X relatively little attention was paid to petty objections, as we can see from the fact that the consultors objected to by Msgr. Turinaz were retained in their posts. In 1906, in fact, Pius X granted the title of "domestic prelate" to Fr. Pillet. Nonetheless, Canon Deshayes was contacted by Msgr. Gasparri and invited to join in the work as a collaborator.[47]

The reply of Msgr. Béguinot, Bishop of Nîmes, was more fundamental. He regretted that "there is no schedule—at least none that has been communicated to the bishops—fixing the points which need to be modified, the texts which are to be revised in the new codification." The danger, thought the Bishop of Nîmes, was that the bishops' replies would be very general. He expressed his fear that "this consultation of the bishops which, according to the Holy Father's grand concept, could be very fruitful, is in danger of being struck by sterility." In Rome they were not unresponsive to these remarks and a reply was sent to Msgr. Béguinot saying that the bishops should not respond with "generalities," but by making "concrete and practical observations," for example, "if there are provisions in the current canon law which, in their opinion, should be corrected or modified."[48]

The task to be done was considerable, and it was organized in a very methodical way. Supplementary consultors were appointed—40 in all. The preparatory work was shared out among all the consultors. One or more consultors or collaborators were charged with preparing a text (a *votum*) on a precise subject. A date was fixed for their work to be sent in. Thus Fr. Pie de Langogne had to work on three items or "titles": *De subiecto s. ordinationis* (for March 1905), *De statut regularium* (for January 1907), and *De indicio in causis professionis religiosae* (for May 1909). On

[46] Letter of Msgr. Turinaz to Cardinal Merry del Val, 25.4.1904, ASV, AA.EE.SS., CIC, scatola 1, busta IV.
[47] The title of *consultor* was reserved to canonists resident in Rome. Canon Deshayes—and others in a similar situation—were employed as *collaborators*.
[48] Letter to Msgr. Béguinot, June 4, 1904, and the Commission's swift reply of June 8, ASV, AA.EE.SS., CIC, scatola 1, busta IV.

the basis of the prepared *votum,* a *schema* was elaborated and submitted to a commission of consultors and the cardinals who were members of the Commission. The corrected *schema* needed a majority of votes to be adopted....[49]

Pius X followed the progress of the work very closely. He attended several sessions of the Commission and, in addition, made his own wishes known through the intermediary of the Commission's secretary. Thus, for instance, in the early stages of the work, Pius X wrote to Msgr. Gasparri to inform him that, "without imposing his will," he would like to see *De Sacramentis* treated before *De personis.*[50] In the end, the Pope's suggestion was not adopted, because *De personis* takes up the second volume of the Code, whereas *De Sacramentis* occupies the first part of the third volume (*De rebus*). It should be noted that this Pope, who is said to have been so authoritarian, knew how to listen, ask for advice, and was quite able to change his mind. We have another testimony to this in these clarifications provided by his Secretary of State:

> In the course of the work, divergences of opinion arose fairly often, making it difficult to take decisions as to whether new legislation should be drawn up on particular points, or whether one should restrict oneself to introducing modifications. Serious arguments were adduced for and against a particular proposal. The views and wishes of the bishops in different parts of the world did not always agree, and the Roman consultors would defend their opinions with tenacity, with the result that a decision of principle was imposed. Then Pius X, with his habitual practical sense, would make a provisional decree whose content seemed to him justified by the more solid arguments and which could eventually be incorporated, or not, in the definitive legislation. In this way the Holy Father gave his collaborators the opportunity of amending this particular provision or withdrawing it and, at an appropriate time, settling the definitive text of the new Code. Superficial observers fail to understand the wisdom of this procedure when they conclude, over-hastily, that Pius X or his successor Benedict XV re-introduced some of their own decisions. Such was not the case, and one can easily find in the Code certain canons which do not express the personal ideas of Pius X. It must not be forgotten that he never imposed his opinion in disputed questions of law if they did not involve the sacrifice of a fundamental principle.[51]

Pius X would have liked to see this great work completed during his lifetime. He often said to Cardinal Merry del Val, "We must insist on the completion of this work, for I am getting old and I would like to see it finished."[52] It could not be. In 1912 the first of the five books of the Code

---

[49] ASV, AA.EE.SS., CIC, scatola 1, busta VIII.
[50] Letter of March 31, 1904, ASV, AA.EE.SS., CIC, scatola 1, busta III.
[51] Cardinal Merry del Val, *Pie X. Impressions et souvenirs,* pp.93-94.

would be sent to the bishops of the entire world. Each bishop had been invited to make his final observations known to the assembly of bishops of his province, which would make a worldwide report to the Roman Commission.

Pius X died before all the draft books of the Code had been sent to the bishops. It was at the end of 1916, after the observations of the whole world's episcopal assemblies had been received, that a complete draft of the Code was printed. Finally the *Codex iuris canonici* was promulgated by Benedict XV on May 27, 1917. It comprised five books, all (except the first) divided into parts, with each part containing several titles and each title containing several canons. In total, the Code contained 2,414 canons.

In the consistorial allocution promulgating the Code of Canon Law (December 4, 1916), Benedict XV paid homage to his predecessor:

> You all know with what great fervor he undertook this gigantic task from the very beginning of his Pontificate and the zeal and perseverance he exercised in striving for its speedy completion. While it was not granted to him to see its completion, the honor of the work is his alone. Therefore his name will be celebrated in the pages of history alongside such eminent names as Innocent III, Honorius III and Gregory IX, who did so much for the development of canon law. It is with the greatest satisfaction that We publish what he created.

In fact, this Code of Canon Law "keeps in its substance the major part of the preceding law," but, at the same time, it "constitutes an absolute novelty in the history of the Church, which had never known a legislation which almost totally absorbed the previously existing discipline and formally abrogated all the former collections."[53] At a more fundamental level, this Code of Canon Law exhibits two characteristics.

Firstly, it is part of the vast movement of Roman centralization which marks the history of the Church, and particularly the history of the Papacy, beginning in the 19th century. In this case, centralization took the form of a structured and complete compilation of all canonical legislation—with the exception of liturgical norms and the different types of agreements with states. The compilation was carried out in Rome and was imposed on the entire Church. This centralization was felt to be a guarantee of unity, creating a communion around the See of Peter, the heart of Christendom. Since that time it has been criticized for imposing on the Church a "uniformity" which threatened diversity.

Secondly, the Code of Canon Law shows a certain adaptation, on the Church's part, to modern conditions by adopting a unique juridical code,

[52] *Ibid.*, p.90.
[53] G. Feliciani, "La codificazione del diritto canonico," p.306.

in imitation of contemporary civil society. At the time, this modernization of ecclesiastical legislation was considered to be a boon, facilitating the development of the Church's life in its different sectors. More recently it has been criticized as inimical to particular conditions and as encouraging a rigid legalism.

Pius X was not unaware of these two dangers—uniformity and legalism. His concern never to impose "his opinion in disputed questions of law," underlined by Cardinal Merry del Val, shows that he was well acquainted with the existence of divergent views and interpretations in the area of canon law. At the same time, however, his care for the Universal Church made him look forward to the establishment of a complete, concise and incontestable compilation, not reserved only to specialists in canon law but easily available to all clerics.[54]

It should be added that, alongside the codification of canon law, Pius X wanted to endow the Church with an official organ for promulgating the acts of the Holy See. Hitherto no official bulletin of the Holy See existed. The custom was simply to regard the constitutions, decrees and other official texts as "promulgated" once they were published in the *Acta Sanctae Sedis*. In origin this was only a publication created—in 1865—on the initiative of a priest, Don Pietro Avanzini.[55] The constitution *Promulgandi Pontificias,* dated September 29, 1908, stipulated that, from 1909 onwards, the Holy See would have an official bulletin: the *Acta Apostolicae Sedis,* described as a *"commentarium officiale."* The first issue appeared on January 1, 1909, and, ever since, *AAS* has been an authoritative reference resource for the Universal Church. Officially, *AAS* is a collection of "all the acts, provisions, decrees and instructions emanating from the Holy See, and which need to be promulgated and published in order to have the force of law." The texts published in *AAS* (often in Latin in the case of pontifical acts) serve as reference documents, and are to be regarded as the

---

[54] A canon lawyer observes: "It was indeed a juridical masterpiece. Now the Church had a collection of laws expressed in the form of concise juridical rules and not a compilation of particular cases (as was often the case in the *Corpus juris canonici*). Furthermore, it was an authentic collection: all the Code's canons had the same legislative authority, whatever their origin may have been. Finally, this new collection of laws had an exclusive character which the earlier collections of canon law did not generally have: all the laws not contained within it, with the exception of liturgical laws, concordats and customs, were abrogated. Previous legislation was null and void except insofar as it was useful for interpreting and supplementing in doubtful cases." Fr. Patrice Laroche, "Le Code de droit canonique, chef-d'œuvre de saint Pie X," *Fideliter,* May-June 1997, no.117, p.10.

[55] Not until May 23, 1904, in a Rescript of the Congregation of Propaganda, was the periodical declared "official."

official source for all the translations subsequently made by the Holy See or by others anywhere else in the world.[56]

The reform of the Curia

If Cardinal Gasparri was the king-pin in the elaboration of canon law, it was Cardinal De Lai who was the king-pin of the reform of the Curia. In both cases Pius X closely followed the work and imprinted his personal mark on it. Not only because he had personal ideas on these subjects, but also because his temperament had always inclined him, in his former responsibilities, to give great attention to questions of law and organization, areas in which he had always been recognized as having great *savoir-faire*.

At the time of his accession to the pontificate, the Roman Curia was still structured according to the principles laid down by Pope Sixtus V in the apostolic constitution *Immensa* (January 22, 1587).[57] At that time the number of Congregations had been fixed at 15. Over the course of time some of them had disappeared and others had been created (such as the Congregation for the Oriental Churches, created by Pius IX in 1862). Commissions had been added, and sometimes there was rivalry between their competence and that of a Congregation. For example, the Oriental Churches had been under the aegis of either the Congregation of Propaganda or the Commission for the Reunion of Dissident Churches. Furthermore, the historical evolution of certain countries meant that the framework of their relations with the Holy See was out of kilter: thus England, Scotland, Ireland, Holland, Canada and the United States were still regarded as mission territories and as such were under the control of the Congregation of Propaganda. Even under the pontificate of Leo XIII there had been calls for a complete reorganization of the Roman Curia. He did not do this, and it fell to Pius X to accomplish the task.

These are the reasons he adduced for reorganizing the Curia:

> The number of the Sacred Congregations grew or diminished depending on the circumstances and the needs of the times. Even the jurisdiction attributed to each of them underwent modifications, either as a result of new prescriptions of the Sovereign Pontiffs, or by the gradual introduction of a usage that was finally ratified. Today, in consequence of this, their respective jurisdiction or competence is not so easily known to all,

---

[56] In fact, particularly where encyclicals are concerned, the original Italian text is translated into Latin and then published in *AAS*. Even in this case the Latin text is the official text to be quoted.

[57] On the history of the Roman Curia and the Congregations, cf. N. Del Re, *La Curia romana. Lineamenti storico-giuridici* (Rome: Edizioni di Storia e Letteratura, 1970), and "Note storiche," published in each edition of the *Annuario Pontificio*, Vatican City, Libreria Editrice Vaticana.

Leonard von Matt

THE PARISH CHURCH AT RIESE

The church is dedicated to the Apostle St. Matthew, and, complete with its fine facade and slender campanile, was consecrated in 1777. In all its main features the building presents the same appearance now as it did to Giuseppe Sarto when he was a boy and a young man.

THE KITCHEN AT HOME

The room, the hearth, the sink, and the plate-racks are still exactly as they were when the Sarto family used them. Even the curtains on the window and the little curtain round the chimney-piece are the ones made by his mother's own hand. The floor used to be merely beaten earth, until Giuseppe Sarto as Cardinal of Venice had a floor of flagstones put in for his mother. The hearth is of the usual pattern in the Veneto, made of bricks and the tiles with the fire inside. The copper cauldron seen on the hearth was for the preparation of *polenta*, the daily dish made from maize.

Leonard von Matt

A SUNDIAL AT FONTANIVA

Don Giuseppe Sarto also had a hobby: he loved sundials–the clocks that notice only the happy hours of sunshine. At least half a dozen sundials that he put up on presbyteries or on churches have been preserved. Such is this one, in the neighboring village of Fontaniva.

Leonard von Matt

Ferretto, Treviso

MSGR. SARTO, AS SPIRITUAL DIRECTOR OF THE
SEMINARY IN TREVISO WITH THE SEMINARY STAFF

This photograph was taken during the academic year 1875-76, before Giuseppe Sarto had become the rector. He is in the second row, third from the left. In the front row is the then Bishop of Treviso, Msgr. Federico Maria Zinelli.

CARDINAL SARTO'S ENTRY INTO VENICE

The new patriarch, preceded by his processional cross, leaving the church of "gli Scalzi" (the Discalced Carmelites) on November 24, 1894, shortly after his arrival at the adjacent railway station.

Leonard von Matt

PONTIFICAL HIGH MASS IN ST. MARK'S
(June, 1953)

CARDINAL PATRIARCH OF VENICE GIUSEPPE SARTO

CARDINAL SARTO IN THE CORPUS CHRISTI PROCESSION

The great procession in honor of Our Lord in the Blessed Sacrament. A rare photograph taken around 1900.

THE POPE RECEIVES SOME YOUNG VISITORS

On July 11, 1904, the Holy Father enjoyed an athletic display given by these visiting Asian boys in the Cortile della Pigna.

Felici, Rome

A PAPAL AUDIENCE IN THE CORTILE SAN DAMASO

On September 13, 1903, four weeks after his coronation, Pius X received in audience the Catholic societies of Rome. On October 4, he gathered the parish of Trastevere in the Cortile San Damaso. There were many subsequent open audiences, at which Pope Pius X preached on the Sunday Gospel like an ordinary priest.

A GYMNASTIC DISPLAY IN THE COURT OF THE BELVEDERE

The audience of September 26, 1908, was a part of the celebrations in honor of the Pope's golden jubilee of his priesthood. On this occasion 2,000 athletes, who had come to Rome from Italy, France, Belgium, Holland, and Canada for an international Catholic congress of physical training, gave a display for the Holy Father in the Cortile del Belvedere.

POPE PIUS X ON THE BALCONY OF THE CORTILE SAN DAMASO

The Holy Father looks down with a friendly smile on the crowd below. Among his attendants, on the extreme right of the picture, is Monsignor Giovanni Bressan, of Treviso, who was his personal secretary at Mantua, in Venice, and throughout his pontificate in Rome.

POPE PIUS X CONSECRATES AS BISHOP
THE FUTURE POPE BENEDICT XV

On December 22, 1907, in the Sistine Chapel, Pope Pius X consecrated as bishop Msgr. Giacomo Della Chiesa, who until then had been *Substitutus* in the Secretariat of State, and was to succeed him in the See of Peter. Three months before the conclave in which the Bishop of Bologna was elected Pope as Benedict XV, Pius X gave him the Cardinal's Hat. It is said that Pope Pius X added with his own hand the name of Della Chiesa to the list of new cardinals prepared for the consistory.

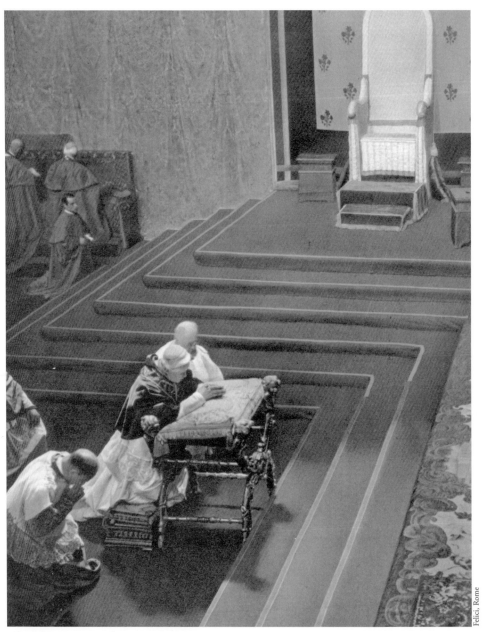

Felici, Rome

CORONATION ANNIVERSARY

According to ancient custom the Pope assists at a Solemn Mass in the Sistine Chapel on the anniversary of his coronation. Here was Pius X praying during this Mass on his ninth anniversary in 1912. The Mass was celebrated by the first cardinal he had created, Merry del Val, his Secretary of State. The Sistine Choir sang Palestrina's Mass "Lauda Sion," under the direction of Don Lorenzo Perosi. Perosi worked in Venice in the time of Cardinal Sarto, and then became conductor of the Sistine Choir, a post he retained until his death in 1914.

THE VATICAN PALACE, RESIDENCE OF THE POPE

The apartments of the Pope were in the story next to the top of the portion of the Vatican shown. The obelisk in the foreground is 162 feet high, and weighs a million pounds. It was brought from Egypt by one of the Emperors of ancient Rome. At the top of the obelisk is a reliquary containing a portion of the True Cross.

LOOKING THROUGH THE DOOR OF THE POPE'S PRIVATE CHAPEL TO ITS ALTAR

Here the Pope celebrated Mass daily at 7am. In this small place he carried on his private devotions, assisted by his private chaplains.

THE POPE IN HIS PRIVATE STUDY

Here His Holiness did his reading and writing. Here he also received the members of his official household and frequently received visits from his sisters.

Felici, Rome

PIUS X AT HIS DESK

The Pope continues his work at his desk in his library, while the Dutch painter Anton van Veel is busy with a portrait of him. Pius X was often painted, largely because he could never refuse, especially if the request came from some obscure and penniless artist. The bronze statue on the desk represents the Curé of Ars, to whom he had a great devotion and whom he beatified on January 8, 1909.

POPE AND PHOTOGRAPHER

He was also kind to photographers who came to him, even though in those early days of photography ordeals of patience were involved, with long periods of sitting motionless. The first photograph of the new Pope was taken on August 12, 1903, by Ferretto of Treviso, the same who had photographed him as newly ordained priest, as bishop, and as cardinal.

GARDENS OF THE VATICAN VIEWED NORTHWARD FROM ST. PETER'S DOME
Normally, the Pope never left the precincts of the Vatican, and spent the summer in this garden, where there is a drive of two and a half miles, as well as many pleasant walks.

PIUS X READING THE NEWSPAPER IN THE GARDEN
On a hot summer day the Pope would seek a shady spot in the garden. He made a point of reading the newspapers regularly, and often became annoyed when he found facts misrepresented. Already as Cardinal of Venice he had declared his devotion of the cause of a good Catholic press.

Felici, Rome

Good Pope Pius X, Who Said, "Remember That I Am Only a Poor Man and That Jesus Christ Is All."

Pope Pius X was the 258th Pontiff. His name was Giuseppe (Joseph) Sarto. He was born of humble parents, June 2, 1835, at Riese, Italy. Ordained priest September 18, 1858. Made Canon and Chancellor of the Diocese of Treviso in 1875, Bishop of Mantua in 1884, and a Cardinal and Patriarch of Venice in 1893. He was chosen as Pope on August 4, 1903.

Pope St. Pius X Taking a Walk in the Gardens of the Vatican

He is accompanied here by Msgr. Giuseppe Pescini, one of his two chaplains. This portion of the grounds was reserved from public intrusion to allow His Holiness an opportunity for rest and quiet in the open air.

CARDINAL MERRY DEL VAL, PIUS X'S SECRETARY OF STATE

Cardinal Merry del Val was of Spanish blood, but was born in London in 1865. He became Italian Archbishop of Nicosia in 1900, and was nominated Papal Secretary of State by Pope Pius X in October 1903, succeeding Cardinal Rampola. He was afterwards created a cardinal.

THE SIGNING OF THE CONCORDAT WITH SERBIA

On June 24, 1914, on the eve of the outbreak of World War I, an agreement was signed by which an ecclesiastical province came into being with an archiepiscopal see at Belgrade; the Church in Serbia received juridical status, and freedom of worship was guaranteed. The document was signed by the Cardinal Secretary of State, Merry del Val, and the Serbian minister in Paris. Behind the cardinal, to the left, stands Msgr. Eugenio Pacelli, then Secretary of the Congregation for Extraordinary Affairs and later Pope Pius XII.

Felici, Rome

HIS SISTERS ANNA, ROSA, AND MARIA

Before these three sister, who remained unmarried, were invited to take a flat in Rome, they lived at Riese. Rosa (center) died at the age of 72, one year before Pius X. Maria (right), died 17 years later at the age of 84. Anna (left), the youngest of the family, died in 1926 aged 76. The three sisters would have liked to have included their beloved brother Beppi in this photograph, but since this could not be they had to be content with a picture of him in the group.

Bigaglia, Venice

HIS SISTERS ANTONIA AND LUCIA

These were the two sisters who kept house for him when he was parish-priest of Salzano. It was here that Antonia (right) married Francesco de Bei, the tailor, and died in 1917, age 74; and Lucia (left), born in 1848, married the sacristan Luigi Boschin, and died in 1924.

HIS BROTHER ANGELO

The Pope's brother Angelo is pictured here (1867) in the uniform of the Austrian military police, in which he reached the rank of sergeant-major. Angelo Sarto became village postmaster at Delle Grazie, near Mantua, Italy. He married Eleonora Siliprandi, of Mantua, who bore him no sons but several daughters. He died in 1916, at the age of 79, like his brother Giuseppe.

THINGS FROM HIS POCKETS

The following items were found in the pockets of his white cassock after Pius X's death: this little wallet with spaces for notes, railway-tickets, and stamps; a small purse, with a figure of the dove of peace on it, and an inexpensive pocket-knife.

THE HOLY FATHER BLESSING PILGRIMS

Pilgrims frequently came from remote parts of Europe and journeyed to Rome under the charge of their parish priest. Some are seen here carrying religious objects upon which they have asked the Pope's blessing.

PIUS X IN PONTIFICAL VESTMENTS
There is a sadness on the Holy Father's features, which was so often
noticed with emotion by those who saw him as *Summus Pontifex*.
This photograph belongs to the earliest days of his reign, and one
notices that the edge of the cope is embroidered near its bottom
edge with the arms of his predecessor Leo XIII.

PIUS X ON HIS DEATHBED

It was reported that before he died the Pope kissed the crucifix here clasped in his hands. The simple iron bedstead and humble furnishings are witness to his personal poverty. On August 2, 1914, Pope Pius X made his last public appearance. From then on his life was spent in almost continuous prayer. Thinking of the world war then engaged, he would exclaim: "I suffer for the wounded, and the sick...I suffer for their families...Oh, that war, it is going to kill me." God called his faithful servant to Himself, August 20, 1914.

THE FUNERAL PROCESSION TO ST. PETER'S

On the morning of August 21, 1914, the Pope's body was taken, clothed in pontifical vestments, for the lying-in-state in St. Peter's. The procession went by the *Scala dei morti* (the "stairway of the dead") by which, traditionally, no living Pope passes.

THE LYING-IN-STATE IN ST. PETER'S

A continuous stream of people came to the Chapel of the Blessed
Sacrament in St. Peter's on August 21-22, 1914, to pay a last homage
and a last farewell to this Holy Father they loved so well. Contrary to
the usual practice of the Vatican but in obedience to Pius X's desire
expressed in his will, the body was not embalmed.

THE BEATIFICATION OF POPE PIUS X

One June 3, 1951, Pope Pius X was beatified. In front of the high altar was the sarcophagus containing his body. After the *Litany of the Saints*, the decree of beatification was read, and the sarcophagus was unveiled together with the picture of the new *Beatus*.

POPE PIUS XII READS THE DECREE OF CANONIZATION

Pope Pius X was declared blessed on June 3, 1951, and was canonized by Pope Pius XII on May 29, 1954.

THE COAT-OF-ARMS OF POPE ST. PIUS X

Pope St. Pius X's design for his papal coat-of-arms incorporated the main elements of his previous coats-of-arms of Mantua and Venice. As his episcopal coat of arms when Bishop of Mantua, he chose an anchor within a sea illumined by a star. The anchor represents hope. (Hope is "like an anchor of the soul, sure and steadfast," [Heb. 6:19] and the star recalling that title of our Lady, *Stella Maris*.) After his appointment as Patriarch-Archbishop of Venice, Cardinal Sarto added the Lion of St. Mark (symbol of the City of Venice) to his episcopal coat of arms in order to show his attachment to his new diocese.

nor is it clearly defined. Several of these Sacred Congregations have to pro-
nounce on identical cases; some have only a few matters to expedite, while
others are inundated with work.[58]

Before proceeding with the complete reorganization of the Curia, Pius
X, by motu proprio, made three gradual simplifications:

—In December 1903 the designation of all bishops—except those
whose dioceses or territories were answerable to the Congregation of Propaganda or the Congregation for Extraordinary Ecclesiastical Affairs—was
entrusted to the Congregation of the Holy Office, presided over by the
Pope.[59] Entrusting the Holy Office with this responsibility, it was possible
to establish a "constant and fixed rule" to be followed in the choice of candidates for the episcopate. As Pius X explained: "We have been at pains to
settle the method to be followed in this matter, by giving an appropriate
instruction. In it, We have ordered that a very serious enquiry be carried
out regarding the faith, life, conduct and wisdom of those priests designated for the episcopate; We have re-introduced the *periculum de doctrina.*"

—In January 1904 the Congregation of Indulgences and Relics of the
Saints was merged with the Congregation of Rites (with the responsibility
of regulating the worship of God and the cult of the saints).[60]

—Finally, in May 1906, the Congregation on Regular Discipline (created in 1695 to maintain the faithful practice of the rule in the convents of
Italy) and the Congregation of the State of Religious Orders (created in
1846 to watch over the discipline of religious orders in the whole world)
were suppressed.[61] Their responsibilities were transferred to the Congregation of Bishops and Regulars.

These limited changes—some of them were to undergo further
change—prefigured the complete reorganization of the Curia which took
place in 1908. Although Pius X more than once underlined the urgency of
a reform, he did not want to rush things. Like all the other great reforms of
the pontificate, this one was preceded by several months' preparatory
work. During the summer of 1907, at the Pope's request, Msgr. De Lai,
then secretary of the Consistorial Congregation, compiled a first memorandum on the subject.[62] In November Pius X himself produced a "draft

---

[58] Apostolic Constitution *Sapienti Consilio* (June 29, 1908), *Documents pontificaux,* vol.I,
    p.525.
[59] This involved suppressing the special Congregation created by Leo XIII for the
    election of the bishops of Italy; motu proprio *Romanis Pontificibus* (December 17,
    1903), *Documents pontificaux,* vol.I, pp.64-65.
[60] Motu proprio *Quae in Ecclesiae* (January 28, 1904), *Documents pontificaux,* vol.I,
    pp.91-92.
[61] Motu proprio *Sacrae Congregationi* (May 26, 1906), *Documents pontificaux,* vol.I,
    p.362.
[62] Giuseppe Ferretto, "La riforma del B. Pio X," *Apollinaris,* 25, 1952, pp.37-81.

plan for the reorganization of the Sacred Roman Congregations" (18 manuscript pages). The draft was precise and well set out.[63] After explaining, in four points, the dysfunctional elements of the Curia in its current state, Pius X defined, in three points, the criteria which should govern a reform. Then, in the draft reorganization plan proper, he reduced the number of Congregations to nine.

A Commission of cardinals was set up to go into things in more depth and present a more developed draft plan. De Lai, created cardinal in December (at the same time as Gasparri), was chosen to preside. Between November 1907 and June 27, 1908, the Commission elaborated several successive versions which modified, corrected and completed the Pope's draft, while keeping to the essential principles he had set out.

Finally, dated June 29, 1908, the apostolic constitution *Sapienti Consilio* proceeded to completely reorganize the Curia.[64] Up to now the Curia had consisted of eleven Congregations (Holy Office, Consistorial, Discipline of the Sacraments, Council, Affairs of Religious, Propaganda, Index, Rites, Ceremonial, Extraordinary Ecclesiastical Affairs, Studies), three Tribunals (Sacred Penitentiary, Holy Roman Rota, and the Apostolic Signatura), and five Offices (Apostolic Chancellery, Apostolic Dataria, Apostolic Chamber, Secretariat of State and Secretariat of Briefs). The duties of the eleven Congregations were well defined and limited. To assess the importance of the reform introduced and to show the concern for clarity which had inspired it, one need only observe the transformations undergone by the first of the Congregations, the Holy Office.

Until that time it had been entitled the *Sacred Congregation of the Universal Inquisition*. It had been created in 1542 by Paul III to defend the Church against heresy. By the reform he introduced, Pius X officially changed its name to the *Sacred Congregation of the Holy Office* (a name which had already been in common use for several centuries). While he retained its original area of responsibility ("to safeguard doctrine touching faith and morals...to judge heresy and other crimes which involve the suspicion of heresy"), he added a further one: "the question of indulgences, both from the doctrinal and the practical points of view." (As we have seen, this responsibility has recently devolved upon the Congregation of Rites). On the other hand, three other responsibilities were withdrawn from it, to be allotted to the Congregations more directly concerned with them:

---

[63] The document is fully reproduced in Ferretto, *ibid.*, pp.38-42.
[64] Text of the Constitution, followed by the "Special law of the Sacred Roman Rota and the Apostolic Signatura" in *Documents pontificaux,* vol.I, 525-559.

—Everything concerning the Commandments of the Church (abstinence, fasting, holy days of obligation, *etc.*) would henceforth come under the Congregation of the Council. This was a logical decision because the Congregation of the Council was responsible for all "affairs concerning the general discipline of the secular clergy and the Christian people."

—The designation of bishops would henceforth come under the Consistorial Congregation.

—Dispensation from the vows of religion would henceforth depend on the Congregation responsible for the Affairs of Religious.

In the event, this Constitution underwent certain minor modifications. For example, in 1912—and this was a sign of Pius X's concern for the lot of emigrants, which we have already noted—a special section was created within the Consistorial Congregation, with responsibility to look after emigrants' spiritual needs.[65] All the same, this reform left unresolved certain problems regarding competence and jurisdiction. Thus the Congregation of the Index was maintained as an independent Congregation, yet its purpose, "to examine...and proscribe dangerous books," was closely linked with that of the Congregation of the Holy Office.[66] Conversely, the Oriental Churches remained under the aegis of the Congregation of Propaganda, *i.e.*, of missions, which—naturally enough—offended their feelings. There was a further imperfection: the Congregation of Studies saw its competence restricted to universities and Catholic faculties, to the exclusion of seminaries. These three problems would be dealt with in the next pontificate.[67]

On account of its wide scope, Pius X's reform of the Curia was the most important ever conducted since the Renaissance. It was characterized by his concern for rationalization and system, with the aim that the Curia "could more easily render service to the Roman Pontiff and the Church,

---

[65] Motu proprio *De Catholicarum in Exteras Regiones Emigratione,* August 15, 1912. On March 19, 1914, another motu proprio, *Iam Pridem,* created a *collegio* in Rome to train priests for the spiritual care of emigrants. This ecclesiastical college was put directly under the aegis of the Consistorial Congregation.

[66] The Constitution *Sapienti Consilio* was not unaware of the problem: it expressly called for collaboration between the two Congregations: "As the prohibiting of books is very frequently with the aim of defending the Catholic Faith, which is also the purpose of the Congregation of the Holy Office, We decree that in future, whenever it is a question of prohibiting books (and solely in such cases) there should be communication between the cardinals, consultors and officers of the two Congregations; and that all should be obliged to the same secrecy on this point."

[67] The motu proprio *Seminaria Clericorum* (November 4, 1915) created a Congregation of Seminaries and Universities. The motu proprio *Dei Providentis* (May 1, 1917) instituted a Congregation for the Oriental Churches. The motu proprio *Alloquentes* (March 25, 1917) suppressed the Congregation of the Index and allotted its sphere of responsibility to the Congregation of the Holy Office.

and lend them more effective help."[68] Not until the reform led by Paul VI, in 1967, do we see a new restructuring of the Curia, this time in the spirit of the Second Vatican Council.[69]

---

[68] Constitution *Sapienti Consilio,* p.526.
[69] Thus, in order to manifest the "collegiality" which should exist in the Church's government, some diocesan bishops would be summoned to be part of Roman Congregations.

CHAPTER 7

THE AFFAIRS OF FRANCE

Throughout his pontificate, the plight of the Church in France and of its faithful was one of the things which most grieved the heart of Pius X. This expression is not too strong if one considers the attention he devoted to the "affairs of France" right from the start, his firmness in matters of principle and, in parallel with this, the great concern he showed for French Catholics and the French clergy.

When Pius X became Pope, France was still living under the regime of the Napoleonic concordat (1801). This concordat stipulated that the "Catholic, Apostolic and Roman religion is the religion of the great majority of French citizens" and, in exchange for the Church's renunciation of the property which had been confiscated from it under the Revolution, the State undertook to assure "proper salaries to bishops and parish priests." In spite of the "Organic Articles" which were unilaterally annexed to this by Napoleon in 1802—articles of a very Gallican tone, which made the Church dependent on the State—the Concordat nonetheless permitted the Church of France to come to life again after the revolutionary turmoil. Throughout the entire 19th century most of the bishops tried to free themselves from state tutelage in order to fulfil their religious mission. They had greater or lesser success in this, depending on the regime in power (the Restoration, the Liberal monarchy of Louis-Philippe, the Second Empire). A relative peace had permitted a visible renewal of the Church: there was the restoration of the great old religious orders, the creation of many new congregations for men and for women, a great readership of the Catholic press, both in Paris and in the provinces. At the same time we can see among Catholics, to an increasing extent in the second half of the 19th century, a steady increase in devotion to the Pope and greater and greater attention being paid to pontifical teaching. However, the hostility to the Church which had been unleashed under the Revolution had not disappeared. It would come to a head in the pontificate of Pius X, in the breaking of the Napoleonic Concordat and in the law separating Church and State.

As early as the end of the second Empire, the republican leader Léon Gambetta, a Freemason, had urged the separation of Church and State in the famous *Programme of Belleville* (1869), which can be considered as the first charter of those who would soon go on to found the third Republic.

Since they could not immediately write this separation into the constitution, the opportunists and then the radicals, who dominated French political life from 1879 to the First World War,[1] multiplied the laws designed to withdraw society from the Church's influence: there were decrees against unauthorized religious congregations (March 29, 1880), a law suppressing the observation of Sunday rest (July 12, 1880), a law on compulsory education and the laicizing of education (March 28, 1882), a law authorizing divorce (July 27, 1884), a law laicizing the personnel in state schools (October 30, 1886), a law on associations (July 1, 1901). This last law, voted for under the government of Waldeck-Rousseau, had been embraced by the latter as "a necessary preface" to the separation of Church and State, *i.e.*, to the breaking of the Napoleonic concordat.[2]

Leo XIII had intervened on several occasions to protest against the policy of the French government. In 1892, in the encyclical *Au milieu des sollicitudes* he had denounced the "vast conspiracy planned by certain men to annihilate Christianity in France."[3] When the draft law on associations was presented to the parliament, with two other draft laws also concerning the Church, Leo XIII wrote to the President of the Republic, Émile Loubet, a Freemason, protesting against plans which, "if sanctioned, would lead to a profound disturbance of religious peace."[4] In reply, Loubet ar-

---

[1] Cf. Jean-Marie Mayeur, *Les débuts de la IIIe République, 1871-1898* (Paris: Éditions du Seuil, 1973), and Madeleine Rebérioux, *La République radicale? 1898-1914* (Paris: Éditions du Seuil, 1975). J.-M. Mayeur situates the Law of Separation within a wider historical context: *La Question laïque, XIXe-XXe siècle* (Paris: Fayard, 1997).

[2] Prior to the Law of Separation the French government published a "yellow book": *Documents diplomatiques. Saint-Siège. 1899-1903* (Paris: Imprimerie Nationale, 1903). This was a collection of 26 documents on the relations between France and the Holy See in the relevant period. The Holy See responded, after the Law of Separation, by publishing a "white book": *La Separazione dello Stato dalla Chiesa in Francia: esposizione documentata* (Rome: Tipografia Vaticana, 1905) (French translation: *La Séparation de l'Église et de l'État en France. Exposé et Documents,* Paris, Éditions des "Questions actuelles," 1906). This collection reproduces 47 documents exchanged between the Holy See and the French government, namely, apart from the Concordat and the organic articles, the official correspondence exchanged between 1900 and 1904. Henceforth we shall cite them as *La Séparation.* This collection is, however, incomplete. Certain documents are not given, and where it is a question of episcopal nominations, the names of persons and dioceses are given by initials only. To acquire a complete view of the exchange of documents it is necessary to consult the Archives of the Ministry of Foreign Affairs (AMAE), Saint-Siège, *Relations avec la France* (1903, January-June 1904, July-December 1904), *i.e.,* respectively, Nouvelle Série 21, 22 and 23, and *Évêques français 1897-1907,* Nouvelle Série 27.

[3] Encyclical *Au milieu des sollicitudes,* February 16, 1892, *Actes de Léon XIII* (Paris: Maison de la Bonne Presse), vol.III, p.112. The encyclical was written and published directly in French so that there could be no contesting of its translation or interpretation.

[4] Letter of Leo XIII to E. Loubet, March 23, 1900, *La Séparation,* p.87.

gued that, constitutionally, he had no power: "The nature of my function does not permit me to intervene personally in a discussion which the law reserves to the ministers responsible."

After the vote on the law on associations (July 1, 1901), forbidding religious congregations to exist unless they were authorized, and making the existence of the others dependent on the good will of the political authorities, Leo XIII ordered his Secretary of State to tender a "note" of protest to the French government. The French government took no account of it and the law was applied.

Combes's "campaign of emancipation"

In June 1902 the radical, Émile Combes, a Freemason, became President of the Council. He also took charge of the Ministry of the Interior and of Cults.[5] He provoked another quarrel, namely the question known as *Nobis nominavit* ("he is named by Us"). In a note sent to the Secretariat of State, the French government demanded the suppression of the *Nobis* in the Bull canonically appointing new French bishops[6]: the Holy See should not claim to nominate bishops in France, since the concordat stipulates that it is the government which nominates bishops, the Pope's power being restricted to instituting and consecrating them. The Holy See replied in a long memorandum giving the historical and theological justification for the formula *Nobis nominavit*: "If, in fact, the Government, in nominating, indicates the subject to the Sovereign Pontiff so that the latter—once he has approved the candidate's suitability—may confer the episcopate upon him in conformity with the obligation assumed by the concordat, it is natural that the Pope should say, in the Bull, *Nobis nominavit*."[7] The quarrel would eventually be one of the pretexts for breaking the concordat.

Émile Combes was determined to achieve the separation of Church and State, but he wanted to prepare public opinion in advance and show "manifestly, and with much supporting evidence, that it is the Catholic clergy themselves who have provoked and willed it by making it inevitable."[8] Three ways, principally, were used to prepare public opinion for this

---

5 Émile Combes (1835-1921), a former seminarian who had embraced atheism, initiated in 1869 in the Lodge "Tolérance et Étoile de Saintonge Réunies," at Pons, "which he frequented until his death," according to Michel Gaudart de Soulages and Hubert Lamant, *Dictionnaire des Francs-Maçons* (Paris: Éditions Jean-Claude Lattès, 1995), pp.277-278. Cf. also Gabriel Merle, *Émile Combes* (Paris: Fayard, 1995), who utilized the Archives Nationales (but not those of the Ministry of Foreign Affairs).
6 Memorandum of Nisard, French Ambassador to the Holy See, to Rampolla, Secretary of State to Leo XIII, December 21, 1902, *La Séparation*, p.111.
7 Memorandum of March 9, 1903, *ibid.*, pp.116-117.
8 Address of Émile Combes to the Senate, March 21, 1903, quoted in *La Séparation*, p.6.

separation. Firstly, the strict application of the laws voted and passed; especially that on "associations," which obliged many congregations to leave France and many non-authorized schools to close (there were 8,200 closures between July 1901 and December 1903). Secondly, the preparation of new laws, notably that presented by the government on December 18, 1903, with the aim of forbidding religious congregations to engage in any teaching. Finally there was the multiplication of draft laws originating with deputies or senators, designed to separate the Church (or churches) from the State. These proposals had no chance of succeeding without the support of the government, but their purpose was to keep the debate before the public and attract the attention of the press to the issue.

Émile Combes, according to the logic of Freemasonry at that time, wanted to set up "a lay society, unencumbered with all clerical subjection."[9] His "campaign of emancipation," as he called it, won the approval of a certain fraction of French and international public opinion. All the messages, letters, telegrams of encouragement received by Émile Combes at this time are preserved in the Ministry of Foreign Affairs.[10] In the last months of 1903, encouragement came from different countries: from Italian, Swiss, North African and English Masonic lodges, from the Mexican Liberal Party, from the Brussels City Council, from students of the Porto Polytechnical Academy, *etc*. Combes could feel that he was the bearer of a mission of "emancipation" that went beyond the limits of France.

Pius X's reaction

It is clear from the foregoing that there had been a deterioration of relations between France and the Holy See well before Pius X's arrival at the Sovereign Pontificate. Pius X was not responsible for the separation, but rather the republican ideology of those times, which was savagely anti-clerical.

The first great protest uttered by Pius X was in December 1903, four months after his accession. In a letter to the President of the French Republic he deplored the consequences arising from the application of the law on associations and the deterioration of relations between France and the Holy See:

> Thousands of religious, men and women, who had worthily served the Church and France, and whose only crime was to have been devoted to their own sanctification and the service of their neighbor by practising the evangelical counsels, have been hounded from their peaceful dwellings

---

[9]   Interview for the London *National Review,* March 1905, quoted in *La Séparation,* p.7.
[10] AMAE, Saint-Siège, *Relations avec la France* (1903), NS 21, fol.397f.

and often reduced to the uttermost wretchedness. And since their own country withdrew from them the right, guaranteed to all citizens by law, to choose their manner of life as seemed good to them, they have been constrained to seek asylum and freedom in foreign lands. If to this we add the repeated attacks made against the Catholic Church and the Holy See itself, in spite of its constantly and particularly peaceful and benevolent attitude towards France and the Government of the Republic, the many instances of suppression of salaries due in justice to bishops and parish priests, and the prolonged vacancy of episcopal sees, no one will be able to deny that the present situation of the Church in France is exceptionally sad and painful.[11]

Pius X had not been slow to see that these various laws were the prelude to a more fundamental struggle: "Confronted with this long series of measures, each one more hostile to the Church," he went on, "it would seem, Mr. President, that the intention is—as certain people believe—gradually to prepare the ground, not only for the complete separation of Church and State, but also, if possible, for the eradication of that hallmark of Christianity which has been France's glory in past centuries."

At the same time—and this is an act of conciliation much to the credit of Pius X—by an exchange of notes dated December 22, the Holy See and the French Government came to an agreement on the question of the *Nobis nominavit*. According to an extant formula, "The Holy See would suppress the *Nobis* in episcopal Bulls, without making any other changes; the President of the Republic would in future request the canonical institution by letters patent."[12]

However, the French authorities were not prepared to entertain any conciliatory moves. In his response to the Pope on the question of the plight of the congregations, Loubet once again pleaded his "constitutional inability in governmental measures" and expressed his wish "to abstain from all personal action."[13] As we shall see, one of his "personal actions"—his official journey to Rome—would be regarded by the Holy See as a grave offence.

In the meantime a new quarrel surfaced. In an allocution he gave the following March 18, replying to the wishes of the Sacred College for a Feast in honor of St. Joseph, Pius X again complained of religious persecution in France.[14] He said that the proposed law forbidding religious congregations to teach was "unjust and odious," and he passed severe judgment on the whole package of laws and measures taken against them in

[11] Letter to Émile Loubet, December 2, 1903, *La Séparation*, pp.106-107.
[12] *Ibid.*, pp.41-42.
[13] Letter of Émile Loubet to Pius X, February 27, 1904, *ibid.*, p.109.
[14] Allocution, *Accogliamo*, March 18, 1904, *Documents pontificaux*, vol.I, pp.147-149.

recent years by the French government. In terms that were by no means diplomatic, he said that "they are essentially contrary to the idea of liberty properly understood, to the country's basic laws, to the inherent rights of the Catholic Church and to the rules of civilization itself, which forbids the molesting of peaceful citizens...."

This allocution, characteristically clear and concise, took the French government by surprise. Delcassé, the Minister of Foreign Affairs, described the Pope's verdict as "inadmissible" and acted in a threatening manner: he ordered the French ambassador to the Holy See to "present to the Cardinal Secretary of State the unequivocal protest of the government, which refuses to accept any responsibility for the consequences which might result from the repetition of similar scenes."[15]

Some weeks later the President of the French Republic made an official visit to Rome. He was returning the visit which Victor-Emmanuel III had paid to Paris. There would have been nothing wrong with this visit if it had not taken place in Rome. Ever since the annexing of the Papal States and the Holy City by the Kingdom of Italy, the Popes considered that they had been unjustly deprived of their territory. So coming to Rome to visit the King of Italy was equivalent to honoring the despoiler in the very place where his despoliation was most grievous. It was made worse by the fact that Émile Loubet stayed in Rome without going to the Vatican to pay a visit to the Pope. After Loubet had left, Pius X's Secretary of State, Cardinal Merry del Val, sent a note to Nisard making "the most formal and the most explicit protest" against the "grave offence" committed against the Pope. He reproached the President of the French Republic with having come—and to Rome itself—to honor the King of Italy who, "against all justice," "shackles the liberty and independence" of the Pope.[16]

Initially the French government was content to "reject...both the views expressed in this note and the form in which they are expressed."[17] There were others, however, who would stoke the fire, French politicians and also—a fact little known—certain cardinals of the Curia.

The Pope's protest to the French government was followed by a protest in similar terms to all governments, communicated through the apostolic nuncios. It contained a passage which is not found in the note given to the French government: "If, in spite of all this, the pontifical nuncio has remained in Paris, this is solely for reasons that are very grave, reasons—in all respects—of a special order and nature."

---

[15] Dispatch of Delcassé to Nisard, March 20, 1904, AMAE, Saint-Siège, *Relations avec la France,* NS 22, f.52.

[16] Note of Cardinal Merry del Val to Nisard, April 28, 1904, *La Séparation,* p.141.

[17] Note of Nisard, French Ambassador to the Holy See, to Cardinal Merry del Val, May 6, 1904, *ibid.,* p.143.

The text of this protest to foreign governments reached Jean Jaurès, a Socialist deputy, the director of the newspaper *L'Humanité*.[18] On May 17 Jaurès published the document in his newspaper, accompanied by an article in which he denounced an "intolerable provocation" on the part of Pius X and urged the severance of diplomatic relations between France and the Holy See, so that France, as he wrote, might be "freed from all political meddling on the part of the Church." He was listened to; or rather, the French government seized upon this pretext to accelerate the process of breaking diplomatic relations and breaking the concordat.

The severing of diplomatic relations

On May 20, in a telegraphic dispatch to Nisard, Delcassé demanded that the Holy See explain itself with regard to the note of protest sent to governments. "If its authenticity is acknowledged," the Minister of Foreign Affairs wrote, "or if they try to avoid a reply," the French ambassador to the Holy See would be recalled to Paris, which could be the prelude to a severance of diplomatic relations.[19] Nisard went to the Vatican, was received by Cardinal Merry del Val, and set forth the demands of the French government. Not having been given the required explanations, he left Rome and an embassy counsellor, Navenne, remained behind to look after day-to-day affairs.[20] The next day Msgr. Lorenzelli, apostolic nuncio in Paris, was recalled to Rome, but his departure was not yet final.

Diplomatic relations, as we see, were close to breaking point, and a certain section of the press accused the Holy See of having offended the French government by refusing to provide explanations. In fact, the following May 24, *L'Osservatore Romano* would give an "authorized" explanation shedding light on the affair: "the Cardinal Secretary of State, far from refusing to reply, wished to have the questions in writing and promised to give a written reply within an hour." Nisard had rejected this.

There is another factor which must be taken into consideration if we are to assess the circumstances leading to a rupture of diplomatic relations between France and the Holy See. There was, of course, as we have seen the French government's anticlericalism, which used different pretexts in order to "emancipate" itself from clerical tutelage. Less well known is the

---

[18] How did he get to know of this text? A Roman informer told the French Ministry of Foreign Affairs that the text had been communicated to Jaurès by the Prince of Monaco (AMAE, Saint-Siège, *Relations avec la France,* NS 22, f.143 and 156). Then he asserted that it was the Prince's secretary, Floquet, who was responsible for what followed (*ibid.*, f.189).

[19] Dispatch of Delcassé to Nisard, May 20, 1904, *ibid.,* NS 22, f.149.

[20] Later the chargé d'affaires would be Robert de Courcel.

hostility of certain cardinals to the policies of Merry del Val and Pius X. These cardinals, by voicing their criticism, would give comfort—perhaps without wishing to—to the French government in its hostility towards Pius X.

On May 25 the French ambassador in Rome, Camille Barrère,[21] sent a telegram marked "very confidential" to the Minister of Foreign Affairs in Paris. In it he reported on the dissensions at the heart of the Vatican with regard to its relations with France: "Among the most influential members of the Sacred College," said the ambassador, "there is absolute condemnation of Cardinal Merry del Val's imprudence and diplomatic inexperience. They are saying that relations with France can only be restored if he is withdrawn from his post. A great effort will be made, therefore, to unseat him despite Pius X's infatuation with his Secretary of State...Cardinal Ferrata would be his successor as Secretary of State."[22]

It must be observed that these anonymous criticisms reported by Barrère were particularly unjust, since even the terms used in the protest of April 28, 1904, had been taken word for word from a note of protest written by Cardinal Rampolla in 1903 when there was a rumor at the Vatican that Loubet might possibly visit Rome.[23] Cardinal Rampolla could not have been accused of being "imprudent" and of "diplomatic inexperience."

Even more significant was the fact that, in a long dispatch elaborating on the aforementioned telegram, Barrère, still quoting Vatican sources, draws a disastrous portrait of Pius X. This time he gives his informer's name: Cardinal Agliardi. Barrère writes to his minister in the wake of what Agliardi told him in confidence:

> The extravagant contradictions presented by current pontifical policies reveal that the successor of Leo XIII is in a strange state of mind that must be of concern both to his friends and his enemies. The memorable events of recent days do not seem to trouble him in the least; his indifference in this regard verges on sheer insensitivity....Lacking culture, ignorant of what is necessary for the Church's prestige and character, he takes no thought for the effects his words and acts may have. He does not know

---

[21] Until 1904 France maintained two ambassadors in Rome: one at the Holy See, and the other to the Italian government (only the latter could be called "French Ambassador to Rome").

[22] Telegraphic dispatch from Barrère to Delcassé, May 25, 1904, AMAE, Saint-Siège, *Relations avec la France,* NS 22, f.183.

[23] Note of Cardinal Rampolla to Nisard, June 1, 1903, *La Séparation,* p.137. Cf. also Rampolla's dispatch to Msgr. Lorenzelli, dated June 8, 1903, which again uses the central phrase, "a grave and manifest offence to the supreme Head of the religion which he professes...," *ibid.,* pp.138-139.

either what a diplomatic note is, nor what is the significance of an interruption of relations with a great power....[24]

The picture of a pope indifferent to, or even scornful of, diplomatic relations with France, did nothing to improve the said relations. This picture, touted by a cardinal who had dreamed of becoming Secretary of State, is false. Pius X did not have the fateful diplomatic note drawn up until after he had asked the advice of the cardinals of the Curia, assembled in an extraordinary session; and, as we have seen, he took as his starting-point the notes recorded on the same subject under the preceding pontificate.

Relations had greatly deteriorated between France and the Holy See. In a few months they would be severed, by action on the part of France. The final pretext was provided by the cases of Geay and Le Nordez. Msgr. Geay was Bishop of Laval, and Msgr. Le Nordez was Bishop of Dijon. For several years, for different reasons, they had both been in grave difficulties in their respective dioceses.

There were complaints that Msgr. Geay had no interest in the affairs of his diocese; there were also rumors accusing him of having blameworthy relations with the superior of the Carmelite nuns in Laval. What is true, at least, is that for some years he had failed to pay the traditional *ad limina* visits which every bishop should make at regular intervals. He had also forbidden the Jesuits to preach and hear confessions. The Congregation of the Holy Office, under the pontificate of Leo XIII, had already had to examine accusations against him.[25] On February 2, 1900, in order to avoid canonical process, he had agreed to resign. Subsequently, however, he had made his resignation dependent on being transferred to another French diocese.

The accusations against Msgr. Le Nordez were of more recent date. The complaint against this republican bishop was that in 1902 he had been one of only three French bishops who refused to sign the petition of the French episcopate urging retention of the schools run by religious congregations. It was also said that he was too fond of receptions, a good table and good wine (he was the object of a jingle which went: "He would rather drink Chambertin than sing Gregorian"). Most important of all, he was accused of being a Freemason.[26] The accusation had been made public by the newspaper *Le Gaulois* (February 9, 1904), repeating confidences com-

---

[24] Dispatch of Barrère to Delcassé, May 31, 1904, AMAE, Saint-Siège, *Relations avec la France,* NS 22, f.218-223.

[25] A lengthy note from Cardinal Merry del Val to Msgr. Lorenzelli, June 10, 1904, retraces the origin of the affair. It does so without making accusations, but speaks of "intimate and personal reasons which tended to compromise the bishop's dignity and honor," *La Séparation,* pp.146-148.

municated by the Archpriest of Dijon cathedral. As soon as the rumor was divulged it started serious antagonisms at the heart of the diocese. The most spectacular protest was the refusal of 58 seminarians to receive holy orders from the hands of Msgr. Le Nordez.

On April 24, 1904, Cardinal Merry del Val, Secretary of State, summoned Msgr. Le Nordez to Rome "as quickly as possible" and on May 17, Msgr. Geay was summoned also, this time by Cardinal Vannutelli, secretary of the Congregation of the Holy Office. The two bishops employed delaying tactics and got the French government to take an interest in their cases. This was the best means of politicizing the affair, and it succeeded. The Combes government was given a further reason to denounce the interference of the Holy See, contrary to the prerogatives conceded to the government in such matters. There was a plentiful exchange of notes between France and the Holy See.[27] Then, since the Pope persisted—as it was his right and duty to do—in his wish to interview the two accused bishops, the Combes government decided to break off diplomatic relations. On July 29 Delcassé sent a message to Courcel, the chargé d'affaires at the Holy See: it was the text of the verbal note designed to effect, definitively and officially, the break between France and the Holy See. It went on: "On receipt of this note, you will understand that we consider the mission of the apostolic nuncio to be ended."[28] On the 30th, Robert de Courcel presented himself at the Vatican and gave Cardinal Merry del Val the note he had received from Delcassé: "Having on several occasions indicated the grave harm inflicted on the rights of the State as expressed in the concordat by the Holy See's action in seeking to exert pressure directly on French bishops...the Government of the Republic has decided to put an end to the official relations which, by the evident will of the Holy See, no longer have any object." The same day Msgr. Lorenzelli, once and for all, left the apostolic nunciature in Paris. In Rome, the French embassy to the Holy See was definitively closed. However, Msgr. Guthlin, who had been this embassy's consultor on canon law for nearly ten years, continued to inform the French authorities very regularly. The archives of the Ministry of Foreign Affairs contain very many short notes written by him at the

---

[26] André Billy made a novel, *Introïbo* (Flammarion, 1939) out of this affair. In it the Bishop of Dijon was given the name of Msgr. Duberville. On the affair (and the bishop's denials) cf. Pierre Leberruyer, *Monseigneur Le Nordez dans un roman et devant l'histoire* (Coutances: Éditions Arnaud-Bellée, 1973), and Joseph Toussaint, *Monseigneur Le Nordez et la rupture des relations diplomatiques entre la France et l'Église* (Coutances: Éditions OCEP, 1976), pp.256ff.; hereafter, *Monseigneur Le Nordez.*

[27] Twenty documents relating to this episode, which led to the severing of diplomatic relations, are reproduced in *La Séparation,* pp.144-170.

[28] Telegraphic dispatch from Delcassé to Courcel, July 29, 1904, AMAE, Saint-Siège, *Relations avec la France,* NS 23, f.159.

request of the French ambassador in Rome, Barrère, or of the Quai d'Orsay. The apostolic nunciature in Paris no longer existed at an official diplomatic level, but a secretary, Msgr. Montagnini, continued to live there and kept up contacts with French political and religious life. He sent in regular reports to the Secretariat of State.

The two bishops who were the ultimate cause of the breakdown in diplomatic relations left their sees. Msgr. Le Nordez finally presented himself in Rome and resigned on September 4.[29] Then he retired to Huberville, his manor in Normandy, while Msgr. Geay retired to Cannes. It should be noted that Pius X, uncertain as to whether the French State would continue to pay them a salary, granted them an annual pension: 8,000 francs for Msgr. Geay, 9,000 francs for Msgr. Le Nordez.[30] In the end the French State gave each of them a life-annuity (of less than half the value of the pension granted by Rome), with the result that the bishops had two sources of income for the rest of their lives.

Separation of Church and State

After the severance of diplomatic relations between France and the Holy See, Pius X's first official act towards France was a magnificent address to pilgrims in which he extolled the greatness of Christian France, "the Church's eldest daughter."[31] This speech contained various allusions to the current difficulties, but above all it was an appeal to fidelity:

> Descendants of those sons of France who were faithful to the Church, devoted unreservedly to the Chair of Peter, always ready to defend and propagate what is true and what is good: do not allow yourselves to be heirs of lesser quality! In all the difficulties and sacrifices which you have to face, particularly today, be always generous; in the certainty that, in this way, you are working not only towards your own happiness, but also towards the prosperity of your country.

---

[29] It is said that Pius X, receiving Msgr. Le Nordez in audience, showed him documents indicating that he was a Freemason. Msgr. Le Nordez is said to have rejected them as crude forgeries. Finally the Secretary of State made public a letter to Msgr. Le Nordez which says: "The Holy Father, anxious to safeguard the good name of your episcopal character and to put an end to all the accusations which might find an echo in the press and elsewhere, has charged me to declare, in his name and in the most explicit way, that the Holy See has neither formulated nor pronounced any judgment against Your Lordship and that, consequently, Your Lordship is leaving his post because he judges it necessary because of the public events of these recent times." The letter is published in Toussaint, *Monseigneur Le Nordez*, p.293.

[30] ASV, Segretaria di Stato, Anno 1905, rubrica 248, f.202-206.

[31] Allocution of September 9, 1904, to the 14th Workers' Pilgrimage ("*Pelerinage de la France du travail*") directed by Léon Harmel, *Documents pontificaux*, vol.I, pp.198-199.

Pius X drew a picture of France's prosperity while she was secure under the wing of the Church:

> Indeed, history proves it. The times when France attained the splendor of glory, when she spread over her children the advantages of a most genuine prosperity united to the pure joys of peace, were those when she listened to the health-giving counsels of the Church. Under the shade of this banner, which brought her victory, she merited the glorious title of the Church's Eldest Daughter, and she extended the benefits of her influence across the whole world. The Church, full of love for her Daughter, was always happy to applaud this glory. Very dear sons, must We repeat that the Holy See has this great love for your country? It continues to live in Our heart, in spite of all. And if necessary We shall accept further suffering in order to assure the good and the greatness of your country.
>
> Instructed by the lessons of the past, enlightened as to the dangers of the present, drawing your inspiration most of all from the precepts of your faith, keep yourselves closely attached to the Church and the Apostolic See, sure that in this way you will attain true prosperity. It is by these means that you will cause Heaven's blessings to descend upon you and your country and hasten the return of days that are less full of sadness and turmoil.

A few weeks later, addressing another group of French pilgrims led by the vicar-general of Paris, Pius X took up the recurring theme of *God loves France* and said that he was certain that France would recover:

> A nation with such sons cannot perish....When you return to France, take with you not only the hope, but the certitude, that Our Lord Jesus Christ, in the infinite kindness of his merciful Heart, will save your country by keeping her always united to the Church; and that through the mediation of the Immaculate Virgin, He will cause the dawn of better days to arise....[32]

For the moment, however, France was preparing for a further step towards the laicization of society. Ferdinand Buisson, a Freemason of Protestant origins and Radical-Socialist deputy for the Seine, was one of the figureheads of the "lay faith" movement; he had said that he wished to "detach the nation, families and individuals from the Church." Three months after the breakdown in diplomatic relations between France and the Holy See, the Radical party, assembled at a congress in Toulouse, unanimously adopted Buisson's report urging the separation of Church and State. This proposal was relayed by the leftist press, by anti-clerical journals (such as *la Raison,* a weekly created by an unfrocked priest, Victor Charbonnel) and by the National Association of Freethinkers, *Libre Pen-*

---

[32] Allocution to the French Pilgrimage to Rome, September 23, 1904, *Documents pontificaux,* vol.I, pp.204-205.

sée, which had been set up three years earlier and had spread even into the villages. What is more, a certain section of the clergy and of Catholics were not actually against the separation; they saw it as an historic opportunity for the Church to recover complete liberty and disengage herself totally from the State's tutelage. In January 1905, in a report sent to the Secretariat of State, Msgr. Montagnini observed that several important parish priests of Paris were favorably inclined towards separation, and were not afraid of it.[33]

The French episcopate was also divided on the issue. Initially the only bishops to say anything were those who were against separation. One of the first was Msgr. Dubois, Bishop of Verdun. He published a pastoral letter on the subject at the very moment when the draft law went before parliament.[34] He saw the projected law as "the supreme assault of impiety against the Church of France." He recalled the "benefits of the Concordat" and demanded that it "be maintained." While "this pact between Church and State is not ideal," it had permitted France's religious rebirth in the 19th century. The pastoral letter, sent to the Secretariat of State, was communicated to the Pope, who was pleased with it and sent his blessing to the Bishop of Verdun.[35] Four years later Pius X would appoint Msgr. Dubois as Archbishop of Bourges. He would be created cardinal and appointed Archbishop of Paris under the following pontificate.

Émile Combes was no longer in charge of the government when the draft law could be presented to parliament. He had been replaced as President of the Council by Maurice Rouvier, also a Freemason. It was the Socialist, Aristide Briand, who presented the draft law to the Chamber of Deputies in March 1905. This draft had undergone lengthy preparation in preceding months at the hands of Léon Parsons, Louis Méjan (a high civil servant and a Protestant, and a director of cults at the ministry) and Paul Grunebaum-Ballin (a Jew and a member of the Council of State). There were long debates and vigorous exchanges in the Assembly. Fr. Lemire and the Catholic right opposed the partisans of separation. In the ranks of the

---

[33] Report of Msgr. Montagnini to Cardinal Merry del Val, January 8, 1905, ASV, Segretaria di Stato, Anno 1905, rubrica 248, fasc.2, f.71-72.

[34] Msgr. Louis Dubois, *Concordat et Séparation* (Verdun: Imprimerie Louis Laurent, 1905).

[35] ASV, Segretaria di Stato, Anno 1905, rubrica 248, fasc.2, f.2-4. Some days after the Bishop of Verdun, the five French Cardinals (Richard, Perraud, Coullié, Lecot and Labouré) intervened, not publicly, in a letter addressed to the President of the Republic dated March 28, 1905. They also asked for the concordat to be maintained and thought that "the plan of Separation would necessarily lead to religious persecution, and does not express the will of the nation" (a copy of the letter was sent to the Secretariat of State, ASV, Segretaria di Stato, Anno 1905, rubrica 248, fasc.2, f.27-28).

left, while there was agreement on the necessity of separation, there was a difference of opinion about the way it should be implemented.

Finally, on July 3, 1905, the draft law was adopted in the Chamber of Deputies by 341 votes to 233. On December 9 the Senate adopted it by 179 votes to 103. On December 11 the law of separation was promulgated in the *Journal officiel.* It proclaimed the freedom of conscience and of worship and affirmed that the Republic "does not recognize" or "remunerate any cult" (Art.2). It stipulated, furthermore, that an inventory of ecclesiastical goods (churches, presbyteries, *etc.*) should be drawn up and should become State property. This property would be granted to locally elected "cult associations."

Vehementer Nos

Among Catholics there were very different reactions to the law separating Church and State. The day after the vote one of the great Catholic figures of those times, Albert de Mun, who had in the meantime gone over to the Republic, published a lengthy article condemning the separation in the first issue of the journal *La Croix*: "Yesterday's event," he wrote, "is the gravest to have taken place in our history for an entire century. Since yesterday, while there is still a Catholic France and Catholic Frenchmen, the French nation has been erased, by its representatives, from the number of Catholic States. *Consummatum est!* The sentence pronounced by the Masonic Sanhedrin has been carried out. Christ has ceased to be officially recognized in France."

The five French cardinals ruling dioceses (Richard, Archbishop of Paris; Coullié, Archbishop of Lyon; Lecot, Archbishop of Bordeaux; Labouré, Archbishop of Rennes; and Perraud, Archbishop of Autun), however, adopted a more pragmatic position. At a meeting in the offices of the Archbishop of Paris, they decided that the law could be accepted. In Rome, Cardinal Mathieu, the only Frenchman in the Curia—he was a member of the Congregation of Extraordinary Ecclesiastical Affairs—also shared the view that an accommodation was possible.[36]

Once Pius X had spoken and acted, however, things changed. He did this over a period of time, which shows that there was no over-hasty action where he was concerned. First there was a doctrinal condemnation of the principle itself (an initial Encyclical against separation), then a high-profile religious response to the law (the consecration of 14 bishops), and only then were the law's practical consequences calmly examined (should the "cult associations" be accepted or not?).

---

[36] Edmond Renard, *Le cardinal Mathieu, 1839-1908* (Paris: J.de.Gigord, 1925), pp.452ff.

The doctrinal refutation of the law of separation arrived on February 11, 1906, in the encyclical *Vehementer Nos,* addressed "to the archbishops, bishops, clergy and all the French people."[37] Pius X's view was that the law of separation "had violently sundered the centuries-old links by which your nation had been united to the Apostolic See" and that it was "equally dire a threat to civil society as it was to religion." Its fundamental basis was erroneous: "The idea that the State should be separated from the Church is an absolutely false thesis and a very pernicious error." The error is four-fold:

> —"First of all, since it is based on the principle that the State should not acknowledge any religious cult, it is gravely offensive to God." For, as the Pope writes, we owe to God "not only private worship, but a public and social cult in order to honor him."

> —"This thesis is a very clear denial of the supernatural order." The State's action should not be limited to public prosperity: it should not hold aloof from eternal beatitude: "the civil power must not hinder the attainment [of eternal beatitude], but rather should help us to attain it."

> —"This thesis, furthermore, overthrows the order most wisely established in the world by God, which calls for a harmony and agreement between the two societies."

> —"Finally this thesis inflicts grave harm on civil society itself, for the latter cannot long prosper or exist once religion is denied its place; religion is the supreme rule and the sovereign mistress where man's rights and duties are concerned."

In its provisions, too (in particular the setting-up of "cult associations"), the law of separation is "contrary to the divine constitution of the Church, her essential rights and her liberty."

A few days later this doctrinal condemnation was followed by a religious act which made a great impression, namely, the consecration of 14 French bishops by the Pope himself. In recent years, due to a lack of agreement with the French government, many episcopal sees had remained without a head. Pius X decided to supply all the vacant sees at once. Five bishops were transferred from one see to another and 14 priests (vicars-general, superiors of seminaries, parish priests) were elevated to the episcopate. These appointments were not made in a hurry, but were kept secret until the last moment. Following a suggestion of Cardinal Mathieu and beginning in October 1905, a new procedure in designating future bishops had been implemented: the bishops of France would be consulted by region ("generally speaking, three ecclesiastical provinces"), and then the

---

[37] *Documents pontificaux,* vol.I, pp.333-342.

names suggested would be submitted to the Pope, who would take the decision himself.[38]

The Encyclical we have referred to was dated February 11, 1906 (although it was not published until six days later). That day and the following day the Secretariat of State summoned the newly promoted priests to Rome.[39] The first men arrived on February 16. As yet, if we are to believe Msgr. Guthlin, it was not known in the Vatican that there would be a Consistory collocating the new bishops and that Pius X had decided to consecrate them himself. Only on February 19 did the Pope announce the convocation of a Consistory for the 21st. As Msgr. Guthlin noted on February 19, "In the annals of the Curia it is unheard-of to organize a collocatory Consistory under such conditions. At such a time as this everyone working here is highly agitated, particularly as the material formalities required are considerable and the carnival holidays have started."

As the newly promoted priests arrived in Rome, the Pope received them in private audience. On February 21 the Consistory took place at which they were officially appointed to their bishopric and then, that same day, they were received in audience together, in the Throne-room. In an address, Pius X recalled the reasons for his opposition to the law of separation, and he also had some memorable words of hope for France:

> The arrogance and iniquity of evil men will never be able to efface the merits won by France, down the centuries, for the sake of the Church. Our hope is that these merits will grow once more when peaceful times return. For this reason We exhort Our cherished Sons not to be discouraged, nor to be cast down by the trials and difficulties of these times. Let them be watchful, firm in faith; let them act like men, recalling the motto of their ancestors: *Christus amat Francos.* The Holy See will always be near them, and the Church's Eldest Daughter will never look in vain for her care and charity.[40]

After this address Pius X received the bishops in his office and gave each of them a pectoral cross, saying: "I summon you, not to joy, but to the cross." The episcopal consecrations took place on February 26 in St. Peter's Basilica. The ceremony was talked about everywhere, because up until then French bishops had generally been consecrated in their own country by two or three bishops. It was the first time for a long time that a pope

---

[38] Renard, *Le cardinal Mathieu,* p.455.
[39] The circumstances of these French consecrations in Rome are narrated by Msgr. Guthlin in two notes addressed to Rouvier, February 19 and 27, 1906. AMAE, Saint-Siège, *Relations avec la France, Évêques français (1897-1907),* NS 27, f.426 and 433-434.
[40] Allocution *Gravissimum Apostolici,* February 21, 1906, *Documents pontificaux,* vol.I, p.347.

himself had consecrated such an important group of foreign bishops in Rome. More than 3,000 French people attended the ceremony. The next day, the French ambassador wrote that it had been a "historic event," but at the same time he reassured his government that "they are religious bishops and not fighting bishops."[41]

The "cult associations"

The law of separation had been condemned; nonetheless, however, the question of the "cult associations" was not resolved. According to the law, these associations, with the task of managing the ecclesiastical goods at the local level, would be elected by the local community. The principle, in itself, had been condemned by Pius X in the encyclical already quoted. These "cult associations," independent of the ecclesiastical hierarchy, could equally well be made up of a majority of laymen hostile to the clergy and the bishop. On the other hand, if the Church refused to accept them, she would risk losing "her fortune, estimated at 331 million francs, her episcopal palaces, great seminaries, presbyteries and even the churches themselves, which the State would have the right to put to some other use."[42] Wasn't there a way of accepting *de facto* these "cult associations" and using them for the Church's benefit?

Contrary to what certain historians have said, Pius X did not initially reject them. He hesitated, waiting to see how the law promulgated in December would be applied. In February 1906, according to Msgr. Guthlin, who was given this information by some of the newly-appointed bishops, when Pius X received the latter in private audience, he was still uncertain what to do: he said that he rejected "all violence, and added that he would not finalize his resolutions on the subject of the cult associations until he knew what effect the administration's regulations would have."[43]

In Rome the cardinals were also asking him about the attitude they should adopt. Cardinal Mathieu, who favored some conciliation between the Holy See and the French government, tried to influence the future bishops: "In Saint-Sulpice, the day before their consecration, he gathered together the 14 bishops newly chosen by Pius X, and strongly urged them to speak to the Holy Father in favor of accepting a mitigated form of the 'cult associations,' in which the French law would be reconciled with canon law."[44] Another cardinal, Arcoverde, Archbishop of Rio de Janeiro, who

---

[41] Dispatch from Barrère to Rouvier, February 28, 1906, AMAE, Saint-Siège, *Relations avec la France, Évêques français (1897-1907)*, NS 27, f.437-439.

[42] Adrien Dansette, *Histoire religieuse de la France contemporaine* (Paris: Flammarion, 1951), vol.II, pp.350-351.

[43] Note from Guthlin to Rouvier, February 19, 1906, AMAE, Saint-Siège, *Relations avec la France, Évêques français (1897-1907)*, NS 27, f.426.

was spending three months in Rome on the occasion of his elevation to the cardinalate, spoke in irenic terms of the separation of Church and State which had been in force in his country since 1889: "During his stay," we read in a note from the French Ambassador,

> this dignitary of the South American Church has frequently been questioned, in Curial circles, about the way in which the regime of separation of Church and State functions in Brazil.
>
> Cardinal Arcoverde d'Albuquerque had no difficulty in acknowledging that, whatever the doctrinal reservations might be regarding the principle of separation itself, it could not be denied that Catholics were satisfied with the way in which they had experienced its operation for more than 15 years...: In Brazil, separation had never led to persecution, as seems to be feared elsewhere.[45]

In France, too, one party of Catholics inclined to accept the law and the "cult associations." On March 26, 1906, *Le Figaro* published a manifesto along these lines, signed by 23 Catholic writers (including Denys Cochin, Henri Lorin, Georges Goyau). This manifesto made quite a stir and showed the importance of the "submissionist" tendency. Since a certain number of the signatories were members of the Académie Française, they were referred to as *green cardinals*, opposing the Pope. In fact, this document had not been intended for publication; it had been addressed to each of the bishops of France, and it reached the newspaper through someone's indiscretion.

Before taking a decision on the "cult associations," Pius X wanted to have the question studied by legal experts and wanted to know the views of the bishops of France. In the first months of 1906, under the presidency of Cardinal Richard, Archbishop of Paris, a commission of civil jurists and another of canonists had a number of meetings at the Archbishop's headquarters "to see whether it would be possible to establish cult associations which were both canonical and legal."[46]

The situation was serious. Beginning in January, inventories of churches were being drawn up. They had given rise to incidents between the faithful, who were trying to prevent revenue agents entering their churches, and the forces of order who were trying to ensure that the law

---

[44] Renard, *Le cardinal Mathieu*, pp.454-455.

[45] Note from the French Ambassador to Rome to the Ministry of Foreign Affairs, March 18, 1906, AMAE, Saint-Siège, *Relations avec les États d'Amérique, II (1901-1907)*, NS 8, f.218-220.

[46] Msgr. Odelin, *Le cardinal Richard, 1819-1908. Souvenirs* (Paris: J. de Gigord, 1922), p.133. Renard, *Le cardinal Mathieu*, p.457, observes that "among the Commission's legal consultors there were some parliamentarians who brought the question into the political arena with the intention of harassing the government and causing it to fall."

would be upheld. The faithful saw these inventories as the prelude to seizure, and feared that sacrileges would be committed.

A plenary assembly of the French episcopate took place in Paris on May 30 and 31 and June 1. Seventy-four bishops and archbishops were present. A letter was read out from Pius X, inviting them to speak according to their consciences and under the gaze of God, and also putting them on their guard against the French government: "Remember the loyal attempts made by the religious congregations after the law of 1901," the Pope wrote. "This law was supposed to permit them the benefit of civil status. In fact they were despoiled and scattered. Furthermore, can one speak of loyalty, can one even imagine a reciprocal loyalty with a government which, as we see, only tries to take by surprise those whom, as yet, it does not wish to attack by violence."[47] The question to be discussed at this meeting had been clearly set out by Cardinal Merry del Val: was it possible to constitute "cult associations" which would safeguard the Church's essential rights, and how could the Church draw practical advantages from them?

The assembly studied the question twice. On the first occasion, after discussions, it pronounced against the cult associations as the December law envisaged them, by a majority of 72 votes to 2. On the second occasion some alternative solution was sought for. After a series of ballots it was decided by 59 votes to 15 to sanction the establishment of what were called *Fabrician* associations, under the control of the hierarchy and given canonical status, which would make it possible to retain ecclesiastical property.

The final decision was the Pope's. The work and results of the plenary assembly of the French episcopate were examined, along with other things, by the Congregation of Extraordinary Ecclesiastical Affairs. On July 12, assembled for the definitive *ponenza*, the cardinal members of this Congregation were divided on the attitude to be adopted and the decision to be taken. Cardinals Rampolla, Mathieu, Ferrata and Di Pietro were in favor of accepting, but five others were hostile to it (Merry del Val, Vivès y Tuto, Vincenzo Vannutelli, Serafino Vannutelli and Steinhüber).

Pius X waited for a further period of time before making his definitive position known. To Cardinal Ferrata, who expressed his anxiety to see the liberty of worship threatened by a refusal to accept the "cult associations," the Pope replied by pointing to a crucifix: "I look at the Cross." Cardinal Ferrata was impressed by this reply and declared: "Most Holy Father, we have given our point of view, but if Your Holiness believes that He must

---

[47] Letter of March 4, 1906, quoted in Renard, *Le cardinal Mathieu*, p.460, which gives a detailed account of the meeting, pp.457-464.

act differently, I will submit to Him in all humility, for the Pope has the assistance of special light."[48]

In saying, "I look at the Cross"—something he was apt to say in such circumstances, as attested by the depositions made at his beatification process—Pius X was unveiling the veritable heart of his thinking: he wanted to judge this question of the "cult associations" principally from a supernatural point of view. Accepting them might perhaps bring some material benefit for the faithful and clergy, provided that they could be accommodated to canon law, but would not such a course bring spiritual danger? The government would be able to rejoice over this concession and increase the pressure on the Church, making it all the easier to stifle her.

So Pius X listened to the views of both sides. But he also prayed a great deal for this special intention, and urged others to pray. He discreetly ordered a triduum of prayers to be made in the convents of Rome. Then, on August 10, 1906, in a short encyclical addressed to the archbishops and bishops of France, he announced that he was against the "cult associations."[49] He also forbade any "attempt to set up...any other kind of association in both civil and canon law...unless it has been ascertained, in a sure and legal manner, that the Church's divine constitution, the immutable rights of the Roman Pontiff and the bishops, as well as their authority over the goods necessary to the Church, and particularly over the sacred buildings, are irrevocably and fully secure in the aforesaid associations."

Pius X was well aware that his rejection of the "cult associations" would result in expulsions, confiscations and a more precarious existence for the Church. He did not look forward to it, but we can imagine that he saw it as a salutary trial for the Church, an opportunity for her to detach herself further from material goods. To someone who asked him how the Archbishop of Paris could exercise his office without a church, a house and an income, the Pope replied:

—"In that case I could give the office to a Franciscan who is bound by his Rule to live on alms and to exercise absolute poverty."[50]

Indeed, there were expulsions. In December 1906 the buildings of the apostolic nunciature were requisitioned and Msgr. Montagnini was ordered to leave French territory. A few days later Cardinal Richard, aged 87,

---

[48] Cardinal Ferrata, "Mémoires inédits," cited by Dal-Gal, *Pius X*, p.173.

[49] Encyclical *Gravissimo Officio*, August 10, 1906, *Documents pontificaux*, vol.1, pp.375-377.

[50] This story, among others, is reported by the Italian politician Vittorio-Emmanuele Orlando, *I miei rapporti di Governo con la Santa Sede* (Milan: 1944), pp.11-12. Orlando regarded Pius X's position as just and right: "Nothing was more noble than the position adopted by the Pope in the struggle with the French government....His decision was magnificent in its apostolic spirit, and, at the same time, it rendered the greatest possible service to the Papacy's political interest...."

was expelled from the quarters of the Archbishop of Paris and had to take refuge in the house of the deputy, Denys Cochin.

At the beginning of 1907, after various new legal solutions had been suggested to him, or had actually been attempted, Pius X, in a third encyclical, solemnly condemned the "law of despoliation, the law of confiscation."[51] The following year he expressed his disapproval of a flawed solution invented by Fr. Lemire, which had been voted in by the Chamber of Deputies: this was the establishment of so-called "mutual societies," officially approved to collect and manage Mass foundations and church pension funds. According to Pius X these mutual societies were dangerous because they were "explicitly lacking in all ecclesiastical character" and because the legislator "forbids all legal intervention on the part of the episcopate."[52]

The parish priests of France, who were obliged henceforth to be "occupiers without title" (as Aristide Briand put it) of their church and presbytery, passed this test in dignity and in submission to the Pope. There was no "Gallican" or "republican" schism, as some had feared. On the contrary, it can be said that the law of separation of Church and State had the effect of attaching the clergy of France more closely to the Holy See and of accentuating an ultramontane tendency that had a long pedigree.

In 1909 the solemn events associated with the beatification of Joan of Arc helped to strengthen this bond between Rome and France.

From Joan of Arc to Maurras

It would be wrong to think that the beatification of Joan of Arc was some kind of religious response to the policies of the French government. The procedure leading to beatification had been begun long before the crisis arose between the French Republic and the Holy See.[53] A diocesan tribunal with the task of conducting a preliminary inquiry into Joan of Arc's reputation for sanctity had been constituted in 1874. The result of its labors had been regarded in Rome as too insubstantial, and two further preliminary inquiries were needed before Leo XIII finally signed the decree introducing the cause in 1894. The canonical process to establish the heroic virtues of Joan of Arc was then set in train. The evidence was examined over three sessions of the Congregation of Rites, and on January 6, 1904, Pius X was finally able to proclaim the heroic virtues of the Maid of

---

[51] Encyclical *Une fois encore*, January 6, 1907, *Documents pontificaux*, vol.I, pp.393-397.
[52] Letter *Le Moment*, May 17, 1908, *Documents pontificaux*, vol.I, pp.518-519.
[53] On the history of this procedure, cf. Yves Chiron, *Enquête sur les canonizations* (Paris: Perrin, 1998), pp.250-255.

Orleans. Now she had the right to be called *venerable,* but as yet she could not be the object of a public cult.

For this to happen, it was necessary that the cures obtained through her intercession were acknowledged to be miraculous. Of the many healings attributed to her, three were substantiated (they took place in 1891, 1893 and 1900 respectively). Their miraculous nature was recognized in 1908, and in 1909 Pius X proceeded to the solemn beatification. She was not canonized until 1920.

On April 18, 1909, in the presence of 30,000 French pilgrims led by 70 bishops, the Pope declared the heroine from Lorraine to be "Blessed." A gesture of Pius X made a great impression: he bent to kiss a French flag that was held out to him. In the Bull of beatification, however, there was no political allusion to France. The Pope praised Joan of Arc for showing mercy; for never shedding blood (even if she "spread terror among the enemy troops"); for being constant in courage and in faith, even at the stake; and for being humble and preserving her purity "in the midst of the carnage and licence of the camps."[54]

On April 20 the Pope received in his private library all the French bishops present in Rome. This time he contrasted the "storm raised by hell" in France with the valiant "struggles for religion and the motherland."[55] He also summoned Catholics to "unite": "Discord among Christians is the triumph of demons."

This concern for the "unity" of Catholics and of the Church's defenders goes some way towards explaining the protection he granted to Charles Maurras, the head of *l'Action Française.* Without going into the whole history of this "non-condemnation," we shall briefly mention those episodes which directly concern Pius X.[56]

Charles Maurras, head of *l'Action Française,* which had acquired a daily newspaper in 1908 and was having a growing influence, was not a practising Catholic. Some of his youthful works, notably *Le Chemin de Paradis* and *Anthinéa,* contained pages pouring scorn on Christianity. But in his later books and articles he had not only taken up the defence of the Church against the persecution offered by the French government, but had praised the "benefits of Catholicism." In the preface to his *Dilemme de Marc Sangnier,* to which we shall return in another chapter, he had called the Church "every man's best friend, the benefactress of the human race."

---

[54] Apostolic Letter *Virginis,* April 11, 1909, *Documents pontificaux,* vol.II, pp.43-46.

[55] Allocution *Significatio Pietatis,* April 20, 1909, *Documents pontificaux,* vol.II, pp.57-59.

[56] Cf. Charles Maurras, *Le Bienheureux Pie X, sauveur de la France* (Paris: Plon, 1953). On the non-condemnation of Maurras in 1914, cf. Yves Chiron, *La Vie de Maurras* (Paris: Éditions Godefroy de Bouillon, 1999; 1st ed. 1991), pp.254-268.

In a number of his writings he had skirmished against all forms of Liberalism and given his support to the Church's struggle against Modernism. Furthermore, once he had left behind the rashness of youth, this unbeliever had never been "contemptuous of the faith" and had never given up his interior metaphysical questioning.

However, there was no shortage of Catholic critics of Maurras and *l'Action Française*. In the first years of the century there was an exchange of polemics—sometimes fiery—between Maurras and Catholic figures, notably Marc Sangnier and Étienne Lamy. From 1908 onwards criticism increased, this time coming from priests and bishops. Fr. Jules Pierre, for example, the author of several works against *l'Action Française*, accused it of being a "school of Nietzscheanism...agnosticism...and naturalism." His first book, according to himself, received the approbation of ten French bishops. Eminent philosophers, Maurice Blondel (under the pen-name of Testis) and Fr. Laberthonnière, criticized more explicitly the philosophy of Maurras. In 1913 Msgr. Chapon, Bishop of Nice, published a pastoral letter against the "skillful Sophists" who "claim to serve the Church while at the same time they attempt to discredit Jesus Christ, his moral teaching and his doctrine." Others tried to have Maurras's works condemned by Rome.

Nonetheless the head of *l'Action Française* enjoyed solid support in the episcopate (in particular, Cardinal Cabrières, Bishop of Montpellier). Both in France and in Rome there were theologians who held him in high regard and came to his defence (for instance, the Jesuits Descoqs and Billot, who was created cardinal in 1911, and the Dominican Pègues).[57] On several occasions the Pope himself showed kindness to Maurras, even going so far as not to promulgate a decree against Maurras drawn up by the Congregation of the Holy Office.

In 1911 Maurras's mother was received by Pius X in private audience. The Pope affirmed: "...I bless his work. It will show results"—although Maurras would not hear about this until later.[58] On July 14, 1913, receiving the musician Camille Bellaigue, a friend of Maurras who was often received at the Vatican, Pius X again said: "Tell him that I share his views in many things. He defends authority, hierarchy and order. He will convert. I firmly hope that he will. But we can do nothing about it; no one can, nor can I. We can only pray. I pray for him very often."

When it looked as though several books by Maurras would be put on the Index, several French theologians and bishops intervened with Pius X

[57] Cf. André Laudouze, *Dominicains français et Action française 1899-1940* (Paris: Les Éditions Ouvrières, 1989).
[58] Statement reported by Maurras, *Le Bienheureux Pie X*, p.52.

and Cardinal Merry del Val, in particular Cardinal de Cabrières. They
were successful for, in January 1914, when the Congregation of the Index
decided to put seven works by Maurras on the list of prohibited books, as
well as the review of *l'Action Française,* Pius X reserved to himself the right
to publish the decree "if some new need to do so presents itself." This was
a way of avoiding condemning Maurras. In fact it was not until 1926, under the pontificate of Pius XI, that the 1914 decree was taken up, amplified and published.

Was this a case of non-condemnation, or of a condemnation not made
public? It is certain that, where it was a case of works and a review which
contained pages offensive to the Christian religion, Pius X was bound to
find them reprehensible. No doubt, however, he also took account of
Maurras's spiritual evolution and did not wish to weaken the Church in
France. If Maurras was not a practising Catholic, other leaders of *l'Action
Française* were. This royalist movement attracted many Catholics. All of
them, in the Pope's judgment, had rendered great service to the Church
and the faith.[59]

An unpublished document shows that Pius X had indeed wanted to
save Maurras from a public condemnation—which would have appeared
to be just as much political as religious—and, in addition, he did not desire to upset the French government. Some days after the meeting of the
Congregation of the Index, when it was certain that the prepared decree
would not be published, Cardinal de Cabrières wrote to Cardinal Merry
del Val to express his satisfaction and thanks. "I beg you," he wrote, "to
express my gratitude to the Holy Father for the extreme kindness with
which His Holiness has deigned to treat M. Maurras."

> I make bold to tell your Eminence, with all the loyalty I have within
> me, that his public condemnation—although most justified—would have
> been a real misfortune for the true friends of the Holy See and an immense
> joy for all the adversaries of the person and conduct of Pope Pius X.
>
> M. Maurras has lost the faith through his own fault, certainly, but he
> bitterly regrets this loss. He has promised me never to write anything
> again which might cause sorrow to Catholics. I even think he will write to
> the Holy Father to thank him, and I would not be surprised if he were to
> go to Rome in the spring or at the beginning of the summer to give his
> thanks in person to Your Eminence and his Eminence Cardinal Billot.

[59] Maurras is a "good defender of the Faith," according to Pius X (Bellaigue, *Pie X et
Rome. Notes et souvenirs*, p.310). This statement has been contested by certain
historians. In defence of its authenticity Fr. André Vincent says this: "Maurras
defended the Faith by defending the mind against the subjectivizing of knowledge, by
re-asserting that the intelligence is objective in its act, in its natural submission to
truth" ("Maurras défenseur de la foi. A propos d'un mot de saint Pie X," *Études
maurassiennes,* 5, 1986, p.510).

You will judge, Most Eminent Lord, whether this son who has been a prodigal for so long, but who is profoundly shaken by the Pope's kindness, should hope to be admitted to his feet.[60]

Cardinal Merry del Val replied to Cardinal de Cabrières urging discretion:

As regards an eventual visit to Rome by M. Maurras and the question of him being granted an audience with the Holy Father and your servant, it is my view that, given the present circumstances and the situation of M. Maurras, such a journey would be inopportune and imprudent, and would cause embarrassment to His Holiness and his Secretary of State.[61]

---

[60] Letter of January 21, 1914, ASV, Segretaria di Stato, Anno 1914, rubrica 220, f.121-122.
[61] Letter of February 7, 1914, *ibid.*, f.123.

CHAPTER 8

THE STRUGGLE AGAINST MODERNISM

It is not easy to define Modernism. There is no single, coherent Modernist teaching. In former times the Church was able to define the Catharist heresy or the Lutheran doctrine which she was combating. She could clearly indicate its origins and its developments. With Modernism, it was different. There was no single centre for Modernism: rather, there were several at the same time. While it is possible to trace influences of one person on another and identify certain personalities on the international scene and at meetings, there was no complete program of doctrine that was adhered to by committed followers.[1]

Sometimes it has been said that, most of all, Modernism was a "state of mind." Modernists were fond of saying that Modernism was a "critical method." But in fact the Modernists did have ambitions in the area of doctrine. The principal French representative of Modernism, Alfred Loisy, felt that it was necessary to "adapt the Gospel to the changing condition of humanity," to work for "harmony between dogma and science, reason and

---

[1] Even the work entitled *Il programma dei modernisti,* published in 1911 in response to the Encyclical *Pascendi,* does not contain a complete program, as we shall see. What is more, it was written by only six authors. The bibliography on Modernism is immense. Without citing here all the works to which we shall refer, the premier historical work on Modernism was that of Jean Rivière, *Le Modernisme dans l'Église. Étude d'histoire religieuse contemporaine* (Paris: Letouzey et Ané, 1929); this work is still of great value. The various works by Émile Poulat are indispensable, notably *Histoire, dogme et critique dans la crise moderniste* (Tournai/Paris: Casterman, 1962; 2nd ed. 1979); *Modernistica. Horizons, physionomies, débats* (Paris: Nouvelles Éditions Latines, 1982); *Critique et mystique. Autour de Loisy ou la conscience catholique et l'esprit moderne* (Le Centurion, 1984). The most recent synthesis is that of Maurilio Guasco, *Modernismo. I fatti, le idee, i personaggi* (Cinisello Balsamo: Edizioni San Paolo, 1995). Italian Modernism has been the object of very many studies, notably those of Lorenzo Bedeschi. Bedeschi, the celebrated author of *Il modernismo italiano. Voci e volti* (Cinisello Balsamo: Edizioni San Paolo, 1995), founded (at the University of Urbino) a *Centro Studi per la storia del modernismo.* Since 1972 this research centre has been publishing collections of documents and studies entitled *Fonti e Documenti.* While these publications are voluminous and contain a wealth of material, they are nonetheless contestable in their very severe judgment of Pius X. French Modernism has been the object of a new approach: Pierre Colin, *L'Audace et le soupçon. La crise du modernisme dans le catholicisme français, 1893-1914* (Paris: Desclée de Brouwer, 1997).

faith, the Church and society."[2] This "adaptation" and "harmony" led to fundamental re-appraisals and questionings. To the historian, therefore, Modernism presents itself as a suite of doctrines or ideas that are more or less new, and in more or less open breach with the Church's teaching. At the time, however, it was not presented in a systematic manner by one or more authors. The Modernist authors supported this or that idea, or several ideas, which the Church was obliged to condemn.

Modernism was very diverse, and it is not always easy to establish its boundaries. Pius X himself, in the encyclical *Pascendi,* clearly pointed out this diversity. As Émile Poulat observes: "Pius X drew a photofit image of the Modernist, in seven forms: the philosopher, the believer, the theologian, the historian, the critic, the apologist, the reformer. No one looks exactly like such a photofit picture, but no individual exhausts it."[3] Of course, the preoccupations of the Modernists differed considerably from one country to another. While the majority of French and German Modernists were "armchair scholars" (as Roger Aubert puts it), in Italy the Modernists were often motivated by "strong pastoral concerns, working not only for the progress of research—though this was indispensable—but also for the growth of the community of believers, and in order to nourish a faith that would be more than external religiosity...."[4]

In this chapter we shall not be presenting a history of Modernism or an exhaustive depiction of all the protagonists and their works. We shall keep principally to Pius X's actions and reactions in this matter, *i.e.,* his successive condemnations of the Modernist ideas and the practical measures he took to combat what he regarded as "not a heresy but the synthesis and poison of all heresies,"[5] as well as his personal attitude *vis-à-vis* the Modernists and those who opposed them.

The crisis antedates Pius X

Many authors have tried to suggest that there is an opposition between the pontificates of Leo XIII and Pius X. In this they were largely mistaken. Almost 30 years ago Émile Poulat warned against this artificial opposition which would fail to recognize the entire basis they had in common:

> One must beware of making too much of an opposition between Leo
> XIII, the political, liberal Pope, open to the modern world, and Pius X,
> the religious Pope, retrograde and outclassed. In the case of both Pontiffs,

---

[2] Alfred Loisy, *L'Évangile et l'Église* (Paris: Alphonse Picard et fils, 1902), p.234.
[3] Poulat, *Modernistica,* p.30.
[4] Guasco, *Modernismo,* p.194.
[5] Pius X, allocution *Accogliamo,* April 17, 1907, *Documents pontificaux,* vol.I, p.412.

it is the same model of Catholicism which is being transmitted and imposed: an "intransigent" Catholicism, as the Italians say, the product of the Counter-Reformation, but forged throughout the whole of the last century in the wake of the ordeal of the French Revolution and the other revolutions, in confrontation with modern times and the modern spirit.[6]

Leo XIII was just as anti-modern as Pius X; one would not go far wrong in surmising that, had his pontificate been longer, he would have carried out the same doctrinal condemnations, and have banned the same books, as his successor. The only difference, in this area as in others, was that Leo XIII was in the habit of procrastinating. Brilliant though his pontificate was in certain fields, it left certain questions unresolved.[7] And one of these was Modernism.

When was Modernism born? Alfred Loisy's *L'Évangile et l'Église* ["The Gospel and the Church"], first published in 1902, is often presented as the manifesto of Modernism. But this book, which is not Loisy's first, is far from dealing with all the subjects treated by the Modernists. In it, exegetical problems are integrated into the question of the development of dogma, but Loisy does not touch on the philosophical questions proper. Should one go back, then, to Ernest Renan, notably in his *Vie de Jésus* ["Life of Jesus"] which caused such a scandal in 1863? No, because Renan, a former seminarian who had become an unbeliever, was a rationalist outside the Church. He was not claiming to be reforming the Church's teaching but, at a higher level, to be "revolutionizing thought." Modernists, for the most part, were priests or former priests who professed the Catholic faith and wanted to transform the Church from within by "harmonizing" her teaching with the modern demands of thought, history, *etc.*

This Modernism, therefore, was born rather in the years 1892-1893 in France, which was experiencing a great intellectual effervescence in the religious domain. Two names, in different areas, stand out in the same period. In 1892 Alfred Loisy, a priest, professor of exegesis at the *Institut Catholique* in Paris, began to publish a review entitled *L'enseignement biblique,* which aroused much polemical response by the audacity of its critical method; it was soon to disappear, while its author was deprived of his professor's chair. The following year the lay professor Maurice Blondel published his philosophical thesis entitled *L'Action: Essai d'une critique de*

---

6   Poulat, "Le modernisme d'hier et d'aujourd'hui," *Recherches de science religieuse,* 1971, 2, reprinted in *Modernistica,* p.230.

7   "When all is said and done, Pius X was taking on a heavy burden in spite of the particularly brilliant character of the former pontificate. He was immediately confronted with serious problems of doctrine and discipline which were left hanging or in crisis by Leo XIII." Joseph Hajjar, *Le Vatican, la France et le catholicisme oriental, 1878-1914* (Paris: Beauchesne, 1979), p.231.

la vie et d'une science de la pratique, which also aroused controversy. (The work was not republished until 1950). Blondel is criticized for his immanentist philosophy and his failure to do justice to the gratuitous nature of the supernatural.[8]

In the first years of Leo XIII's pontificate, the Modernist ferment became more visible in Paris and attracted the first sanctions against its authors.

In July 1901 a priest of the Paris archdiocese, Marcel Hébert, director of the *École Fénelon,* was relieved of his post by the Archbishop of Paris, Cardinal Richard, because two years previously he had published (anonymously) a book entitled *Souvenirs d'Assise,* in which he explained the Christian dogmas as symbols. The following year, far from retracting his errors, Marcel Hébert raised the stakes by publishing an article in the *Revue de métaphysique et de morale* entitled "*La dernière idole*": the dogmas are contradicted by historical criticism, and everyone must be "allowed freedom to interpret them as symbols according to his temperament and his religious sense; no importance should be attached to any rite or formula except insofar as these *means* help us effectively to become better people." Hébert soon left the Church.[9]

In March 1902 a priest who originated from the diocese of Angers, Albert Houtin, published a work entitled *La question biblique chez les catholiques de France au XIXe siècle,* in which he showed "the conflict between scientific teaching and Church teaching," and concluded that, sooner or later, science would triumph. Some months later, however, Alfred Loisy's *L'Évangile et l'Église* stirred up a far greater controversy.

In 1896 Fr. Loisy had founded a new publication, the *Revue d'histoire et de littérature religieuses.* In 1901 and 1902 he published four studies which aroused growing controversy[10]: in 1901 he published *La Religion d'Israël* and *Études bibliques;* some of the chapters in *La Religion d'Israël* had been published before, under the pseudonym of "Firmin," in the *Revue du clergé français.* The Archbishop of Paris had ordered that its publication should be stopped. As for *Études bibliques,* it was severely criticized in the *Bulletin de littérature ecclésiastique* of the *Institut Catholique* of Tou-

---

[8]   One of his first critics, Fr. Schwalm, O.P., described him as a "neo-Kantian." Pierre Colin shows the absurdity of such a charge, *L'Audace et le soupçon,* pp.209-210.

[9]   Cf. Rivière, *Le Modernisme dans l'Église,* pp.140-153, and Poulat, *Histoire, dogme et critique dans la crise moderniste,* pp.318-326.

[10] Alfred Loisy published his *Mémoires pour servir à l'histoire religieuse de notre temps* (Paris: Émile Nourry, 1930-1931, 3 vols.), which are a mine of information and documents, even if they are used as an argument to support his own case and cannot be taken without certain precautions. Cf., on this subject, the critical study written by Fr. Lagrange, *M. Loisy et le modernisme. A propos des "Mémoires"* (Juvisy: Les Éditions du Cerf, 1932).

louse. The review warns readers against an author who shows "too much equivocation, too much individualism, too much irony." In November 1902, nonetheless, Fr. Loisy published two new books: a collection entitled *Études évangéliques* and, most notoriously, *L'Évangile et l'Église,* called the "little red book" because of its orange-red cover.

This latter work claimed to be a reply to *Das Wesen des Christentums* ("What is Christianity?"), a collection of lectures published by a famous German Protestant, Professor Harnack. Loisy's book immediately provoked a great controversy: some received it enthusiastically and others were scandalized by it.[11] It caused all the more commotion since it was produced in small format, with a reduced number of pages (234 pages in the first edition), and was easy to read. In five chapters (The Kingdom of Heaven; the Son of God; the Church; Christian dogma; Catholic worship) Loisy saw himself as refuting the theses of Harnack, the liberal Protestant, by using the same methods, namely, objective history. These are the conclusions he draws at the end of each of his five chapters: the Gospel is not "a unique and immutable truth, but a living faith, concrete and complex" which undergoes an "evolution";[12] the divinity of Christ and his resurrection are acts of faith: "the resurrection is not a fact that could have been directly and formally established";[13] the Church is nothing other than the "collective and continuous life of the Gospel," and "the decisions taken by authority only sanction, so to speak, and consecrate the movement of the community's thought and piety";[14] "the Church does not demand belief in its formulas as if they were an adequate expression of absolute truth," and there is an "unceasing evolution of Christian doctrine";[15] finally, the Church endeavors to "regulate" the external forms of devotion: they must not be seen as opposed to true piety and faith, but as forms of "the immense development which has gone on in the Church," a development which has not come to an end, "for it has always been necessary to adapt the Gospel to the changing condition of humanity, and today it is even more necessary."

A bishop, Msgr. Mignot, Archbishop of Albi, known for his liberal ideas and who had been in touch with Loisy for a long time, had read the book before it was published and declared that he was "very satisfied" with

---

[11] We shall quote it according to the first edition which appeared in November 1902, Alphonse Picard et Fils, éditeurs. In spite of the most recent studies on the subject, the standard work remains Émile Poulat's *Histoire, dogme et critique dans la crise moderniste* (we cite this work according to the 2nd revised edition, Casterman, 1979).

[12] Loisy, *L'Évangile et l'Église,* p.38.

[13] *Ibid.,* p.74.

[14] *Ibid.,* p.125.

[15] *Ibid.,* p.174.

it.[16] It was otherwise with the majority of bishops and theologians in France. Loisy's ideas immediately provoked a storm of controversy. One of the great theologians of the time, the Jesuit Fr. Grandmaison, wrote an extensive presentation of the work in *Études*.[17] He acknowledged that the work contained a number of "original ideas" and described it as a "powerful essay," but he concluded with a warning: "...the author's philosophical ideas need to be treated with explicit reservation, and this applies even more to the way he presents the doctrine of the Person of the Saviour. I fear that the Christ presented to us here is neither the Christ of theology nor the Christ of history (and for a Catholic the latter follows from the former)."

At the beginning of 1903 Cardinal Perraud, Archbishop of Autun, pressed Cardinal Richard, who was hesitant about the attitude he should adopt, to intervene.[18] The Archbishop of Paris convoked a commission to study the question and prepare a ruling. On January 17 the Paris archdiocesan *La Semaine religieuse* published a ruling condemning Loisy's book:

> ...considering:
>
> 1. that it was published without the *imprimatur* required by the law of the Church;
>
> 2. that it is of a nature tending gravely to trouble the faith of the faithful regarding the fundamental dogmas of Catholic teaching, notably on the authority of the Scriptures and of Tradition, on the divinity of Jesus Christ, on his infallible knowledge, on the redemption achieved by his death, on his resurrection, on the Eucharist, on the divine institution of the Sovereign Pontificate and the episcopate;
>
> —We condemn this book and forbid it to be read by the clergy and faithful of our diocese.

Seven bishops—some will be disappointed that there were only seven—reproduced this ruling in their diocesan bulletin. Loisy seemed to submit; at least, this is how his letter to the Archbishop of Paris was interpreted.[19] In Rome, according to the witness of Fr. Lepidi, Master of the Sacred Palace, many were reluctant to condemn him. Leo XIII himself prevaricated, if we are to believe other sources, at a time when the Congregation of the Index had examined several of Loisy's works.[20]

---

16   Quoted by Poulat, *Histoire, dogme et critique*, p.60.

17   Fr. Léonce de Grandmaison, "L'Évangile et l'Église," *Études*, January 1903, pp.145-174.

18   Cf. Roger Aubert, "Aux origines de la réaction antimoderniste. Deux documents inédits," *Ephemerides theologicae Lovaniensis*, 37, 1961, pp.557-578.

Loisy's works are put on the Index

Seven months after Loisy's condemnation by the Archbishop of Paris, Pius X became Pope. He was to show himself far more determined than his predecessor in fighting against Modernism, which he saw as a grave peril for the Church. As we have seen, ever since his time as Patriarch of Venice he had become acquainted with Loisy's writings. They seemed to him to represent a danger to the faith. Once he was Pope he took up the struggle against Modernism; he combatted it in different ways, but he himself, at least, never abandoned either charity towards the persons involved, or the intellectual labor required to "defend the truth."

In his very first encyclical Pius X had uttered a warning:

> ...We shall take the greatest care to see that the members of the clergy do not allow themselves to be taken in by the insidious maneuvers of a certain new science which dons the mask of truth and from which one does not discern the fragrance of Jesus Christ; it is a mendacious science which, using fallacious and perfidious arguments, tries to beat a path to the errors of rationalism and semi-rationalism, and against which the Apostle was already warning his beloved Timothy when he wrote: "Guard the deposit, avoiding profane novelties in language as well as in the arguments of a knowledge falsely so-called, whose enthusiasts, with all their promises, have failed in the faith.[21]

This warning against the Modernists must also be understood as an appeal to vigilance. Later, and even today, the Pope would be accused of having thus opened the way to a narrow-minded repression of Modernism, and of having fettered all intellectual research in the Church for a long time ahead. In fact, as we have noted, Pius X would go on to encourage various initiatives and labors of considerable value in the field of exegesis and in other fields; but in any case we must recognize that the sanctions and condemnations against Loisy and Modernism were initiated by cer-

---

[19] On February 2, 1903, Loisy wrote to Cardinal Richard: "It goes without saying that I condemn and reprove all the errors which people have managed to deduce from my book by interpreting it from a point of view that is different from the one I had to adopt, and did adopt, when writing it." On February 7, the journal *La Semaine religieuse* of the Diocese of Paris referred to this letter: "...the author has written a letter to His Eminence in which he says that he has halted the second edition of this work (which was on the point of being published), that he accepts the judgment given and censures the errors which some have deduced from his book. His Eminence, gladdened by this action on the part of Fr. Loisy, has expressed his complete satisfaction to him." Texts cited by Loisy, *Autour d'un petit livre*, pp.vii and p.263. See p.194, note 23.

[20] Testimony cited in Aubert, "Aux origines de la réaction antimoderniste," pp.570-571.

[21] Encyclical *E Supremi Apostolatus*, October 4, 1903, *Documents pontificaux,* vol.I, p.38.

tain members of the clergy of France itself, appalled at the currency achieved by the new and dangerous theses.

A few weeks before Pius X's first encyclical, M. Letourneau, a Sulpician and former superior of the major seminary of Angers, parish priest of the parish of St. Sulpice in Paris, took steps to have Loisy's erroneous ideas condemned by Rome. He had already been the mainspring of the Parisian commission of January 1903. This time he addressed Cardinal Perraud: "I told him that the Holy See seemed unhappy with the idea of a condemnation by the Index, and that it might perhaps accept the idea of condemning specific propositions submitted to the Holy Office...."[22] The Archbishop of Autun approved this approach. M. Letourneau set to work with a Jesuit, Fr. Bouvier, who was already author of a study against Loisy. They also consulted Fr. Billot, another Jesuit and a great Thomist, who was professor of dogmatic theology at the Gregorian University, currently staying in Paris.

They had already drawn up a first list of 18 condemnable propositions drawn from the writings of Loisy, when the latter published a new "little red book" entitled *Autour d'un petit livre*.[23] This was a reply, in seven open letters and 13 documents, to those who had criticized *L'Évangile et l'Église*. Far from retracting, as people had thought after his letter to the Archbishop of Paris, Fr. Loisy drew a distinction between the "Christ of history" and the "Christ of faith"; he denied that the divinity of Jesus was "a fact of Gospel history whose reality could be verified critically" (it is "a belief: the historian can only establish its origin and development"); and he developed his theory of the increasing "chasm" between "the truth of history, which is better known as every day goes by, and what is understood materially by the theological datum."[24]

Such a book did nothing, of course, to cool the controversy down. It would be wrong to think that the entire French episcopate was hostile to the leader of Modernism. Having read Loisy's last book Msgr. Lacroix, Bishop of Tarantaise, wrote to him: "The publication of this work will be a celebrated date in the history of the Church of France."[25]

M. Letourneau and Fr. Bouvier did not share this view. They extracted more condemnable propositions from Loisy's new book, and altogether there were 41 propositions, described as "gravely offensive to divine revela-

---

[22] Georges Letourneau, "Mes souvenirs personnels sur le mémoire présenté au pape Pie X le 1er novembre 1903 par le cardinal Richard sur les écrits de M. Loisy," archives du séminaire Saint-Sulpice, Paris, quoted by Aubert, "Aux origines de la réaction antimoderniste," pp.563-564.

[23] Alfred Loisy, *Autour d'un petit livre* (Paris: Alphonse Picard et fils, 1903), 290 pages.

[24] *Ibid.*, pp.113, 130 and 258.

[25] Cited by Poulat, *Histoire, dogme et critique*, p.250.

tion,"[26] drawn from the two "little red books" in the memorandum submitted to Cardinal Richard on October 17, 1903. The following November 1 the Archbishop of Paris, who had come to Rome, presented the memorandum to the Pope. Cardinals Perraud, Langénieux and Coullié had supported this step by letters sent to the Secretariat of State. Pius X told Cardinal Richard that he would study the memorandum and pass it on to the Holy Office.

However, certain people stepped in to ensure that no condemnation would be pronounced. Msgr. Lacroix, who was in touch with the Council President, Waldeck-Rousseau, solicited a diplomatic intervention from France at the Holy See, warning of "the wretched impression which such a condemnation would make in France..."; Msgr. Mignot, Archbishop of Albi, and Msgr. Le Camus, Bishop of La Rochelle, who were in Rome at the time, endeavored to dissuade Pius X from condemning Loisy's writings.[27] In vain. Dated December 16, 1903, a decree of the Holy Office put five of Loisy's works on the Index of prohibited books: *Études évangéliques, L'Évangile et l'Église, Le Quatrième évangile, Autour d'un petit livre* and *La Religion d'Israël.*[28]

There followed a rather painful exchange of letters.[29] On January 11, 1904, and then on January 24 Loisy wrote to Cardinal Merry del Val, Secretary of State, giving his letters of "adherence" to the decrees which put these books of his on the Index. They were judged insufficient, since they did not constitute a retraction of the errors expressed. On February 28, therefore, Loisy wrote directly to Pius X:

---

[26] Full text of the memorandum (in Latin) in Aubert, "Aux origines de la réaction antimoderniste," pp.572-578. Cf. also Paul Dudon, "Origines françaises du décret *Lamentabili* (1903-1907)," *Bulletin de littérature ecclésiastique,* 1931, pp.73-96, which gives many details on the genesis of the memorandum and its consequences.

[27] Reported in Poulat, *Histoire, dogme et critique dans la crise moderniste,* pp.250, 247. It should be added that the motives of the two camps were different. Msgr. Le Camus had no sympathy for Modernism, but he preferred refutation to condemnation. In order to reply to the first "little red book" he had published a booklet entitled *Vraie et fausse exégèse* (True and false exegesis), and to refute the second "little red book" he published *Fausse exégèse, mauvaise théologie* (False exegesis, bad theology), to which we shall return.

[28] *Index Librorum Prohibitorum* (Rome: Typis Polyglottis Vaticanis, 1948), pp.286-287. On the previous December 4 the following books of two other Modernists had also been put on the *Index: Un Carême apologétique sur les dogmes fondamentaux* and *L'Église et l'État, les leçons de l'heure présente* by Fr. Charles Denis (editor of the *Annales de philosophie chrétienne*), and *Mes difficultés avec mon évêque* and *La question biblique chez les catholiques de France au XIXe siècle* by Albert Houtin.

[29] On Loisy's "submission" in 1904, cf. his *Mémoires,* vol.II; Lagrange, *M. Loisy et le modernisme,* pp.136-151, and Poulat, *Histoire, dogme et critique,* pp.253-254.

Most Holy Father,

I am well acquainted with Your Holiness's kindness, and it is to his heart that I am speaking today.

I wish to live and die in the communion of the Catholic Church. I do not wish to contribute to the ruin of my country's faith.

It is not in my power to destroy in myself the results of my labors.

As far as in me lies, I submit to the judgment of my writings made by the Congregation of the Holy Office.

In testimony of my good will, and for the calming of minds, I am ready to abandon my teaching role in Paris, and I will also suspend the publication of the scholarly work which I have in preparation.

A cursory reading of this might suggest that Loisy was making his submission, and that he had given a good profession of faith in the Church. Pius X was not deceived. He did not reply directly to Loisy but, in a letter to Cardinal Richard dated March 7, he observed: "He appeals to my heart, but he did not write this letter with heart" (*col cuore*). Pius X saw perfectly well that the mental reservations Loisy made—"It is not in my power to destroy in myself the results of my labors," "As far as in me lies..."—could be understood as a refusal to acknowledge that he had been wrong. Finally Loisy gave in. On March 12, in the presence of Cardinal Richard, he allowed an unconditional surrender to be "wrested" from him, as he was later to put it. "Monsignor, I declare to Your Eminence that, in a spirit of obedience to the Holy See, I condemn the errors which the Congregation of the Holy Office has condemned in my writings."

This submission, however, as Loisy's foes would say, was superficial, cowardly and hypocritical. In reality Loisy did not renounce any of his ideas. His reaction to the two pontifical acts condemning Modernism, the decree *Lamentabili* and the encyclical *Pascendi,* showed this clearly.

Lamentabili

The condemnation of certain of Loisy's books had elicited a considerable echo. First in the press, and then in the official responses of certain bishops. One of the latter did more: Msgr. Le Camus, Bishop of La Rochelle. He was a solid exegete; before becoming a bishop he had published a *Life of Jesus* in refutation of Strauss's rationalistic work. After Loisy was put on the Index, Msgr. Le Camus wrote a book refuting his errors: *Fausse exégèse, mauvaise théologie* (False exegesis, bad theology). This work merited a letter of praise from Pius X, who was delighted with the quality and solidity of the refutation. In this letter the Pope praised the bishop for having employed "true science, not that which puffs up, but that which rejects the dreams of delirious minds and holds firmly to the truth which God has revealed."[30]

Pius X well knew that Loisy's case was by no means an isolated one. He saw, behind the theses propounded by the French exegete, a tendency, a "system" raising its head. He expressed this at the beginning of 1905 in a letter addressed to the rector of the *Institut Catholique* of Paris. After having praised the *Institut*, its "select masters, who were capable of bringing honor to scholarship and religion," he deplored the fact that some in the Catholic Church "seem to want unreservedly to approve the current dictum that *what is false today will be held as true tomorrow. This explains the system, which has spread everywhere, of removing everything that is ancient and promoting everything that is new, almost for no other reason but its novelty; as if scholarship ought to consist in a kind of disdain for antiquity."[31] Indeed, both in philosophy and in literature, what would soon be termed "Modernism" manifested itself as a critique of "blind traditionalism."[32]

Pius X's unease in February 1905 was to find striking confirmation in the following weeks. In March the chargé d'affaires at the Paris nunciature, Msgr. Montagnini, wrote to Cardinal Merry del Val, saying that Loisy, "who had been keeping quiet for some time," had published an article which "seems to me to be just as bad as his previous works."[33] On April 16, Édouard Le Roy published an article in the *Quinzaine* entitled "*Qu'est-ce qu'un dogme?*" (What is a dogma?), which was to trigger a lively controversy. The author, a mathematician and philosopher, reduced dogmatic truth to the level of an orientation for the believer's practical living. The day after the article appeared, even Blondel regretted that it exaggerated the "anti-intellectual tendency" and "suppressed truth's realist meaning."[34] As Pierre Colin observed: "Insofar as it deals with the status of religious language and the problem of truth, this controversy does not have a direct bearing on the problems posed by Loisy's exegetical work. On the other hand, there are connections. It seems to be the case that the dogmatic

---

[30] Letter of Pius X to Msgr. Le Camus, June 27, 1904, *Bulletin religieux du diocèse de La Rochelle,* July 9, 1904, pp.13-14.

[31] Letter *Solemne Illud,* February 22, 1905, *Documents pontificaux,* vol.I, pp.271-272.

[32] This phrase was used by Fogazzaro, the Italian novelist, in a letter to Paul Sabatier, November 13, 1903, published in Poulat, *Histoire, dogme et critique,* p.249.

[33] Letter from Msgr. Montagnini to Cardinal Merry del Val, March 13, 1905, ASV, Segretaria di Stato, anno 1905, rubrica 248, f.237. The article "Le Message de saint Jean-Baptiste" was published in the *Revue d'Histoire et de Littérature religieuses.* Montagnini added: "I could not find out exactly which party the *Review* represented..." Cardinal Merry del Val replied that he regularly received this publication—a sign that people at the Vatican were better informed than the Modernists thought.

[34] Letter to Auguste Valensin, April 17, 1905, in Maurice Blondel/Auguste Valensin, *Correspondance,* (Paris: Aubier, 1957), vol.I, p.209.

structure is being attacked both in the area of history and in the area of philosophy, as if these attacks were convergent."[35]

This same year the Oratorian, Fr. Laberthonnière, took over the direction of the *Annales de philosophie chrétienne* and followed the path blazed by his predecessor, Fr. Charles Denis, of whom we have already spoken. His aim was to make it a forum for conciliation "not between philosophy and religion, but between the free initiative of the philosopher and the docile heart of the believer."[36] There can be no doubt, however, that the Modernist publication with the greatest readership in 1905 was the novel *Il Santo* by the Italian, Fogazzaro.[37] Fogazzaro, a talented novelist and a personal friend of the English Jesuit, Tyrrell, was acquainted with the works of Loisy and the "reformers." He praised Loisy as the "most valiant promoter of this renewal of the old formulas of the Catholic faith, whereas a blind traditionalism would like to bind us to accepting the letter as an exact representation of supernatural truth."[38] His novel, which people described as "Modernism's *Divine Comedy*,"[39] presents us with a lay philosopher, Giovanni Selva, the central figure among a group of Catholics of different countries who aspire to reform the Church. These "progressive Catholics" (*cattolici progressisti*) find an old Benedictine, Benedetto, a "saint" who, in his life and thought, best expresses the ideal that inspires them. One night Benedetto succeeds in entering the Vatican and there meets the Pope. At some length he points out to him the "four evil spirits" which have invaded the Church and are "warring against the Holy Spirit": the spirit of untruth, which has reduced many clerics to being nothing more than "worshippers of the letter" and which charges the defenders of a living faith with heresy; the spirit of domination which animates the clergy; the spirit of avarice; and finally, the spirit of immobility which makes the clergy "idolaters of the past."[40]

The work was very successful. Published in Italy in November 1905, it was translated in the following months into French, German and English. The *Revue des Deux-Mondes* serialized it; in *Le Figaro* the Vicomte de Vogüé, a liberal Catholic, gave it an enthusiastic reception. Nor was the sanction slow to fall: in a decree dated April 5, 1906, the novel was put on the *Index* of prohibited books. A few months later, in an encyclical ad-

---

[35] Colin, *L'Audace et le soupçon*, p.244.
[36] "Our program," revised and corrected by Blondel, cited in a note in the Blondel/Valensin *Correspondance*, vol.I, p.224.
[37] We cite it here according to the 1925 edition (54th thousand): Antonio Fogazzaro, *Il Santo* (Milan: Baldini & Castoldi).
[38] Letter to P. Sabatier, November 13, 1903, published in Poulat, *Histoire, dogme et critique*, p.249.
[39] The phrase used by the Jesuit Fr. Maurice de La Taille in *Études* (1907), p.662.
[40] Fogazzaro, *Il Santo*, pp.270-277.

dressed to the Italian bishops and the clergy in general, Pius X reproved what he regarded as a dangerous tendency. Without mentioning Fogazzaro, and no doubt having other Italian figures in mind as well,[41] the Pope issued a warning: "As regards Catholic publications, it is necessary to reprove all language which, animated by a spirit of unhealthy novelty, mocks the piety of the faithful and speaks of *new orientations of the Christian life,* of *new directions for the Church,* of *new aspirations of the modern soul,* of a *new social vocation for the clergy,* of a *new Christian civilization* and other similar things."[42]

Here we shall not mention all the authors associated with this Modernist trend, nor all the works which were published and the reviews which were founded. They were sometimes published anonymously or under pseudonyms, which rendered them doubly suspect. The twofold general and systematic condemnation of Modernism which came in 1907 was no surprise. In the Pope's eyes, we may say, every day brought further reasons for a solemn intervention on his part.

On April 17, in an allocution at the ceremony of giving the hat to new cardinals, Pius X deplored the "terrible war" waged by certain "rebellious spirits." He referred to the popularization of errors "in pamphlets, reviews, books of spirituality, and even in novels." This time it was quite clear that he was thinking of Fogazzaro's *Il Santo.*[43] Without mentioning the word "Modernism," the Pope described the whole complex of ideas and new methods in exegesis, philosophy, theology and history as an "assault which constitutes, not a heresy, but the synthesis and poison of all heresies." The Pope distinguished four major principles in Modernism:

    —dogma must undergo evolution in its formulation;

    —there must be return to the "pure Gospel";

    —people must be emancipated from the Church's authority;

    —the Church must adapt her teaching to the present time.[44]

---

[41] Notably the campaigns of Fr. Murri who, in one of his most famous addresses, given at San Marino on August 24, 1902, had expressed his vision of a "great deliverance" of the Church, whereby she would reject "semi-pagan, varnished customs, juridical concepts based on Roman law, philosophical and theological ideas elaborated in our schools, monastic institutions in a state of fatal decay and incapable of rejuvenation, political systems, views and sympathies...," quoted in Rivière, *Le Modernisme dans l'Église,* pp.281-282.

[42] Encyclical *Pieni l'animo,* July 28, 1906, *Documents pontificaux,* vol.I, p.371.

[43] The reviews Pius X had in mind were the following: *Cultura sociale,* founded by Fr. Murri in 1908; *Studi religiosi. Rivista critica e storica promotrice della cultura religiosa in Italia,* founded in 1901 by Salvatore Minocchi (one of its principal editors was Fr. Semeria, a Barnabite); *Rivista storico-critica delle scienze teologiche,* founded in January 1907 by Alessandro Casati, Tommaso Gallarati-Scotti, and Stefano Jacini, lay associates of Fogazzaro.

This allocution alarmed the Italian Modernists. A priest of the diocese of Perugia, Luigi Piastrelli, associated with Murri and Buonaiuti, replied to it in an open letter to Pius X. Piastrelli did not sign this letter, which was ostensibly drawn up by a "group of priests." Entitled *A Pio X. Quello che vogliano* (To Pius X: What we want), this letter was a plea of innocence in the face of the grave accusations the Pope had made in his allocution to the cardinals.[45] More precisely, it concluded with an appeal to clemency with regard to Don Murri.

This letter acquired a certain currency and was immediately translated into English (the fact that it was not immediately translated into French was because the translator was looking for too high a fee). In any case, however, it could do nothing to alter the condemnations that were in preparation. The first solemn condemnation took the form of a long decree of the Holy Office, dated July 3 and entitled *Lamentabili Sane Exitu* ("By a truly lamentable misfortune"). It appeared on July 17 on the front page of the *Osservatore Romano.* Now we know how this famous document came to be written. As we have seen, the list of errors in the writings of Loisy drawn up in 1903 by the Frenchmen Letourneau, Bouvier and Billot had provided the basis on which five of the exegete's books had been put on the *Index.* This synopsis of Loisy's errors had not disappeared from sight. The Holy Office received other memoranda from Belgium, Austria and England.[46] Finally, without citing any particular author, the Holy Office produced a list of 65 propositions to be "reproved and proscribed."[47] Loisy later affirmed that his works had provided "the majority" of the theses condemned by the Holy See. But in his commentary on the decree he also identified propositions extracted from the works of Msgr. Hinot, Houtin, Tyrrell and Le Roy, or "interpretations" of some things they had said.[48] He even identified propositions which, he said, could have been drawn from the works of Newman.[49]

---

[44] Allocution *Accogliamo,* April 17, 1907, *Documents pontificaux,* vol.I, p.412: "... these rebels profess and repeat, in subtle formulas, monstrous errors on the evolution of dogma, on the return to the pure Gospel—that is, as they say, a Gospel purified of theological explication, Council definitions, and the maxims of the moral life—and on the emancipation of the Church. This they do in their new fashion: they do not engage in revolt, lest they should be ejected, and yet they do not submit either, so that they do not have to abandon their convictions. In their calls for the Church to adapt to modern conditions, in everything they speak and write, preaching a charity without faith, they are very indulgent towards believers, but in reality they are opening up for everyone the path to eternal ruin."

[45] Guasco, *Modernismo,* p.152.

[46] This fact is recorded in an unpublished memorandum of M. Letourneau, cited by Dudon, "Origines françaises du décret *Lamentabili,*" p.94.

[47] Decree *Lamentabili Sane Exitu,* July 3, 1907, *Documents pontificaux,* vol.I, pp.779-783.

Wherever these condemned theses originated, the decree *Lamentabili* constituted a "new *Syllabus*" (the term was therefore current at the time), *i.e.,* a catalogue of errors that were to be condemned and not professed. Unlike the *Syllabus* of Pius IX (published in 1864), the decree did not arrange the condemned theses thematically. Nonetheless, on reading it, it can easily be seen that seven types of errors are quoted: those relating to the interpretation of the Scriptures (propositions 1-8); those concerning the inspiration and historicity of the Scriptures (propositions 9-19); those concerning Revelation and the definition of dogmas (propositions 20-26); those relating to the Person of Christ (propositions 27-38); those concerning the Sacraments (propositions 39-51); those relative to the Church (propositions 52-56); and those relative to doctrine and science (propositions 57-65).

The decree's reception

Nowadays, when the "repression of Modernism" is stigmatized by the majority of historians, it is hard to appreciate the eager welcome accorded to this first condemnation. The archives of the Secretariat of State contain hundreds of enthusiastic and grateful letters.[50] It is noticeable that the majority of them came from France, even if there are significant letters from certain other countries. Bishops, priests and religious superiors sent letters (individually or collectively), pastoral addresses and reports also.

One of the first was Msgr. Turinaz, the Bishop of Nancy, an ardent champion of orthodoxy, who addressed "a hymn of gratitude and admiration" to the Pope, reminding him that he had asked for a condemnatory decree of this kind ("Your Holiness deigned to promise me one..."[51]). Among other collective addresses from the clergy of France there was that, dated July 23, of the Bishop of Belley and his clergy, "assembled in congress," who "joyously acclaimed the latest instruction." On July 31 it was Msgr. Douais, Bishop of Beauvais, on retreat together with his clergy, who sent Pius X a telegram to show their "obedience" and express their "heartfelt and unreserved adherence to the decree *Lamentabili*." The Bishops of Maurienne and of Gap were glad to report that their respective dioceses were free of Modernism. Msgr. Eyssautier, Bishop of La Rochelle (the successor of Msgr. Le Camus, who had died a year earlier) was more uneasy.

---

[48] Alfred Loisy, *Simples réflexions sur le décret du Saint-Office "Lamentabili sane exitu" et sur l'encyclique "Pascendi Domini gregis,"* published by the author at Ceffonds, 1908 (2nd ed.), pp.40, 45, 69, 70, 123.

[49] *Ibid.,* pp.69, 95, 97, 99.

[50] ASV, Segretaria di Stato, anno 1908, rubrica 82, f.1 and 2. All the letters we cite here come from this archive.

[51] Letter of July 19, 1907.

In a letter to the Secretary of State he complained that "women subscribe to these dangerous notions in order to seem to be in the know." He also reported that, to "destroy these tendencies," he had given an address to the town's *Mères chrétiennes* (Christian mothers). In addition, he complained of the lack of submission of one of his priests, Fr. Couriade, who was appealing to the "judgment of the public." The bishop admitted, "I do not know what else I can do to bring back this priest."[52]

On August 6, Msgr. Guillibert, Bishop of Fréjus and Toulon, wrote a letter to the Pope, in Latin, accompanying a pamphlet he had just published on the decree, *Le Jugement du Saint-Siège* (The Judgment of the Holy See). There was also a joint letter from all the bishops of Brittany, assembled for the Feast of St. Anne d'Auray (five Breton dioceses and three other invited dioceses).

There were also important joint letters from the potential breeding-grounds of Modernism: seminaries and the Catholic Institutes. The letter from the *Alliance of Major Seminaries* is enthusiastic, yet anodyne: 125 directors of major seminaries and professors, meeting in Paris under the leadership of Msgr. Péchenard, Bishop of Soissons and former director of the Institut Catholique de Paris, addressed a letter expressing "full and entire adherence to the condemnation issued by Your Holiness."[53] The Institut Catholique de Toulouse expressed its "unreserved, unanimous and glad submission"; the rector, Msgr. Batiffol, and the dean of the Faculty of Theology, Maisonneuve, underlined their role as precursors in the battle against Modernism: "The errors condemned by the decree of the Holy Office are the same which we have not ceased to combat since 1900, in our teaching and writing, and particularly in the *Bulletin,* the monthly journal of our Institute. We were the first to discern this cloud of errors forming and to warn people against it."[54] The professors of philosophy, theology and history at the Catholic University of Louvain and the Belgian seminaries associated themselves with the joint letter of the Belgian bishops at their annual meeting. But it seems that, for some of the professors concerned, this expressed adherence to their bishops' letter had a therapeutic purpose, as the Apostolic Nuncio to Brussels wrote: "By this act on the part of the professors the bishops are hoping that, if any of the professors

---

[52] Letter of Msgr. Jean-Auguste Eyssautier to Cardinal Merry del Val, August 2, 1907.

[53] Letter to Pius X, July 23, 1907.

[54] Letter to Pius X, July 21, 1907. Coincidentally, five days later, one of the signatories of this letter, Msgr. Batiffol, had one of his works, *L'Eucharistie,* put on the Index; he resigned from the Institut Catholique the following December. This inclusion in the Index was not made official until 1911: his resignation is more likely to have been connected with personal problems than with this condemnation. Cf. Marcel Bécamel, "Comment Monseigneur Batiffol quitta Toulouse, à la Noël 1907," *Bulletin de littérature ecclésiastique,* 1971, pp.258-288.

has an inclination towards the condemned errors, his signature will oblige him to get back on the right path."[55]

Some of the bishops and religious superiors adopted a tone of reassurance. Cardinal Bourne, Archbishop of Westminster, wrote: "In England, happily, only a few Catholic writers have involved themselves in this dangerous tendency, and their influence seems to be on the decline."[56] Fr. Fiat, superior-general of the Congregation of the Mission (Vincentians), related the measures he had taken even prior to the publication of the decree:

> It had come to my knowledge that certain of the missionaries had a general tendency towards Modernism. The colleagues in question were warned in charity and at an opportune time, and certain disciplinary measures were taken. As a last resort, on April 25 this year, I believed it my duty to address a circular letter to the entire Company, warning the missionaries against the modern ideas and prescribing the means to be used to preserve intact, not only our faith, but also the reputation of orthodoxy which, up to now, has been the glory of the family of St. Vincent.[57]

Without mentioning all the letters of adherence arriving in Rome from various countries, it is worth mentioning that of Cardinal Svampa, Archbishop of Bologna, on August 3; that of the Archbishop of New York and ten bishops of the ecclesiastical province of New York, on August 31; and that of Msgr. Laguarda y Fenorella, Bishop of Jaen, in Spain; these three letters salute the decree of the Holy Office as a "new Syllabus."

The comparison was also made by the decree's opponents. In *La Tribuna*, under the pseudonym of *Rastignac*, Vincenzo Morello wrote on July 19, 1907: "The new *Syllabus* only confirms what has been evident for some time: it is only possible to be faithful to the Church by not thinking; and, vice versa, one can only use one's mind if one is unfaithful to the Church. Where thought comes to a full stop, Faith begins, and Faith can only start once thought has succumbed." In *L'Humanité* of July 23 the Socialist leader Jean Jaurès took up the same phrase, adding that the Church had rejected "the last opportunity of reform offered it by Modernism."[58]

We cannot give a complete picture of the negative reactions to the Holy Office's decree here, but we must mention the reaction of the Italian Modernists who endeavoured to give a collective response. One of them, Salvatore Minocchi, reacted clumsily in an article published the day after the decree:

> I am not well acquainted with the works of Loisy, and I do not have the time to examine closely those of Laberthonnière. But, as regards the

---

[55] Letter from the Apostolic Nuncio to Cardinal Merry del Val, July 27, 1907.
[56] Letter of Msgr. Francis Bourne to Cardinal Merry del Val, July 21, 1907.
[57] Letter of Fr. Fiat to Cardinal Merry del Val, July 29, 1907.
[58] Quoted by Dal-Gal, *Pie X*, p.269.

propositions attributed to them, I think that neither of them ever dreamed of expressing errors of this kind, contrary to the most elementary demands of modern historical and philosophical criticism. The errors must have been deduced from their works and propagated by others, greatly harming the truth and the Catholic Church.[59]

More significant was the meeting organized at Molveno, in the Trentino, at the end of August.[60] The organizers of this meeting were two Perugia priests, Luigi Piastrelli, whom we have already met, and Umberto Fracassini, rector of the Perugia Seminary. This meeting had already been arranged several months before the publication of the decree, and the latter only redoubled the determination of the interested parties. The two Perugia priests had drawn up a program for discussion in collaboration with Murri and Buonaiuti. They were to do two things: they were to study certain philosophical and theological problems (knowledge, revelation, Christology, authority in the Church, the Sacraments, public worship) and coordinate action and reaction (*i.e.,* the attitude to be adopted *vis-à-vis* the hierarchy's decisions, the organization of regular meetings and the setting-up of a general secretariat in Rome). The location of the meeting, which was secret, was provided by the directors of the *Rinnovamento.* Finally, ten Modernists assembled at the end of August; all were Italians (Fogazzaro, Buonaiuti, Fracassini, Piastrelli, Mari, Casciola, Murri, Casati and Gallarati Scotti) except Baron von Hügel, who was regarded as the representative of foreign Modernists.

This meeting, which lasted from August 27 to 30, did not produce a final agreed statement. The participants did not succeed in working out a common program either in the area of doctrine or at the practical level. By contrast, the encyclical *Pascendi* would soon provide an ample definition and a very detailed synthesis of Modernism, and would indicate the practical ways of combatting it.

Pascendi

The encyclical was dated September 8, 1907, and was published on the 16th. It was doubtless the most famous pontifical act of Pius X (but by no means the most read).[61] During the process of beatification, as if to enhance the figure of Pius X as "defender of the faith," Cardinal Canali maintained that "the condemnation of Modernism was decreed by Pius X, who had himself spent a long time drawing up the plan of the encyclical *Pascendi.*"[62] In reality things were not so simple.

---

[59] Article published in *Il Giornale d'Italia,* July 21, 1907, quoted by Dal-Gal, *ibid.,* pp.269-270.

[60] The most accurate account of this meeting is that of Nicola Raponi, "I veri promotori del convegno di Molveno," *Fonti e documenti,* 1987-1988, vol.XVI-XVII, pp.348-449.

No doubt, as we see from the history of the writing of *Pascendi,* Pius X had a clear idea of what he wanted to see in the document, namely, a doctrinal synthesis of Modernism, followed by practical measures for opposing it. But it cannot be said that he himself laid down the plan for the doctrinal part of the document (which is by far the longest part). It is entirely normal for the Pope to request the help of collaborators in a document of this importance. The work of the collaborators is read, modified to a greater or lesser extent, and finally the Pope makes it entirely his own by signing it.

There has been much guesswork regarding the churchmen who participated in the preparation of the encyclical. By turns, people have seen in it the hand of Cardinal Vivès y Tuto; of Fr. Pie de Langogne (both Capuchins); Fr. Billot, the Jesuit theologian who was already associated with the origins of the decree *Lamentabili;* of Frs. Malebrancq, Barbieri, Mattiussi (Jesuits); and of Msgr. Benigni, who would be involved in the affair of *La Sapinière.* Two months after the publication of the encyclical, *La Croix* saw in it the work of Msgr. Sardi, secretary of the "Briefs to Princes" section. In reality, even if some of these figures were associated with the project, it has now been established that it was a French religious, Fr. Joseph Lemius, who, at the instigation of Cardinal Merry del Val and Pius X, prepared a draft encyclical. Both the doctrinal and the disciplinary parts of the pontifical document owe a great deal to him.[63]

---

[61] Research needs to be done on references to *Pascendi* in subsequent pontificates. At the Second Vatican Council St. Pius X was hardly quoted at all (he was the least quoted pope of the 20th century), and there was no reference to *Pascendi.* Paul VI, who, during a general audience on January 19, 1972, referred to "Modernism which, under different names, is still a reality," was also the pope who abolished the "anti-Modernist oath." In his first Encyclical *Ecclesiam Suam* (1964), however, he had portrayed Modernism as a "danger that is threatening," "an episode of oppression, emanating from psychologico-cultural tendencies that are proper to the secular world, inflicted on the faithful and pure expression of the doctrine and rule of the Church of Christ." This definition, which is somewhat obscure, was the last mention of Modernism as such in any encyclical until the 14th encyclical of John Paul II, *Fides et Ratio,* September 14, 1998, where we find not only a reference to *Pascendi* but also a justification of it. John Paul II writes: "Here the pronouncements of Pope St. Pius X are pertinent, stressing as they did that at the basis of Modernism were philosophical claims which were phenomenist, agnostic and immanentist." *Faith and Reason* (Dublin: Veritas, 1998), p.81.

[62] Deposition of Cardinal Canali at the Roman ordinary process, quoted by Dal-Gal, *Pie X,* p.268.

[63] François Veuillot, "Jugement d'un journaliste," *Missions de la congrégation des Missionnaires oblats de Marie Immaculée,* vol.LVII, 1923, pp.748-751; Jean Rivière, "Qui rédigea *Pascendi?*" *Bulletin de littérature ecclésiastique,* April-September 1946; letter of Fr. A. Perbal, *Bulletin de littérature ecclésiastique,* 1946, pp.242-243; François Marcotte, "Le Père Joseph Lemius et l'encyclique 'Pascendi,'" *Études oblates,* vol.VI, 1947, pp.144-147. We shall also use various unpublished documents.

Fr. Joseph Lemius was born in Montfort, in the Landes, in 1860.[64] After spending a little more than two years in the major seminary of Aire, in 1882 he entered the Oblates of Mary Immaculate. He was sent to pursue his studies in Rome. He was ordained priest two years later and then obtained successively a doctorate in philosophy, a doctorate in theology and a licence in canon law. He was professor and then superior of the OMI scholasticate in Rome before being appointed procurator-general of his congregation in 1894. He exercised this office until his death. He was also a consultor of several Roman Congregations. From 1888 he was consultor of the Sacred Congregation for Studies. It was in this capacity that he intervened successfully on several occasions in favor of Fr. Mercier, who was establishing a college of Thomist philosophy in Louvain (the future Leo XIII College). Fr. Joseph Lemius remained closely associated with the future Cardinal Mercier. As 1904 approached, the Congregation for Studies also entrusted him with the task of preparing a reply to Msgr. Batiffol, rector of the Institut Catholique de Toulouse, who had requested "a very clear direction with regard to modern ideas." For two years running, furthermore, he was appointed to deliver a lecture to the Academy of St. Thomas on the danger of the modern errors.

These tasks prepared him for direct collaboration on the encyclical against Modernism. Roman theologians had first been consulted, as well as professors of the University of Freiburg. Fr. Jean-Baptiste Lemius, Fr. Joseph's brother, explains: "The Sovereign Pontiff, having decided to condemn Modernism, consulted eminent professors of the University of Freiburg. He thought that, being at the centre of Europe, they would be familiar with what was being said in France, Germany and elsewhere, and asked them to draw up a thesis on the current errors." These different drafts for an encyclical were not judged satisfactory by the Pope and his collaborators.[65] They were submitted by Cardinal Merry del Val to Fr. Jo-

---

[64] Fr. Jean-Baptiste Lemius, who also was a religious of OMI, wrote a long biographical notice on his brother (36 typed pages, Archives OMI, Rome). This unpublished document also gives information on the relations between Fr. Joseph Lemius and Pius X; this information complements what is found in the articles cited above.

[65] We can imagine that one of the reports sent to Rome was a report by Professor Gaspard Decurtins (1855-1916). He was the leader of the "German party" at the Catholic University of Fribourg, quite distinct from the "French party," which later was accused of Modernism. In 1911 Descurtins published *Le modernisme littéraire* which was honored by a very warm Brief of Approbation by Pius X (letter *Tuum Opus*, September 15, 1910, *Documents pontificaux,* vol.II, pp.286-287): "... once again you show yourself to be the Church's very dear son and valorous champion, who has always merited the special esteem and affection of Our illustrious predecessor and of Ourselves."

seph Lemius. He took over the entire work and, in four days, set forth a new draft.

The encyclical is in two distinct parts. The longer, doctrinal part presents the errors of Modernism in a detailed and systematic way. The shorter, disciplinary part gives, in seven points, the practical measures which must be taken to combat Modernism. Cardinal Vivès y Tuto has been credited with the encyclical's disciplinary part.[66] In fact, without excluding the possibility that the latter had made some corrections to this part of the encyclical, it is certain that Fr. Lemius, following the Pope's directives, prepared a complete draft, in two distinct and unequal parts.[67] The draft was judged satisfactory and Pius X, after having refashioned the text's doctrinal part a little, and its disciplinary part rather more, made the text his own.

It has often been forgotten that this great doctrinal text had a pastoral purpose. As the encyclical's title makes clear, it is in order to protect "the flock" that Christ has given the Pope's intervention to the Church.[68] First of all, the encyclical systematically sets forth Modernism's principles. Such an exposition is necessary, the Pope writes, because "It is one of the cleverest devices of the Modernists" (he rightly gives them a generic name) "to present their doctrines without order and systematic arrangement, in a scattered and disjointed manner, so as to make it appear as if their minds were in doubt or hesitation, whereas in reality they are quite fixed and steadfast...."

This is not the place for a detailed analysis of this long encyclical: we shall simply give its broad outline. At base, the Pope explains, Modernism is founded on philosophical principles that are incompatible with Catholic faith, namely, agnosticism and immanentism. According to the Modernists, "God can never be the direct object of science; God is not a historical person"; it follows that "faith, which is the basis and foundation of all religion, must consist in a certain interior sense, originating in a need of the divine." Theology's purpose is therefore to render intelligible this "in-

[66] Marcotte, reporting the testimony of Fr. J.-B. Lemius, "Le Père Joseph Lemius et l'encyclical 'Pascendi,'" p.147.

[67] The original text of the draft encyclical, in Italian, "consists of 62 pages on the doctrinal part and 20 pages on the 'moral' or disciplinary part....I have compared the Italian text of the Encyclical and the text submitted by Fr. Lemius. As far as I am concerned there can be no doubt: the doctrinal part is clearly based on the text of Fr. Lemius. The order of contents is essentially the same, and often whole phrases and paragraphs are identical. On the other hand, it cannot simply be said that the Encyclical's final text is Fr. Lemius's: his text has been shortened here and there, his Italian amended in many places. This seems to me to be very normal in the procedure of drawing up an encyclical." Letter of Fr. Aloysius Keidl, archivist general OMI, to the author, June 23, 1998.

[68] Encyclical *Pascendi Dominici Gregis,* September 8, 1907, *Documents pontificaux,* vol.I, pp.432-468.

terior sense"; it is an endless task and its results are always provisional and inadequate, because dogmas "do not contain absolute truth": they are "images of truth, and must therefore in their turn be adapted to man in his relation to the religious sense." "Individual experience" is the primary foundation of religious certitude, and, as time goes by, it is translated into "symbols" and "religious formulas" which are bound to be ceaselessly changing. Tradition, the Pope explains in the encyclical, is thus "totally ruined," and in all areas: "when they treat of philosophy, history, and criticism, acting on the principle that science is no way depends upon faith, they...are wont to display a manifold contempt for Catholic doctrines, for the Holy Fathers, for the Oecumenical Councils, for the ecclesiastical Magisterium."

The Pope points out "the passion of such men for innovation. In all Catholicism there is absolutely nothing on which it does not fasten." The Modernists, Pius X writes, want to reform everything: the teaching of philosophy, of theology, of history, the catechism, the Church's discipline, her government, even her moral teaching.

And so we come to the most famous formula of the encyclical: Modernism is "the synthesis of all the heresies."

> Undoubtedly, were anyone to attempt the task of collecting together all the errors that have been broached against the faith and to concentrate into one the sap and substance of them all, he could not succeed in doing so better than the Modernists have done. Nay, they have gone farther than this, for, as We have already intimated, their system means the destruction not of the Catholic religion alone, but of all religion.

At the core of the encyclical we find an important and very severe rejection, not only of the Modernist ideas, but also of those who profess them. Since *evolution* is "the principal doctrine of their system," the Modernists are convinced that one day the Church will recognize the "progress" of the ideas they represent. In the meantime, the Pope writes,

> they go their way, reprimands and condemnations notwithstanding, masking an incredible audacity under a mock semblance of humility. While they make a pretence of bowing their heads, their minds and hands are more boldly intent than ever on carrying out their purposes. And this policy they follow willingly and wittingly, both because it is part of their system that authority is to be stimulated but not dethroned, and because it is necessary for them to remain within the ranks of the Church in order that they may gradually transform the collective conscience....

Is this portrait of the Modernist perhaps too severe? Is it unjust, or a caricature? To answer this question one would have to examine the case of each Modernist individually. However that may be, we have already observed Loisy's evasive reactions to ecclesiastical authority between 1903 and 1907, and the very widespread habit of writing anonymously or under pseudonyms. For example, the French priest Turmel, a prolific writer, who declared that he had lost the faith at the age of 26, used at least 14 pseudonyms from 1906 onwards, although in 1908 he swore that he had nothing to do with "Antoine Dupin" and "Guillaume Herzog," two of his *noms de plume*![69]

It is no surprise, therefore, that the practical recommendations which form the second part of the encyclical are very precise. There are seven of them, each of them attended by lengthy explanations. It should be remembered that this encyclical was addressed to the bishops of the entire world, and that, in the spirit of the Pope, they were charged with putting his directives into operation:

—"We will and strictly ordain that scholastic philosophy be made the basis of the sacred sciences." Here Pius X is placing himself in the line of his predecessors, Pius IX and, above all, Leo XIII, whom he quotes at length four times.

—In the seminaries and Catholic universities, extreme care must be taken in the choice of directors and professors: "Anyone who in any way is found to be tainted with Modernism is to be excluded without compunction from these offices, whether of government or of teaching, and those who already occupy them are to be removed. The same policy is to be adopted towards those who openly or secretly lend countenance to Modernism either by extolling the Modernists and excusing their culpable conduct, or by carping at scholasticism, and the Fathers, and the magisterium of the Church, or by refusing obedience to ecclesiastical authority in any of its depositaries; and towards those who show a love of novelty in history, archaeology, biblical exegesis; and finally towards those who neglect the sacred sciences or appear to prefer to them the secular."

—Bishops must prevent the reading and sale of evil books, even, if necessary, using "solemn interdict" and depriving those who stubbornly persist in selling condemned books of "the title of Catholic booksellers."

—As well as the *imprimatur* (the permission to publish), books which cannot be published without the bishop's authorization must have obtained a *nihil obstat* (no objection) given by a specially appointed diocesan censor.

—"Priests' congresses" can be authorized only "on very rare occasions" and "on condition that matters appertaining to the Bishops or the Apostolic See be not treated in them, and that no resolutions or petitions be

---

[69] Jacqueline Lalouette, "Turmel Joseph," in *Les Sciences religieuses,* vol.IX of *Dictionnaire du monde religieux dans la France contemporaine* (Paris: Beauchesne, 1996), pp.646-647, and Émile Poulat, "Turmel (Joseph)," *Catholicisme,* vol.LXX, col.400-404.

allowed that would imply a usurpation of sacred authority, and that absolutely nothing be said in them which saviors of Modernism, Presbyterianism, or Laicism."

—A "Vigilance Committee" shall be established in each diocese, composed of priests chosen by the bishop. "They shall meet every two months on an appointed day in the presence of the bishop....[T]heir functions shall be as follows: They shall watch most carefully for every trace and sign of Modernism both in publications and in teaching, and, to preserve from it the clergy and the young, they shall take all prudent, prompt and efficacious measures."

—A report on the whole observance and success of these different prescriptions must be sent to the Holy See by the bishops within one year, and every three years thereafter. Superiors-general of religious orders must do the same.

Reactions to the encyclical

The reactions to the encyclical were of two kinds. On the one hand, it received a wholehearted welcome, from that expressed even by people relatively distant from the Church, to the deferential enthusiasm of priests and bishops, an enthusiasm which reiterated the reception given to the decree *Lamentabili*. On the other hand, most of the Modernists and their supporters rejected the encyclical; in certain cases this rejection caused them to go to the lengths of breaking with the Church.

In Italy the great Italian newspaper *Il Giornale d'Italia*, reputed to be "vehicle and organ of Modernism,"[70] published a reply to the Pope by two Modernists. On September 26 the Irish ex-Jesuit Tyrrell published a "Reply to the Encyclical *Pascendi* of Pius X."[71] On October 11 the Italian Salvatore Minocchi gave his reaction in the same newspaper, saying that he did not feel concerned by the encyclical's condemnations. By contrast, another Italian Modernist, Buonaiuti, privately admitted: "As for me, what the encyclical describes are my most unshakable scientific and philosophical convictions."[72]

---

[70] Letter of Msgr. Zanecchia-Ginetti, Bishop of Teramo, to Cardinal Merry del Val, February 18, 1908, ASV, Segretaria di Stato, Anno 1908, rubrica 82, f.179-183.

[71] Tyrrell had been excluded from the Society of Jesus on February 1, 1906, following an interview, under cover of anonymity, which he had given to the *Corriere della sera* of the previous January 1. After his indignant protest against *Pascendi* which was published in *Il Giornale d'Italia*, September 26, 1907, he published another long protest in the *Times* of September 30 and October 1. In virtue of this he was "deprived of the sacraments" (excommunicated) on October 22. He died in 1909 without being reconciled to the Church (Fr. Bremond was suspended *a divinis* for having prayed at his grave during the funeral).

[72] Letter from Buonaiuti to Gallarati Scotti, cited in Guasco, *Modernismo*, p.165.

It would be wrong, however, to think that on the one side was ranged an inflexible Pius X and his more or less obscurantist court, and on the other side learned Catholics, whether churchmen or not, who were being unjustly persecuted, attracting the sympathy of all "enlightened" men. Paradoxically, it was a non-Catholic, the renowned philosopher Benedetto Croce, who took up the defence of *Pascendi* and of Pius X in the very same *Giornale d'Italia*. On October 15 he wrote:

> Modernism, according to Minocchi, claims to distinguish between dogma's real content and its metaphysical expressions, which he regards as something accidental, just as the different forms of language which can translate the same thought are accidental. This comparison is the first and principal sophism of the Modernists.
>
> It is true, of course, that the same concept can be translated in different ways. But metaphysical thought is not a form of expression: it is logic. Consequently, a dogma translated into a different metaphysical form is no longer the same dogma, just as a concept transformed into another concept is no longer the same concept.
>
> Modernists are free to transform dogmas according to their ideas. I myself exercise this freedom....The difference is that when I do it, I am aware of being outside the Church, outside all religion, whereas the Modernists stubbornly proclaim to be not only religious, but Catholics. If, trying to escape from the consequences of their principle, and sympathizing with positivists, pragmatists and empiricists of all kinds, they claim not to believe in the value of thought and logic, they will necessarily end in *agnosticism* and *scepticism,* doctrines which can be harmonized with a vague religious sentiment, but are hostile to all positive religion....My good Modernist friends must excuse my enjoying this situation; I shall hardly have such good fortune again to be in agreement with the Pope.

Later, the other great Italian philosopher of the time, Giovanni Gentile, also a layman, would salute the coherence of *Pascendi*:

> Catholicism will never be able to turn into the negation of itself, as Tyrrell and Loisy wished. This truth, so distasteful to the Modernists, resounds throughout the Encyclical of September 8, 1907, from beginning to end. It is a magisterial summary and magnificent critique of the philosophical principles of all Modernism. The Encyclical's author has utterly penetrated and very exactly interpreted the doctrine which is found disseminated in Modernism's philosophical, theological, apologetical, historical, critical and social demands; he can be said to have judged it from a higher point of view. As for Loisy's ripostes, they make a pitiful showing in the face of the philosophy expressed in the Encyclical....The Modernists must learn that a Pope's work cannot be judged according to the criteria of that rationalism which, down the centuries, has always ended up in heresy. To make such a judgment would be as logical as approving a king's achievement insofar as it contributed to the proclamation of a republic.[73]

The far-reaching reply to *Pascendi* welcomed by certain Italian Modernists was *Il programma dei Modernisti. Riposta all'Enciclica di Pio X.* The first Italian edition appeared in the month following the pontifical document. There were two further editions in succeeding years. In 1908, French, English, German and American translations of this "program" were made. Apropos of this reply to the Pope, which was published anonymously, Émile Poulat observes: "The whole idea of the *Programma* should be attributed to Buonaiuti, who undertook to write it on the basis of a memorandum he had requested from his friend Fracassini; it echoes, more or less, the discussions of the small circle of Roman Modernists."[74] On October 29, 1907, a decree of the Vicariate of Rome forbade anyone to "sell, read, or keep this same book, under pain of mortal sin" and excommunicated "the authors and writers and any other persons who, in whatever way, have collaborated in the production of this book."[75]

As for the French Modernists, in January 1908 Alfred Loisy published a new "little red book" entitled *Simples réflexions sur le décret du Saint-Office "Lamentabili sane exitu" et sur l'encyclique "Pascendi Dominici Gregis."* In the first part of his book Loisy took the decree's articles one by one and set against them, as we have seen, his own theses. In the book's second part he radically contradicted not only the encyclical's argumentation, but also its method. The encyclical's point of departure is mistaken, Loisy explained, because the Modernism exposed by Pius X does not exist: "the exposition he gives of the *modernist* doctrines is practically a fantasy of the theological imagination."[76] Whatever the falsity of its premises, the encyclical, according to Loisy, has the merit of "proclaiming officially" and "in the voice of its head" that "the divorce is complete" between the Roman Church, which "rejects all concessions" and "the modern spirit, modern science, modern society."[77]

Dated February 14, an order of Msgr. Amette, the new Archbishop of Paris, condemned the book (as well as another work of Loisy's, *Les Évangiles synoptiques*). On February 19 Loisy was threatened with excommuni-

---

[73] The article by Croce and that by Gentile (which appeared in *Critica,* May 20, 1908) are quoted at length in Dal-Gal, *Pie X*, pp.284-286.

[74] Poulat, *Histoire, dogme et critique,* p.675.

[75] Decree of the Vicariate of Rome (October 20, 1907), *Documents pontificaux,* vol.I, p.483.

[76] Loisy, *Simples réflexions,* p.149. This criticism is taken up, in different terms, by the most recent historian of Modernism, Colin, *L'Audace et le soupçon,* p.249: "the synthesis constructed by the Encyclical is so impressive that this text can be considered to be the veritable *invention* of 'Modernism.'...When we speak of individual initiatives that were not part of a concerted plan, we are therefore rejecting the Encyclical's whole thesis."

[77] *Ibid.* p.289.

cation if he did not retract within ten days. Since no expression of submission was made, he was excommunicated on March 7.

Of course, these Modernist voices which could not be made to submit to the teaching of Pius X, although they were relayed by some elements of the press, remained largely a minority in the Church. The Vatican archives, once again, enable us to assess the adherence (and not merely the obedience to a command) which *Pascendi* evoked from the clergy of the entire world.[78] The bishops and archbishops had not been requested to manifest their adherence, and that of their clergy, by writing personal letters. But very many did so. To imagine that they did this out of fear of being suspected of compromising with Modernism, or out of lukewarm acquiescence, would be unjustly to cast a slur on the whole of the Catholic episcopate under Pius X.

A significant example of sincere zeal is that of Cardinal Mercier, Archbishop of Malines, the great protector of the celebrated Catholic University of Louvain. No one could have suspected him of servile submission to the Holy See and yet, two days before *Pascendi* was made public (September 16, in the *Osservatore Romano*), he wrote a letter to the Holy Father and had it printed. It was a letter of submission to the decree *Lamentabili* and to the encyclical; he had copies of it signed by the professors of the University of Louvain, and of the diocesan seminaries under his aegis, and by all the members of the teaching orders. A total of 254 signatures of clerics were collected. Three months later Msgr. Rumeau, Bishop of Angers, the seat of another Catholic university, also had sheets printed to receive the signatures of adherence of all the priests of his diocese.

Msgr. Shanahan, Bishop of Harrisburg, Pennsylvania, USA, published a letter, dated December 26, on the *Doctrines of the Modernists,* and announced that he was putting in place an anti-Modernist *Vigilance Committee* as the encyclical had demanded; in addition he announced that he would give conferences to his clergy—which had not been requested—on the divinity of Christ, the Church, the Sacraments, the Trinity, the Incarnation and the Holy Scriptures. This kind of initiative was also undertaken in Scotland at the same time. On December 20 Msgr. Maguire, Bishop of Glasgow, wrote to Cardinal Merry del Val, informing him that he had established a *Vigilance Committee* and the Corps of Censors demanded by the encyclical, and that, in addition, he had given two conferences to his clergy: the first, beginning the previous April, dealt with "novelties in theology," and the second, on December 3, addressed the "doctrines of the Modernists."

---

[78] There is a vast unedited archive—hundreds of documents (letters, addresses, *etc*).—in ASV, Segretaria di Stato, anno 1908, rubrica 82, f.2-5.

Elsewhere, in Italy, the Bishop of Teramo showed his acceptance of the pontifical teaching by publishing a circular forbidding the priests of his diocese to read the Modernist reviews and the local newspapers which, he said, were supporting Modernism.[79]

These few examples of complete adherence to the teachings and directives of *Pascendi* from different countries—many others could be cited—augmented the current fostered by the decree *Lamentabili*. All this makes it clear that Pius X's condemnation of Modernism met with the quasi-unanimous support of the episcopate, the clergy and the religious orders.

Eradicating Modernism

We have already indicated the canonical sanctions taken against the Modernist authors who stubbornly refused to retract their errors. In fact, these individual sanctions attached to named people were only the official form, the public manifestation of the severe penalties which Pius X had decided to invoke *latae sententiae* against the Modernists. Two months after the publication of *Pascendi*, a motu proprio applied excommunication *latae sententiae* to all those who "by all kinds of sophistry and artifice endeavor to evacuate the force and efficacity" of the decree *Lamentabili* and the encyclical.[80]

Pius X did not publish any further doctrinal text on Modernism. No doubt he thought that he had exposed and refuted the doctrine in sufficient detail. In various different circumstances, however, he would renew his warnings: on December 16, 1907, in a consistorial allocution at the creation of four cardinals (two of whom were French: Msgr. Luçon, Archbishop of Rheims, and Msgr. Andrieu, Bishop of Marseilles); on January 2, 1909, in a public letter to Msgr. De Busch, Bishop of Speyer, thanking him for a letter in which the latter had expressed his "submission" to the anti-Modernist teachings and directives; on January 10, 1910, in a public letter to Msgr. Franceschini, Bishop of Fano, in which he takes up a term used by the latter ("the contagious plague of Modernism"); on September 15, 1910, in a public letter of approbation of a book by the Freiburg professor, Descurtins, on the subject of *literary Modernism*; on December 31, 1910, in a letter to Cardinal Fischer, Archbishop of Cologne; on January

---

[79] Letter of Msgr. Zanecchia-Ginetti to Cardinal Merry del Val, February 18, 1908. The Modernist reviews which the Bishop of Teramo prohibited his priests from reading are *Nova et Vetera* (Rome), *Rinnovamento* (Milan), *Cœnobium* (Lugano) and *Gioventù Nova* (Città di Castello). According to the Bishop, the local newspapers supporting Modernism are: *Lotta* and *Libertà* (Fermo), *Sario* (Cesena), *Adriatico e Roma* (Ascoli Piceno), and the famous national daily, *Il Giornale d'Italia*.

[80] Motu proprio *Praestantia* (November 18, 1907), *Documents pontificaux,* vol.I, pp.486-488.

7, 1911, in a letter to the Austrian episcopate and in another to the Bishop of Acerenza Materacereta.

Three years after *Pascendi,* however, and after having put many books on the Index, Pius X judged it necessary solemnly to reaffirm and amplify the encyclical's practical prescriptions. On September 1, 1910, the motu proprio *Sacrorum Antistitum* reiterated the seven prescriptions of 1907 (the setting-up of *Vigilance committees* in every diocese, *etc.*) and imposed "special measures for seminarians and novices" and their professors.[81]

In the seminaries, the formation of the mind and the perfection of the soul should go hand in hand. "We have no right to regard these establishments as being for study alone, or for piety alone." In the choice of candidates for the priesthood, seminary superiors and bishops must demand both "innocence of life" and "the possession of sound doctrine." The acquisition of "many and varied" areas of knowledge is a necessity, "as the very situation of our times shows us." The cleric must "acquire higher knowledge than that of ordinary men and strive more than others for the excellence of doctrine." But "the passion for learning must be moderated," as St. Paul teaches ("For I say...not to be more wise than it behoveth to be wise, but to be wise unto sobriety," Rom 12:3); furthermore, "it is important for the young men not to waste their time with other questions, and not to be distracted from their principal studies; for this reason We absolutely forbid the reading of all newspapers and reviews, however excellent they may be."

"To prevent Modernism having any opportunity of insinuating itself unnoticed," the professors should present their course text to their superior at the beginning of the academic year, and their "method of teaching" will be examined during the year: "if it seems to be straying from sound doctrine, the teacher responsible must be removed immediately."

However, the most important novelty of the motu proprio was the prescription of an oath, which immediately became known as the anti-Modernist oath, since part of it consisted of a profession of faith in five points, and the other part contained a detailed censure of the Modernist doctrines and methods. This anti-Modernist oath had to be taken by all clerics in major orders, confessors, preachers, parish priests, canons and holders of benefices, members of episcopal curias and ecclesiastical tribunals, members of the Roman Congregations and Roman ecclesiastical tribunals, superiors and professors of religious congregations before taking up office.[82]

---

[81] Motu proprio *Sacrorum Antistitum* (September 1, 1910), *Documents pontificaux,* vol.II, pp.266-284.

Finally the motu proprio devoted many pages to sacred preaching and the care with which preachers should be chosen. Pius X took up an instruction issued by the Congregation of Bishops and Regulars under his predecessor, who had sent it solely to the bishops and religious superiors of Italy, and had it sent to all bishops. The instruction was reprinted in its entirety, and the Pope completed it by adding certain recommendations to preachers. The Pope rejected "subtleties of language" and "fair words" that were too often given from the pulpit with "a certain theatrical delivery," and also the profane subjects that, too often, were broached, and recommended preachers to return to "the incontestable and most abundant source of sacred eloquence, the Bible." The Holy Scriptures "represent for sacred preaching an excellent source, indeed, one of the most fruitful," and the Pope is displeased to see it neglected by a great number of preachers. He urges them, moreover, not to be content with a pragmatic view of religion: "They proudly boast of the advantages which the Christian religion has brought to human society; but they omit to speak also of the obligations to which men are committed; they set forth the charity of Christ the Saviour, but they are silent about his justice."

Bishops and religious superiors must "oppose, with apostolic courage, this form of preaching and do all they can to suppress it." Paying great attention to the choice of preachers is essential if sacred preaching is to regain its "sacredness" and "effectiveness."

The promoter of biblical studies

The prescriptions of *Pascendi* and the motu proprio *Sacrorum Antistitum* should not cause us to forget that, at the same time, Pius X was very concerned to promote authentically Christian progress in religious studies. It would be a grave mistake to think that, because he was an ardent defender of the faith against the Modernists who were imperilling it, he was hostile to all research which questions the methods hitherto employed and the knowledge so far acquired. His ideas on theology, philosophy and exegesis were not rigid. To take Holy Scripture as a case in point, the solemn acts of his pontificate and the initiatives he took show that it was the same Pius X who condemned rash exegetical works who, at the same time, was a resolute promoter of biblical studies.

This aspect of Pius X's constant concern is too often ignored or obscured; a letter of his to Msgr. Le Camus, Bishop of La Rochelle, who was

---

[82] Without going into complicated historical detail, it should be noted that, in the end, Pius X exempted all the ecclesiastical professors of the State Universities of Germany from taking the oath. Cf. Émile Poulat, *Catholicisme, démocratie et socialisme* (Tournai/Paris: Casterman, 1977), pp.425-435.

also an exegete and a defender of "true exegesis," shows this side of the Pontiff:

> Just as one must condemn the temerity of those who, more anxious to follow the taste for novelty than the teaching of the Church, employ critical procedures that are excessively free; one must also disapprove of the attitude of those who will not, in any way, risk breaking with the current scriptural exegesis, even when—providing that the faith remains sound—the wholesome progress of studies commands them to do so; you have set your course, most felicitously, between these two extremes.[83]

It was with a view to the "wholesome progress" of biblical studies that, in 1909, Pius X founded the Pontifical Biblical Institute.[84] True, this initiative on the Pope's part was wholly in continuity with his immediate predecessor, Leo XIII, who had already done much to develop and establish biblical studies. Pius X, however, had long been attracted, even since his time as a student in the Padua Seminary, to the study of and meditation on Holy Scripture. When he became Pope, the Holy Scriptures remained central to his teaching. As Cardinal Lercaro remarked, 40 years after Pius X's death, "the number of documents relating to Holy Scripture which the holy Pope issued with his authority, was greater than any other pope had published."[85]

The final years of Leo XIII's pontificate had been marked by a new impetus in biblical studies. Protestant exegesis had overturned people's grasp of Holy Scripture by the use of the historico-critical method (David Friedrich Strauss, Ferdinand Christian Baur, Julius Wellhausen). This exegesis, tending to rationalism, represented a danger to the faith, and the Dominicans responded in 1890 by founding, in Jerusalem, the *École Biblique* (which published the *Revue biblique* from 1892 onwards). In 1892 this first important initiative was officially blessed, in a way, by the publication of the encyclical *Providentissimus Deus,* which dealt with biblical

---

[83] Letter of Pius X to Msgr. Le Camus, January 11, 1906, cited in Lagrange, *M. Loisy et le modernisme,* p.134. Émile Le Camus (1839-1906) was an exegete before being appointed Bishop of La Rochelle in 1901. He was co-author of two works in the controversy with Loisy: *Vraie et fausse exégèse* (1903) and *Fausse exégèse, mauvaise théologie* (1904); cf. Yves Blomme, "Le Camus," *Les sciences religieuses,* under the direction of François Laplanche, vol.IX of *Dictionnaire du monde religieux dans la France contemporaine,* pp.398-400.

[84] On the origins and development of this Institute, one can consult three retrospectives published by the same Institute. The first two are in Latin: Léopold Fonck, *Primum quinquennium Pontificii Instituti Biblici* (Rome: Sumptibus Pontificii Instituti Biblici, 1915); Agostino Bea, *Pontifici Instituti Biblici de Urbe. Prima quinque lustra* (Rome: Pontificio Instituto, Biblico, 1934); various, *San Pio X, promotore degli studi biblici, fondatore del Pontificio Istituto Biblico* (Rome: Pontificio Istituto Biblico, 1955).

[85] Giacomo Lercaro, "S. Pio X e la Sacra Scrittura," in *San Pio X, promotore degli studi biblici,* p.15.

studies. In it, Leo XIII affirmed that three things were necessary: a critical edition of the sacred texts; reliable norms for interpretation; and the training of masters. On October 30, 1902, in the Apostolic Letter *Vigilantiae*, the same Pope created the Pontifical Biblical Commission, whose task was to discuss biblical questions and give answers subject to the Pope's approbation.

At the same period the projected Biblical Institute, to be established in Rome, took shape. In 1903 two French exegetes, the Sulpician Fulcran Vigouroux, secretary to the Biblical Commission, and the Jesuit Ferdinand Prat, consultor to the same Commission, were entrusted by Leo XIII with the task of designing a project. The former established a program of studies and the latter drew up a plan for the organization of the future Institute. Leo XIII was enthusiastic about this project, but his death prevented it being carrying out.

Pius X took up the project some years later and laid down its threefold mission. On February 23, 1904, by the Apostolic Letter *Scripturae Sanctae*,[86] he affirmed his desire to "promote the study of Sacred Scripture more and more among the clergy, particularly in these times when We see this source of divine revelation and faith under heavy attack everywhere and more than heretofore, as a result of the intemperance of human reason." He also spoke of his predecessor's plan to set up "a kind of special faculty" in Rome. He made the plan his own, but he also said that "at present We do not have the resources to implement this project...We have the firm hope and certainty that, one day, We shall be supplied with these resources by the generosity of Catholics." This was not a mere delaying tactic, as history would show.

While he was waiting for this day to come, Pius X, in the Apostolic Letter, gave the Biblical Commission power to confer licentiate and doctoral diplomas in Sacred Scripture. He established the precise conditions governing the awarding of these diplomas. Only those who were priests and doctors of theology could present themselves for the licence in Sacred Scripture. An oral and a written examination were required for both the licence and the doctorate; the Biblical Commission decided which subjects should be prescribed for the examinations. At first, the doctorate in Sacred Scripture was at a high level, being granted only after an oral defence of a written thesis, whereas at the same period the doctorate in philosophy or in theology could be obtained after only a single oral examination.

---

[86] Apostolic Letter *Scripturae Sanctae* (February 23, 1904), *Documents pontificaux*, vol.I, pp.115-116.

Fr. Prat, the French Jesuit, an exegete and a collaborator of the Biblical Commission, closely involved with Leo XIII's plan, was called to Rome by Pius X himself. He played a dominant part in drawing up the program of examinations.[87]

Pius X was not only concerned to train good teachers of Sacred Scripture; he also made sure that all future priests should receive a complete biblical education. Leo XIII, in the encyclical *Providentissimus,* had already prescribed the study of Sacred Scripture in the seminaries. Pius X worked out a precise course of study for this. In 1906 he published an Apostolic Letter on this one topic.[88] Until then there had been no detailed regulation on the subjects to be taught and learned in biblical studies. In 18 very clear points, Pius X laid down the program to be followed. Every year spent in the seminary was to include a course of biblical instruction. Without going into all the recommendations and regulations, it is enough to note that the Pope remembered his time as a young seminarian, when he had so wanted to study Oriental languages. Also, since he was well aware of the need for it, he stipulated that "pupils who show the best promise should be trained in Hebrew and biblical Greek and also, insofar as it is possible, in another Semitic language, such as Syriac or Arabic."

It is worth noting, furthermore, that Pius X did not have fixed ideas about biblical teaching. The professor of Old Testament, "drawing profit from recent discoveries, will show the course of events and the relations which linked the Hebrew people with the other peoples of the Orient." In general, the professor of Sacred Scripture "will assimilate all the genuine progress of this science and all the discoveries of modern scholars, but he will leave to one side the adventurous commentaries of innovators."

Pius X would soon say that "No (enterprise) is more salutary, or corresponds more to the needs of the times"[89] than to give access to the greatest number of people to the riches and the truth of Revelation. Furthermore, having urged preachers to return to Sacred Scripture, having encouraged and ordered its teaching in the seminaries, he encouraged the spread of translations of the Gospel. Several years before, the *Society of St. Jerome* had been created, with the aim of printing and widely propagating the Gospels in Italian. Five hundred thousand copies had already been printed and propagated in Italy and among the Italian immigrants in America. On Jan-

---

[87] Ernest Vogt, "S. Pio X fondatore del Pontificio Istituto Biblico," in *S. Pio X, promotore degli studi biblici,* pp.26-27. Later on, however, Fr. Prat was not associated with the Pontifical Biblical Institute, because in 1907 he was removed from the Biblical Commission.

[88] Apostolic Letter *Quoniam in Re Biblica* (March 24, 1906), *Documents pontificaux,* vol.I, pp.354-356.

[89] Letter *Noi che fin* (January 21, 1907), *Documents pontificaux,* vol.I, pp.401-402.

uary 21, 1907, in a public letter to Cardinal Cassetta, protector of the Society, Pius X encouraged the enterprise: "To give everyone a simple means
of reading the Gospel and meditating on it—this is a special need nowadays, when people's eagerness to read is much greater than heretofore, and
often leads to dangerous excesses."

The year 1907 also saw the launch of a long-term project—the revision of the Vulgate—and the reinforcement of the authority of the Biblical
Commission.[90]

The Council of Trent had already hoped for a new, critical edition of
the Vulgate (the Latin translation of the Bible, made in the fourth century
by St. Jerome). Pius X set the work going. On April 30, 1907, Cardinal
Rampolla, president of the Biblical Commission, in a letter to Dom Hilde-
brand de Hemptinne, Abbot Primate of the Benedictines, entrusted this
task to his order. The Benedictines had a tradition of learning and a
knowledge of the manuscripts, and were accustomed to long-term work;
this rendered them particularly apt for the task. Some months later Pius X
created a Biblical Commission for the revision of the Vulgate. It was presided over by Dom Aidan Gasquet, Abbot General of the Benedictines of
England.[91] This Commission, composed of five Benedictine monks of different nationalities (including Dom Henri Quentin, a monk of Solesmes,
who would be the Commission's mainspring) was initially housed in the
monastery of St. Anselm, the primatial abbey of the Benedictines in
Rome. Then, when Dom Gasquet was created cardinal in 1913, the Commission moved to the Palace of St. Callistus. "The preparatory work for
this huge undertaking required years. It involved research into, and examination of, the manuscript bibles which were to be used; the working-out
of a method of establishing a good text; and, most of all, it meant travelling to the different libraries of Europe to study these biblical manuscripts
on the spot or to photograph them."[92] Pius X died without seeing the first
published volume of this revised Vulgate.[93] The work was not completed

---

[90] The strengthening of the authority of the Biblical Commission was marked by the
motu proprio *Praestantia,* to which we have already referred. Pius X orders that "all,
without exception, are bound in conscience to obey the doctrinal decisions of the
Pontifical Biblical Commission, those which have been promulgated and those which
will be, in the same way as they obey the decrees of the Sacred Congregations approved
by the Sovereign Pontiff." Under the pontificate of Pius X, the Biblical Commission
published 13 "decisions" concerning precise points in the field of biblical studies. The
full text is in *Documents pontificaux,* vol.I, pp.845-850 and vol.II, pp.663-682.

[91] Letter *Delatum Sodalibus* (December 3, 1907), *Documents pontificaux,* vol.I, pp.489-
490.

[92] Pierre Brottier, "L'Abbaye Saint-Jérôme de Rome," *De Cliärrwer Kanton,* 1997 (special
number on the Abbey of Clervaux) p.29.

until 1995...It will be a long time before this monument of erudition, this reference edition, will be replaced.

The last great undertaking of the pontificate in the area of biblical studies was the establishment of the Biblical Institute, which had been projected so long ago. Beginning in the academic year 1908-1909, with the approval of Pius X, a Higher Course of Sacred Scripture for clerics already possessing diplomas in theology was set up at the Pontifical Gregorian University, which was directed by the Jesuits. Fr. Leopold Fonck, a German exegete, had been given the task of organizing this course. He was received in audience by Pius X on January 10, 1909, and was struck by the Pope's enthusiasm for the courses given at the Gregorian and by "the exact nature of his knowledge" on biblical studies. During this audience the Pope gave words of encouragement which recall those he gave Msgr. Le Camus, which we have already cited: the Pope said,

> I do not think that we can be content to teach the ancient doctrines with old methods, spurning genuine progress. Without distancing ourselves from antiquity in matters of principle, we must nevertheless take account of new approaches in matters of form and method, not following the modernist method, but in a modern way in a good sense.[94]

In the Higher Course of Sacred Scripture, Fr. Lucien Méchineau taught Old Testament, Fr. Leopold Fonck New Testament, and Fr. Enrico Gismondi Hebrew and Syriac.[95] However, this teaching could not take the place of a complete program of biblical studies (exegesis, archaeology, ancient languages, geography and history) which could be offered by an institute entirely devoted to this area. So the superiors of the Gregorian quickly decided, in the very first months, that this Course should be transformed into a Biblical Academy which would be autonomous, but still linked to the University. On February 14, 1909, Pius X received Fr. Fonck in audience again and immediately made the project his own, seeing it as a way of finally realizing the Biblical Institute to which Leo XIII, and then he himself, had looked forward. Instead of creating an academy within the framework of the Gregorian University, however, he decided to create a

---

[93] The first volume of this revised Vulgate was published in 1926 (the Book of Genesis); two other books (Exodus and Leviticus) appeared in 1929. From 1933 onwards the monks of the Abbey of Clervaux in Luxemburg were given the task of continuing the enterprise and moved to the Abbey of St. Jerome which Pius XI had specially built for this purpose. The 18th and final volume (the two books of Maccabees) appeared in 1995.

[94] Account of the audience of January 10, 1909, quoted by Vogt, "San Pio X, fondatore," p.29.

[95] All three were subsequently professors at the Pontifical Biblical Institute. Enrico Gismondi (died in 1912) was consultor to the Sacred Congregation of the Index and the Pontifical Biblical Commission.

totally independent Institute, directly linked to the Holy See. Fr. Fonck was given the task of drafting a program and a corpus of regulations, basing himself on the work done by Vigouroux and Prat. The Jesuits would be the pillars of the future Institute. In the same way that Pius X had entrusted the revision of the Vulgate to religious of a single order (the Benedictines), he wanted to entrust the training of teachers of biblical studies to religious of a single order, namely, the Jesuits, who, by their Constitutions, were particularly subject to the pope.[96] This dependence on the pope, which is written into their Rule and which forms the Jesuit fourth vow of religion, would allow these religious to accept the two first articles of the Institute's constitution without questions of conscience arising:

1. The Pontifical Biblical Institute will be directly subject to the Apostolic See, whose laws and prescriptions will be its rule.

2. The direction of the Institute will be entrusted to a president appointed by Us, and who, in virtue of his charge, will represent the Institute; he will refer to Us in all important affairs of the Institute and give Us an account, every year, of his administration.[97]

The project may, at last, have been in a fair way to start up, but the necessary financial resources were still lacking. During this same audience on February 14, Pius X decided to make the Sacred Heart the Institute's Patron, and to make a continuous novena (three *Our Fathers* and three *Hail Marys* every day) "to obtain from the Sacred Heart the necessary funds for the foundation and development of the work."[98]

The Pope received Fr. Fonck on four other occasions, examining in detail the successive projects and the proposed program. On May 7, 1909, the Pontifical Biblical Institute was created and its regulations were set forth.[99] On June 11, Fr. Fonck was appointed president of the new Institute, being inaugurated the following November 5. The staff consisted of 12 professors, and 117 students were enrolled in the first year—numbers

---

[96] A. Vaccari, "Pio X e gli studi biblici," in *Pio decimo novello beato*, special number of *Palestra del Clero*, June 15, 1951, p.567.

[97] Apostolic Letter *Vinea Electa*, May 7, 1909, *Documents pontificaux*, vol.II, p.86.

[98] On different occasions Pius X desired to recall the Sacred Heart's patronage of the Institute. The Institute's coat of arms bears an image of the Sacred Heart surrounded by the *Alpha* and *Omega*. The Letter of Foundation, published on May 30, 1909, in the *Osservatore Romano*, was ante-dated 7 May, the first Friday of the month, traditionally consecrated to the Sacred Heart. The future professors of the Institute were received in audience by Pius X on October 17, 1909, the Feast of St. Margaret Mary Alacoque. The Institute opened its doors on the following November 5, first Friday of the month. Finally, in thanksgiving for the happy result of the "perpetual novena," Pius X had a large statue of the Sacred Heart placed in the *aula* of the Institute.

[99] *Vinea Electa* (May 7, 1909), *Documents pontificaux*, vol.II, pp.85-89.

which were totally unexpected, as Pius X himself observed. Only 20 or 30 had been expected for the first year. The Institute's 117 first students (properly speaking, 47 students, 18 auditors and 52 "guests") came from 17 countries. 46 were doctors of theology and about ten had already been professors of Sacred Scripture in seminaries or religious institutes. The new Institute was clearly responding to a need. Donations from diverse sources gave the Institute a stable basis on which to function. One month after the opening of the Institute, Fr. Charles du Coëtlosquet, a French Jesuit who had returned from his mission in Madagascar—and who had learned of the Institute's foundation from the newspapers!—communicated a very generous gift from his family.[100] The Coëtlosquet family gave other gifts too. From the list of generous donors we can mention Msgr. Kohn, Archbishop of Olmütz [Olomouc], and Msgr. O'Connell (later Cardinal), Archbishop of Boston.[101]

On March 13, 1910, the professors and students of the Institute were received in audience by the Pope. Notably, Pius X urged them to take no notice of the criticisms which had inevitably surrounded this work ever since it was announced. Five years after its opening, 35 professors of Sacred Scripture had been trained in the bosom of the Biblical Institute. (Fourteen were serving in Italy, in seminaries or religious congregations, six in Spain, six in the United States, two in Austria, two in Germany, two in Holland, one in Bavaria, one in Ireland, one in Canada).

From its very foundation, Pius X had appointed a twofold aim for the Pontifical Biblical Institute: "to develop biblical scholarship and all the ancillary studies in the most effective way, according to the spirit of the Catholic Church," and "against the false, erroneous, rash and heretical opinions largely propagated by the moderns, to defend, promulgate and promote the sound doctrine concerning the Sacred Books, in absolute conformity with the rules already established or which will be fixed by the Apostolic Holy See."[102] To attain this twofold aim, the Pontifical Biblical Institute gave courses in different disciplines: exegesis of the Old and New Testaments, biblical history and geography, Greek, Hebrew, Aramaic and other Oriental languages.[103] From the outset, however, it had been envisaged that there would be open lectures addressed to a wider public, and a spe-

---

[100] Bea, *Pontifici Instituti Biblici de Urbe,* pp.8-9, who speaks at length about the Coëtlosquet family.
[101] Fonck, *Primum quinquennium,* p.32.
[102] *Vinea Electa, Documents pontificaux,* vol.II, p.86.
[103] From the first year 1909-1910 there were courses in Assyrian, Arabic and Coptic. Other languages were added as the years went by: Sumerian and Egyptian from 1910-1911, Ethiopic from 1911-1912, Syrian from 1912-1913. Soon the journals *Orientalia* and *Analecta Orientalia* began to appear.

cialized library (by 1914 it had reached 50,000 volumes) and a biblical museum, and that the work of the Institute professors would result in the publication of scholarly studies. This latter objective well shows the desire for learning and for progress in scholarship which characterized the new Institute; this objective was on a par with its concern to "defend Catholic truth regarding the Sacred Books." As the years went by, high-quality scholarly studies were published, recognized as such by all biblical exegetes and historians. In 1915, 19 volumes had already appeared. Their diversity makes it clear that the Institute's horizon of scholarship was far from being narrowly restricted. For instance there were studies on the origins of Islam by Fr. Henri Lammens, a synoptic edition of the Gospels in Polish, a study on the Babylonian pantheon, exegetical studies properly so-called, and an edition of the Syriac works of St. Ephrem.

On March 12, 1911, in the Apostolic Letter *Iucunda Sane,* Pius X rejoiced in the first results that had been achieved and laid down certain norms for the examinations. The following year, in the Apostolic Letter *Ad Pontificium,* he granted the Institute the faculty of awarding diplomas. Until then the Institute's students had had to take their examinations before the Biblical Commission.

Anti-modernist "repression" and "integrism"

Even today certain historians still think that, in the battle he waged against Modernism, Pius X exhibited an intellectual narrowness of view that was utterly harmful to the progress of Catholic scholarship, and encouraged a "system of surveillance which laid itself open to the practice of informing against people who were all too carelessly suspected of 'modernizing' deviations...."[104] It must be said that this twofold accusation has been around for a long time.

The very next day after the election of Pius X, Maurice Blondel was already of the opinion that this Pope was an intellectually unenlightened "reactionary." He wrote to Fr. Wehrlé: "One's first impression is that 'reaction' has triumphed, albeit in the most benign form. In this world everything follows a rhythm. Even his choice of a name is an indication. The Holy Spirit can only have recourse to living human beings, and so it would take a miracle to give us an intellectual leader....We have, and we will have, much to do, and even more to suffer."[105] According to him, Pius X's election presaged dark days for Catholic intellectual life.

---

[104] Jacques Gadille, "Face aux nouvelles sciences religieuses. Le modernisme," in *Histoire du christianisme,* vol.XI, 1830-1914 (Paris: Desclée, 1995), p.461.

[105] Letter of Maurice Blondel to Fr. Johannes Wehrlé, August 5, 1903, in Blondel/Valensin, *Correspondance. 1899-1912* (Paris: Aubier), vol.I, p.94.

The Italian Modernist Fogazzaro shared this point of view exactly at this same period. Pius X had not been Pope for three months and had not yet taken any step against the Modernists, nor had he published any text condemning their doctrines, nor had he even published his first encyclical, but Fogazzaro predicted that Loisy would be condemned and he deplored Pius X's lack of intellectual breadth: "Pius X does not understand anything concerning these questions; he is not informed about them, due to a lack of modern culture; his intellectual milieu has always been rigorously traditionalist."[106]

"Traditionalist"—this was the gibe. Later, the favorite epithet would be "integrist." However, this word did not emerge in the period of Pius X. It had been used at the end of the 19th century in Spain: a political party had coined it in connection with the *Syllabus*. At the beginning of the century, still under the pontificate of Leo XIII, the word appeared in France, but with a different meaning: in matters of biblical exegesis, *integrism* was opposed to *progressism*.[107] As time went on, the two words would be applied to other areas of the Church's life and teaching.

The assertion that Pius X "did not understand anything" concerning biblical questions is contradicted by the testimony of Fr. Fonck, which we have already cited, and by the very foundation of the Pontifical Biblical Institute. But what of the other charge: did he not encourage or give his authority to a complex system of delations, denunciations and suspicion? What some people have in mind here are the Apostolic Visitations of the Italian dioceses and seminaries, as well as the *Sodalitium pianum,* which certain authors have portrayed as a kind of integrist "freemasonry." We shall examine both of these, restricting ourselves to the direct part played by Pius X.

---

[106] Letter of Antonio Fogazzaro to P. Sabatier, November 13, 1903, cited in Poulat, *Histoire, dogme et critique*, p.249. This was the general opinion in Modernist circles. Fogazzaro's verdict was repeated by the same Sabatier three years later: "Among the cardinals no one understands anything of the present crisis. The only way to keep in step with the current defenders of orthodoxy would be to do nothing and, most of all, to stop thinking" (letter to Tyrrell, May 7, 1906, quoted by Bedeschi, *Il modernismo italiano*, p.38).

[107] On integrism, the two standard reference works are still Jean Madiran, *L'Intégrisme. Histoire d'une histoire* (Paris: Nouvelles Éditions Latines, 1964), and Émile Poulat, *Intégrisme et catholicisme intégral* (Paris-Tournai: Casterman, 1969). Cf. also Émile Poulat, "Un couple maudit. Modernisme et intégrisme," in *Modernistica* (Paris: Nouvelles Éditions Latines, 1982), pp.32-57, and Roger Aubert, "Intégrisme," *Dictionnaire d'histoire et de géographie ecclésiastiques* (1995), vol.CXLIV-CXLV, col.1352-1367.

The Apostolic Visitations

We have already described the Apostolic Visitations in the chapter concerning Pius X's first great reforms. In fact, these Apostolic Visitations (of the Italian dioceses, beginning in 1907) were not aimed primarily against Modernism, but had a much wider scope. They were one of the favored means of the reform of the clergy undertaken by Pius X. Nonetheless, since they took place when the Modernist crisis was at its height, they were also, to quote Roger Aubert, "one of the instruments of what may be called institutional anti-Modernism."

We are beginning to get a better idea of the way these Apostolic Visitations took place and what they achieved.[108] Here we shall limit ourselves to what they show regarding Modernism's penetration among the clergy and the measures taken to counter this, and, most of all, the part which Pius X played in it. As we have already observed, most of the Apostolic Visitations were conducted by religious. In a certain number of cases we know that they had been chosen by the Pope personally. In the dioceses they visited it was their task to gather information about the spiritual and intellectual life of the clergy, and about their conduct. Though officially confined to priests, the Apostolic Visitations of the dioceses often concerned bishops too. The Apostolic Visitations of seminaries concerned the seminarians as well as their professors and superiors. First of all the Visitors compiled voluminous reports (*relazioni*), and then these were reduced to summaries (*sunti*) which were published in a limited edition. These summaries were destined chiefly for the cardinals' Commission for the Apostolic Visitations, but they were also sent to the relevant Congregations (in the case of dioceses, the Congregation of the Council, and then, after the reform of the Curia, the Consistorial Congregation; in the case of seminaries, the Congregation of Bishops and Regulars, then, after the reform, the Consistorial Congregation). There can be no doubt that Pius X was informed of the execution and results of each of these Visitations, and he actually read the reports of some of them.

With regard to the battle against Modernism, we see first of all that, in certain circumstances Pius X intervened personally, even in the execution of the Visitation. In 1905, for instance, during the long Apostolic Visitation of the Diocese of Florence (of which we spoke in an earlier chapter),

---

[108] In addition to the studies and documents published by *Fonti e Documenti* (vol.IX, pp.55-95; vol.XI-XII, pp.7-78; and vol.XX-XXI, pp.343-385), there is the article by Giovanni Vian, "Sviluppi ed esiti dell'antimodernismo durante il pontificato di Pio X attraverso le relazioni delle visite apostoliche," *Rivista di Storia e Letteratura religiosa*, 32, 1996, pp.591-615; this study contains a wealth of material although its conclusions are debatable. The same author's doctoral dissertation, defended in 1995, was published by Herder in 1998.

the Visitor felt obliged to tell the bishop, Msgr. Mistrangelo, that the Pope would prefer him to part company with his secretary.[109] Some time later, on a visit to Rome, the Bishop of Florence asked the Pope for confirmation of this, and the Pope replied that he had never made any such request. Did Pius X contradict himself here, or—more probably—did someone presume knowledge of his feelings? The latter seems to have been the case, for the secretary in question, Don Andrea Cassulo, was to become vicar general of the diocese and would be nominated by the Pope, in 1914, as Bishop of Fabriano and Matelica.

A different situation, of a different order, arose during the Apostolic Visitation of the Diocese of Cremona carried out by the head of the Discalced Carmelites, Fr. Rousset. The bishop of the diocese, Msgr. Bonomelli, was suspected of Modernist tendencies. Pius X intervened personally on several occasions, specifying in writing the points which the Congregation of the Council should put to Msgr. Bonomelli in its correspondence with him. When the Consistorial Congregation took up its duties of supervising the dioceses and the seminaries, Pius X communicated his personal decisions and orders through its secretary, Cardinal De Lai. Thus, in May 1907, in the wake of the Apostolic Visitation carried out in the Diocese of Vicenza, Pius X told Cardinal De Lai to recommend the diocesan bishop "to remove professors Don Caldana and Don Quaresima from the seminary, since both of them are decided Modernists."

As Giovanni Vian observes, the information assembled by the Apostolic Visitors on the spread of Modernism in the dioceses and seminaries probably reinforced Pius X's conviction that the Church, and in particular the clergy, were undergoing a grave crisis of faith and were being dangerously infiltrated.

It would be a mistake, however, to think that Pope and Curia had been submerged by a tidal wave of suspicion, leading to indiscriminate measures and sanctions. In 1908 the four Apostolic Visitors dealing with the 18 dioceses of the Piedmont were not determined to find culpable persons at any price. In his report, for example, Msgr. Fantozzi, Apostolic Visitor to the Diocese of Ivrea, having interrogated two priests suspected of Modernism, defended them in these terms: "Canon Boggio, professor of philosophy, has been accused of Modernism by certain people, but unjustly so...," and as for Don Giuseppe Marchisio, secretary to the bishop: "I have heard, from certain persons outside the diocese, that this young priest entertained some Modernist ideas; but since the Pope's warnings he has

---

[109] The affair was referred to by Msgr. Mistrangelo in a letter to the secretary of the Congregation of the Apostolic Visitation, June 4, 1906; this very long letter is published in *Fonti e Documenti,* vol.XI-XII, 1982-1983, pp.69-78.

changed his mind."[110] In 1908, again, La Fontaine (future Cardinal of Venice), in his report of his Apostolic Visitation in the Archdiocese of Pisa, exculpates Cardinal Maffi of the accusation of Modernism. Nor was Cardinal Maffi—a man of moderate views who had been in conflict with the Curia over the Catholic press—kept under suspicion, for the following year he was entrusted with the Apostolic Visitation of the Dioceses of Livorno and San Miniato.[111]

Again, in 1911 the Apostolic Delegate for the Venetian seminaries, Döbbing, did not hesitate to contradict a former Apostolic Visitor who had accused Concordia seminary's vice-rector of Modernism. Döbbing reported: "The opposite is the case. (The vice-rector) is a young and active man who enjoys everyone's confidence. No Modernist could last long in this seminary, because of the extreme vigilance of the Bishop, the rector and the prefect of studies."

On the other hand, in 1907 it was an Apostolic Visitation which obliged Don Fracassini to leave the Perugia Seminary. He had been one of the organizers of the Modernist meeting of Molveno. Another participant at this meeting, Don Francesco Mari, professor of Sacred Scripture and ecclesiastical history in the seminary of Nocera, was also removed from the seminary. One month after the Molveno meeting, Pius X wrote a letter to the Bishop of Nocera requesting him to dismiss Don Mari from his teaching post.[112] However, Don Mari was not left without resources or responsibility, for he was made a canon and was called to preach the Spiritual Exercises. In 1910 the Apostolic Visitor described him as a Modernist but, after having a discussion with him, thought that he could be brought back to the "right path" because he had a "good heart," and that "it would be a pity to risk losing a cultivated priest, such as are rarely to be found in this diocese."[113]

These different cases show that there was vigilance and there were sanctions, but no widescale unleashing of injustice and suspicion. On the other hand it is clear that there was a great concern to root out Modernism from the seminaries. This was even more evident in 1911-1912, i.e., after the real extent of the influence of the new ideas—despite the various pontifical acts and measures—had been assessed. In the wake of a new series of

---

[110] Report on the Apostolic Visitation of Ivrea (October 1908), extracts published in *Fonti e Documenti,* vol.IX, pp.93-95.

[111] Extracts from his report on the Apostolic Visitations of Livorno and San Miniato were published in *Fonti e Documenti,* vol.XVIII-XIX, 1989-1990, pp.26-30 and 59-62.

[112] The facts are reported by F. Mari in a letter to A. Houtin, November 19, 1911, in a letter published in *Fonti e Documenti,* vol.XVIII-XIX, 1989-1990, p.121.

[113] Extracts from the report on the Apostolic Visitation (July 1910), published in *Fonti e Documenti,* vol.XX-XXI, 1991-1992, pp.383-384.

Apostolic Visitations, ordered for all the regional seminaries of Italy in 1911, the Consistorial Congregation which supervised seminaries decided to modify the *ratio studiorum* introduced in 1907. As we have seen, the 1907 reform of studies was not a superfluous exercise but a coherent and determined response to the developments of modern culture which were getting further and further away from Christianity. Compared with the 1907 program of studies, the modifications called for in the circular letter which Cardinal De Lai sent to all the bishops of Italy in 1912[114] do not signify a retreat; rather, they introduce greater precision; the structure of seminary studies remains the same. "Now that the results of the Apostolic Visitations have been collated,"—at length, in 14 points—"the Holy Father asks for the attention of the Most Reverend ordinaries." After stressing the necessary distinction between minor and major seminaries, and giving instructions on the organization of the former, the Pope goes on to points 11 to 14, which deal with studies properly so-called, in the major seminaries. It is here that we find the Pope's concern to prevent Modernism penetrating into the seminaries, without his turning his back on the legitimate progress of religious scholarship.

In the study of theology, there was a reaffirmation of the obligation to follow the scholastic method, "supplemented by use of modern scholarship—insofar as it is sound—in history and Sacred Scripture." All theological manuals which had not received the Holy See's approbation should be forbidden. Also, it was recommended (but not made obligatory) for dogmatic and moral theology to be taught in Latin, and philosophy too if possible. As regards the study of history, "care should be taken...not to omit the part played by the supernatural," without which the Church herself "is incomprehensible." The role of Providence should be stressed, on the basis of the philosophy of history developed by St. Augustine, Dante and Bossuet. The teaching of the other subjects (Biblical Greek, Hebrew, sacred eloquence, patristics, liturgy, archaeology, sacred art and Gregorian chant) is not suppressed or reduced, but must be divided up among the four years of theology, lest it be provided to the detriment of theology.

It should be added that, parallel to this circular on the seminaries, the Consistorial Congregation published several circulars or decrees forbidding seminarians to read certain works judged dangerous or suspect. In this category the following works were mentioned: on September 1, 1911, the translation of the *Histoire ancienne de l'Église* by Msgr. Duchesne; on June 29, 1912, various works on Holy Scripture[115] and "many writings" by

---

[114] Circular letter on seminaries, July 16, 1912, *Documents pontificaux*, vol.II, pp.608-613.

[115] *Kurzgefasstes Lehrbuch der speziellen Einleitung in das Alte Testament* by Karl Holzhey, and *Die Heilige Schrift des Neuen Testaments* by Fritz Tillmann.

Fr. Lagrange; on July 16, 1912, the history manuals by Funk and Kraus, and the manual of patrology by Rauschen. It should be noted that, depending on the case, the Consistorial Congregation's limited interdiction either preceded the book's posting on the *Index* (which meant that it was generally banned)—this was the case with Msgr. Duchesne's work—or was only a cautionary move, not followed by any other sanction. Historians of Modernism often present the banning of a book by means of the *Index* as a terrible sanction, a sign of the "obscurantism" of the Congregations concerned and of the Pope; to counter this view we can cite a case which shows, on the contrary, that putting a book on the *Index* did not always mean that it was consigned to absolute oblivion. Msgr. Batiffol, whose case we have already mentioned, saw one of his books on the history of dogma, *L'Eucharistie,* put on the *Index* in 1907. He sent in his letter of submission to Rome. The official announcement that it had been put on the *Index* was not made until 1911. But Msgr. Batiffol was not reduced to silence. Together with Pierre de Labriolle he founded the *Bulletin d'ancienne littérature et d'archéologie chrétienne* and, in 1913, he obtained permission from Pius X in person to publish a revised and corrected edition of his work on the Eucharist.[116]

Whether it is a question of the *Index,* canonical sanctions or Apostolic Visitations, anti-Modernist repression should not be represented by caricature and exaggeration. Giovanni Vian's verdict, in concluding his study of the Apostolic Visitations to the seminaries and dioceses, is that they were one of the many forms of "anti-Modernist repression" which led to "a culture of suspicion, based on anonymous delations and spying, and on the presumption of culpability...."[117] Lorenzo Bedeschi speaks of "inquisitors" and underlines the "fundamentally repressive character" of the Apostolic Visitations.[118] These verdicts, and the adjectives used, are more than excessive. Certainly, there were untoward instances due to over-zealousness. We have already cited some of them in this book, and shall mention other cases later. But Pius X cannot be held directly responsible for the excesses of either party. This can clearly be seen in the case of *La Sapinière*.

La Sapinière

Was *La Sapinière* the spearhead of an anti-Modernism that was all the more virulent because its activities were more or less secret? And as for Pius X, by encouraging *La Sapinière* and protecting its founder, Msgr. Benigni,

---

[116] Bécamel, "Comment Monseigneur Batiffol quitta Toulouse," pp.278-279; Poulat, *Modernistica,* p.219, and Pierre Riché, "Batiffol Pierre," in *Les sciences religieuses,* vol.IX of *Dictionnaire du monde religieux dans la France contemporaine,* p.37.

[117] G. Vian, "Sviluppi ed esiti dell'antimodernismo," p.613.

[118] Bedeschi, "Antimodernismo piemontese," p.55.

was he not guilty of promoting "an integralist plot" (*eine integralistische Verschwörung,* in the words of the German historian Schmidlin in 1936) and an odious system of denunciations? For more than 70 years the historical controversy has gone on and on. The works of Émile Poulat, with their unparalleled detail and erudition, have shed light on the functioning of *La Sapinière* and the personality of Msgr. Benigni.[119] Pius X's attitude to *La Sapinière* and Msgr. Benigni was the object of various serious "objections" (*animadversiones*) by the Promoter of the Faith during his beatification process. The defenders of Pius X's cause for beatification gave a lengthy reply, an important element in the dossier, which has rarely been used by historians.[120]

Umberto Benigni was born in 1862 in Perugia. Ordained priest in 1884, he became secretary to the city's Archbishop. At the same time, since he was very interested in the social question, he founded a weekly paper, *La Rassegna sociale.* Then, as Émile Poulat says, he cut the figure of a "priest of the left." So he began his career as an ecclesiastical journalist, which he pursued in Genoa, and then in Rome from 1894. Simultaneously he began to publish significant historical works which enabled him to teach ecclesiastical history in different Roman institutions, notably in the Academy of Noble Ecclesiastics, where the Holy See's future diplomats received their education. In November 1904 he started a career in the Roman Curia which came to an abrupt end seven years later. First he was *minutante* (attaché or secretary) to the Congregation for the Propagation of the Faith; then in 1906 he joined the Congregation of Extraordinary Ecclesiastical Affairs, a post he retained when, in 1908, the Congregation became part of the Secretariat of State. As under-secretary in this Congregation he was particularly occupied with the press service. His huge knowledge of the world of journalism and his familiarity with various foreign languages made him particularly apt for this position.

---

[119] In addition to *Intégrisme et catholicisme intégral,* one should consult *Catholicisme, démocratie et socialisme. Le mouvement catholique et Mgr Benigni de la naissance de socialisme à la victoire du fascisme.*

[120] It is sometimes cited, but seems to be even more rarely read. The author—generally well-informed—of the most recent synthesis on Modernism (Guasco, *Modernismo,* p.188) speaks of it as a *fascicolo* (a "booklet"), whereas the work consists of 323 pages. The *Disquisitio circa quisdam obiectiones modum agendi Servi Dei respicientes in modernismi debellatione* was published in a limited edition by the Sacred Congregation of Rites in 1950. It was recently published in French translation under the title *Conduite de saint Pie X dans la lutte contre le modernisme* (Versailles: Publications du Courrier de Rome, 1996). Pages 219-317 examine in more detail Pius X's attitude towards *La Sapinière* and Msgr. Benigni, and many documents are reproduced in full.

On May 23, 1907, Msgr. Benigni launched the publication of a bulletin entitled *Corrispondenza romana* (which in 1909 was renamed *Correspondance de Rome*). Thanks to correspondents and friends based in different countries, Msgr. Benigni was able to publish religious news and information on cultural, intellectual, social and political life. The news items published by *Corrispondenza* were principally intended for newspapers. This publication had no official status, although its founder was still under-secretary at the Secretariat of State.[121] His enemies, however, saw it as a semi-official Vatican organ, just as they saw *La Sapinière* as a kind of semi-official secret network of anti-Modernism.

In fact *La Sapinière* (which comes from its real name, *Sodalitium Pianum*, "Sodality of St. Pius V," abbreviated as SP) was founded in 1909; it was a kind of secular institute before its time. The SP was directed by a Diet of four members: in addition to Msgr. Benigni, the director, there were two French religious who lived in Rome (Fr. Saubat, procurator-general of the Priests of the Sacred Heart of Bétharram, and Fr. Charles Maignen,[122] future procurator-general of the Brothers of St. Vincent de Paul) and Msgr. Speiser, Bishop of Freiburg. The SP was a federation of "integral Roman Catholic groups," local groups which could admit both priests and laity. In a lengthy program drawn up in 1913, the SP defined itself: "The integral Roman Catholic," it says in point 1, "accepts integrally the Holy See's doctrine, discipline and directions and all their legitimate consequences for the individual and society. Thus it is 'papalist,' 'clerical' and anti-Modernist, anti-liberal and anti-sectarian. It is therefore integrally counter-revolutionary, since it is opposed not only to the Jacobin Revolution and sectarian radicalism, but equally opposed to religious and social Liberalism."

The Roman Diet sent different documents to its groups, *i.e.*, a weekly letter—for a time—and confidential circulars, *etc*. In return it received information and reports from them. Since secrecy was required of its members and between correspondents, they used a code. Later, their oppo-

---

[121] He lost this post in 1911 following what Poulat has called "the enigma of March 7, 1911" (*Catholicisme, démocratie et socialisme*, pp.358-436). He was succeeded by Msgr. Pacelli, the future Pius XII. Stripped of all official responsibility because of his tactlessness and excesses in the Secretariate of State, Msgr. Benigni nonetheless did not become *persona non grata:* he was regarded as being still useful in the anti-Modernist battle.

[122] Fr. Maignen was closely involved in the crisis which shook his congregation in 1907 and which, after an Apostolic Visitation, resulted in the departure of the superior general, Fr. Anizan, and many religious. Jean-Yves Moy, in his very searching study, *Le Père Anizan, prêtre du peuple* (Paris: Cerf, 1997), uncovers the various causes of this crisis. One can only say that Fr. Anizan was one of the victims of the anti-Modernist witch-hunt.

nents—and some historians too—spoke of the SP as a kind of secret society, an army solely in the (quasi-paranoid) service of anti-Modernism.[123] This accusation was first made in 1921 in an anonymous memorandum; it actually originated with Fr. Mourret, author of a *Histoire générale de l'Église* which enjoyed a certain authority.

On the other side it must be mentioned that Msgr. Benigni was at pains to have his association canonically recognized. He never succeeded in this, in spite of the dossiers which were presented to the all-powerful Cardinal De Lai. True, Msgr. Benigni was proud of having obtained three written approbations from the hand of Pius X himself (July 5, 1911; July 8, 1912; and July 6, 1914), but it must be said that these handwritten blessings (and the Pope's annual subvention of 1,000 lire to the SP) did not constitute anything unusual. It was only a case of a few brief lines of encouragement, in a stereotyped formula; the first autograph letter urges him to "fight the good fight of faith, particularly against the errors and wiles of Modernism in all its forms." This was not a complete approbation of everything that was done, said and written by the SP.

SP's opponents have vastly overestimated its importance and influence. In 1921 Fernand Mourret put its membership at 1,000. Msgr. Benigni, who at that time did not know the identity of the author of the anonymous memorandum, refuted this claim at length in a letter to Cardinal Sbarretti and gave more modest figures: "The really active members can be counted on the fingers of two hands; and the other members and friends are hardly more numerous. In all, *i.e.,* including friends who are not affiliated but are in sympathy with our aims, we have less than 100."[124] So there were few active members, and no cardinal among them, no bishop (apart from Msgr. Speiser, already mentioned) and no prelate of the Curia.

In a memorandum in his defence, Msgr. Benigni asserts that Cardinal Merry del Val, Secretary of State, Cardinal De Lai, secretary of the Consistorial Congregation, and Msgr. Bressan, particular secretary to Pius X, "for years, almost daily, received reports, extracts from the press, *etc.*, both on the general situation and on particular facts; and they needed only to say the word to be provided with the best we could supply with our feeble forces." At the same time, however, we can deduce from a particular remark of Msgr. Benigni that he was received in audience by the Pope only

---

[123] One example among others of the "anti-Modernist espionage" practised by the SP is this: when Fr. Semeria, a Barnabite of Genoa who had links with the Modernists, was exiled to Brussels, Msgr. Benigni sent a photograph of the Barnabite to his correspondent in Belgium "so that he could keep him under special surveillance."

[124] Official reply of Msgr. Benigni to Cardinal Sbarretti, November 16, 1921, reproduced in Poulat, *Intégrisme et catholicisme intégral,* p.582.

once a year.[125] What is more, he was given warnings, and at the highest level. On March 1, 1913, Msgr. Benigni and Fr. Saubat were received by Cardinal De Lai. The previous February 25 they had received written encouragement for the SP from the Consistorial Congregation, and now they had come to present new documents (the SP's program and statutes) with a view to the canonical approbation for which they were still hoping. Cardinal De Lai gave them a warning on this occasion, and felt it important to keep a written record of it on the back of one of the proffered documents: "I pointed out to them that the SC (Sacred Congregation) could approve neither a secret society nor a secret inquisitorial body over the bishops. They are in agreement with this, but..."[126]

This "but..." says it all: the SP would never acquire canonical status.[127] As this note shows, Cardinal De Lai was not convinced that Msgr. Benigni and the SP always used irreproachable methods; he was afraid that, despite their disinterested concern and their good faith, they might go beyond the limits they had set themselves. In the absence of documents written by Pius X on this subject, we can only conjecture that he shared the views of Cardinal De Lai.

However, even if it seems certain that Pius X only received Msgr. Benigni in private audience three or four times, it would be ridiculous to say that Pius X only had distant relations with the SP and its director. He entrusted certain missions to it.[128] It gave him information which could go towards helping him to make certain decisions.[129] The SP was not, therefore, an entirely secret society, an entirely private initiative; the Pope and his closest collaborators (notably Msgr. Bressan, Cardinals Merry del Val, De Lai, Vivès) entrusted it with tasks, gave it directives, but also imparted counsel and warnings. So, as Jean Madiran put it, it was "a kind of 'supple-

---

[125] Pius X "gave me 1,000 lire per year....One year, since I had no opportunity for an audience, the Pope had the kindness to send the money to me by his secretary."

[126] Note published in *Conduite de s. Pie X*, p.279.

[127] The further history of the SP after the death of Pius X goes beyond the scope of this book. We merely observe that, the day after the Pope's death, Msgr. Benigni dissolved the SP, on August 22, 1914; he re-established it in June 1915. In November 1921, within less than two weeks, an inquiry of Cardinal Sbarretti resulted in the dissolution of the SP.

[128] Thus, in 1910, through the intermediary of Cardinal Merry del Val, Pius X requested the SP to send one of its members to Berlin for the International Congress of Liberal Christianity and Religious Progress. Modernists from various countries (Murri, Lilley, Funk) and the unfrocked Carmelite, Loyson, were to give addresses along with several Protestants. Pius X was satisfied with the reported material.

[129] So, in 1909, the information provided by Don Pietro Perciballi, an associate of Benigni, contributed to the condemnation of the Roman Modernists, Ernesto Buonaiuti and Mario Rossi.

mentary' organ that was occasionally of use, in very exceptional circumstances and for a very limited period."[130]

It would be a mistake to overestimate the importance and influence of the *Sodalitium Pianum* and Msgr. Benigni. They had less power than people surmised after the event. The Modernist peril had been identified long before they began their anti-Modernist activities. The struggle against Modernism used many other means besides the SP network, and primarily these were the institutional means we have already mentioned: Apostolic Visitations, diocesan committees of vigilance, the anti-Modernist oath, the *Index, etc.* Finally we must remember that, as the pontifical acts demonstrate, Pius X had arrived at an exhaustive grasp of the many doctrinal dangers of Modernism before the SP came on the scene. The SP was used as an instrument; it did not have a directing role.

The same thing can be said of another anti-Modernist group which was openly active at the time: the International Priestly League *Pro Pontifice et Ecclesia* (PPEE). It owes its origin to something said in confidence, in April 1912, to Msgr. Archi, Bishop of Como, who had been very close to the Pope ever since his time in Venice. Pius X, quoting the Book of Isaiah (*De gentibus non est vir mecum*), had said that he felt alone, lacking in support from certain bishops and even in the Vatican.[131] Some time later, Fr. Chiaudano, a Jesuit from Turin who had formerly worked on the *Civiltà Cattolica,* the great Jesuit review published in Rome, had the idea of an international league of priests with the aim of helping the Pope materially and supporting him doctrinally. For its patron it had the great Jesuit theologian, Billot (who had been created cardinal the year before); its official founder and director was Cardinal Dubillard, Archbishop of Chambéry. The latter, who had made his mark in the fight against the law of Separation, against Modernism and the *Sillon,* had been created cardinal at the same time as Fr. Billot and had been hailed by Pius X as a model bishop, "*episcopus firmus et custos verae fidei.*"[132] In August 1912 the weekly *La Semaine Religieuse* of the Diocese of Chambéry presented the League as an organization for "promoting among the clergy, and—through them—among the laity, generous devotion to the Apostolic Holy See." Its members undertook to celebrate one Mass every year for the Pope's intentions,

---

[130] Madiran, *L'intégrisme,* p.131.

[131] *La Vigie,* the anti-Modernist and anti-Liberal weekly, published under the direction of Henri Merlier from December 5, 1912, alluded to this private remark in its "Programme" (no.1). Cf. Poulat, *Intégrisme et catholicisme intégral,* p.100. The latter contains information, in different places, on the League PPEE.

[132] Cf. Christian Sorrel, *Les Catholiques savoyards. Histoire du diocèse de Chambéry, 1890-1940* (Montmélian: Éditions La Fontaine de Siloë, 1995), which refers to the PPEE on pp.272-274.

to give 20 francs to Peter's Pence, to take out "new subscriptions for journals that are integrally Catholic and papal," to "make known as widely as possible the acts of the Holy See condemning modern errors" and "to oppose the conspiracy of silence with regard to the Roman question." In Italy the League's national director was Bartolomeo Chiaudano, brother of the founder and director of the Turin Seminary.

At the end of 1912, when Cardinal Dubillard made his *ad limina* visit, Pius X publicly praised the League, and in April 1913 he gave it his official approbation.[133] The League gave its support to the "intransigent," anti-liberal and anti-Modernist press. In France it was particularly linked with *L'Univers,* and in Italy to *La Riscossa,* edited by the Scotton brothers. At the end of 1913 the Pope appointed the man who had inspired it, Fr. Chiaudano, as director of the *Civiltà Cattolica.* In June 1914 a special section for laypeople was started. Lorenzo Bedeschi describes the League as "an organization of anti-Modernist espionage."[134] This expression is more than exaggerated, for the League operated quite openly and its aim was simply to give public support, financial and doctrinal, to the Pope. Émile Poulat, who has revealed the part played by the League, along with others, in having the Fr. Brémond's *Sainte Chantal* put on the *Index,* is more correct when he speaks of it as "a medium and channel of resistance to the new ideas, which hid nothing and led a normal life, which was above all suspicion, widely spread and ramified, and ultimately representative of the dominant spirit."[135] It should be added that several priests belonging to the League became bishops, also under the succeeding pontificate.

If we are fully to understand Pius X's relations with the anti-Modernist movements, we need to examine the Pope's personal attitude towards the Modernists—something which is rarely done.

His personal attitude towards the Modernists

From his very first encyclical, Pius X urged charity even towards "those who oppose us and persecute us, and perhaps seem worse than they really are." This charity was not a sign of weakness, but was grounded in hope: "the hope," wrote the Pope, "that the flame of Christian charity, patient and kind, will dissipate the darkness of their souls and bring God's light and peace."

Pius X also had this hope—of seeing the Church's adversaries mending their ways and renouncing their errors—as regards the Modernists.

---

[133] Letter *Laudare Satis,* April 28, 1913, *Documents pontificaux,* vol.II, pp.514-515.
[134] Lorenzo Bedeschi, "Spionaggio antimodernista a Perugia e in Umbria," *Fonti e Documenti,* vol.XX-XXI, 1991-1992, p.318.
[135] Poulat, *Modernistica,* p.218.

The testimonies we shall quote will prove this beyond dispute. But Pius X did more: he discreetly gave financial assistance to some of them or found them other posts; in other cases, he showed himself prudent before condemning them. Is this generosity, which was not exceptional, incompatible with his determination to fight against Modernism? How can the same man who imposes sanctions, dismisses clergy, excommunicates, simultaneously show himself charitable or forbearing? During the beatification process, the Promoter of the Faith presented a series of objections; one of them was this: "Let us be frank: the question, the only question which, in my view, seems to be raised in this great inquest, is to know whether Pius X, in his struggle against Modernism, overstepped the boundaries of prudence and justice, particular in his latter years...."[136] To this, the Postulator of the Cause replied with a voluminous dossier of more than 300 pages in which he showed that Pius X was "firm in his principles, right in his intentions, and patient and kind with those he dealt with, even when he had good cause to show his distress on their account."[137]

We now turn to this question of Pius X's personal attitude towards the Modernists, and will cite a number of cases. Pius X's contemporaries were perhaps unaware of these gestures of charity and justice on the part of the Pope. The day after the Pope's death, Msgr. Mignot, who was close to the Modernists, reproached the deceased in these terms: "Pius X was a saint, with a disinterestedness which is rare for an Italian, but his absolute ideas paralyzed his heart....He broke many souls, whom a little kindness would have kept on the right path."[138] Modernism's historians do not mention Pius X's gestures of charity or justice, or only in passing. The number and consistency of these deeds show, however, that they were not the result of exceptional decisions on his part, but manifested a state of mind and a spiritual attitude. In the struggle against the *phenomenon* of Modernism, all methods were used, and without pity, because Pius X considered that the faith of believers was in danger and that what was at stake was the Church's future; on the other hand, where the fate of *Modernists* was concerned, Pius X, when he knew of it, was at pains to be as just, prudent and charitable as possible.

An examination of Pius X's relations with Loisy, the most famous of the Modernists, gives us a good idea of his profound feelings. As we have already seen, when Loisy manifested a willingness to submit, Pius X was demanding, insisting that the French exegete should make a complete and sincere submission "with his heart." Loisy, who persisted in his errors after

---

[136] *Novae Animadversiones,* quoted in *Conduite de s. Pie X,* p.14.
[137] *Ibid.,* p.20.
[138] Letter from Msgr. Mignot to Hügel, September 9, 1914, quoted by Poulat, *Histoire, dogme et critique,* p.480.

Pascendi, was finally excommunicated. He lived in retirement at Ceffonds in the Haute-Marne, and would soon be elected to the Collège de France. However, Pius X did not regard him as a son lost to the Church. In 1908, receiving the new Bishop of Châlons, Msgr. Sevin, Pius X commended Loisy (whom he had excommunicated some time previously) to him. The Pope's words were reported by Loisy himself: "You are going to be Fr. Loisy's bishop. If you have the opportunity, treat him kindly; and if he makes one step towards you, make two towards him."[139]

Another case was that of Fr. Murri. As we shall see, the National Democratic League which he had founded had been condemned by the Pope. He had known links with Modernists. In April 1907, in the wake of a series of articles in which Murri had bitterly criticized the Vatican's policies in France, Pius X had sent a letter to the bishop of the diocese of this democratic leader, instructing him to inform the latter that he had been suspended *a divinis.* When, some months later, the Encyclical *Pascendi* was about to be published, there was a certain expectation that Murri would be immediately excommunicated, since it was quite clear that the turbulent Christian Democrat leader was going to oppose the encyclical. The question was put to Pius X, who preferred to be patient. On August 25, 1907, he wrote to the Congregation of the Holy Office: "If everything is in order with Fr. Romolo Murri's *celebret,* he cannot, without grave injustice, be prevented from saying Mass insofar as he has not performed any act condemned by the Encyclical."[140] Murri, however, persisted publicly in his views and was finally excommunicated in 1909. Subsequently he experienced grave financial difficulties; Pius X learned of this and had him paid a monthly subsidy.[141]

The Italian Barnabites had become embroiled in the Modernist crisis. We refer to three cases in which priests benefited from Pius X's attention. Fr. Alessandro Ghignoni published, in Rome, a popularizing review entitled *Pagine buone,* and collaborated on *La Vita,* "which can be regarded as the expression of ethico-religious Modernism according to the categories laid down in *Pascendi.*"[142] He was forbidden to preach in Rome and, finally, he was sent to Venice. His superior general obtained an intervention in his favor from Pius X. In October 1910 Pius X wrote a letter to Cardinal

---

[139] Loisy, *Mémoires,* vol.III, p.27. Fr. Lagrange gives another version of these words, a version he had from the mouth of Msgr. Sevin; when the Bishop of Châlons asked the Pope what attitude he should adopt towards Loisy if the latter showed repentance, the Pope replied: "Receive him with open arms. I tell you that he, my son, will return." (Lagrange, *M. Loisy et le modernisme,* p.138).

[140] Quoted by Dal-Gal, *Pie X,* p.404.

[141] Deposition of Cardinal Merry del Val, *Summarium,* p.195.

[142] Bedeschi, *Il Modernismo italiano,* p.107.

Cavallari, Patriarch of Venice, commending Fr. Ghignoni to his care.[143] When the anti-Modernist Venice Committee of Vigilance met, under the aegis of the Patriarch, it was less gentle, suspending Fr. Ghignoni *a divinis.*

Initially, Pius X showed the same patience with regard to Fr. Semeria, a colleague and friend of Fr. Ghignoni. Fr. Semeria was living in Genoa, and for a long time he had been connected with Loisy and other Modernists.[144] He himself had published books which caused a stir in certain circles. (None of them, however, was put on the *Index.*) In 1908 he was forbidden to preach. That same year, on the advice of his superior general, he wrote a very deferential letter of submission to Pius X, expressing his acceptance of the teachings of *Pascendi.* In 1910, when the anti-Modernist oath was imposed, Fr. Semeria applied to the Holy Office, and then to the Consistorial Congregation, requesting to be dispensed from it. When he received no satisfactory answer from that quarter, Fr. Semeria approached the Pope. He wrote him a long letter setting forth his case as a matter of conscience: while he could adhere fully to "dogmatic and defined truths," he could not give "firm interior and unconditional adherence" to "historico-critical opinions...that do not bear the august character of infallibility."

The Pope replied personally, authorizing him to swear the oath "with the reserves he had indicated." This confidential concession on the part of Pius X quickly became known in Modernist circles and allowed many clerics to swear the oath in that spirit.[145] It should be added—without imputing the decision with any certainty to Pius X—that in 1912 Fr. Semeria was sent to Brussels, where he lived as an exile.

A third religious of the Barnabite congregation, close to the Modernists, was Fr. Gazzola. He was a parish priest in Milan, closely connected with Loisy and other Modernists, and was considered as the inspiration behind the group of young intellectuals and aristocrats who published the review *Rinnovimento.*[146]His sermons, in which his Modernist ideas were quite plain, were much applauded. Ultimately his faculties for preaching and hearing confessions were withdrawn, and in 1908 his superiors transferred him to Cremona, where he was put in charge of the spiritual direction of the Barnabite college. As a result of a conference he gave on the

---

[143] Facts reported by Antonio Niero, "La formazione della spiritualità del clero e del popolo," in *La Chiesa veneziana dal 1849 alle soglie del novecento,* p.124, n.85.

[144] A. Gentili and A. Zambarbieri, "Il caso Semeria, 1900-1912," *Fonti e Documenti,* vol.IV, 1975, pp.54-527.

[145] Letter of Fr. Semeria to Pius X, November 17, 1910, published in *Fonti e Documenti,* vol.IV, 1975, pp.314-316. Pius X's reply is known indirectly by a quotation (*ibid.,* p.365).

[146] Maurilio Guasco, "Gazzola (Pietro)," *Dictionnaire d'histoire et de géographie ecclésiastiques,* vol.XX, col.197-199.

notion of miracle, and of the publication of a collection of sermons, he was expelled from his congregation. Subsequently this measure was revoked, and Fr. Gazzola was sent to Livorno. There his authorization to preach was restored to him, under the watchful eye of the city's bishop and of his religious superiors.

Another case shows how Pius X could be protective of those in his care, namely, that of Fr. Genocchi.[147] Born in Ravenna in 1860, he had entered the French congregation of the Missionaries of the Sacred Heart of Issoudun. First of all he was a missionary in Syria, in Constantinople and in New Guinea. His foreign postings enabled him to learn Arabic, Syriac, Aramaic, Turkish, and modern Greek (he had already mastered Hebrew and classical Greek). Having returned to Europe for health reasons, he was appointed professor of Sacred Scripture and moral theology at the scholasticate of the Missionaries of the Sacred Heart of Chezal-Benoît, in France. It was at that point that he became acquainted with Loisy. In 1897 he returned to Italy and was appointed professor of Sacred Scripture at the Apollinaire, at the same time holding the post of superior of the Barnabite monastery of the Via della Sapienza. The following year, however, Leo XIII, in connection with Cardinal Mazzella's opposition, suppressed the chair of Sacred Scripture. When the Pontifical Biblical Commission was created by Leo XIII in 1902, the name of Fr. Genocchi was proposed as a consultor, but, as he said, he "was passed over as being inclined too far to the left." Finally, the following year, he was appointed consultor, a post which he retained up to the early time of Pius X's pontificate. Although, during the discussion of many "responses," he adopted advanced positions, in 1905 he received two new responsibilities which show that the Pope still had confidence in him (and also that Pius X was able to acknowledge intellectual merit): the Pope appointed him a member of the special commission for reorganizing the Italian seminaries, and also an *Apostolic Examiner of the Clergy* (whose task was to examine candidates for Holy Orders in the Rome Vicariate). Soon, however, he would be accused of Modernism. In 1907 he wrote a review of the *Profezie di Isaia* by the Italian Modernist, Minocchi, which was judged to be too favorable. This was shortly before the publication of the Decree *Lamentabili* and the Encyclical *Pascendi*. The accusation of Modernism grew louder. Fr. Genocchi decided to write directly to the Pope. Without abandoning his convictions "in matters of scholarship and history," he implored the Pope's "pardon" and said that he was prepared to leave Rome, and even Europe, if his pres-

---

[147] Turvasi, *Giovanni Genocchi e la controversia modernista*, and "Genocchi (Giovanni)," *Dictionnaire d'histoire et de géographie ecclésiastiques*.

ence and activity was an "obstacle." This letter, suffused with frankness, filial respect and self-abnegation, found favor with Pius X. The very next day he sent Fr. Genocchi a very long letter in which, having praised him as "a good priest and an excellent religious," he related the accusations which had been brought against him, advising him to break off all relations with Modernists: "If many, unfortunately, accuse you falsely, dear Father, strive not to say anything which might give the least indication of such relations, resolutely closing the door against all those who claim to be masters in Israel and who, under the pretext of suppressing defects and abuses, are the first to neglect their own obligations.

"This, and this only, is what We recommend to you, and not that you should leave Rome, where We are sure that, with your spirit and your heart, you will be able to do much good yet."[148]

Relations between Fr. Genocchi and Pius X stayed characterized by affection and esteem. Some months after this exchange of letters, Pius X received Fr. Genocchi in audience on the occasion of the 25th anniversary of his ordination, giving him a photograph with a dedication and an Apostolic Blessing. In other circumstances the Pope took up the defence of Fr. Genocchi, and in 1911 he appointed him Apostolic Visitor to South America, with a twofold mission of which we shall speak in another chapter.

Many other cases could be mentioned, notably that of Fr. Lagrange.[149] In this case, as in others, Pius X had to take many things into consideration: the safeguarding of the faith and the good of the Church, the necessity and legitimacy of study in religious matters, the personal good and the good faith of the persons involved, as well as the maneuvering, the ambitions and the jealousies of some of the parties. As Pope, his first duty was the first of these; as a Christian, he was obliged to follow charity, prudence and justice. Pius X had to reconcile all these things. Msgr. Duchesne, who had seen one of his books put on the *Index*, uttered a mischievous remark when he said that "Pius X governs the Church with a boat-hook" [*à la gaffe*]. This was intended as a hurtful irony, but it fails to do justice to a complex reality. Pius X felt it his duty, as the guardian of the faith, to combat Modernism, and to do so using the most varied methods and without

---

[148] Genocchi's letter (December 27, 1907) and the Pope's reply (December 28) are published in full in Turvasi, *Giovanni Genocchi e la controversia modernista*, pp.346-347.

[149] Cf. the edition (with commentary) of his correspondence with his master general: *Exégèse et obéissance. Correspondance Cormier-Lagrange, 1904-1916*, edited by Bernard Montagnes (Paris: J. Gabalda et Cie., 1989). As we have seen, the Consistorial Congregation issued a warning regarding "several works" of Fr. Lagrange, and he could not publish his study on Genesis; however, he continued to direct the *Revue Biblique*.

weakness, because, as he saw it, the very existence of the Church was threatened. At the same time, without making any concession to error, he was at pains to help people who were incriminated or under suspicion, and he took care to limit the excesses of the anti-Modernists. One of his favorite maxims was, "we must combat error without injuring the persons concerned."

The Catholic press

It would be a distortion of its spirit to illuminate only one aspect of the battle against Modernism. The same can be said of the Catholic press. Pius X most certainly gave public support and approval to the "papal" or "intransigent" newspapers and to anti-Modernist publications.

As regards Italy, we shall mention only three of the most famous publications which took part in the very lively controversies, and which were much criticized by their opponents and by the Catholic moderates, namely, *La Liguria del populo,* directed by Don Boccardo; *L'Unità cattolica,* which was transferred from Turin to Florence; and *La Riscossa,* published in Bragantia by the Scotton brothers, all priests, Andrea, Gottardo and Jacopo. Pius X supported these newspapers and, conversely, criticized the liberal Catholic press, which he regarded as "infiltrated." This applied particularly to the closely allied papers of the so-called "trust": *L'Osservatore Cattolico* of Milan, *L'Avenir d'Italia* of Bologna, *Il Momento* of Turin and Rome's *Il Corriere d'Italia.* Pius X wrote:

> The Pope condemns all these so-called Catholic newspapers which complacently accept *faits accomplis*, which never say a word about the liberty and independence of the Church, which, just like the others, report items that are inedifying, praise books that should be condemned, and put on a pedestal those men who have done so much harm to Religion. These newspapers can be neither supported nor recommended, because they are more murderous than those which are openly very evil, and because they infiltrate the poison of Modernism into people's minds, and particularly into the minds of the Clergy.[150]

In France *La Foi catholique* comes to mind, a monthly review founded by Canon Gaudeau in 1908. Its watchword was something which Pius X had said at a private audience on March 9, 1907: *"Il kantismo è l'eresia moderna"* (Kantianism is the modern heresy). The review saw its principal task as providing a critique of Kantianism. Bernard Gaudeau had initially been a Jesuit, successively professor of the history of philosophy at the Institut catholique of Toulouse, of dogmatic theology at the Gregorian Uni-

---

[150] Letter of Pius X to Msgr. Archi, Bishop of Como, May 15, 1911, published in *Conduite de s. Pie X,* p.147.

versity in Rome, and then at the Institut catholique in Paris. His review quickly acquired great intellectual authority, and was hailed by Pius X and his successors Benedict XV and Pius XI. In 1913, in the name of Pius X, Cardinal Merry del Val wrote a public letter of "special congratulations" to Canon Gaudeau for his "zeal in establishing the truth and unmasking error in all its forms" and for his battle against "a false philosophy which denies the value of the human reason and asserts that it has no power to know a personal Creator God."[151]

In France, among the anti-Liberal and anti-Modernist publications encouraged by Pius X, we can also mention *La Critique du libéralisme religieux, politique et social,* and *La Vigie.* The former review was founded in 1908 by Fr. Barbier, an erstwhile Jesuit, whom we have already met. Initially he had been an educator, the founder of the College of St. Louis Gonzaga in Paris. He had been chaplain to the ACJF [*Association catholique de la jeunesse française*], and joined the secular clergy in 1905. His first works also date from this time. He was the principal anti-liberal French author of the period. He opposed the *Sillon,* the Christian-Democratic movement, Freemasonry and Modernism. After founding his review he was received by Pius X, who encouraged him. *La Vigie,* with its watchword, *"Ubi Petrus ibi Ecclesia"* (Where Peter is, there is the Church), was a weekly paper for "integral Roman Catholics." The first issue came out in December 5, 1912. Its director was Henri Merlier and its general secretary was Roger Duguet (the pen-name of Fr. Paul Boulin). The latter received an Apostolic Benediction from Pius X on March 26, 1913.

Such prominent support given to organs of the "integral" press (which its opponents called "integrist") did not prevent Pius X from stepping in several times, directly or through his collaborators, against the excesses of certain "intransigents" and anti-Modernists. In 1908, in several letters to Msgr. Mistrangelo, Archbishop of Florence, he required him to intervene with the chief editors of *L'Unità cattolica.* Of Don Cavallanti and Don De Töth he observed: "...they too have fallen into error by giving their polemics a subjective and personal character. I recommend them to refrain from gathering and retailing the gossip people bring them. Nor should they keep repeating that their mission is from the Pope, for in fact the Pope has given them no mandate."[152] Again, a further message for De Töth: "Urge him again to be moderate: errors must be combatted, but without injuring the persons concerned."[153]

---

[151] Letter from the Secretariate of State, March 11, 1913, *Documents pontificaux,* vol.II, p.506.
[152] Letter to Msgr. Mistrangelo, March 13, 1908, *ibid.,* p.134.
[153] Letter to Msgr. Mistrangelo, November 21, 1908, *ibid.,* p.135.

This was a consistent line with Pius X. In 1912, when *La Liguria del populo* had strongly criticized the clergy of the Diocese of Milan, who, along with their Archbishop, Cardinal Ferrari, were suspected of being too tolerant of Modernism, the Pope had a letter sent to the newspaper's editor:

> The publication of matter of this kind has been censured by the Holy Father because it creates an atmosphere that is everything but serene, and contains portrayals which are not only savage in their form and exaggerated in their substance, but also because it clearly infringes the honor of those concerned...it is possible to defend the good cause without having recourse to such means and without going to such extremes. He wishes you to remedy this situation as far as within you lies.[154]

Sanctions were applied even against an anti-Modernist and anti-liberal of considerable stature, namely, Fr. Barbier. Before he founded *La Critique du libéralisme,* which we have already cited, he saw two of his works put on the Index on May 25, 1908: *Le progrès du libéralisme catholique en France sous le Pape Léon XIII. Histoire documentaire,* and *Ne mêlez pas Léon XIII au libéralisme.* These writings were judged too critical of Leo XIII and certain French bishops. Fr. Barbier submitted to the decree of the Congregation of the Index. A short time later he launched his review. Fr. Barbier was received in private audience by Pius X and the review appeared until 1914.

To conclude this long chapter on Pius X and Modernism we shall mention a little-known fact. In the penultimate paragraph of *Pascendi* (1907), Pius X had expressed his intention of creating "a special Institute in which, through the co-operation of those Catholics who are most eminent for their learning, the advance of science and every other department of knowledge may be promoted under the guidance and teaching of Catholic truth." This project did not remain a dead letter.[155] Even before the encyclical appeared, it had been the idea of Professor Toniolo, who had been particularly close to Pius X since his time in Mantua. Cardinals Mercier and Maffi, and then Cardinal Rampolla, had been involved in it, as well as the German historian, Pastor, and the Belgian historian Kurth. A draft statute was published in *L'Osservatore Romano* and a provisional committee was formed. The project did not prosper because of internal disagreements, notably concerning the list of those to be admitted to the institution; Pius X vetoed several names, in particular that of Msgr. Duchesne. Cardinal Rampolla resigned from the provisional committee.

---

[154] Letter of Cardinal Merry del Val to Don Boccardo, June 30, 1912, *ibid.*, p.150.
[155] Cf. the very detailed study (including correspondence) by Roger Aubert, "Un projet avorté d'une association scientifique internationale catholique au temps du modernisme," *Archivum historiae pontificae,* 16, 1978, pp.223-312.

In November 1909 Pius X gave his verdict: "Let us leave the project suspended. It is better to have no Institute than to see it setting off on the wrong track." R. Aubert observes: "It is only right to point out that the proposed lists included a series of indisputable scholars who were of international renown at the time and are still respected nowadays. Moreover, they included some men who were very far from being *personae gratae* at the Vatican, such as von Hertling and Baeumker, against whom considerable pressure had been applied. Here again we can see that the reality is more complex than people's *a priori* ideas."

In conclusion we quote the judgment of an opponent, Fr. Semeria. As we have seen, he was exiled to Brussels because of his Modernist sympathies. However, with the passing of time, almost twenty years after the events, he came to understand the religious and ecclesial intention behind Pius X's struggle against Modernism:

> The rhythmical movement of studies in philosophy, history and natural science which was promoted by Leo XIII, even if it was temporarily slowed down, was not stopped by the action of Pius X, let alone by his intention. In fact, the condemnations uttered by Pius X were already anticipated in the warnings and anxieties of Leo XIII. The Church remains courageous in condemning error and facing up to every truth. Each phase of her 2,000 year history brings battles to be fought, duties to be embraced, for the glory of the Father and for the good of humanity. In the Pope of the Encyclical *Pascendi*, and in other acts of his pontificate condemning Modernism, we see the vibrant reality which St. Paul so well describes as *sollicitudo omnium ecclesiarum*—which is the charge committed to Peter.[156]

---

[156] P. Semeria, *I miei quattro Papi* (Milan, 1930), p.217, quoted in *La Conduite de s. Pie X,* p.34.

CHAPTER 9

FOR THE SOCIAL KINGSHIP OF CHRIST

It is often the case, in works discussing the Church's social teaching, and even in recent pontifical documents on the same subject, that the name of St. Pius X is forgotten or, at best, mentioned only in passing.[1] This is unjust.

For Pius X's addresses and writings, as well as his varied initiatives, show that his work in the social sphere was not inconsiderable. We have already seen that, as Bishop of Mantua and as Patriarch of Venice, he was a bishop who was greatly concerned with the social question. Once he became Pope, his earlier experience was very useful to him.

Certain authors, caricaturing the different personalities of Leo XIII and Pius X, make the former into an innovator and the latter into a backward-looking spirit, as if, in the question of social teaching, there were an opposition between the two pontificates. The truth is that, in this area, Pius X was always in line with Leo XIII.

The heritage of Leo XIII

Leo XIII was not the first pope to seek eagerly to put forward the Church's social teaching. His immediate predecessor, Pius IX, while he did not publish any encyclical exclusively devoted to this subject, encouraged the different movements and schools in Europe which took an interest in the question. In various documents, furthermore, he condemned erroneous social doctrines: economic liberalism and socialism. Leo XIII gave a full presentation of the Church's teaching on this matter. The most famous was *Rerum Novarum* (May 16, 1891), "on the condition of the workers."[2] It affirmed the legitimacy of the Church's intervention in social matters, and, while condemning once more the errors of socialism, it deplored the

---

[1] A most recent example: in his voluminous "*Synthèse de la doctrine sociale de l'Église*" entitled *Construire la civilisation de l'Amour* (Paris: Téqui, 1998) (830 pages), Fr. Marc-Antoine Fontelle does not once mention Pius X in his "brief historical sketch of the Church's social teaching" (pp.133-141). Nonetheless three pontifical documents of Pius X are cited in the bibliography.

[2] *Rerum Novarum, Actes de Léon XIII* (Paris: Maison de la Bonne Presse, 1927), pp.18-71. (English version cited from the Daughters of St. Paul edition, Boston, 2000.)

unjust conditions in which many workers lived after decades of naked economic liberalism ("the workers, isolated and defenseless, have seen themselves progressively handed over to the mercy of inhuman masters and to the cupidity of unbridled competition"). While the Pope pleaded for an improvement of the conditions of work, a just wage, Sunday rest, and the right to create employer-employee corporations or trades unions, he also defended private property and the State's duty to intervene in economic and social matters.

It is often forgotten that, if Leo XIII was concerned for an improvement of the condition of the workers, what he meant by this was not merely a material improvement, but also a moral and religious betterment. This twofold perspective is very clear, for example, when the Pope sets forth what the workers' associations (corporations or trades unions) should be: they should

> be so constituted and so governed as to furnish the most suitable and most convenient means to attain the object proposed, which consists in this, that the individual members of the association secure, so far as possible, an increase in the goods of body, of soul, and of prosperity.
>
> It is clear, however, that moral and religious perfection ought to be regarded as their principal goal, and that their social organization as such ought above all to be governed completely by this goal. For otherwise they would degenerate in nature and would be little better than those associations in which no account is ordinarily taken of religion. Besides, what would it profit a worker to secure through an association an abundance of goods, if his soul through lack of its proper food should run the risk of perishing?

This religious perspective on social action was affirmed at the same period, as we have seen, by Msgr. Sarto. Once he became Pope, it would be one of the dominant themes of his writings and addresses on the subject. Another important teaching of Leo XIII would be reaffirmed by Pius X, namely, the meaning to be given to the term *Christian democracy.* The term became very current after the Encyclical *Rerum Novarum* alongside other, older expressions such as *social Christians* or *Christian popular action.* In different countries, various movements or personalities embraced the term "Christian democracy." Thus there was the *Democrazia Cristiana Italiana* (DCI), which was not yet a party, and was founded in 1900 by Fr. Murri, whom we have already mentioned;[3] the "Democratic League" in Belgium; and Frs. Lemire and Gayraud in France, who were elected as deputies in 1893 and 1896 respectively.[4] In his Encyclical *Graves de Communi* (Janu-

---

[3] Cf. Lorenzo Bedeschi, *Murri, Sturzo, De Gasperi, Ricostruzione storica ed epistolario, 1898-1906* (Cinisello Balsamo: Edizioni San Paolo, 1994).

ary 18, 1901), Leo XIII made it clear in what sense the use of the term *Christian democracy* was legitimate.[5] The term, he observed,

> offends many good people, to whom it seems equivocal and danger-
> ous; they reject this appellation for more than one reason. They fear that
> this word is a poor disguise for popular government, or suggests a prefer-
> ence for such government over other forms. They fear that the virtue of
> the Christian religion seems restricted to the interests of working people,
> leaving the other classes of society out of consideration. Finally, they fear
> that, under this deceptive name, there lies hidden an intention to decry
> any kind of legitimate power, be it civil or sacred.

Thus Leo XIII makes it clear that it is only possible to use the term *Christian democracy* "if all political connotation is removed from it, so that it means nothing more than benevolent Christian action among the people." One year later a long and very precise instruction from the Congregation of Extraordinary Ecclesiastical Affairs, sent to all the bishops of Italy, gave very detailed directives, most of which were based on earlier pontifical documents, quoted in great number.[6] "Christian Democratic institutions, of whatever kind," must not be "instruments for the attaining of political ends, or designed to bring about a change in the form of government." Christian Democrat newspapers should not claim to be speaking "in the name of the Church when they are discussing purely political matters," and they should be submissive to the bishops. The instruction also reminded Catholics in Italy that they were forbidden to "participate in any political action": elections at the national level were forbidden; only local elections, which were regarded as merely "administrative," were authorized.

The Encyclical of 1901 and the Instruction of the following year were received with disappointment by the Christian Democrats who wished to give a political aspect to their struggle. *Domani d'Italia,* the DCI review, lost half its readership. The day after the publication of the Congregation's Instruction, Fr. Murri wrote to Don Sturzo, a young priest who had been one of the founders of the DCI: "I am very upset at the way we have been treated, after so much enthusiasm and so much work." At the same time, however, he said that he was determined to carry on the struggle as before: "Greet the friends and tell them that nothing is lost, provided that our program maintains an adequate spirit of initiative and autonomy."[7]

---

[4]   Cf. Jean-Marie Mayeur, *Des Partis catholiques à la Démocratie chrétienne, XIX-XX siècles* (Paris: Armand Colin, 1980), and *Catholicisme social et démocratie chrétienne* (Paris: Cerf, 1986).

[5]   Encyclical *Graves de Communi, Actes de Léon XIII,* vol.VI, pp.204-227.

[6]   *Instruction sur l'action populaire chrétienne ou démocratique chrétienne en Italie,* January 27, 1902, *Actes de Léon XIII,* vol.VI, pp.262-272.

The defiant attitude manifest here would be exacerbated under the pontificate of Pius X which was shortly about to begin.

The Italian Catholic Movement

In his very first encyclical, Pius X outlined the limits he was setting for what, like many other authors or men of action before him, he would soon call "Christian popular action." Like his predecessors, he praised and encouraged the Catholic associations, the various "works"—and Pius X was primarily thinking of the *Opera dei Congressi* to which we have already referred. In addition, however, his first teaching on the subject as Pope sounds a note of warning: "The first and principal object of these associations is to make sure that their members faithfully fulfill the duties of the Christian life. There is no point, to be sure, in sharpening one's intellect on many questions and talking eloquently about rights and duties, unless this results in action."[8]

Pius X defined this action in three terms: "Full and scrupulous observance of the divine laws and Church's regulations, open and bold profession of religion, and the exercise of charity in all its forms." We can say that the order of this list constitutes, in itself, a further piece of instruction. The Pope himself says as much later in the Encyclical: once the faith and religious practice are soundly restored in individuals and in society, "temporal interests and public prosperity will feel the beneficial effects....The nobility and the wealthy will know how to be just and charitable to the little ones, and the latter will peacefully and patiently endure the hardships of their indigent condition."

According to Pius X, therefore—and he had often said as much before becoming Pope—religious action and social or economic action must be linked by the same principle and the same goal: "the restoration of all things in Christ." This expression is, in all fields, the watchword of this pontificate.

The Pope was not slow to ascertain that this principle and this goal were not accepted by all those (clergy or laity) who were involved in the Italian Catholic Movement.[9] One month after the publication of the Encyclical, the 19th Congress of Italian Catholics was held at Bologna. It took place from November 10 to 13, 1903, and was attended by some 2,000 delegates of charitable societies, newspapers and Catholic associa-

---

[7] Letter of Romolo Murri to Luigi Sturzo, January 27, 1902, published in Bedeschi, *Murri, Sturzo, De Gasperi*, p.194.

[8] Encyclical *E Supremi Apostolatus*, October 4, 1903, *Documents pontificaux*, vol.I, p.40.

[9] On the evolution of the Catholic movement seen by a bishop who was not a "conciliationist," cf. Carlo Snider, *L'Episcopato del cardinale Andrea C. Ferrari*, vol.II, pp.373ff.

tions. The Congress opened with the reading of a Brief of Pius X written to Count Grosoli, president of the *Opera dei Congressi*.[10] In it, the Pope summoned them to "concord" and to that "union of all Catholic forces which is so much desired." He feared that there could be opposition and agitation from Don Murri's circle. Quoting the three texts of Leo XIII to which we have referred, Pius X warned: "It is essential to hold fast to these very important documents and never, under any pretext, to stray from the interpretation of them which is given by the Apostolic See and Our venerable brothers, the bishops."

However, the Congress discussions were very animated. From an institutional point of view, the DCI was attached to the 2nd section of the *Opera dei Congressi*. Its spokesman, Don Murri, dominated the debates, in which there were clashes between many personalities and views, *e.g.,* the president, Grosoli, Count Paganuzzi, former president of the *Opera,* and Professor Toniolo of the University of Pisa, a specialist in social questions. President Grosoli was confirmed as head of the *Opera dei Congressi,* thanks to the support of Don Murri and his party. The latter, by his enthusiasm, seemed to rouse a majority of the Congress participants to advocate the necessity of using new methods.[11] As for Professor Toniolo who, as we have already seen, had long been associated with the Pope, he had a "moderating" influence on the proceedings—if we are to believe the long report which the French ambassador made to his government.[12] At all events, he put forward practical proposals which were bold and also tended to appeal to everyone, thus encouraging that "concord" which the Pope had hoped for: namely, the creation of collective rented farmland to replace the system of large agricultural properties (the *latifundia*); the building of low-rent "worker's houses"; and the participation of Catholic teachers in the National League of Italian Teachers (a non-confessional organization) so that their voice and their concerns could be heard.

Initially Pius X seemed satisfied with the work of the Congress. The French ambassador notes in his report:

> We are assured that Pius X is not at all unhappy with the result of the Bologna Congress. It is said that he relies on Count Grosoli's firm hand to exercise discipline, without too much difficulty, and to pull together

---

[10] Brief *Instaurandum in Christo,* dated November 6, 1903, *Documents pontificaux,* vol.I, pp.42-43.

[11] Cf. Bedeschi, *Murri, Sturzo, De Gasperi,* pp.101ff., and Georges Jarlot, *Doctrine Pontificale et Histoire. L'enseignement social de Léon XIII, Pie X et Benoît XV vu dans son ambiance historique, 1878-1922* (Rome: Gregorian University Press, 1964), pp.279ff.

[12] Dispatch from Nisard, French Ambassador to the Holy See, to Delcassé, Minister of Foreign Affairs, November 20, 1903, AMAE, Saint-Siège, Politique étrangère, NS 12, f.40-46, 14 pages.

the somewhat disorganized, but undoubtedly vibrant forces which Don Murri succeeded in enrolling as his followers. Don Murri's friends like to see him in the role of a "Sieyès of the fourth estate."[13]

Immediately after the Congress, Pius X received in audience Count Paganuzzi and some of his friends, who had come to complain of the innovatory tendencies of Don Murri. The Pope listened to them kindly, but three days later he received Count Grosoli and his colleagues. Shortly afterwards an authorized note appeared in the *Osservatore Romano* (November 25, 1903) to the effect that the president of the *Opera dei Congressi* "continues to enjoy the full confidence of the Holy See."

Nonetheless, as we have seen in other areas, Pius X simply wanted to give himself time for reflection. A little more than a month after the Congress there appeared an important motu proprio on "Christian action among the people."[14] In it, Pius X regretted that the 19th Catholic Congress had produced the spectacle of "certain dissensions" and "too agitated polemics," and he judged it useful to "re-affirm the principles which should inform all Catholic action." He did this by setting forth a long *Regulation for Christian action among the people* in 19 points. Each of these points referred to a document, *i.e.,* a teaching, of Leo XIII. There was nothing in this Regulation which could appear to be a novelty, a new demand or a new prohibition. Pius X was continuing to affirm that the foundation and goal of social action were by nature religious, and that this social action, even if it used very diverse practical means, must hold aloof from all political action.

Murri and his friends regarded this re-affirmation of principles as a step backwards. The Christian Democrat publications contained articles and views which diverged more and more from the pontifical directives. In March 1904, in a Brief to Count Medolago Albani, president of the 2nd section of the *Opera dei Congressi* (to which the DCI and Murri were attached), Pius X gave a warning: "Let the 2nd section of the *Opera dei Congressi* take care to keep its young people, in particular, within proper limits. The latter, led by their generosity, do not always have the requisite maturity of judgment and, wanting to reform everything, aspire to dangerous projects. Striving for what is better, they fail to reach the good. If they do not show themselves docile to friendly guidance, you must exclude them from your work. For what is important is not the number of collaborators, but the warm concord of spirits, without which the true good can never be realized."[15]

---

[13] Allusion to the Abbé Siéyès (1748-1836), who, in 1789, was elected to the Estates-General by the Third Estate and not by the clergy, and who played a determining role at the beginning of the French Revolution.

[14] *Fin dalla Prima,* December 18, 1903, *Documents pontificaux,* vol.I, pp.66-69.

The conflict became so intense that the entire work of the *Opera dei Congressi* was dissolved. On July 2 the General Assembly of the Permanent General Committee of the *Opera dei Congressi* met in Bologna. The 38 members present were divided into two parties, "rigid" and "broad." In particular, the latter wanted the Catholic Movement to be less dependent on the bishops; they wanted Catholics to be able to take part in political life at a national level; and they also desired that religious considerations in matters of social actions should not take precedence over economic considerations.[16]

Divided, the Permanent Committee turned to the Pope. Count Grosoli wrote a report to the Secretariate of State. Cardinal Merry del Val replied by a public letter regretting the lack of "concord" and "unity of purpose." Finally Grosoli handed in his resignation. On July 28, 1904, all the groups of the *Opera dei Congressi* were wound up, with the exception of the Second Group, which remained under the presidency of Count Medolago Albani; he was now responsible for the whole of Christian Action.[17]

This was an important event, and subsequently it has been severely judged by many historians. Yet it must be borne in mind that the dissolution of the *Opera dei Congressi* did not mean the end of all Catholic movements and all Catholic social action in Italy. It can even be said that it liberated the Italian Catholic movement from the bonds of a complicated superstructure. For the present it was replaced by a more decentralized mode of organization. The dissolved large-scale groupings were replaced by "regional and diocesan groups" and would be under the authority of the bishops. The following year, the "Unions" would be put in place.

Don Murri noted the disappearance of the *Opera dei Congressi* and took the opportunity of carrying out his long-term ambition of forming a political party. Since Murri had announced a meeting of a "constitutive congress" in Bologna for March 1905, Pius X wrote a public letter to Cardinal Svampa, the Archbishop of Bologna, condemning this initiative, forbidding Catholics to take part in it and threatening with canonical sanctions the priests who might participate in it.[18] Don Murri paid no heed. A few months later he founded the *National Democratic League* (LDN). This was the first Italian Christian Democratic party. While its title contained no reference to Christianity, article 4 of its Statutes invited its members to

---

[15] Brief *Fra le Tante Dimostrazioni*, March 19, 1904, *Documents pontificaux,* vol.I, p.151.

[16] Jarlot, *Doctrine pontificale et histoire,* pp.283-284, and dispatch of the chargé d'affaires of the French Embassy to the Holy See to Delcassé, July 6, 1904, AMAE, Saint-Siège, Politique étrangère, NS 12, f.133-135.

[17] Letter of the Secretariate of State *La Santità di Nostro Signore,* July 28, 1904, *Documents pontificaux,* vol.I, pp.190-192.

[18] Letter *La lettera circolare,* March 1, 1905, *Documents pontificaux,* vol.I, pp.275-276.

behave "in a Christian spirit." It proposed to give "a democratic direction to the public activity of Catholics" and to defend "the interests of workers." Jean-Marie Mayeur points out that, like the Belgian Democratic League and the League of the Young Republic in France (the successor of the *Sillon*), "the term 'League' indicates a desire to carry on political action in a different way from that of the parties."[19] It also claimed to promote reforms in the Church. This brought Murri even closer to the Modernists, as we have seen in the preceding chapter.

Murri and the LDN were bound to move further and further away from the Church. In 1906 Pius X formally forbade priests to belong to the LDN.[20] Murri was forbidden to write for the press. He avoided this prohibition by giving newspaper interviews. In 1907 he was suspended *a divinis*, and on March 22, 1909, after his election to the Chamber of Deputies, he was excommunicated.

As for Pius X, he endeavoured to guide the Catholic movement towards a broader goal. One year after the dissolution of the *Opera dei Congressi* he published a long Encyclical "on Catholic Action."[21] "Having removed, insofar as it depends on Us, all obstacles in the field," Pius X wished to inspire Catholics with a new determination: "The field of Catholic Action is immense; in itself, it excludes nothing that, in one way or another, directly or indirectly, belongs to the Church's mission." The Pope recalled the aim of this Catholic Action—a word which was to be heard more and more: "this work is so important for the sanctification of our souls, but also in order to spread and promote the reign of God in individuals, families and society." Later, using different terms, he defined it thus: "Catholic Action, which has as its aim to restore all things in Christ, constitutes a true apostolate for the honor and glory of Christ himself."

Drawing inspiration from the *Volksverein*, the German Catholics' organization, Pius X urged the formation of *Popular Unions*. He laid down three areas of privileged action: "current social needs," "social and economic studies," and "the conditions of civil society, the public life of states." As regards this last area, Pius X made a substantial concession: in certain cases, "for the supreme good of society, which must be saved at all costs," the bishops would be able, after obtaining the permission of the Holy See, to authorize Catholics to "participate in the legislative power." This concern to "save society at all costs" may be seen as an allusion to the

---

[19] Mayeur, *Des Partis catholiques à la Démocratie chrétienne*, p.96.
[20] This prohibition is formulated in the Encyclical *Pieni l'Animo*, July 28, 1906, *Documents pontificaux*, vol.I, pp.371-372. The Encyclical deals with the different aspects of the mission of the clergy.
[21] *Il Fermo Proposito*, June 11, 1905, *Documents pontificaux*, vol.I, pp.296-306.

serious unrest which had broken out the previous year in Turin, Naples, Genoa and Milan, provoked by Socialist movements.

This concession on the participation of Italian Catholics in national political life was a break, although a limited and controlled break, with the former rule of "Neither electors, nor elected." It meant that Italian Catholics, with the agreement of the bishops and the Pope, would be able in certain circumstances to participate in national elections and present candidates. Thus Catholics had "the duty to prepare themselves prudently and seriously for political life, for the time when they would be summoned to enter it."

The organization of the Popular Unions envisaged by the Pope was entrusted to Professor Toniolo, Count Medolago Albani and Commander Paolo Pericoli, president of the Society of Italian Youth. Three such Unions were created at a congress in Florence in February 1906. They were the *Christian Popular Union,* directed by Toniolo, with particular responsibility for propagating Christian social teaching; the *Economic and Social Union of Italy,* directed by Medolago Albani, which was to coordinate the activities of the existing (or of future) associations in the economic or social fields—without losing sight of its members' spiritual interests; and finally, the *Electoral Union,* directed by Pericoli, with the task of preparing Catholics for political life and giving support to candidates who had been granted the right, by the ecclesiastical hierarchy, to offer themselves for election.

The entry of Catholics into Italian political life took place in a gradual manner. In the Encyclical which set forth the possibility of this development, Pius X had defined the "high principles" which should guide the Catholic engaged in politics:

> In all circumstances he must be, and must show himself to be, truly Catholic: he must assume and exercise his public responsibilities with the firm and constant resolve to promote, as much as he can, the social and economic good of his country and particularly of the people, following the principles of avowedly Christian civilization, and at the same time defending the supreme interests of the Church, which are also the interests of religion and justice.

In fact, individual Catholics had already taken part in election contests even prior to Pius X's concession. At the November 1904 elections the Liberal, Giolitti, who was head of the government, had received the support of many Catholic votes in his struggle against the Socialists. The policy of abstentionism had weakened significantly, and Catholic votes had been given to moderate candidates; a Milanese Catholic, Cornaggia, had even been elected a deputy.[22] In Venice, the local Catholic paper *La*

Difesa, probably with ecclesiastical authorization, had supported the candidature of the Liberal (and Catholic), Girolamo Marcello.[23]

Once the *Electoral Union* had been set up, the entry of Catholics into national political life was even more significant. In 1908 Pius X made a further breach in the former policy of *Non expedit* by urging Catholics to vote for "good candidates." On January 13, in a private letter, he authorized Msgr. Origo, Bishop of Mantua, to choose the most suitable candidates so that, if elected, they would undertake *"not to vote for laws contrary to the laws of the Church, like divorce, secular schools, the suppression of ecclesiastical goods, etc."*[24] Pius X also wrote urging "the collaboration of Catholics with other good men who were defenders of order." In the 1909 elections the support of Catholic votes for moderate Liberals was decisive, and 16 Catholics were elected as deputies, though they were "elected Catholics" rather than "Catholic deputies" insofar as they did not officially represent the Church.

Pius X always refused to authorize a Catholic party. Nonetheless he encouraged the *Electoral Union* and approved its strategy, notably in the 1913 elections, when its new president, Ottorino Gentiloni, invited all Catholics to support the moderate candidates if they would undertake to defend the Church's rights. The *patto Gentiloni* (the Gentiloni pact) calls to mind the alliance concluded by Cardinal Sarto in Venice in order to oust the leftists from the municipality. In 1913 the results were equally satisfactory: the number of "elected Catholics" doubled—33—and, according to Gentiloni, 228 governmental candidates were elected thanks to the support of Catholic votes.

The Roman question

In the matter of elections, therefore, Pius X managed gradually to break with the *Non expedit* rule fixed by Pius IX. On the Roman question, similarly, he succeeded in making practical concessions without yielding on principles.

Pius X could not accept the despoliation of 1870 as a *fait accompli* any more than his predecessors could. What remained of the Papal States and the City of Rome had been occupied and annexed by the Italian State, without any discussion or antecedent negotiation. In Pius X's case, this refusal to accept the *fait accompli* did not result from some nostalgia for the

---

[22] Mayeur, *Des Partis catholiques à la Démocratie chrétienne,* pp.95-96.

[23] Bruno Bertoli, "Una diocesi all'ombra di Pio X," in *La Chiesa di Venezia nel primo novecento* (Venice: Edizioni Studium Cattolico Veneziano, 1995), p.33.

[24] Letter published in full by Stefano Siliberti, "La figura e l'opera di Mons. Giuseppe Sarto a Mantova, 1884-1893," in *Giuseppe Sarto. Un Vescovo e la società mantovana alla fine dell'Ottocento* (Mantua, 1995), pp.123-124 (italics in text).

former Papal States. He never made any reference to his "temporal power." In the last years of his pontificate he remarked to Msgr. Bonomelli:

> In all my pontificate I was concerned that there should be no mention of temporal power in any letter or allocution, lest our adversaries should have been given a pretext for calumniating the Church and the Pope....Ah! If those in government had really desired the Church's liberty, they would have treated the Apostolic See and the Pope's person differently these last 40 years![25]

In fact, Pius X would gladly have embarked on a course of reconciliation with the Italian State if, on the one hand, he had been presented with a government which was respectful towards the Church, and if, on the other hand, he had been certain that the Church would find "another means" of keeping her independence. "What Pius IX and Leo XIII would have done," he said, "would eventually be done by the present Pope if he could be certain of finding another way of guaranteeing the liberty and articulation of the government of the Universal Church. It is not a question of intransigence, but of the absolute necessity of asserting a right which admits of no limits or diminution. The Pope will never submit to an act constituting an outrage against the Church, for by doing so he would make himself the accomplice of an unpardonable fault."[26]

Without submitting to the *fait accompli* of the despoliation, Pius X showed, by various gestures and decisions, that he was disposed to engage in more normalized relationships. Diplomats based in Rome and the foreign press did not fail to point out this new orientation of Roman politics.

In May 1904, King Victor-Emmanuel III made an official visit to Bologna to inaugurate an exhibition of tourism. Bologna, in former times a legation, had been the most important city of the Papal States after Rome. This royal visit could therefore have a certain symbolic value. As it turned out, Cardinal Svampa, Archbishop of Bologna, an "intransigent" by reputation, not only paid a visit to the King but accepted the invitation to the official dinner. Subsequently it was learnt that he had made these two gestures with the Pope's express authorization. The Paris newspaper, *Le Temps,* furious on account of the Cardinal's visit to the King, published a major article which ended with the crude jibe: "when last summer's Conclave went to the vote, under the heel of the Germanic boot, it seems that the Holy Spirit was on holiday."[27] The French Ambassador to Rome, how-

---

[25] Letter to Msgr. Bonomelli, October 15, 1911, published in Guido Astori, "Pio X ed il vescovo Bonomelli," *Rivista di storia della Chiesa in Italia,* X, 1956, p.258.

[26] Letter to Count Apponiyi, Hungarian Minister of Religion, November 9, 1910, cited by Dal-Gal, *Pie X,* p.372.

[27] Article dates May 29, 1904. The *Osservatore Romano* replied on June 2 in an article deploring the "highly inappropriate tone."

ever, had a more realistic view of the event. According to him, it illustrated
"the continuation of Pius X's personal policy, which favors, not conciliation above everything else, but a *de facto* rapprochement with Italy."[28]

In March 1907 it was Msgr. Bonomelli's turn to be received, first by
the Pope in the Vatican, and then by the King in the Quirinal Palace. This
event was important: it was the first time, since the Kingdom of Italy had
been established and had taken possession of Rome, that a bishop was authorized to pay a visit to the King.

This rapprochement was again marked officially by an important declaration by the president of the *Popular Union*. At the 8th Social Week of
Italian Catholics, which took place in Milan from November 30 to December 5, 1913, he declared, with the Pope's consent, that "peace between
the State and the Church can always be realized by the constitutional will
of the country, without compromising the State's civil sovereignty."[29]

It can be said that the goodwill gestures towards normalization which
Pius X showed, or caused to be shown, prepared the way for the Treaty of
the Lateran. Signed during the pontificate of Pius XI, it gave a definitive
ruling on the dispute between the Holy See and the Italian State.

The Sillon

Pius X did not limit himself to setting the correct course for the social
and political action of Italian Catholics. Clearly, the doctrine set forth on
these matters applied to all the faithful. Furthermore, the Pope intervened
very directly in the Catholic social organizations of two countries: the Sillon, in France; and the trades unions in Germany.

In October or November 1893 Marc Sangnier, a student at the Collège Stanislas in Paris who was preparing for the entrance examination for
the École Polytechnique, had started an open association for all the pupils
and students at the Collège.[30] In their meetings they discussed intellectual,
religious and social problems. The governing body of the Collège had put
at the group's disposal a room in the basement, which gave rise to its name:
The Crypt. In January 1894 some members of the group launched a review
entitled *Le Sillon* ["The Furrow"], edited by Paul Renaudin, which intended to identify itself with the line of Maurice Blondel and Ollé-Laprune.
Gradually, the review's name became more and more attached to Marc
Sangnier's association. In 1899, at the age of 26, he abandoned his studies

---

[28] Dispatch from Barrère to Delcassé, May 30, 1904, AMAE, Saint-Siège, Relations avec
l'Italie, NS 12, f.74.
[29] *Civiltà Cattolica*,1913, pp.739-745.
[30] The standard book remains that of Jeanne Caron, *Le Sillon et la démocratie chrétienne,
1894-1910* (Paris: Plon, 1967). Cf. also *Marc Sangnier*, testimonies presented by Jean-
Claude Delbreil (Paris: Beauchesne, 1997).

at the École Polytechnique in order to devote himself entirely to "the cause of Christ and the People." He was a good orator, and organized small meetings in various parts of Paris for working people, laborers and students. Study circles were set up, and an *Institut populaire* was created. Marc Sangnier enjoyed disputations, where his task was to convince his opponents, socialist or anti-clerical.

The Sillon grew rapidly and spread throughout France. At its first Congress in 1902 there were only 45 delegates. But the next year there were 300, and in 1904 there were 800. In 1904 five regional Sillons, each one publishing an independent review, took over from the Paris Sillon. The 1905 Congress brought together 1100 delegates from all over France, and there were 1500 at the 1906 Congress. At that date the Sillon had some 4000 subscriptions.

The Sillon was a Catholic movement, but it wanted to differentiate itself from existing Catholic organizations, in particular the important ACJF (Catholic Association of French Youth). While the ACJF saw its task as deepening the religious formation of its members, the Sillon had the aim of addressing society's de-christianized elements by undertaking a program of winning people over one by one. In the process, it wanted "to stop putting the emphasis on Catholic dogma and hierarchy—which only meets with indifference or hostility—and to find a perspective for re-introducing the Church into society."[31] It also saw itself as a defender of democracy and looked forward to a reconciliation between the Church and the Republic.

Initially this effort did not encounter hostility from the Church. In France in 1903 there was hardly more than one bishop, Msgr. Turinaz, Bishop of Nancy, displaying public opposition to the Sillon. When Pius X was elected, Marc Sangnier wanted to make a pilgrimage to Rome. He himself had a sincere attachment to the Papacy, but also hoped to see the Sillon recognized in Rome.

There has been much speculation concerning the favorable reception he received by the Pope on this occasion, and on his condemnation which took place in 1910. In fact, the Sillon did not make a pilgrimage to Rome as an independent group in 1903. It joined the annual pilgrimage called *La France au travail* which was organized by Léon Harmel. There were only about 20 from the Sillon. They were presented to the Pope. Also, on September 29, Pius X received Marc Sangnier in a private audience. The latter has told how the Pope invited him to recite the *Angelus* and gave him some words of encouragement. Marc Sangnier was also able to meet Cardinal Merry del Val and Cardinal Vivès.

---

[31] Caron, *Le Sillon et la démocratie chrétienne*, p.258.

The motu proprio of December 1903 on "Christian popular action," to which we have already referred, aroused certain reservations among the Sillon membership. Marc Sangnier delayed publishing it. A Christian-Democratic program that was limited to "benevolent action among the people on the part of the Church" did not satisfy him. Without neglecting the latter, he insisted on his attachment to democracy as such, defined as "that social organization which tends to maximize every citizen's conscience and civic responsibility."

This reticence regarding an important pontifical document, in addition to other incidents, reinforced the various criticisms made in France in connection with the Sillon. Newspapers such as *L'Action française* and *La Vérité française* did not fail to point out Marc Sangnier's contradictions regarding the Christian acceptance of democracy. Then, in July 1904, Bishop Turinaz published an essay entitled *Encore quelques mots sur les périls de la foi et de la discipline dans l'Église de France* ['Further words on the danger to faith and discipline in the Church of France']. The substance of his remarks was directed against the Sillon. Msgr. Turinaz's essay was received favorably by various provincial Catholic newspapers, but the other French bishops continued to give their approval to the Sillon (by taking part in its Congresses, for instance), or waited to see how things would turn out.

Next, Sangnier decided to organize a new pilgrimage to Rome in order to strengthen his position. It took place in September 1904. This time the Sillon pilgrimage, although still a part of the pilgrimage of *La France au travail,* had some 500 participants. Marc Sangnier met Cardinal Merry del Val five times, and the group was received in audience by Pius X. His allocution on that occasion was very warm.[32] He had grasped the essential aim of the Sillon apostolate, exercised "among those who are of your own age, are pursuing the same studies or profession as yourselves, but who are not yet of your number." However, the allocution also contained a clear allusion to the ACJF, which the Sillon must not oppose, and a reminder that it was necessary for the Sillon to be submissive to the bishops.[33]

---

[32] Allocution *Chaque Fois,* September 11, 1904, *Documents pontificaux,* vol.I, pp.200-201.

[33] "The soldiers of a powerful army do not all use the same arms or the same tactics. But they must all be united in the same enterprise, maintain a spirit of brotherhood, and promptly obey the *authority which directs them.* So may the charity of Christ reign among you and among the other young Catholics of France! They are your brothers; they are not against you, but with you. When your forces meet on the same ground, have regard to one another, and never let holy rivalry degenerate into an *opposition* that is inspired by human passions or by personal views that are not sufficiently lofty" (our italics, *ibid.*, p.201).

The disagreement was to grow, and the Sillon continued more and more to follow an autonomous path. 1905 was a turning point for the Sillon. Marc Sangnier published a book entitled *L'Esprit démocratique,* and the Sillon broke with the French Christian Democrats and moved politically to the left. Henceforth, Sangnier asserted, "We have resolved to put Christianity in the service of democracy"; and this democracy "is more the goal of an indefinite evolution than a moment accessible to history." Without going into the history of the Sillon up to its condemnation by the Pope, it is worth pointing out that, from 1907 onwards, Marc Sangnier would try to expand the movement to include what he called "the greater Sillon," *i.e.,* a grouping which went beyond the boundaries of the Church, endeavoring to attract men of "goodwill"; what united them was the defence of the same conception of democracy. The ultimate objective was to create "a republican and democratic party."

Criticism grew. In 1906 Fr. Barbier, who had published a "critical study" entitled *Les idées du Sillon* the previous year, wrote a long, three-part study called *Les erreurs du Sillon* (religious and social errors, errors of polemics and of conduct).[34] The same year, under the title *Le dilemme de Marc Sangnier,* Charles Maurras published a collection of the many articles he had been writing over a period of three years about the Sillon and its leader.[35] Sangnier saw the democratic republic as "the historical and logical goal of French national evolution" and appealed to everyone's conscience and heart to realize it; Maurras, the leader of *L'Action française,* confronted him with realities and presented a different way of resolving them (the "nationalist position"). Maurras also succeeded in drawing a distinction between Marc Sangnier's religious motivation and his democratic ideas, and observed that this religious motivation was not in harmony with the Church's pontifical teaching. The official condemnation which ensued four years later seemed, to Maurras, to be a confirmation of his view of the matter.

Meanwhile the Sillon had kept affirming its autonomy *vis-à-vis* the Church. It became more and more embroiled in opposition to the French bishops. In May 1907 Marc Sangnier decided to go to Rome again. He was received by Cardinal Merry del Val and by Pius X. But his reception was not as cordial as before. In a note of his conversation with the Secre-

---

[34] In February-March 1908, with the support of Msgr. Turinaz, Fr. Barbier went to Rome to present a memorandum on "the state of mind of the Catholics of France." This memorandum was very critical, among other things, regarding the Sillon. Pius X received Fr. Barbier in audience and gave him testimonies of his good will (which did not prevent two of Fr. Barbier's books being put on the Index the following May, as we saw in the chapter on Modernism).

[35] Cf. Chiron, *La Vie de Maurras,* pp.202-205.

tary of State, Sangnier indicated four points which, he felt, were reassuring; he published these in the movement's journal, and they were widely circulated. In fact, Pius X had shown his severe side. At the same time, after visiting Rome, the Bishop of Bayonne, Msgr. Gieure, published in his diocesan bulletin an account of his audience with Pius X. At one point the conversation touched on the question of the Sillon. Pius X showed his fears:

> I am anxious about the Sillon. Several French bishops have written asking what I think about it. I have read Marc Sangnier's addresses, and I have also read some of his articles: it is all very disquieting. These young people are following a fateful path: *Viam sequuntur damnosam.* I am not happy about priests entering this association; they seem to allow themselves to be led by laymen....The priests should not get involved in this movement....All the same, be kind to these youngsters; they are sincere and generous....[36]

Other bishops confirmed the reticence expressed by Pius X: Msgr. Bougoüin, the new Bishop of Périgueux; Msgr. Marty, Bishop of Montauban. The latter revealed what Pius X told him about his conversation with Sangnier. The Pope had told the leader of the Sillon: "What you have done is a defection. You have desired to have a purely political and lay association."[37]

It is not difficult to see the difference between "Christian popular action" such as Pius X wished it—action that was primarily religious, and then social, aiming at the "restoration of all things in Christ"—and the action of the Sillon as Marc Sangnier came to define it as the years went by, which was to develop the "social and civic virtues" by gathering together, beyond the limits of the Catholic Church, "a party with democratic ideals."[38]

Many had been looking forward to Rome's condemnation of the Sillon. Visiting Rome in February and March 1908, Fr. Barbier urged the Holy See to take up a position in the conflict between certain French bishops and the Sillon. Two personalities who had influence with the Pope agreed with him wholeheartedly: Cardinal Vivès, and in particular Fr. Pie de Langogne, who said, "I would go further: it is necessary to declare that the Sillon is not a Catholic movement."[39] A short while later Fr. Desgrang-

---

[36] *Semaine religieuse* of the Diocese of Bayonne, May 25, 1907, cited by Barbier, *Histoire du catholicisme libéral et du catholicisme social en France*, vol.IX, p.439.

[37] Statement quoted by Barbier, *ibid.*, p.442.

[38] Quotations taken from an article by Marc Sangnier which appeared May 29, 1910 in *L'Éveil démocratique.*

[39] Statement reported by Fr. Barbier in a letter to Msgr. Turinaz, March 9, 1908, cited in Caron, *Le Sillon et la démocratie chrétienne*, p.656.

es, an ardent "popular preacher" who had broken with the Sillon, visited Msgr. Benigni in Rome. The anti-Modernist prelate did not hide his hostility to Sangnier:

> It is impossible, at the present time, to be both with Marc Sangnier and with the Pope. Marc Sangnier does not seem to be capable of changing his attitude. If by prostrating myself at his feet I could get him to change his attitude, I would do it straight away. Alas, he is incurable, because he is abnormal. The more powerful his personality, the more serious the deviation it produces. Men like this must be pulverized....[40]

In 1909 things moved from indirect warnings from Rome to an official admonishment uttered by one of the highest authorities in the episcopate. On February 13, Cardinal Luçon, Archbishop of Rheims, published a pastoral letter warning people against the "erroneous" and "dangerous" theories of the Sillon. The Cardinal wrote, "We believe that it is time to warn our diocesan faithful, by an official declaration, so that no one may remain in ignorance, that we are publicly denouncing the leaders of this Movement which, in its initial stages, seemed so promising."[41] This pastoral letter was reproduced in *La Croix* and in a great number of diocesan bulletins.

The same year Marc Sangnier's involvement in the field of elections reinforced the opposition to his movement and his personality. He presented himself as a candidate in an election at Sceaux, where he faced only candidates of the left. He was ballotted and beaten at the second ballot by a Socialist (7,132 votes to 6,007). The following year, in the general elections, he was again a candidate, presenting himself in the constituency of Les Batignolles. This time, however, he faced two candidates of the left and a Catholic candidate. At the first scrutiny of votes he was in third position, behind the Catholic. He withdrew for the second scrutiny, refusing to call on voters to vote for the Catholic candidate (who was nonetheless elected).

However, Sangnier still had supporters in the episcopate. In turn, and by a concerted effort, Msgr. Gibier, Bishop of Versailles, Msgr. Chapon, Bishop of Nice, and Msgr. Mignot, Archbishop of Albi, intervened on behalf of the Sillon. This was in the first months of 1910. Msgr. Gibier did so by replying to the *Osservatore Romano*, which had published a critical article; Msgr. Chapon wrote to Cardinal Merry del Val to forestall any condemnation of him; and Msgr. Mignot tried to mobilize as many bish-

[40] Fr. Desgranges, *Carnets intimes,* entry May 17, 1908 (Geneva/Paris: La Palatine, 1960), p.144.
[41] *Bulletin du diocèse de Reims,* February 13, 1909, cited in Caron, *Le Sillon et la démocratie chrétienne,* p.661.

ops as possible in favor of the Sillon, and also provided support for a large-scale press campaign.

The first issue of the Sillon's daily newspaper, *La Démocratie,* appeared on August 17. Less than ten days later—although the document had been in preparation for a long time—Pius X's long letter condemning the Sillon appeared.[42] Many of the arguments given by Pius X were drawn from adversaries of the Sillon (Fr. Barbier and M. Charles) or from critics (Fr. Desgranges), but it seems that the substance of the document is largely due to Msgr. Sevin, Bishop of Châlons, who, the previous year, had written a report on the subject for Cardinal Vivès.[43]

The theories of the Sillon were condemned because "under their brilliant and generous appearances, they too often lack the clarity of logic and truth, and thus fail to represent the specific genius of Catholicism and of France." The first error of the Sillon is "the claim to be outside the control of ecclesiastical authority." Its social theory is gravely erroneous. Pius X sums it up as "what it calls the democratic education of the people, that is, raising to its maximum the conscience and civic responsibility of every one, from which will result economic and political Democracy and the reign of Justice, Liberty, Equality, Fraternity."

The Sillon sees liberty and conscience as the foundation of its action. But, as the Pope reminds us in a series of affirmations that were to become famous:

> The City cannot be built otherwise than as God has built it; society cannot be set up unless the Church lays the foundations and supervises the work; no, civilization is not something yet to be found, nor is the New City to be built on hazy notions; it has been in existence and still is: it is Christian civilization, it is the Catholic city. It has only to be set up and restored continually against the unremitting attacks of insane dreamers, rebels and miscreants. *Omnia Instaurare in Christo.*

This Letter on the Sillon was an opportunity to remind people of important things, notably that the Church cannot subordinate herself to any particular type of regime. The Sillon regarded democracy as "that form of government which is most favorable to the Church"; but Pius X insists, "We do not have to demonstrate here that the advent of universal Democracy is of no concern to the action of the Church in the world; we have already recalled that the Church has always left to the nations the care of giving themselves the form of government which they think most suited to their needs." He points out how far the Sillon has contradicted the

---

[42] Letter *Notre Charge Apostolique,* August 25, 1910, *Documents pontificaux,* vol.II, pp.252-266.
[43] Caron, *Le Sillon et la démocratie chrétienne,* p.711.

Church's teaching: "there is no true civilisation without a moral civilisa-tion, and no true moral civilisation without the true religion: it is a proven truth, an historical fact." However, the Sillon sees itself—within the con-text of the "Greater Sillon"—working together with non-Catholics and non-believers:

> When we consider the forces, knowledge and supernatural virtues which were necessary to establish the Christian City,...it is frightening to behold new apostles eagerly attempting to do better by a common inter-change of vague idealism and civic virtues. What are they going to pro-duce? What is to come out of this collaboration? A mere verbal and chimerical construction in which we see, glowing in a jumble, and in se-ductive confusion, the words of Liberty, Justice, Fraternity, Love, Equal-ity and human exaltation, all resting upon an ill-understood human dignity. It will be a tumultuous agitation, sterile for the end proposed, but which will benefit the less Utopian exploiters of the people. Yes, we can truly say that the Sillon, its eyes fixed on a chimera, brings Socialism in its train.

Accordingly, Pius X insisted that the leaders of the Sillon renounce their position in the movement, and that the membership put themselves in each diocese under the authority of the bishops, constituting "Catholic Sillons" ("in order to show clearly that they have broken with the errors of the past").

On September 10 Marc Sangnier published a letter to Pius X in which he announced his submission and his resignation from the leadership of the Sillon. In accordance with the Pope's wishes "Catholic Sillons" were set up in certain dioceses. Sangnier, however, had no intention of abandoning his struggle. He obtained permission from the Secretariate of State to con-tinue to edit the newspaper *La Democratie,* which he had launched a few days prior to his condemnation. The fact that the Sillon's ideas persisted in spite of their being condemned belongs to another historical theme, namely, that of the Christian-Democrat movement. In 1912 the former leader of the Sillon started a new movement, *La Jeune République,* ["The Young Republic"], which took a deliberately and officially non-confes-sional stance. Marc Sangnier was a deputy from 1919 to 1924, and then again in 1945 under the banner of the MRP—the *Mouvement Républicain Populaire,* founded in 1944, and of which he was honorary president.

Christian trade-unionism

We must examine one final aspect in Pius X's work in the social field: the question of trades unions. We have left it to the end of this chapter because, although it was a constant theme throughout the pontificate, it was in 1912-1914 that it was given a definitive response—and an unexpected one—at least as far as Germany was concerned.

The Church recognized the legitimacy of professional associations, whether they were organizations where employers and employees worked together (corporations) or separate organizations (trades unions). But—and this teaching is constant from Leo XIII to Pius X—such professional organizations must be, above all, Catholic, because their goal must be religious and moral before being economic. The first thing, in the mind of the popes, was not the improvement of the running of enterprises or of the workers' social conditions, but the moral and religious perfection of everyone, employers and employees; the rest would follow naturally.

Particularly in Germany, however, a debate arose: must the professional organizations be exclusively Catholic, or should they be open to non-Catholics, *i.e.,* should they be inter-denominational trades unions?[44] Since the 19th century there had been *Arbeitervereine,* workers' associations, under the control of the clergy, to provide for the religious formation of the workers and also in order to defend their rights and interests. More recently, beginning in Cologne, "Christian trades unions" had been set up that were open to Protestants. In 1909 a conflict erupted between the leadership of the *Arbeitervereine* in Berlin and the advocates of an inter-denominational trade-unionism, supported by the powerful *Bachem* press. (Julius Bachem was the editor of the *Kölnische Volkszeitung.*) Each of the two parties said that they had received encouragement from the Pope and the Holy See.

In 1912, in an effort to put an end to this quarrel which seemed to be going on and on, Pius X published an encyclical addressed to the German bishops.[45] This was the 17th of his pontificate, and his last.

After affirming that "even in the temporal order, the Christian does not have the right to put supernatural interests in second place," Pius X praised the "purely Catholic workers' associations which exist in Germany." In the Pope's eyes, these constitute the best means of resolving the "social question." However, "having regard to the particular situation of Catholicism in Germany" (in many regions Catholics were fewer in numbers than Protestants), the Pope made an important concession: Catholics could belong to "mixed," or inter-denominational trades unions.

This concession, which surprised certain "integralists," shows that, in this area also, Pius X was not as rigid and intransigent as his opponents have said. But, as usual with this Pope, the practical accommodations in

---

[44] Émile Poulat gives a fine analysis of the debate in "La dernière bataille du pontificat de Pie X," in *Rivista di storia della Chiesa in Italia,* XXV, 1971, pp.83-107.

[45] *Singulari Quadam Caritate,* September 24, 1912, *Documents pontificaux,* vol.II, pp.472-475.

no way signified that he was abandoning principles and opting for doctrinal evolution. The concession he had given was to be hedged about with "guarantees." Pius X laid down the principal guarantees required. Firstly, the Catholic workers who wanted to belong to "mixed" trades unions would have to enroll in the Catholic workers' associations as well. Only in the latter would they receive the necessary teaching which would enable them to act, in the trades unions, according to the law and principles of Catholic doctrine. Secondly, if Catholics were to enroll in "mixed" trades unions, they would have to "reject every theory and every act which is contrary to the teaching and commands of the Church or of the competent religious authority."

The Catholic trade union remained the rule, therefore, and the "mixed" or inter-denominational trade union was a matter of toleration, always under the exclusive control of the bishops and with well-defined practical precautionary measures.[46]

The Pope's intervention to resolve the German controversy on trades unions had been closely followed in different countries. Could what had been conceded to German Catholics not be conceded to others too? In Italy the Economic-Social Union, led by Count Medolago Albani, as we have seen, consisted exclusively of Catholic associations. Some people were unsettled at the prospect of independent associations developing, with their inherent dangers. At the beginning of 1914 a controversy began which, without adopting the terms of the German debate, sharpened it, so to speak: Is Christian trade-unionism legitimate?

The question was posed in two resounding articles in the *Civiltà Cattolica* (February 21 and March 7, 1914).[47] Following the custom of the journal, the articles were not signed. In fact they were by the Jesuit, Fr. Giulio Monetti, a theologian who was influential with the Pope and Cardinal Merry del Val. On the basis of analyses of largely French cases, Fr. Monetti judged Christian trade-unionism to be "false in its presuppositions, pernicious and illusory in its aims, and both immoderate and destructive in its means."

Should this have been seen as preliminary announcement of a pontifical document on trades unions? Both Cardinal Merry del Val and Pius X

---

[46] Pius X returned to this subject, in very clear terms, in what was to be his last consistorial allocution: "You must say clearly that mixed associations and alliances with non-Catholics for the promotion of material well-being are permitted under specific conditions, but that the Pope's preference is for unions of the faithful who, having banished all human respect and shut their ears to all flattery or threats..., flock to that banner which, war-torn though it may be, is the most splendid and the most glorious because it is the banner of the Church," Allocution *Il grave dolore,* May 27, 1914, *Documents pontificaux,* vol.II, pp.575-577.

[47] Cf. Poulat, "La dernière bataille du pontificat de Pie X."

seem to have approved of the ideas expressed in the two articles. The controversy was lively, in Italy and abroad. However, the War and the Pope's death meant that no pontifical document on trade-unionism saw the light of day. Feared by some and welcomed by others, it would not, in any case, have been a condemnation of trade-unionism as such, and even less a condemnation of Christian trade-unionism. As Émile Poulat has written, "what missed being condemned in 1914...[was] a particular evolution of Christian trade-unionism in a new direction," *i.e.,* a Christian trade-unionism which, in places, was already losing its Christian character and was abandoning its prime goal: moral and religious perfection.

In the absence of an encyclical or motu proprio on trade-unionism, we have a final intervention of the Pope on Catholic social associations. It comes from his last consistorial allocution on May 27, 1914. In it, the Pope re-affirmed very precisely the doctrine which had always been his on this matter: "Never stop repeating," he told the last cardinals he created, "that, if the Pope loves and approves the Catholic associations which aspire even to material welfare, he has always repeated that, in these associations, moral and religious welfare should always have pride of place. The desire to improve the lot of the worker and the peasant, just and praiseworthy as it is, must always be united to a love of justice and the application of legitimate means, so that harmony and peace may be maintained between the different social classes."[48]

---

[48]   Allocution *Il Grave Dolore,* May 27, 1914, *Documents pontificaux,* vol.II, pp.575-577.

CHAPTER 10

THE CARE OF THE UNIVERSAL CHURCH

We are not writing an exhaustive history of the Church under the pontificate of Pius X. In this chapter, therefore, we shall not be tracing the entire evolution of the Church on the different continents. We are restricting ourselves to the Pope's decisions and direct interventions, and where necessary this will naturally involve a certain amount of history of the countries concerned.

Pius X's decisions and interventions were of two kinds: on the one hand, faced with governments who entered into conflict with the Church, the Pope demonstrated his doctrinal firmness while attempting to find practical accommodations; on the other hand, in his relations with local ecclesiastical hierarchies, he endeavoured to promote the Church's vitality.

In the face of anticlericalism

In addition to France, which we have already mentioned, several countries entered into conflict with the Church by conducting anticlerical politics, often inspired by Freemasonry. Sometimes, but not always, a compromise was found after the Pope had protested.

In Spain in 1910 a conflict between the civil authorities and the bishops had taken a grave turn. For several years the legal status of religious congregations had provoked differences between Church and State. At the beginning of Pius X's pontificate an agreement had been reached.[1] The Church had made large concessions, in particular, agreeing that "houses or convents of religious orders and congregations in which less than 12 persons are leading a life in common, shall be suppressed," and stipulating that "no new order or new congregation may be established in Spain without authorization from His Holiness and the prior agreement of the government...." In 1910 a new anticlerical government, led by Canalejas, challenged this agreement. He decided to treat religious congregations as ordinary associations and, as in France, to make them subject to prior authorization by the Minister of Justice. The conflict came to a head with the

---

[1] *Accord entre le Saint-Siège et l'Espagne,* June 19, 1904, *Documents pontificaux,* vol.I, pp.184-186.

breaking-off of diplomatic relations between the Holy See and Spain. Pius X did not want to let the situation fester. In 1911, in a letter to the Bishop of Vieh, congratulating him on having taken a stand against the government's policies, he recalled the traditional doctrine: "the twin powers, ecclesiastical and civil, should agree"; "it is never permitted to ignore the authority of the Roman Pontiff when dealing with questions concerning the Church of an entire country."[2] At the same time, however—and this is characteristic of Pius X's policy in this area of relations with states—the Pope declared that he was ready to be conciliatory: "the Church, by her very nature, is inclined to be receptive to the expression of good and just requests...at all times the Sovereign Pontiff has been full of indulgence and inclined to concord." That is what happened. In January 1913, under a new government led by Dato, an agreement was reached between the Holy See and the Spanish state. One important concession had been made: for the space of two years no religious house, even of religious in simple vows, could be founded in Spain without special authorization from the Holy See. The resolution of these differences allowed the resumption of diplomatic relations.

In Portugal things took a very different course. On February 1, 1908, the King, Don Carlos, and the Crown Prince were assassinated. In 1910 a republican regime, with the support of Freemasonry, was put in place. Religious congregations were dissolved and many religious were expelled from the country. Divorce was legalized. Religious holy days were erased from the calendar of national holidays. The Bishops of Porto and Beja were deposed from their sees. On January 15, in a letter to the Portuguese episcopate, the Pope exhorted them to be faithful and courageous. The following April 20, the Portuguese government proclaimed the separation of Church and State. Then Pius X published an encyclical solemnly condemning this "absurd monstrosity...exempting the State from divine worship, as if all men, individuals and society, were not dependent on Him who created and maintains all things."[3] He also denounced the legal provisions which deprived the clergy of all revenue, put lay associations in charge of religious worship, and placed the Church's entire life under state control (including the internal organization of the seminaries). A few months later, in a consistorial allocution, Pius X again referred to the dismal fate of the Church in Portugal, denouncing "the Sect" (Freemasonry) which was responsible for revolution and persecution.[4] Again in 1913, in a public letter to the Patriarch of Lisbon, Pius X denounced the persecutions

---

[2]   Letter *Medias Inter,* May 1, 1911, *Documents pontificaux,* vol.II, pp.336-337.
[3]   Encyclical *Jamdudum,* May 24, 1911, *Documents pontificaux,* vol.II, pp.344-348.
[4]   Allocution *Gratum Quidem,* November 11, 1911, *Documents pontificaux,* vol.II, p.392.

which continued to afflict the Church: emprisonment of priests, deposition and expulsion of bishops, and various kinds of despoliation.

All the Portuguese bishops were deprived of their revenue. The Pope charged Msgr. Pacelli, the future Pius XII, who at that time was secretary in the section of Extraordinary Ecclesiastical Affairs, with the task of working out a financial project in support of the Portuguese bishops. The amount involved was a million lire. Pius X succeeded in collecting this sum, and the very day he handed the money over to Msgr. Pacelli for the Portuguese bishops, he unexpectedly received a visit from a stranger who gave him a check for an identical sum. "You see," Pius X humorously told Msgr. Mella, the duty secret chamberlain that day, "it goes out like this and comes back like that!"[5] It took many years for the Church in Portugal to return to a satisfactory state of affairs.

In Latin America, too, the Church was confronted with hostile policies at the beginning of the century. In Ecuador, at the start of Pius X's pontificate, the anticlerical and laicist legislation got worse. In particular it included the legal recognition of divorce, the confiscation of the goods of the clergy, the dispersion of religious orders, and restrictions on the right to profess vows of religion. In his consistorial allocution of March 27, 1905, Pius X deplored this persecution. The following May 14 he addressed a public letter to the bishops of Ecuador complaining that the government's policies were aiming at "the utter destruction" of the Church; he exhorted them to be courageous and faithful.[6]

In Bolivia also, but on a lesser scale, Pius X had to deplore the introduction of the freedom of religious worship and the legalization of divorce.[7] In 1908, however, Pius X could rejoice at the re-establishment of diplomatic relations between Bolivia and the Holy See.

In fact, in Latin America, the long conflict which had often caused the Church to clash with the State throughout the 19th century (after decolonization) tended to abate between 1910 and 1914, except in Mexico.[8] The Church did not resume her former position, which was characterized by patronage (patronato real), but "found herself free and ultramontane; for the first time in her history she was no longer linked to state power, and

---

[5] Anecdote reported by G. Fornari in his deposition, *Summarium*, p.266, also reported in *Articoli*, p.121.

[6] Letter *Acre Nefariumque*, May 14, 1905, *Documents pontificaux*, vol.I, pp.294-295.

[7] Letter *Afflictum Proprioribus* to the bishops of Bolivia, November 24, 1906, *Documents pontificaux*, vol.I, pp.383-384.

[8] On December 8, 1910, in the letter *Sollicitis Nobis* (*Documents pontificaux*, vol.II, pp.296-299) to the Archbishop of Caracas, Pius X expresses his "gratitude to the members of the Republic (of Venezuela), and in particular to the noble President whom, in virtue of the universal zeal shown for justice, We see to be well-disposed towards the Church."

could develop her European ideas directly. This was something revolutionary, and explains how Catholics were in a good position to attack liberalism, positivism and utilitarianism in the name of religion and patriotism."[9]

This new authority enjoyed by the Church was also manifested in the mediating role that the Papacy was called to exercise in many Latin American countries at the beginning of the century. In 1905 a disagreement arose over the delimitation of the frontier between Bolivia and Brazil. Both countries appealed to Pius X to act as arbitrator; he entrusted the matter to the Apostolic Delegate in Brazil. The same year, Colombia and Peru had a dispute over the territory of Putamayo; they too decided to appeal to the Pope.

As we have said, in the years 1910-1914 it was only Mexico, of all the Latin American countries, which embarked upon a long-lasting conflict with the Church, a conflict that was to be a very bloody one. President Porfirio Diaz, who had been in power from 1876 onwards, was toppled in 1910. In this context it is interesting to read the letter which Pius X had addressed to the Mexican episcopate some time earlier.[10] On the occasion of the centenary of the institution of the Republic of Mexico, the Pope had exhorted the bishops to develop a program of teaching of the faith to all the faithful. He recommended them to "hold religious meetings to study the precepts of the faith and education in the faith, but also to establish durable organizations providing Christian instruction for the people, particularly the youth." The Pope, aware of the growing influence of political forces hostile to the Church, also recommended the bishops to create or develop social organs "permitting Christian charity to play its part" and "protecting the humblest people...from the trap of *socialism*." Finally, in relation to the elections, he exhorted the bishops: "You must make every effort to ensure that Catholics support only the candidature of those whose writings are wholesome...and who respect religion." Pius X had clearly recognized the menace threatening Mexico. The Mexican revolution exploded and, in the 1920's, was to reach its peak in a pitiless persecution and civil war.

---

[9]   Jean-André Meyer, "L'Amérique latine," in *Histoire du Christianisme,* vol.XI (1830-1914) (Paris: Desclée, 1995), p.956. The author does not once cite the name and acts of Pius X.

[10] Letter *Per Solemnia Saecularia,* February 23, 1910, *Documents pontificaux,* vol.II, pp.193-194. The following June 16, in the Apostolic Letter *Gratiae Quae Sunt* (II, pp.244-245), Pius X granted a plenary indulgence to the faithful who, on the day of the Renewal of the Consecration to Our Lady of Guadalupe, made their confessions, received communion and went to a church to pray "for unity between the leaders of Christian states, the destruction of heresies, the conversion of sinners and the exaltation of our Mother, Holy Church."

One of the most striking instances of Pius X's action in Latin America was his intervention on behalf of the Indians. Once he had been alerted by the reports of missionaries and bishops concerning the grim fate, in many places, of people of Indian origin, Pius X, on July 6, 1911, appointed Fr. Genocchi as Apostolic Visitor in South America. Fr. Genocchi, whom we have already mentioned as a protagonist in the Modernist crisis, also had long experience as a missionary.[11] The Pope gave him a twofold mission: to enquire into the living conditions of the Indians, and into the situation of the Catholic missions in the South American continent. From July 1911 to March 1912 Fr. Genocchi visited many Latin American countries. He entered into contact with the Indian populations and drew up several reports which he sent to the Vatican during the course of his travels. Back in Rome, he was received by the Pope on April 26, 1912. We can imagine that he was directly associated with the preparation of the Encyclical "On the amelioration of the deplorable condition of the Indians" which Pius X published two months later.[12] In this encyclical, the penultimate of his pontificate, the Pope expressed his "profound pity" for "this unfortunate people," and was not afraid to go into detail in denouncing the terrible treatment the Indians were still undergoing. Pius X told the bishops of Latin America to develop programs of instruction and social work for the Indians, and exhorted the faithful of different origins to show charity towards this minority. He also expressed his determination to set up "new missionary stations where the Indians will find refuge and salutary protection."

In fact, Fr. Genocchi was charged with organizing, together with Cardinal Merry del Val, a missionary expedition to the region of Peru where the Iquitos Indians lived. This expedition was entrusted to English Franciscans.

The Missions

While we cannot give a complete history of the missions under the pontificate of Pius X, it is possible to outline his general thrust and the important decisions he took in this matter.

From the beginning of his pontificate Pius X demonstrated the great importance he attached to the missions by giving St. Francis Xavier as the patron saint of the work of the Propagation of the Faith, and by raising his feast to that of a major double.[13]

---

[11] Turvasi, *Giovanni Genocchi e la controversia modernista*, and "Genocchi (Giovanni)," *Dictionnaire d'Histoire et de Géographie Ecclésiastique,* vol.XX, col.488.493.
[12] *Lacrimabili Statu Indorum,* June 7, 1912, *Documents pontificaux,* vol.II, pp.435-438.

For half a century the missions had been undergoing continual development. Under the pontificate of Pius X this missionary expansion allowed the erection of many apostolic vicariates on different continents: in Morocco (1908), Egypt (1909), Eritrea (1911), the Caroline Islands and the Island of Guam (1911), Korea (1911), two in China (1911 and 1912), the Solomon Islands (1912), Africa (the region of Kivuen in 1912 and of Banguelo in 1913), and Libya (1913). The development of the apostolic vicariate of western Ho Han, in China, enabled it to be erected into an apostolic prefecture (1911). In the territories adjacent to north-west India and eastern Pakistan, the expansion of the Catholic communities necessitated the creation of the ecclesiastical province of Simla in 1913 (it consisted of an archdiocese, a diocese and an apostolic prefecture).

In order to facilitate the vitality of the Catholic communities in countries which had no diplomatic relations with the Holy See, Pius X was willing to receive extraordinary ambassadors, who came to him bringing messages from their sovereigns. So, in 1907, he received an envoy from the Emperor of Japan, and then one from the Shah of Persia; in 1909 he received an envoy from the Ottoman Sultan Mahomet V. In 1914 he also received the King of Uganda in private audience. This sovereign was not a Catholic and his country had only known Catholic missionaries since 1879. But Pius X, remembering the terrible persecution of 1886 (in which tens of Christians had been burned), thought it profitable for the peace of the country to receive its sovereign, even though still a pagan.

In Ethiopia, a country where Christianity had been planted in very ancient times, Pius X had to intervene because Catholics in the region of the Harar had been imprisoned and their goods had been confiscated. The Capuchin missionaries in charge of this country appealed to the Pope to intercede with the Negus, Menelik. So, on July 18, 1906, Pius X wrote a letter to the Emperor of Ethiopia.[14] He demanded that he should put an end to the persecutions in which Catholics of Lume, Salale and Bercket had been victims: "Have not the Catholics of the Harar been very faithful subjects of Your Majesty? If Your Majesty permits his other subjects to profess this religion, to which the voice of Heaven has called them, why will you not exercise tolerance in respect of Your Catholic subjects?"

This latter argument refers, no doubt, to the protection which Negus Menelik had granted the missionaries of the Anglican Church Missionary

---

[13] Apostolic Letter *In Apostolicum,* March 25, 1904, *Documents pontificaux,* vol.I, pp.156-158. The association of the Propagation of the Faith had been founded in Lyons in 1822 to collect alms from the faithful and distribute them to Catholic missions all over the world. It became a Pontifical Association under the pontificate of Pius XI.

[14] Letter *Il Nostro Predecessore,* July 18, 1906, *Documents pontificaux,* vol.I, p.365.

Society and the Swedish Lutheran missionaries.[15] At any rate, Menelik was impressed by the Pope's letter and intervened so that the Catholics of the Harar should have complete freedom to exist. Some months after the Pope's letter, he sent a French Capuchin missionary, Fr. Marie-Bernard, to the Vatican to assure the Pope of his good will.[16]

The Oriental Christians

Generally, historians are severely critical of Pius X's attitude to oriental Christians, whether Orthodox or Oriental Catholics. In a most interesting study, Joseph Hajjar speaks of "the Pope's systematic antipathy and prejudice towards the Christian orient."[17] Fifteen years later, Jean-Pierre Valognes is equally severe, deploring the "Latinizing reaction" and the "new thrust of Roman imperialism" which, supposedly, marked the pontificate of Pius X.[18]

This severely critical view is not convincing. In fact, it measures Pius X's action *vis-à-vis* the Christian orient by the standards of ecumenical politics which have been pursued for the last number of decades. This lack of perspective causes Pius X's policy towards Oriental Christians to seem rigid or retrograde. We will demonstrate that, on the contrary—without, of course, abandoning the desire that Orthodox Christians should return to the Catholic Church—Pius X succeeded in reaching agreements with non-Catholic governments. And as for the Oriental Catholics, far from imposing an enforced latinization, he was able to make important concessions for the good of the faithful.

We begin with the Constitution *Tradita ab Antiqua*, which is concerned with the reception of the Eucharist in the different rites.[19] Nowadays this Constitution is often interpreted as restrictive, as a step backwards.[20] In fact it clarifies and simplifies a question which had undergone many developments during the centuries. Pius X decrees that all the faithful, of whatever rite they may be, shall be able to receive communion at whatever rite they are attending. At the same time, priests must celebrate exclusively according to the rite proper to their Church, and shall not be

---

[15] Jacques Gadille and Jean-François Zorn, "L'Afrique," in *Histoire du christianisme*, vol.XI, pp.1021-1022.

[16] Cf. the allocution *Au Milieu des Douleurs, Documents pontificaux*, vol.I, p.408.

[17] Hajjar, *Le Vatican, la France et le catholicisme oriental, 1878-1914*, p.263.

[18] Jean-Pierre Valognes, *Vie et mort des chrétiens d'Orient. Des origines à nos jours* (Paris: Fayard, 1994), pp.359 and 497.

[19] September 14, 1912, *Documents pontificaux*, vol.II, pp.465-470.

[20] *E.g.,* Catherine Mayeur-Jaouen, "Les chrétiens d'Orient au XIXe siècle," in *Histoire du christianisme*, vol.XI, p.828, who sees this as a sign of Pius X's "reticence to follow his predecessor's eastern policy."

able to change from one rite to another for the sake of the group of faithful who happen to be present. This last point, which today seems to be a restriction—a priest of the Latin rite, for instance, could not celebrate according to the Greek rite—in fact manifested a great respect for the rites and traditions proper to each Catholic Church, for the Constitution's final decree was as follows:

> Everyone shall remain in the rite in which he was born, even if he has been in the habit of communicating in another rite for a long time; no one will be permitted to change from one rite to another without just and legitimate reason, of which the Sacred College of Propaganda for the affairs of Oriental Rites will be the judge.

In our view this last point seems to give the lie to the accusation levelled against Pius X nowadays, that he wanted increasingly to latinize the Oriental Catholic Churches. Other facts will show the same thing.

He made many concessions to Catholics of other rites. In 1906, when, as we shall see, there was a vast movement of return, on the part of Uniates, to Latin rite Catholicism, the Secretariate of State authorized the use of Russian in preaching, catechism, prayers and canticles; it confirmed the legitimacy of using Polish for the same "ceremonies complementary to worship."[21] Even more significantly, on February 17, 1908, in a personal indult to the Ukrainian Metropolitan of Lemberg (Lvov), Msgr. Szeptickij, Pius X extended to the entire Slavic world the particular measures conceded by Leo XIII to the Oriental Churches.[22]

Pius X also instituted a hierarchy for the Ukrainian Catholics in the United States and Canada, and in 1912 he conceded the erection of a diocese of the Greek Catholic Rite in Hungary, the diocese of Hajdudorog, composed of parishes from six existing dioceses.[23] This latter concession was important, because it included the authorization of the use of Hungarian in extra-liturgical functions (catechism, church music, etc.). This authorization had already been requested in the past, when the parishes concerned were dispersed among different dioceses. Three times (in 1897, 1898 and 1899) the Congregation of Extraordinary Ecclesiastical Affairs had forbidden this practice, under pressure from the Austro-Hungarian government, which was endeavoring to stifle all manifestation of nationalism within the Empire.[24]

---

[21] Letter from the Secretariate of State to the Bishops of Russia, October 13, 1906, *Documents pontificaux,* vol.I, pp.379-380.

[22] This fact is cited by Roger Aubert, "Pio X tra restaurazione e riforma," in *La Chiesa e la società industriale, 1878-1922,* vol.XXII/1 of *Storia della Chiesa,* p.124.

[23] Apostolic Letter *Christi Fideles,* June 8, 1912, *Documents pontificaux,* vol.II, pp.439-444.

[24] Hajjar, *Le Vatican, la France et le catholicisme oriental,* pp.139-140.

In the same field, we should note the concession granted to the dioceses of Gorizia, Zara and Zagreb to use Glagolitic (the ancient Slavonic language). Finally there was the favor granted to the Romanian bishops of the Greek rite (the bishops of the ecclesiastical provinces of Fagares and Alba Julia). They had asked for a church in Rome with a residence beside it for their *Procurator* (their representative, who proposed questions relating to their rite to the Roman Curia). On March 31, 1914, Pius X granted them the church of San Salvatore alle Coppelle.

As regards the Oriental Catholic Patriarchates, the results of Pius X's pontificate are quite diverse. This follows from the complicated evolution which these churches had undergone over the centuries.

The Armenian Catholic Church had lived through considerable upheavals under the pontificate of Pius IX and then under that of Leo XIII. In August 1904 Paul Sabbaghian, Bishop of Alexandria, was elected Patriarch, taking the name of Paul Peter XII. At a consistory the following November Pius X confirmed the election.[25] At that time relations between Rome and the Armenian Catholic Church experienced a period of harmony. On January 18, 1906, Pius X received the Patriarch of the Armenians in audience at the Vatican. However, Paul Peter XII died in 1910. Paul Terzian was elected to succeed him and took the name of Paul Peter XIII. He got into difficulties with some prominent members of his community. Pius X convoked an Armenian Synod in Rome in order to ease the conflict. On this occasion, exercising his own authority, he named nine new bishops. The Synod was held in 1911 in the presence of the Patriarch, "in an atmosphere of blind resistance, to which the many defections bore witness."[26] Once he had returned to Constantinople in 1912, Paul Peter XIII was dismissed from his civil functions by the Ottoman government, and the Armenian Catholic Church was torn by internal dissension until the First World War.

As for the Syrian Catholic Church, it was experiencing an expansion which was in contrast to the strife found in the Armenian Church. From 1898 to 1929 it was led by the Patriarch Ephrem II Rahmani, a great liturgist. In 1913 many Syrian Orthodox bishops rejoined the Catholic Church together with a good number of their clergy and faithful. These spectacular returns are due, no doubt to a large degree, to the zeal and great moral authority of Ephrem II, but one can imagine that it was also the doctrinal and spiritual personality of Pius X which succeeded in attracting

---

[25] Allocution *Duplicem,* November 14, 1904, *Documents pontificaux,* vol.I, pp.215-216.
[26] Valognes, *Vie et mort des chrétiens d'Orient,* p.497.

these Orthodox dignitaries and inducing them to place themselves under his jurisdiction.

Mention should also be made of the Chaldean Catholic Church of Malabar. Leo XIII had erected three apostolic vicariates, which were soon entrusted to Chaldean bishops. To respond more adequately to the traditional social organization of this region, Pius X agreed in 1911 to create a special vicariate for the caste of the *sudra* at Kottayam.

Pius X had solemnly expressed his concern for the Oriental Catholic Patriarchates during the celebrations in Rome for the 15th centenary of the death of John Chrysostom. A Patriarch and many bishops had been invited. During an audience given to them all at the end of the solemnities, Pius X, in a way that many present found moving, expressed his admiration for the Oriental Churches, and encouraged them in these terms:

> It is you, Venerable Brethren, living in poverty and subject to all manner of privations, continuing to hold in honor the sacred traditions of your ancestors, sparing no pains to convert your brothers—it is you who are Our joy and Our crown. As you return to your countries, tell everyone that the dignity and splendor of the Orient is nowhere so much loved as in Rome. Tell them that here the different Oriental rites are treated with honor, and that they are regularly celebrated in many churches, often joining in the Papal ceremonies.[27]

More surprisingly—and without failing to refer to practical considerations—the Pope also desired to express Rome's respect for the Oriental Churches:

> Tell them that a special Congregation is charged with the task of watching over their continued existence and their orthodoxy. Tell them that every year the Congregation of Propaganda sends out into the whole world young indigenous priests, whom she has nourished and formed according to the orthodox traditions of their countries. These priests are bound by law to remain faithful to the rites of their respective nations. Tell them that Rome takes such care to banish all pretexts for division that she firmly resists the ardent zeal of those neophytes who would like to embrace her discipline.

True, in the same allocution, Pius X had severe things to say to the Orthodox who were separated from Rome. He referred to "the pre-eminence which Constantinople had usurped from the Apostolic Patriarchs of the Orient," the "rebellious sons" who preferred "a harsh yoke (that of Islam) to the tenderness of their mother," the "prelates who have forsaken Catholic unity."

---

[27] Allocution *Ringraziamo Vivamente,* February 14, 1908, *Documents pontificaux,* vol.I, pp.514-515.

In fact Pius X distinguished two Orients: that of the Catholic communities, which he admired and whose rites and traditions he wished to preserve; and that of the Orthodox communities, separated from Rome, who ought to return to her. This position comes out very clearly in the solemn condemnation he made regarding an article which was too ecumenical.

In 1910 the Basilian monks of Grottaferrata, south of Rome, published the first issue of a review dedicated to Oriental Christians: *Roma e Oriente.* Since 1882 the head of the Abbey, which was founded in the 11th century, had been Abbot Arsenio Pellegrini.[28] As agreed with Leo XIII, he had resumed the Greek rite, and in 1910 he began publishing the aforementioned review. The first issue included an article in French by the Rev. Fr. Prince Max of Saxony, professor of liturgy at the Catholic University of Freiburg. This study, entitled "Observations on the Question of the Union of Churches," contained statements which were scandalous, in terms of both history and theology, *i.e.,* on the causes of the 1054 Schism, on the Crusades, on the Catholic Church's efforts to unite the Churches, on the *Filioque,* on Purgatory and on the Immaculate Conception. The author concluded his study by envisaging union between the Catholic Church and the Orthodox Churches on the basis of beliefs held in common prior to the Schism.

The scandal caused by this article moved Pius X to publish a long letter refuting "such grave theological and historical errors."[29] The letter, dated December 26, 1910, was published on January 3, 1911. In order to prevent the Oriental Catholic Churches from being infected by "such a pernicious plague" he directly addressed a copy of this letter to the Apostolic Delegates in Constantinople, Greece, Egypt, Mesopotamia, Persia, Syria and India. The Prince made his submission. The review was allowed to continue to appear (it only went out of existence after the First World War) and took a critical stance towards the Pope's decision.[30] This is proof enough, if proof were needed, that Pius X did not put a muzzle on all liberty of expression.

Relations with Orthodox states

While Pius X was intransigent *vis-à-vis* the Orthodox Churches in matters of doctrine, he sought and obtained accords with Orthodox states.

---

[28] Cf. Giuseppe M. Croce, *La badia greca di Grottaferrata e la rivista "Roma e l'Oriente." Cattolicismo e ortodossia fra unionismo ed ecumenismo* (Vatican City: Libreria Editrice Vaticana, 1990), 2 vols.

[29] Letter *Ex Quo,* December 26, 1910, *Documents pontificaux,* vol.II, pp.308-311.

[30] *E.g.,* in 1912 Professor Baumstark published a series of articles on the reform of the Breviary carried out by Pius X, in which he was very critical of the latter's work "in the light of the history of comparative liturgy."

Tensions persisted between the Russian Empire and the Holy See with regard to the Polish territories under Russian jurisdiction (where more than 90% of the population was Catholic), and with regard to the Belorussian, Ukrainian and Russian Catholics. Political considerations—the Russian Empire's refusal to recognize a Polish national identity—were mixed up with religious considerations, *i.e.*, the Orthodox Church's desire to maintain its own supremacy. Pius X intervened in different ways. In the wake of the initial Russian revolution which began in January 1905, and then of the "October manifesto" which made the Russian autocracy into a parliamentary monarchy, Tsar Nicholas II made certain concessions in religious matters, as regards both Russian territory and the other territories of the Empire. Two edicts, of April 30 and October 30, 1905, assured all the Empire's subjects of liberty of conscience in matters of religion.

These edicts had a double effect. They allowed the return of about 300,000 Belorussian Uniates to Latin Rite Catholicism,[31] and they brought about a tangible improvement in the situation of Polish Catholics. Many Poles were associated with movements seeking national redress, and some had taken part in the revolution of 1905. Furthermore, at the end of the year, Pius X published an Encyclical addressed "to the Archbishops and Bishops of Poland, subject to the Russian Empire."[32] This is an important document, showing the clarity and courage of the Pope. After praising Polish Catholicism ("It will be the eternal glory of your ancestors to have generously offered their breasts as a rampart in the defence of Catholicism"), Pius X set himself to define the conditions of "this peace and concord to which the best of you have dedicated all their efforts, albeit without result, up to the present day." At some length he condemned (without naming them) the Communist-inspired revolutionaries who had attracted a certain following among the Poles.[33] He also condemned the "national radicalism" which "paraded an often unintelligent patriotism" which aimed at "creating and nourishing political passions in people's hearts." Noteworthy was his condemnation of the "horrible crimes that cause the barbaric nations themselves to blush, such as—to name but one—the recent, blatant massacre of Jews, a massacre which is reproved and condemned by the law of the Gospel, which commands us to love all men."

---

[31] Constantin Simon, "L'Église orthodoxe russe à la fin du XIXe et au début du XXe siècles: isolement et intégration," in *Histoire du christianisme* (Paris: Desclée, 1995), p.777.

[32] *Poloniae Populum,* December 3, 1905, *Documents pontificaux,* vol.I, pp.323-327.

[33] "These conspiratorial groups of desperate men have been set up everywhere, seeing it their task to overthrow law and rights. By using propaganda, insinuation and daring plots, they try to gain control of the people by terror so that they may plunge them into the most abominable crimes, inflicting the greatest harm on society."

To all these "disturbers of religion and of political and social order"[34] Pius X preached submission to the civil authority. As Leo XIII had done before him, he exhorted Polish Catholics to maintain "the calm of peace." But he also urged them to "group together in associations and societies in which, sharing their ideas and combining their efforts, they can fight effectively for religion and for their country."

This appeal was heard. Historians observe the birth of a vast and diversified movement of rebirth in the Poland of 1905-1920:

> One discerns a current of moral rebirth, which is the indispensable condition for independence. Circles of young Christians were established in many large cities: these were the beginnings of the movement of the Catholic *intelligentsia* which was to be so important during the 20th century. The great success of the Polish Scouts just prior to 1914, the religious (but not confessional) movement in the service of God and the motherland, meant a great deal to this new generation: the formula proved an inspiration to successive generations of young Poles in the 20th century.[35]

Poland owes this, in part, to Pius X.

The encyclical of 1905 was favorably received by the Russian government. Eight months later Cardinal Merry del Val gave the chargé d'affaires of Russia in Rome a promemoria concerning a revision of the curriculum of studies in the Polish seminaries. The study of Russian language, history and literature were obligatory for Polish seminarians. Up to then, the curriculum for these studies had been set by the Russian government and the examinations had been carried out by Russian officials. In July 1907 the Holy See's negotiations resulted in an agreement which conceded to the Russian civil authorities only the right of inspection.[36]

A new accord with another Orthodox state was concluded in 1914: on June 2 a concordat was signed with the Kingdom of Serbia. Until then only one bishopric had existed and, in this country where the vast majority were Orthodox, Catholics were faced with a number of obstacles. As a result of the concordat, the freedom of Catholic worship was assured and an

---

[34] We may mention here, along the same lines, an encyclical published a few months earlier in order to condemn a sect, the Mariavites, Catholic by origin, which enjoyed great success in Poland. (In 1910 it still had 100,000-150,000 adherents.) *Tribus Circiter,* April 5, 1906, *Documents pontificaux,* vol.I, pp.357-360.

[35] Jerzy Kloczowski, "Christianisme et nationalité dans l'Europe du Centre-Est," in *Histoire du christianisme,* vol.XI, p.714. Strangely, the author does not mention Pius X's 1905 Encyclical and the influence it could have had on this moral renaissance in the years before the First World War.

[36] *Accord du Saint-Siège avec la Russie,* July 9-22, 1907, *Documents pontificaux,* vol.I, pp.428-429.

ecclesiastical province was created, consisting of an archdiocese (Belgrade, with about 10,000 faithful) and the suffragan diocese of Usküb.

CHAPTER 11

PASTOR OF SOULS

The name of Pius X has long been associated with that of the catechism, commonly called the *Catechism of Pius X,* and then *of St. Pius X,* and with the "liberating" decrees on Holy Communion—on the communion of children and on frequent communion. Nowadays these aspects of his legacy are even more forgotten. The Catechism of Pius X has been forgotten because "catechesis," particularly after the Second Vatican Council, has undergone considerable evolution—which Pius X could have neither allowed nor even imagined. On the other hand, his decrees on the communion of children and on frequent communion have been so integrated into the religious life of Catholics (that is, practising Catholics) that no one remembers which Pope they are due to.

In this chapter we shall examine this twofold work of Pius X, the Pope of the catechism and the Pope of the Eucharist. The two things are intimately linked, because both of them, on different levels, constitute essential nourishment for the life of faith. Catechism is knowledge of the faith; Eucharist is participation in the divine life. In both cases, by taking important decisions, Pius X labored as a "pastor of souls," concerned for the development of the life of faith, the spiritual life, in the everyday life of the faithful.

We shall refer to other aspects of Pius X as a "pastor of souls," and this will lead us, naturally, to his death on the threshold of the First World War. For it was not as a temporal leader or as an Italian that Pius X reacted to the threat of war, but as a pastor of souls.

The Pope of the catechism

The catechetical concern which Pius X had shown as parish priest of Salzano, as Bishop of Mantua, and then as Patriarch of Venice, reached its high-point during his pontificate.

A few months after his elevation to the pontificate, he wrote a public letter to Cardinal Richard, Archbishop of Paris, giving his encouragement to a catechetical work that had been started in France some decades before.[1] This *Œuvre des catéchistes* (Catechism Project) had been founded in 1884 in Paris by pious laypeople inspired by Msgr. d'Hulst, Rector of the

---

[1] Letter *Opus a Catechismis,* December 8, 1903, *Documents pontificaux,* vol.I, p.62.

Institut Catholique: it involved catechists helping parish priests in the religious instruction of children.[2] Nine years later it was erected into an archconfraternity. It was intended primarily for children of public (state) schools who were not able to receive religious instruction there. Pius X was to develop this collaboration between lay catechists and priests in all countries. It was one of the innovatory aspects of his work in this field.

In 1905 he dedicated an encyclical to the teaching of Christian doctrine.[3] The encyclical opens by identifying the existence of a "religious crisis": "many Christians are completely ignorant of the truths necessary to eternal salvation: this commonly expressed complaint is—alas!—only too well founded." This religious ignorance leads to perdition after death and, in this life, it is the cause of the decadence of societies: "Why, I ask you, should we be surprised that moral corruption and depravity are so prevalent and are increasing day by day, not only among barbaric nations, but even in those states which bear the Christian name?"

After establishing this fact, Pius X exhorts the bishops, following the precepts of the Council of Trent, to carry out their "first and principal duty" of giving religious instruction to the Christian people. They are to do this in two ways: by preaching (explaining the Gospel) and by the teaching of Christian doctrine. There was nothing new, of course, in this exhortation to give religious instruction. On the other hand, no pope before Pius X had so clearly and exhaustively defined the means that were to be employed; and he did so with that practical spirit which was so much his own. The encyclical gives six prescriptions.

1. Every age group, including adults, should be given appropriate instruction.

2. Parish priests should teach the catechism to children "for one full hour on all Sundays and Holy Days of the year, without exception."

3. Children and young people should be given instruction and exhortations preparing them to receive the sacraments of penance and confirmation, and to receive their first communion.

4. In every parish a Congregation of Christian Doctrine should be canonically established, consisting of laypeople who are to be used by parish priests as "auxiliaries in the teaching of the catechism."

5. In towns where there are universities, secondary schools and colleges not under Church authority and where no course of religious instruction is given, "schools of religion" must be set up in a supplementary role.

---

[2] G. Jacquemet, "Catéchismes (Archiconfrérie de l'Œuvre des)," and A. Boyer, "Catéchistes," *Catholicisme,* vol.II, col.656-660.
[3] Encyclical *Acerbo Nimis,* April 15, 1905, *Documents pontificaux,* vol.I, pp.281-289.

6. Finally, all the adults of the parishes should be summoned to come and hear religious teaching, over and above the homily at Mass, at some other time:

> All parish priests and all who have a cure of souls shall give catechism to the faithful in simple language, adapted to their intelligence. For this purpose they will use the *Catechism of the Council of Trent* in such a way that, in the space of four or five years, they will have covered everything concerning the Creed, the Sacraments, the Ten Commandments, Prayer, and the Commandments of the Church.

At this stage there is no question of lowering the age of first communion. Pius X speaks of the necessity of giving a good preparation to "young people...so that they may approach the holy Table in a holy manner on the first occasion." Similarly, the only reference to the catechism of adults is that to the *Catechism of the Council of Trent*. However, concern for Christian instruction, to be given to all the faithful, had always been uppermost in the Pope's desire "to restore all things in Christ." It was Pius X's "merit to have awakened in the clergy the awareness of their catechetical ministry, and to have acknowledged the central role of catechesis in pastoral work."[4]

The terms of the Encyclical would be included, sometimes word for word or in an elaborated form, in the *1917 Code of Canon Law*.[5] In the meantime, Pius X's order for the establishing of a Congregation of Christian Doctrine in every parish was followed in different ways. In France, for example, this work was based on the Archconfraternity of the *Œuvre des Catéchistes:*

> Most of the dioceses responded to Pius X's call by establishing, not parish Confraternities—which, alas, were felt to be neither useful nor effective—but, which was easier, diocesan Confraternities, affiliated to the Paris Archconfraternity. The latter supported them as much as it could, while it was not actually the stimulus which caused them to blossom.[6]

During the pontificate of Pius X two national Congresses of Catechists were held in France, one in 1908 and the other in 1912. For the latter, Pius X sent a letter of encouragement and mentioned the number of 40,000 "pious women who are working effectively for the good education of children."[7]

---

[4]   Luigi Guglielmoni, "Il pioniere della catechesi," in *L'ultimo papa santo Pio X*, p.155.
[5]   Canons 1330-1336 and 1372-1373.
[6]   Boyer, "Catéchistes," col.658.
[7]   Letter *Alias Nos,* January 25, 1912, *Documents pontificaux,* vol.II, p.410. Prior to this Pius X had already sent his encouragement, through Cardinal Merry del Val, to a catechetical congress organized in Calabria (Letter of the Secretariate of State, December 13, 1909, *Documents pontificaux,* vol.II, p.183).

The other great initiative of Pius X in catechetics was the publication of a new catechism. Two months after the Encyclical to which we have referred, he had printed for the dioceses of the Roman Province a *Summary of Christian Doctrine,* which would commonly be called the *Roman Catechism.* The core of this "summary of Christian doctrine" was a text derived from the catechism published in 1765 by Msgr. Michele Casati, Bishop of Mondovi. This catechism had spread through many dioceses in the north of Italy and it had given rise to a new version, published in 1896, which had been adopted by all the dioceses of Lombardy, Liguria and Piedmont (subsequently it was also adopted by those of Aemilia and Tuscany).[8]

Thus the 1905 *Summary* was a revised version of the old catechism of Casati. Expressions which could have been given a false or heretical interpretation had been revised and others had been given greater precision, particularly matters touching on dogmas proclaimed in the 19th century. It had been complemented by specific items. The complete edition comprises five parts: "Fundamental Notions of the Catechism"; "Little Catechism"; "Greater Catechism"; "Instruction on the Principal Feasts"; and "A History of Religion." Instruction was to be given in the two major sections, the "Little Catechism" for children who had not yet made their first communion; and the "Greater Catechism" for other children and adolescents.

According to the Pope's wish, this *Roman Catechism* was "obligatory for public and private instruction in the Diocese of Rome and in all the other dioceses of the Roman Province," but he was also "confident that the other dioceses would also wish to adopt it, so that all would be using a single text, at least in the whole of Italy, which is something to be desired by all."[9] In fact it did spread over the whole of Italy, but was also translated into some foreign languages. In 1906, in France, the Bishop of Langres had this catechism translated.[10]

Pius X himself, however, was not entirely satisfied with this *Summary of Christian Doctrine.*[11] The book was too long. Combined, the "Little Catechism" and the "Greater Catechisms" totalled 1,567 questions and answers. There were certain defects in its overall plan. What is more, it was

---

[8]   Pietro Stella, "Alle fonti del catechismo di San Pio X: il catechismo di Mons. Casati," *Salesianum,* XXIII, January/March 1961, pp.43-65.

[9]   Letter to Cardinal Respighi, Vicar of Rome, June 14, 1905, which is prefaced to all the editions of this abridged catechism.

[10] *Catéchisme de Rome ou Abrégé de la Doctrine chrétienne* (Langres: Éditions Martin-Berret, 1906). It was followed by another edition: Paris, Lethielleux, 1907. This 1906 translation was reprinted in the edition made for the review *Itinéraires* (No.116, September/October 1967) under the title *Catéchisme de saint Pie X.*

[11] Guglielmoni, "Il pioniere della catechesi," in *L'ultimo papa santo Pio X,* p.153.

designed for children and young people, not for adults. Where adults were concerned, as we have seen, Pius X had to recommend the *Catechism of the Council of Trent.*

In 1909 the Pope created a Catechetical Commission with the task of preparing a new catechism according to his directives. This Commission consisted of three members (including Fr. Pietro Benedetti, and Msgr. Faberi). The Pope said that this catechism should be "much shorter and more adapted to today's requirements."[12] Five versions were elaborated between 1909 and 1911. In November 1911 the last of these versions was submitted to 50 Italian cardinals, bishops and prelates for their observations. The Commission took account of the remarks made. It is worth noting that a poet, Guido Salvadori, was asked to read the work and improve it from the stylistic point of view.[13] Finally, in October 1912, the *Catechismo della dottrina cristiana* was published.

In his letter of approbation of this new catechism, Pius X clearly indicated the improvements which had been introduced:

> We are confident that, with the Lord's blessing, this new text will be more practical. It will offer as many advantages as the old one, or even more. The smaller compass of the book, and the smaller number of questions to be learned, will be less daunting to the young, who are already overburdened with their school work; with the help of their teachers and catechists they will be able to learn it in its entirety. In spite of its brevity, it contains better explanations and sheds clearer light on the truths which today, to the great harm of souls and society, are most attacked, or most misunderstood, or most forgotten.
>
> Furthermore, We are confident that it will be found useful even by adults who wish, or who—because of their duty to live a better life and to improve the education of their families—are bound to revive in their souls that fundamental knowledge on which the spiritual life and Christian morality are grounded.[14]

Two versions of the catechism were published. There was a short version entitled *A Primer of Christian Doctrine*, which would be called, more simply, the *Little Catechism*; it was designed for children preparing for confession and first communion. It consists of the text of the prayers and basic ideas of the Christian Faith, followed by 188 questions and answers. The long version, entitled *The Catechism of Christian Doctrine*, consisted of 814 questions and answers, following the same plan as that of the *Catechism of the Council of Trent*: I. The Faith (the Creed); II. The Law (the

---

[12] Letter *Fin dai Primordi*, October 18, 1912, *Documents pontificaux*, vol.II, p.477.
[13] Guglielmoni, "Il pioniere della catechesi," in *L'ultimo papa santo Pio X*, p.157.
[14] Letter *Fin dai Primordi*, p.478.

Commandments of God, the precepts of the Church, the Virtues); III. Grace (the sacraments, prayer).[15]

In approving this catechism, Pius X made it obligatory only for the Diocese of Rome and the dioceses of the Roman ecclesiastical province. But, as in the case of its predecessor, he expressed the wish that the other dioceses of Italy would adopt it also. That is what happened. Its clarity, as well as its coherent organization, found admirers beyond the frontiers. In 1913, translations were made into Spanish, German, French (one in Paris and one in Annecy) and English. But not all the countries adopted it officially. In France, for example, beginning in 1930, there was an attempt to produce a "unitary" catechism that would apply to all the dioceses. At any rate, all the Italian dioceses used the 1912 catechism for several decades, and most of the Spanish-speaking countries did the same.

Finally it should be mentioned that, in 1913, Pius X had the idea of producing a universal catechism for the use of the entire Church.[16] Even at the First Vatican Council this idea had been proposed, but nothing came of it because the Council was suspended. It was John Paul II, 80 years after Pius X's project, who would initiate the project of the *Catechism of the Catholic Church.*

The Pope of the Eucharist

No pope in modern times did so much to encourage more Christians to receive the sacrament of the Eucharist. He did this partly by lowering the age for first communion, and partly, in different ways, by urging the faithful to more frequent communion.

The Eucharistic Congresses represented one of the means used to revive eucharistic devotion and the practice of communion. In Venice, as we have seen, the future Pius X had organized the Fifth National Eucharistic Congress. During his pontificate a Eucharistic Congress was organized in Rome, June 1-6, 1905.

It opened with a Mass celebrated by the Pope in St. Peter's Basilica and concluded with a eucharistic procession in the same basilica, during which Pius X himself wished to carry the Blessed Sacrament. On June 5, in a short address to the participants, Pius X urged the bishops and priests present to be apostles of the Eucharist: "I pray and urge you all to encourage the faithful to approach the divine Sacrament....The divine Sacrament of the Eucharist assures us of eternal life and gives us confidence in fight-

---

[15] We refer to the last Italian edition: *Catechismo di San Pio X* (Salpan Editore, Matino, 1991).

[16] Gilbert Adler and Gérard Vogeleisen, *Un siècle de catéchèse en France, 1893-1980* (Paris: Beauchesne, 1981), pp.23-24.

ing to victory against our enemies." He also exhorted the priests present "to make sure that Jesus, the greatest benefit given to sorrowing humanity, is not left abandoned through cowardice and ingratitude...."[17]

In the following years, whenever there were International Eucharistic Congresses in different countries, Pius X sent a pontifical legate and a message: Tournai (1906), Metz (1907), London (1908), Cologne (1909), Montreal (1910), Madrid (1911), Vienna (1912), Malta (1913), and Lourdes (1914). At the Congress held in Madrid, for example, Pius X wrote a letter in which he particularly recommended two things: he urged the wider use of the custom "already established in many places" of celebrating Benediction of the Blessed Sacrament every Sunday and Holy Day; and he urged those who were "gravely ill," and their families, not to call the priest at the very last moment for Extreme Unction, but to call him sufficiently early so that the dying person could receive the sacrament of confession and last communion (*viaticum*) while lucid.[18]

Most of all, Pius X did much to modify the eucharistic practice of the faithful; he did this through a series of decrees, notably those on frequent communion and on the communion of children.

The decree on "the daily reception of the Holy Eucharist," issued at the start of Pius X's pontificate, was not a novelty, but it cut across a tendency which had become widely established in the Church, namely, that the vast majority of the faithful only communicated on rare occasions. Recommending frequent, and even daily, communion was not new, however. The Council of Trent itself, in a provision which recalls the attitude of Pius X, had hoped that "at each Mass, the faithful who are present should communicate, not only in spiritual desire, but also by the sacramental participation of the Eucharist, that thereby a more abundant fruit might be derived to them from this most holy sacrifice."[19]

In more recent times, in order to counter the Jansenist tendency which suggested that people should only approach communion rarely, writers had been trying to spread the practice of frequent communion and to indicate its spiritual fruits. Thus in 1860 Msgr. de Ségur published his *La très Sainte Communion*—a work approved by Pius IX.[20] Under this same pontificate Cardinal Antonelli, Secretary of State, wrote a letter to the Bishops of France encouraging them to admit children and seminarians to communion more frequently.

---

[17] *ASS,* XXXVII, p.678.
[18] Letter *Qui Propediem,* June 5, 1911, *Documents pontificaux,* vol.II, pp.351-352.
[19] Council of Trent, Session XXII, ch.VI.
[20] Letter of Pius IX to Msgr. de Ségur, September 29, 1860, BN ms. NAFr. 22833, f.24-25.

Under the pontificate of Leo XIII it was Msgr. de Ségur and a lay-woman, Émilie Tamisier, who had been the initiators of the International Eucharistic Congresses, of which the first was held in Lille in 1881. "The Eucharistic Movement pursues a twofold objective: on the one hand, adoration and reparation; and on the other hand, frequent communion."[21]

In 1890 a decree of the Congregation of Bishops and Religious once again recommended that seminarians should receive frequent communion. Yet these recommendations were far from being followed everywhere. In Venice, for example, "there were complaints"[22] that confessors only authorized communion once a week for the youngest seminarians. Conversely, also in Venice, in the parish of San Martino di Burano, frequent communion was already widely practised at the beginning of the 20th century (prior to Pius X's decree), thanks to the spiritual zeal of a succession of parish priests—more than 100 communions being given each day.[23] Again, in 1902, in his Encyclical *Mirae Caritatis,* Leo XIII encouraged regular communion and wished to "dissipate the prejudices" and "banish the specious reasonings" which held Christians back from more frequent communion.

In historical context, therefore, the decree of the Sacred Congregation of the Council, published in December 1905, simply continues and amplifies an antecedent line of thought and practice. Nonetheless by issuing this decree Pius X wished to give the long-established recommendations a more general and universal application and, by doing so, to break definitively with an attitude that was still prevalent in the Church.[24] The decree recalls the witness of the Holy Scriptures themselves, according to which, every day, the first Christians "persevered in the Apostles' teaching and fellowship, and in the breaking of bread" (Acts 2:42). In order to counter the slackening of devotion and "the poison of Jansenism," the decree laid down the conditions under which the faithful could communicate daily: they should be in the state of grace (not having committed any mortal sin) and have a right intention (this *right intention* was defined as "approaching the Holy Table, not by habit or by vanity, or for human reasons, but to satisfy the will of God, to unite themselves more intimately to Him by charity and, thanks to this divine remedy, to fight against their faults and

---

[21] André Haquin, "Les décrets eucharistiques de Pie X. Entre mouvement eucharistique et mouvement liturgique," *La Maison-Dieu,* 203, 1995, p.63.

[22] These two expressions are found in the *relazione* of the Apostolic Visitor in December 1906, cited by Bertoli, "Una diocesa all'ombra di Pio X," in *La Chiesa di Venezia nel promo novecento,* p.22.

[23] Figure quoted by the Apostolic Visitor in his *relazione, ibid.,* p.23.

[24] Decree *Sacra Tridentina Synodus,* December 20, 1905, *Documents pontificaux,* vol.I, pp.673-676.

weaknesses"). They were also recommended to seek the advice of their confessor before embarking upon frequent communion and to make sure that every communion was followed by some "suitable act of thanksgiving."

Soon, other decrees would be issued by the same Congregation, encouraging the frequent communion of children who had already made their first communion, and to facilitate the communion of those who were seriously ill (by reducing the rule of the eucharistic fast).[25] The Congregation of Indulgences would even give a dispensation from the obligation of weekly confession for those who communicated daily, provided they were "not aware of any mortal sin since their last confession."[26] These various recommendations and provisions were not sufficient, however, to ensure that the decree on frequent and daily communion was unanimously accepted and followed. It would be necessary to examine the influence of these Roman directives in each country and each diocese. During a Eucharistic Congress in Venice in 1913, a priest, explaining why frequent communion was not yet widely practised in all the parishes, gave four reasons: "The inadequacy or absence of religious instruction; ignorance of the pontifical decrees; Jansenist traditions...; the belief that the whole eucharistic cult should consist in adoration alone...."[27]

Identical reticence attended the fixing of the age for children's first communion. Here too, however, the pontifical directives eventually came into force everywhere and permanently replaced established practices. In the 19th century it had become customary in most countries to defer the age of first communion until 12-14 years. It was Pius IX who was the first to challenge the custom of deferring communion until this late age.[28] In 1851 the Congregation of the Council corrected a chapter of the Rouen provincial council which had prohibited the admission of children to communion before the age of 12 years. In 1866, in a letter to the Bishops of France, Cardinal Antonelli, Secretary of State to Pius IX, reproved the custom of "deferring the first communion until a fixed, late age."

By a decree dated August 8, 1910, Pius X laid down rules which were to apply to the whole Church.[29] After describing the many disadvantages

---

[25] Decision of the Sacred Congregation of the Council, September 15, 1906, and the Decree on Communion of the Sick and the Eucharistic Fast, December 7, 1906, *Documents pontificaux*, vol.I, pp.679-685 and 686.

[26] Letter of the Sacred Congregation of Indulgences, February 14, 1906, *Documents pontificaux*, vol.I, p.739.

[27] Address of Don Luigi Cerutti at the Venice Eucharistic Congress (1913), quoted by B. Bertoli, "Una diocesa all'ombra di Pio X," in *La Chiesa di Venezia nel promo novecento*, p.23.

[28] Cf. Yves Chiron, *Pie IX, pape moderne* (Étampes: Éditions Clovis, 1995), p.494.

[29] Decree *Quam Singulari* (of the Sacred Congregation of the Sacraments), August 8, 1910, *Documents pontificaux*, vol.II, pp.651-656.

and dangers of a delayed first communion, the decree recalls the traditional teaching, which is that of St. Thomas Aquinas: "But when children once
begin to have some use of reason so as to be able to conceive some devotion
for the sacrament, then it can be given to them" (*Summa Theologica*, III,
q 80, a.9). Therefore, "so that children may approach Jesus Christ at an
early age, live his life and there find protection against the dangers of corruption," the Congregation of the Sacraments laid down precise rules.
First communion and first confession should take place when "the child
has begun to reason, that is, at about seven years, more or less." The essential condition is that the child should "know how to distinguish the eucharistic bread from ordinary, physical bread."

To encourage all the dioceses to apply these new rules, the decree stipulated that every five years the bishops must give an account of the way in
which the decree had been implemented.

The application of this decree on first communion, and of that on
daily communion, were matters of constant concern to Pius X. Hardly had
it been published when a French bishop, the Bishop of Laval, made known
his and his clergy's enthusiastic adherence to the decree. Pius X thanked
him publicly by letter.[30] In this letter the Pope well expresses the profound
motive behind his eucharistic decrees: they were one of the supernatural
means of "restoring all things in Christ." He writes: "While the sons of
perdition cry, 'We will not have Him to reign over us,' God himself estab-
lishes a more worthy reign over the souls of those to whom the Kingdom
of Heaven belongs."

Pius X knew that the decree on the age of first communion would
encounter some reluctance in France. One day he received Msgr.
Chesnelong, Bishop of Valence, and told him, "In France they sourly crit-
icize Our decree on communion; but, you will see, there will be saints
among these children."[31] On the other hand, France was also one of the
countries where a powerful movement developed in favor of early communion. In April 1912, 400 young French communicants went on pilgrimage to Rome and gave the Pope an album containing the signatures of
135,000 children who had made their first communion for the Pope's intentions. In the allocution he made to them, Pius X set forth the benefits
of the Eucharist with great simplicity and clarity: "By communicating
Himself to us in this way, our adorable Saviour gives truth to our minds,
justice and holiness to our wills, and goodness to our hearts."[32] Again, "the
faithful who are united to Jesus Christ in the holy Eucharist find every

[30] Letter *Quamvis Explorata*, September 5, 1910, *Documents pontificaux*, vol.II, p.285.
[31] Deposition of Msgr. Chesnelong, Archives of the Postulation, quoted by Dal-Gal, *Pie
X*, p.305.
[32] Allocution *Je Vous Remercie*, April 14, 1912, *Documents pontificaux*, vol.II, p.427.

perfection and all holiness in the virtue of this sacrament. From this well they can draw strength to rise above themselves and to aspire to eternal happiness, despising this world's false goods since they cannot satisfy their desires."

Liturgical reforms

As one of the first historians of the Liturgical Movement rightly underlined,

> With Pope Pius X the Liturgical Movement entered into an entirely new period. Up to then, in effect, it had been the monopoly of individual people and groups in the Church. Voices had been raised here and there expressing their consensus in response to the invading secularism; they urged a return to the sources as the true way of re-Christianizing the world. Some monasteries had become centers of liturgical vitality, and a certain number of priests and laypeople, sharing the same ideas, tended to group together and become, indirectly, the propagators of these ideas.[33]

With Pius X, things changed. The clergy who, until then, had largely kept aloof from the liturgical renewal, was now receiving directives from the Pope himself. We have already seen the first great initiative of the liturgical reform, namely, that regarding sacred music and the restoration of the Gregorian chant. Other reforms were undertaken in the last years of the pontificate, namely, the reform of the liturgical calendar and the reform of the Breviary.

By the motu proprio *Supremi Disciplinae* the number of holy days of obligation (when it is obligatory to attend Mass and rest from work) was reduced.[34] As he said, the Pope wished to take into account "the changed conditions of the times and of civil society." It was necessary to reduce the number of holy days because of the social and economic constraints of modern life. Sundays apart, there were only eight Feasts during the year, when the Christian was obliged "to hear holy Mass and abstain from servile work."

More fundamentally, the liturgical calendar was entirely reformed by the motu proprio *Abhinc Duos Annos*.[35] Pointing out that the offices of saints had multiplied so much in the liturgy that they had largely obliterated the cycle of Sundays and Feasts, Pius X desired to re-establish the temporal cycle (the cycle of the life of Christ) and reduce the sanctoral cycle (the cycle of saints). Fixed Feasts occurring on Sundays were suppressed

---

[33] Olivier Rousseau, *Histoire du mouvement liturgique* (Paris: Éditions du Cerf, 1945).

[34] *Supremi Disciplinae,* July 2, 1911, *Documents pontificaux,* vol.II, pp.361-362.

[35] Latin text of the motu proprio (dated October 23, 1913) and of the General Decree of the Congregation of Rites (dated October 28, 1913), translation and commentaries by Dom Lambert Beauduin, in *Les Questions liturgiques,* no.1, December 1913, pp.3-26.

and transferred to another day of the week. For example, St. Joachim, which was celebrated on the Sunday after the Assumption, was henceforth to be celebrated on August 16.

It is worth noting that Pius X had envisaged fixing the date of Easter.[36] In 1913 a questionnaire was sent to bishops in all countries. The Holy See received a majority of positive replies. The Congregation of Rites, at a meeting on December 9, 1913, gave its judgment against the project since there was a risk of "naturalizing the great event of Christ's resurrection." Pius X abandoned the project.

Closely linked with this reform of the liturgical calendar was the reform of the Breviary. The Apostolic Constitution *Divino Afflatu,* with its 13 chapters, was chiefly concerned with the re-casting of the liturgical Psalter.[37] The Pope recognized that the multiplication of the offices of saints made it more and more difficult to accomplish a complete weekly recitation of the Psalms—to which every priest is bound. He announced a reform of the Breviary, with the aim of restoring "the ancient custom of reciting the whole Psalter every week." The Pope did not do this simply to re-establish an ancient discipline, but also because the Psalms were composed "under divine inspiration,"—they were not merely old texts. The Pope quoted many Fathers of the Church, notably St. Augustine: "So that He could be worthily praised by man, God has praised Himself; and it is by this praise, the fruit of the divine condescension, that man finds the right manner of praising Him."

The regulations laid down by the Pope constituted a veritable reform of the Breviary. These were the principle modifications: 1. The length of the Breviary offices was reduced (*e.g.,* instead of the 18 Psalms to be recited on Sundays, there would be never more than nine Psalms or parts of Psalms); 2. The Psalter was once again to be recited in its integrity during the week, without suppressing the feasts of saints; 3. The Proper of Sundays and feasts was re-established; 4. The readings of Scripture proper to the time of year were privileged.[38]

In liturgical matters, Pius X was animated by two great concerns: to restore the dignity, beauty and coherence of worship; and to promote "active participation in the Church's sacrosanct mysteries and her public, solemn prayer."[39]

---

[36] Honoré Vinck, "Une tentative de Pie X pour fixer la date de Pâques. Quelques documents inédits," *Revue d'histoire ecclésiastique,* April-June 1975, pp.462-468.

[37] *Divino Afflatu,* November 1, 1911, *Documents pontificaux,* vol.II, pp.379-390.

[38] A. Mollien, "L'office dans le bréviaire romain," in *Liturgia* (Paris: Bloud et Gay, 1931), pp.606-607.

[39] *Tra le Sollecitudine,* November 22, 1903, *Documents pontificaux,* vol.I, p.50.

Great celebrations

If Pius X held that "the divine Eucharist is the centre of the faith, the final goal of every other devotion,"[40] he also regarded the other devotions with great esteem and urged the faithful to take part in them. The first years of his pontificate were marked by great Marian festivals. Looking forward to the 50th anniversary of the proclamation of the dogma of the Immaculate Conception, his predecessor had created a commission of cardinals with the task of preparing for it. One of the first pontifical acts of Pius X was to confirm the mission and composition of this commission. It consisted of Cardinals Vannutelli, Rampolla, Ferrata and Vivès.[41] For this event Pius X also composed a prayer to the Immaculate Virgin, and attached to it an indulgence of 300 days. The 50th anniversary year (1904) was indicated by an Extraordinary Jubilee, announced by the Apostolic Letter *Quae Catholico Nomini*,[42] and marked by the Encyclical *Ad Diem Illum Laetissimum*.[43] Pius X also crowned the painting of the Immaculate Conception which is found in the Vatican Basilica and accorded the celebration of the Mass of the Immaculate Conception to the whole world. In February 1908 there was also the celebration of the 50th anniversary of the apparitions of the Virgin at Lourdes. Pius X appointed Cardinal Lecot, Archbishop of Bordeaux, as legate, to represent him at the ceremonies.

The beatifications and canonizations performed during the pontificate were also opportunities to remind the faithful of the different ways of imitating Christ. Pius X undertook 73 beatifications and 4 canonizations:[44]

He beatified these:

December 18, 1904: Gaspare del Bufalo, an Italian who died in 1837, the founder of a congregation of priests;

December 27, 1904: Stefano Bellesini, an Italian Augustinian of the 18th century;

January 1, 1905: Agathange de Vendôme and Cassien de Nantes, two French Capuchins of the 17th century who died as martyrs;

January 8, 1905: Jean-Marie Vianney, Curé of Ars, who died in 1859;

January 15, 1905: Mark Crisin, Stephen Pongracz and Melchior Grodecz, Jesuits martyred by Protestants in Hungary in the 16th century;

---

[40] *Je Vous Remercie*, April 14, 1912, *Documents pontificaux*, vol.II, p.428.
[41] Letter *Se è Nostro Dovere*, September 8, 1903, *Documents pontificaux*, vol.I, pp.30-31.
[42] Dated December 7, 1903, *Documents pontificaux*, vol.I, pp.56-57.
[43] Dated February 2, 1904, *Documents pontificaux*, vol.I, pp.94-104.
[44] Listed in *Index ac Status Causarum* (Vatican City: Congregatio pro Causis Sanctorum, 1988). The date given is that of the solemn beatification or canonization ceremony.

May 13, 1906: Julie Billiart, the Belgian foundress of a religious congregation, who died in 1816;

May 20, 1906: Francis Gil de Federich and seven other Dominicans, martyred in Tonkin in the 18th and 19th centuries;

May 27, 1906: Thérèse de Saint-Augustin and 15 other Carmelites of Compiègne, martyred during the French Revolution;

June 10, 1906: Bonaventure of Barcelona, a Spanish lay Franciscan of the 17th century;

May 17, 1908: Marie-Madeleine Postel, a Frenchwoman who founded the Sisters of Mercy of Christian Schools in the 19th century;

May 24, 1908: Madeleine-Sophie Barat, a Frenchwoman, foundress of the Society of the Sacred Heart in 1800;

May 31, 1908: Gabriele dell'Addolorata, an Italian Passionist of the 19th century;

April 18, 1909: Joan of Arc;

April 25, 1909: John Eudes, the founder of the Congregation of Jesus and Mary in the 17th century;

May 2, 1909: Francisco de Capillas, a Spanish Dominican who was martyred in China in 1648, and 33 other martyrs of the 19th century, killed at Tonkin, in Annam and in Cochin-China.

Pius X canonized the following:

December 11, 1904: Alessandro Maria Sauli, an Italian Barnabite of the 16th century venerated by Pius X when he was Bishop of Mantua;

December 11, 1904: Gerard Majella, an Italian Redemptorist brother of the 18th century;

May 20, 1909: Johannes Clemens Maria Hofbauer, an Austrian Redemptorist who died in 1820;

May 20, 1909: Joseph Oriol, a Spanish priest of the 17th century.

The anniversary dates of certain of Christendom's great figures also furnished opportunities for ceremonies or encyclicals. In 1904 the 13th centenary of the death of St. Gregory the Great was marked by an encyclical. This centenary and, later (in 1907), the 15th centenary of the death of St. John Chrysostom, were accompanied by the important liturgical ceremonies to which we have already referred. In 1907, on the seventh centenary of the "heavenly birthday" of St. Elisabeth of Hungary, the Pope wrote the Letter *Tempus Prope Diem* to the Cardinals and Bishops of Hungary. In 1909 the eighth centenary of the death of St. Anselm was the occasion for a very lengthy encyclical, *Communium Rerum*. Pius X had a particular affection for this Italian, a native of Aosta, who became a monk in Bec (Normandy) and then Archbishop of Canterbury. He was both a great defender of the Church's rights *vis-à-vis* the Kings of England, and a philosopher and theologian whose doctrine and method are fundamental to medieval Scholasticism. In his first encyclical Pius X had extensively quoted him, and he would do so on many subsequent occasions.

We should also mention the encyclical *Editae Saepe Dei,* published on the occasion of the third centenary (in 1910) of the canonization of St. Charles Borromeo, and the Letter addressed to the Carmelite Order on the third centenary (1914) of the beatification of St. Teresa of Avila. In this latter document, in the last year of his pontificate, Pius X explains why he attributed such importance to commemorating Christendom's great figures, as he had done in Mantua and Venice:

> Ever since God, in His goodness, elevated Our humble person to the Sovereign Pontificate, it seemed to Us that it was Our apostolic duty eagerly to seize every opportunity offered to Us to celebrate the sons of the Church who have been distinguished by their virtues and knowledge, and by the glory of their lofty deeds. This We have always done with much zeal. Deeds, in fact, impress souls much more strongly than do words, and We have always been persuaded that, to attain the goal for which We are striving, to "restore all things in Christ," Our exhortations are less effective than the examples of those who, by contemplating Christ himself in order to imitate him, have magnificently reproduced in themselves his model of sanctity.[45]

Example is better than exhortation; the past must illuminate the present; and the goal is always the same: *Instaurare omnia in Christo.* This is the theme which unifies the entire pontificate of Pius X.

The War and the death of Pius X

In 1889, at a ceremony to honor St. Aloysius Gonzaga who, among other things, was a great peacemaker, the then Bishop of Mantua had given a beautiful sermon in praise of Christian peace—which has nothing in common with contemporary pacifism:

> Ah yes, let us ask for peace, peace as it is understood and desired by the children of God; this is a peace worthy of the name, which holy Scripture in no way separates from Truth, Justice and Grace; this is the peace of the Church: it is the tranquil performance of the Christian law, the peaceful development of works of faith and charity, the public affirmation of the truth and precepts of the Gospel, the conformity of human laws and institutions with the doctrine and moral teaching of Jesus Christ, the unceasing resistance to the prince of darkness and all those who propagate his perverse maxims.[46]

---

[45] Letter *Ex Quo,* March 7, 1914, *Documents pontificaux,* vol.II, p.558.
[46] Address of September 3, 1889, quoted in Dal-Gal, *Pie X,* p.129.

There was no lack of opportunities for peacemaking during the pontificate. In Latin America, as we have seen, the Holy See offered on several occasions to mediate between two countries. Pius X thought that the Pope should promote peace in all circumstances, in so far as he was able. In 1911 he did not hesitate to give his public approval to the *Carnegie Endowment for International Peace,* an organization endeavoring to encourage peace among nations. "To promote concord between minds," wrote the Pope, "to restrain bellicose instincts, to remove the dangers of war, and even to alleviate the anxieties of what is called the 'armed peace,' is a very noble enterprise."[47]

In 1911, when Italy was still engaged in a war against the Ottoman Empire over control of Tripolitania, and at a time when Catholic newspapers, the clergy, a number of bishops, and even the *Civiltà Cattolica* were already comparing this war to a new crusade and seeing in it a parallel to the Battle of Lepanto, Pius X intervened by having the following note published in the *Osservatore Romano*: "It is missionaries, not soldiers, who bring Catholic doctrine to infidels...the Tripolitanian enterprise is an absolutely political affair from which religion holds aloof"; Catholic newspapers, therefore, should not encourage people "to think that it is a holy war."

At this time Pius X feared that there would be an all-out war in Europe. "I see a great war," he told his sisters from time to time.[48] Cardinal Merry del Val gives the same witness: "I can testify that Pius X on many occasions predicted the unleashing of the Great War in Europe....As early as 1911 and 1912 the Holy Father spoke of an imminent conflict, and he referred to it in terms which made a deep impression on me."[49] He affirmed that a "great war" (in Italian: *il guerrone*) was approaching.

When it became clear in 1914 that a war was imminent between the Great Powers, Pius X was profoundly shaken. The immediate cause of the conflict was the assassination of the Austrian Archduke Franz Ferdinand (and heir to the Imperial throne) in Bosnia-Herzegovina. Austria accused Serbia of having armed the assassins, and addressed an ultimatum to Serbia. A European war was to be feared, given the web of bilateral alliances.

---

[47] Letter *Libenter,* to Msgr. Falconio, Apostolic Delegate to the United States, June 11, 1911, *Documents pontificaux,* vol.II, p.356.

[48] Depositions of Maria Sarto and Anna Sarto at the Roman ordinary process, quoted by Dal-Gal, *Pius X*, p.221.

[49] Cardinal Merry del Val, *Pie X. Impressions et souvenirs*, p.105.

Some months earlier the Holy See had signed a concordat with Serbia, as we have seen. At the same time, however, Pius X and Cardinal Merry del Val had a great affection for Austria-Hungary:

> Austria, which, after France's break with Rome, remained the only great Catholic state in Europe, seemed to the Vatican to be a rampart against German Protestantism on the one hand and Orthodox Slavism on the other.[50]

While he believed that Austria-Hungary was right to act with severity against Serbia, the Pope was very much afraid of a European conflict. Certain witnesses say that he wrote a letter to Emperor Franz Josef, imploring him to avoid a war. Subsequently Cardinal Merry del Val himself said that he had no knowledge of this letter; there is no trace of it in the Austrian or Roman archives.

On July 28 Austria declared war on Serbia. According to Msgr. Bressan, when the Austrian Ambassador came to announce the news to the Pope and asked him to bless the Imperial armies, Pius X replied: "Tell the Emperor that I can bless neither war, nor those who have desired war. I bless peace."

Then the Ambassador requested a personal blessing for Franz Josef. "I can only pray that God may pardon him," replied the Pope. "The Emperor should consider himself lucky not to receive the curse of the Vicar of Christ!"[51]

On August 1, Germany declared war on Russia, and then, on August 3, on France also. Meanwhile, on August 2, Pius X published an exhortation which was his last pontifical act. He exhorted Catholics of the entire world, whichever camp they belonged to, to turn "to Him from whom alone help can come, to Christ, the Prince of Peace and mankind's all-powerful Mediator with God." The Pope also said that his "soul was torn by the most painful sorrow for the salvation and life of so many individuals and peoples."[52]

This was not a mere rhetorical formula. The outbreak of the World War coincided with a sudden worsening of the Pope's health, which was to prove fatal. All the testimonies agree that the outbreak of this War profoundly shattered Pius X. As Cardinal Merry del Val says: "The horror of

---

[50] Aubert, "Pio X tra restaurazione e riforma," in *La Chiesa e la società industriale, 1878-1922*, vol.XXII/1 of *Storia della Chiesa*, p.153.

[51] Testimony of Msgr. Bressan, cited by Cigala, *Vie intime de S.S. le pape Pie X*, p.221. In connection with this same event the beatification process quotes a similar, but more substantial reply: "I do not bless arms, but peace!"

[52] *Dum Europa Fere*, August 2, 1914, *Documents pontificaux*, vol.II, p.584.

war tormented and obsessed him day and night. The invasion of Belgium and the news of the first battles overwhelmed him with suffering."[53]

From August 15 Pius X felt increasingly unwell. It was attributed to the suffocating heat of the time of year. Initially the pontifical doctors Amici and Marchiafava decided that the illness was not particularly grave, and advised the Pope to stay in bed. But Pius X's health did not improve.[54]

Brother Faustino Giulini of the Order of St. John of God, who was the Pope's nurse, drew up a detailed account of the Pope's last hours.[55] On the morning of August 19 the doctors were summoned to the Pope's bedside. They diagnosed a bronchio-pulmonary condition and prescribed various medicines. The patient's state of health was evidently deteriorating by the hour.

According to Professor Marchiafava, Pius X then said: "I am offering my miserable life as a holocaust to prevent the massacre of so many of my children." He asked to make his confession to Msgr. Bressan. At 11p.m. he received viaticum and extreme unction from the hands of Msgr. Zampini, Sacristan of the Apostolic Palaces. In the afternoon and evening, still in bed and in pain, he gave his last farewell to the Cardinals present in Rome, and to his sisters. On August 20, at 1:15 in the morning, he breathed his last. His final words, in Venetian dialect, were an act of trust: *"Gesù, Giuseppe e Maria, vi dono il cuore de l'anima mia!"*

---

[53] Cardinal Merry del Val, *Pie X. Impressions et souvenirs,* p.110.

[54] At the beginning of 1913 Pius X's health had already given cause for concern; he had had to stay in bed for a while. Certain newspapers in New York had even announced his death....His return to health on the Feast of St. Joseph (March 19) and then on the Feast of St. Pius V (May 5) prompted innumerable telegrams and letters which arrived from the whole world from bishops and from Catholics and Catholic associations (*ASS,* Segretaria di Stato, anno 1913, rubrica 1, fasc.1-3.).

[55] *Summarium,* p.246.

CHAPTER 12

BLESSED AND SAINT

The day after the Pope's death the praise for him was unanimous. In Rome the great liberal daily *Il Giornale d'Italia,* which had so often echoed the principles and catch-phrases of Modernism, gave pride of place to an article which well expressed the common feeling: "History made him a great Pope, and the Church will make him a great Saint." Even the great Paris Socialist newspaper, *L'Humanité,* gave an admiring bow before the mortal remains of Pius X:

> The Pope is dead. It must be said that he was a great Pope. His policies were very simple, namely, to restore the values of faith with an apostolic firmness. He was able to conduct these policies with authority because of his simplicity of soul and the indubitable sincerity of his virtues. However he is judged, it must be said that Pius X has been a great Pope.

Even while he was alive, his prestige was very great. Guillaume Apollinaire, a poet far removed from classicism, wrote in one of his poems:

> *Seul en Europe tu n'es pas antique ô Christianisme*
> *L'Européen le plus moderne c'est vous pape Pie X.*[1]
>
> [You alone in Europe, Christendom, have not grown old and ancient; Of all Europeans, you, Pope Pius the Tenth, are the most modern.]

Immediate veneration

After his death, in conformity with the express terms of his will, Pius X's body was not embalmed. This meant that the lying-in-state was very short, from the first evening of the day he died until the following morning. For one whole night the mortal remains of Pius X, clothed in a white pontifical habit, were exposed in the throne-room of the Vatican. The crowd of anonymous faithful filed uninterruptedly past the coffin. Many had brought small objects (a rosary, holy pictures, a crucifix) in the hope of touching them against the body of a Pope who, in popular piety, was already considered to be a saint. Two prelates willingly offered their services

---

[1]   *Zone* (first published in 1912, reprinted in the collection *Alcools*). Apollinaire used the term "modern" again, later, to explain why he preferred Pascal to Claudel: "What, nowadays, is more fresh, more modern, more laid bare and weighed down with riches than Pascal? You taste this, I'm sure, and rightly. We can love him," Guillaume Apollinaire-Pablo Picasso, *Correspondance* (Paris: Gallimard, 1992), p.181.

for this devotional rite, and touched Pius X's mortal remains with these proffered objects.

According to his wishes, Pius X was interred in the crypt of St. Peter's Basilica. Thus he broke with the tradition of his predecessors who were buried in one of the great Roman basilicas: Pius IX in St. Laurence-outside-the-Walls and Leo XIII in St. John Lateran. Pius X wanted to associate himself with a longer tradition, *i.e.,* that of the many popes in the past who had regarded it as important to be buried close to the remains of St. Peter.

On the evening of August 23 the body of Pius X was taken down to the Vatican Grotto. The marble tomb was simple, austere and without ornament. Only the tympanum bore the monogram of Constantine and the name: PIUS PAPA X. The Pope's wish to have a poor and simple tomb was respected. However, an addition was placed on a small stone tablet in front of the tomb, in the form of this inscription in Latin:

> Pope Pius X
> Poor in riches
> Gentle and humble of heart
> A firm defender of the Catholic faith
> who desired
> to restore all things in Christ
> Died a holy death on August 20, 1914
> *Fama sanctitatis*

Pius X's reputation for holiness went back a long way. Even while he was alive, he was reputed to have the gift of healing. Here we mention just three cases from the time of his pontificate. One day, a Belgian nun who was suffering from consumption was admitted to a public audience with the Pope. When she came out, she found that she was completely cured and had no relapse. On another occasion, after a public audience, a German who had been blind from birth gained his sight after Pius X put his hands over his eyes and exhorted him to have trust in God. Similarly, a blind child was immediately cured after the Pope put his hand on its head and said to the mother: "Pray to the Lord and have faith."[2]

As soon as Pius X's body had been placed in the tomb, the pilgrimages began. Soon reports came in of miraculous favors and graces received, attributed to his intercession. In February 1923 all the Cardinals resident in Rome—the only time in history—signed a request for the introduction of his cause for beatification. A postulator was appointed: Dom Benedetto

---

[2]   Deposition of Msgr. R. de Samper, *Summarium*, p.991.

Pierami, the Procurator General of the Benedictines of Vallombroso. In St. Peter's, a few months later, on June 28, 1923, Pius XI inaugurated a monument in honor of Pius X. A marble statue shows him with his arms outstretched and his eyes lifted to heaven. At the base of the moment there are eight bronze panels representing the most prominent aspects and events of his pontificate: 1. The Pontiff of the Eucharist; 2. The Defender of the Faith; 3. The Supporter of Catholic France; 4. The Patron of the Arts; 5. The Guardian of Biblical Studies; 6. The Reorganizer of Canon Law; 7. The Reformer of Sacred Music; 8. The Father of Orphans and the Abandoned.

The beatification process

The diocesan processes (or "ordinary processes") began. They took place in Pius X's diocese of origin and in the dioceses where he had exercised his different functions. They were organized under the authority of the individual bishop responsible. There were four "ordinary processes": in Treviso, 1923-1926; in Mantua, 1924-1927; in Venice, 1924-1930; and in Rome, 1923-1931. These processes began less than ten years after the Pope's death, and so it was possible to question people who had known him: some of his sisters, some friends of his childhood and youth, some ecclesiastics who knew him in his different priestly and episcopal responsibilities, and also certain Vatican prelates and cardinals. In total, 205 witnesses to his life were interrogated and their statements, under oath, were collated. Each witness was asked the same questions (63 questions in all).

The collated statements from the ordinary processes (more than 10,000 manuscript pages) were published in the form of large extracts—*summarium*—in the *Positio super introductione causae* (Report on the introduction of the Cause). This *Positio,* which was finally edited and produced in 1941, has 1,130 pages. It was examined by the Congregation of Rites, which published the Decree for the introduction of the Cause in 1943. This meant that the cause for beatification and canonization had officially been judged worthy of being studied by the Holy See.

Now the new processes, termed *apostolic,* would be repeated in the same places as the "ordinary processes." These apostolic processes lasted from 1943 to 1946. Eighty-nine witnesses were called, each having to reply to 81 questions. While some of the witnesses for the ordinary processes were no longer to be had, new witnesses were available to make their statements. In total, in this twofold series of processes, some 240 witnesses were interrogated and gave statements on the life and virtues of Pius X. A new *Positio* was drawn up, composed of extracts of the twofold series of processes; this was called the *Positio super virtutibus.* Published in 1949, it consisted of 897 pages. The "objections" (*animadversiones*) raised by the Promoter of the Faith—called the *devil's advocate*—resulted, in 1950, in a *Nova Positio super virtutibus* and a *Novissima positio super virtutibus* (82 and 17 pages).

Meanwhile, a canonical examination of the remains had taken place. The remains of Pius X were removed from his tomb on May 19, 1944, and brought to the Vatican Basilica. The lead coffin was placed in the Chapel of the Holy Crucifix and was opened in the presence of the prelates who were members of the Tribunal of the Apostolic Process. The purpose of this examination is to be sure that the remains in the tomb are those of the person who is a candidate for beatification. By long tradition, however, the ceremony has also been to establish whether the corpse may be incorrupt. This non-corruption is not an additional proof of sanctity, but it is a miracle which can confirm a reputation of sanctity that has been otherwise established. This was the case with the remains of Pius X. One witness who was present at the exhumation and examination describes the state of incorruptibility discovered on May 19, 1944:

> Opening the coffin they found the body intact, clothed in the papal insignia as it had been buried 30 years before. Under the taut skin which covered the face the outline of the skull was clearly recognizable. The hollows of the eyes appeared dark but not empty; they were covered by eyelids much wrinkled and sunk. The hair was white and covered the top of the head completely. The pectoral cross and pastoral ring shone brilliantly. In his last testament Pius X had specially requested that his body should not be touched and that the traditional embalming should not be done. In spite of this the body was excellently preserved. No part of the skeleton was uncovered, no bones were exposed. While the body was rigid, the arms, elbows and shoulders were quite flexible. The hands were beautiful and slender and the nails on the fingers were perfectly preserved.[3]

Once the canonical examination had been completed, Pius X's remains stayed in the Chapel of the Holy Crucifix, open to the veneration of the faithful, until the morning of July 3. Then they were placed in another chapel of the Vatican Basilica, the Chapel of the Presentation, the first on the left when one enters the Basilica, where they are still to be found, situated below the altar.

The beatification process continued. Some consultors of the Congregation of Rites felt that the testimonies regarding Pius X's struggle against Modernism were too numerous and too controversial: they raised detailed objections on this subject and requested a supplementary report with documentary research. This work was carried out by the Reporter General, Antonelli, a Franciscan, who produced his *Disquisitio circa quasdam obiec-*

---

[3] J. Dal-Gal, *Pius X*, p.235.

tiones modus agendi Servi Dei respicientes in modernismi debellatione una cum summario additionali ex officio compilato, 1950. This long collection of documents and commentary (303 pages) won the support of the Congregation and of Pope Pius XII.

Blessed and saint

On September 3, 1950, the decree was signed acknowledging that Pius X had practised *heroically* the theological virtues of faith, hope and charity and the cardinal virtues of prudence, justice, fortitude and temperance. All that remained, for beatification, was the canonical recognition of two miracles that had been the result of the Pope's intercession. Among the hundreds of cures registered by the Postulator of the Cause, that could not be attributed to medicine, two were selected for canonical recognition.

One was that of a French nun, Marie-Françoise Deperras, who had been suffering from a cancer of the left femur, and who was cured spectacularly after the imposition of a relic of Pius X and two novenas to the Sovereign Pontiff. The other was that of another nun, an Italian, who had been suffering from a malignant tumor in the abdomen. The healing took place in February 1938 after the imposition of a relic of Pius X and when the convent had begun a novena to ask his intercession. After a scientific study of the two cases, conducted by medical experts of the Congregation of Rites, the cures were declared to be instantaneous, perfect and definitive. Since they had been due to recourse to the intercession of Pius X, they were declared to be of the supernatural order, and on February 11, 1951, they were acknowledged, by decree, to be authentic miracles. On June 3, 1951, Pius XII was able to proceed with the solemn ceremony of beatifying his predecessor.

Finally, on May 29, 1954, after the examination of a further miracle, Pius XII proceeded to the canonization of Pius X. In his address, the Pope said:

> Sanctity, which was the inspirer and guide of Pius X in all his undertakings, shone even more brilliantly in his everyday actions. The task he set before him, to unite and bring back all things in Christ, was something he made a reality in himself before bringing it about in others.[4]

---

4   Pius XII, *Discours de canonization de Pie X,* May 29, 1954, *Documents pontificaux,* vol.I, p.21.

SOURCES

ARCHIVES

The only archives listed here are those which we have utilized. In particular, the Secret Vatican Archives possess a great wealth of material regarding St. Pius X and his pontificate. These archives, which have only recently been open to researchers, are still in the process of inventorization. Some of the sections are not yet accessible.

SECRET VATICAN ARCHIVES (Vatican City)

S.Congregazione AAEESS: Codex Juris Canonici, scatola 1 (busta I,III,IV,VIII), scatola 4.

S.Congregatio Concilii: Relationes, 485B.

S.Congregatio Consistorialis: Processus consistoriale, 275, no.30.

Segretaria dei Brevi: 5908.

Segretaria di Stato: Anno 1903, rubrica 229, fasc.1.

Anno 1905, rubrica 248, fasc. 1,2,3.

Anno 1908, rubrica 82, fasc. 1,2,3,4,5.

Anno 1913, rubrica 1, fasc. 1,2,3.

Anno 1914, rubrica 220, fasc. 1,2,3,4,5.

ARCHIVES OF THE MINISTRY OF FOREIGN AFFAIRS (PARIS)

Nouvelle Série 1897-1918 Saint-Siège:

NS 3: Gouvernement intérieur de l'Église, janvier-juillet 1903.

NS 4: Gouvernement intérieur de l'Église, août 1903-décembre 1907.

NS 8: Relations avec les États d'Amérique, 1901-1907.

NS 12: Relations avec l'Italie, 1903-1907.

NS 21: Relations avec la France, 1903.

NS 22: Relations avec la France, janvier-juin 1904.

NS 23: Relations avec la France, juillet-décembre 1904.

NS 24: Relations avec la France, 1905-1907.

NS 25: Relations avec la France, 1910-1913.

NS 26: Relations avec la France. Cardinaux français, 1897-1907.

NS 27: Relations avec la France. Évêques français, 1897-1907.

ARCHIVES OF THE ABBEY OF ST. PIERRE DE SOLESMES

Letters of Don Perosi to Dom Moquereau.

ARCHIVES OF THE OBLATE MISSIONARIES OF MARY IMMACULATE (ROME)

Dossier J. B. Lemius (autobiographical, *etc.*).

Bibliography

The numerous footnotes show all the printed sources used.

As yet there is no complete bibliography on Pius X and his pontificate. In the meantime one may refer to that published by Quirino Bortolato, "Scheda bibliografica essenziale su Pio X," in *Sulle orme di Pio X. Giuseppe Sarto (1835-1914) dal microcosmo veneto alla dimensione universale* (Amministrazione Comunale di Salzano, 1986), which is very full, though not exhaustive. Cf. also that given in Gianpaolo Romanato, *Pio X* (Milan: Rusconi, 1992).

INDEX

A reference to a footnote is indicated by *n* after the page number.